T0350863

MEGAPROJECT MANAGEMENT

MEGAPROJECT
MANAGEMENT

MEGAPROJECT MANAGEMENT

LESSONS ON RISK AND PROJECT MANAGEMENT FROM THE BIG DIG

Virginia A. Greiman

Cover Design: Wiley

Cover Images: (from left to right) © xenotar/iStockphoto; © Genyuan Huang/iStockphoto; © Steven Phraner/iStockphoto

This book is printed on acid-free paper.

Published by John Wiley & Sons, Inc., Hoboken, New Jersey

Published simultaneously in Canada

For general information about our other products and services, please contact our Customer Care Department within the United States at (800) 762-2974, outside the United States at (317) 572-3993 or fax (317) 572-4002.

Wiley publishes in a variety of print and electronic formats and by print-on-demand. Some material included with standard print versions of this book may not be included in e-books or in print-on-demand. If this book refers to media such as a CD or DVD that is not included in the version you purchased, you may download this material at http://booksupport.wiley.com. For more information about Wiley products, visit www.wiley.com.

Project Management Institute (www.pmi.org) is the leading advocate for the project management profession globally. Founded in 1969, PMI has more than 650,000 members and credential holders in 185 countries. PMI's Project Management Professional (PMP) credential is globally recognized as the gold standard credential in project management.

Library of Congress Cataloging-in-Publication Data:

Greiman, Virginia A.
  Megaproject Management : lessons on risk and project management from the Big Dig / Virginia A. Greiman.
     pages cm
  Includes bibliographical references and index.
  ISBN 978-1-118-11547-3 (cloth : acid-free paper), ISBN 978-1-118-41634-1 (ebk.); ISBN 978-1-118-41887-1 (ebk.); ISBN 978-1-118-56765-4 (ebk.); ISBN 978-1-118-67109-2 (ebk.)
  1. Central Artery/Third Harbor Tunnel Project (Mass.)–Case studies. 2. Tunnels–Massachusetts–Boston–Design and construction–Case studies. 3. Public works–Massachusetts–Boston–Management–Case studies. 4. Project management–Case studies. 5. Risk management–Case studies. I. Title.
  HE356.5.B6G74 2013
  658.4′04—dc23

                                                                              2012040855

Printed in the United States of America

V10017697_022020

This book is dedicated to the creativity, imagination, and perseverance of all the engineers and construction workers on the Big Dig, and to all those who come after them in creating the great engineering projects of the world.

Contents

Author's Perspectives

There are many reasons for writing about megaprojects, but perhaps one of the most significant is to share the important lessons learned for future projects so that the workers, engineers, contractors, government policy makers, project management professionals, and the communities impacted by these large-scale projects will benefit from the challenges that others before them faced. Having served on the Big Dig for the better part of nine years, as both deputy chief counsel and head of risk management, I am grateful for the opportunity of working with a devoted team of professionals who everyday faced unprecedented risks, made difficult and often unpopular decisions, and, despite the public criticism, burdens, and numerous hurdles, implemented those decisions because it was the right thing to do. As James Tobin, in his popular book *Great Projects*, notably writes, "Americans have admired their engineers from afar. But few have learned much about them."

Hopefully, this book will enlighten the reader not only about the many technical marvels of the Big Dig but, more important, about the day-to-day obstacles, challenges, and uncertainties faced by the engineers and many other participants in this megaproject. Rarely are the successes of these mammoth projects noticed, as the stories that are told are too frequently focused on what went wrong. The goal of this book is to provide some balance.

I am most appreciative of the participants in the Big Dig and other megaprojects who willingly agreed to be interviewed for this book, so that projects of the future can have even better outcomes. This book, of course, is itself an ongoing research project, and I hope the lessons herein will encourage others to share their experiences, so that we all may learn how to build a better and safer world through the advancement of innovative ways of thinking about and managing the projects of the future.

Acknowledgments

There continues to be a desperate need for innovative project managers, as evidenced by the numerous endeavors to improve the quality of life for so many, particularly those from the poorest and most war-torn countries in the world. Academic scholarship, sometimes overlooked in the urgent desire to get things built, plays an important role in the improvement of projects. As I explored the tremendous amount of research that has already been done on large projects, I was truly grateful for the honest evaluations and thoughtful analysis of so many diverse projects in our universe—from deepwater and underground tunneling to livable communities for the poorest of our society, the great space explorations, and the Next Generation Air Transportation Systems (NextGen).

I have many to thank for their tremendous contributions to this book in bringing the story of the management of the world's largest inner-city engineering project to life. The names of those to whom this book is indebted are legion. They include my students, who instill in me my passion for teaching and enlighten me with their enthusiasm, dedication, and creativity. I am also thankful to my fellow professors and colleagues, especially those who provided insight and new direction and guided me when I went astray.

To my talented and dedicated research assistance, Nora Estrella, who coordinated thousands of documents, explored every avenue of research on megaprojects, and labored over every detail, there are no words to express my appreciation. I could not have done it without her devotion and encouragement. To my colleague Dorothy Tiffany, who meticulously reviewed every chapter and provided sound advice based on her many years of experience in project and program management at NASA, I owe my deepest gratitude.

To my colleagues on the Big Dig, I will always be grateful for your support and devotion to seeing this project through, despite its many obstacles and challenges. I owe a special thanks to those who generously shared their experiences and perceptions and gave sound advice on best practices and lessons learned, as highlighted throughout this book. Among my many other colleagues at the Big Dig who contributed to this book, a special thank-you to Richard Schoenfeld, Nicole Hunter, Keith Diggans, and Yoke Wong for sharing their insights and valuable knowledge.

To Fred Salvucci, the master planner of the Big Dig, I am tremendously thankful for your generosity with time and for the knowledge you have given me about a project that has forever changed the face of Boston. To Mary

Connaughton, a devoted member of the Massachusetts Turnpike Board, thank you for all you did to raise the voice of the people a little louder. Thanks also to all my colleagues who served in various capacities within the federal and state government, to Bechtel/Parsons Brinckerhoff, and to those members of the risk management and safety and health teams. I am also most appreciative of the many who served on great projects throughout the world and kindly shared their experiences with me.

To Dean Halfond, Dean Zlateva, Dean Chitkushev, professors Vijay Kanabar, Wally Miller, Tamar Frankel, Kip Becker, Roger Warburton, Sam Mendlinger, Barry Unger, and Stephen Leybourne, and to all my colleagues, thank you for your support and guidance in this effort and for sharing your love of projects with me. Thank you to my diligent reviewers, Khang Ta, John Martin, Diane Hemond, Tom Kendrick, Charles W. Bosler, Jr., Star Dargin, Jim Hannon, and Joann Frantino, for your critical analysis and thoughtful recommendations. To Nancy Coleman and her staff, thank you for your valuable perspectives on teaching methodologies and learning in cyberspace.

To my student researchers, Bran Crudden, Heng Zhang, Ming-Hwa Wu (Fiona), Visutthep Thammavijitdej (Tang), Silvano Domenico Orsi, and Sergei Tokmakov, thank you for never missing a beat and for keeping me motivated and excited about this project in the midst of the collection of massive amounts of research and overwhelming documentation. To Martha Totten, Fiona Niven, Susan Sunde, and Lucille Dicker, thank you for your unrelenting administrative assistance and support.

A special thanks to my publisher, John Wiley & Sons; to Executive Editor Robert Argentieri and Dan Magers for your willingness to take on this project and your constant support; to Amanda Shettleton for preparing this book for production; to Renata Marchione, Marketing Manager; Robert Wall, Supervisor (Project Creative Services); and to my production editor Nancy Cintron and my copy editor Ginny Carroll for their diligent review of this book. Also, much appreciation to the Project Management Institute (PMI), especially Barbara Walsh and Steve Townsend, for their excellent insights into PMI standards and practices.

I would like to thank my wonderful family for their constant support and inspiration throughout this lengthy endeavor and for their incredible assistance with graphics and design.

My apologies to anyone I may have forgotten to mention here.

Finally, to the readers of this book, I would like to encourage you to continue to explore the reasons why some projects fail and others succeed, what makes megaproject management so inspiring and challenging, and how we can better prepare for the projects of the future.

Responsibility for errors or omissions in this book remains mine alone.

Introduction to This Book

What we think, or what we know, or what we believe is, in the end, of little consequence. The only consequence is what we do.

—*John Ruskin*

OVERVIEW

In 1956, an interstate highway was built across the United States, which ended abruptly at the edge of Boston and connected with an elevated highway known to Bostonians as the "Highway in the Sky." Almost 50 years later, America's most ambitious infrastructure project, the Big Dig, was substantially completed. This was the largest, most complex urban infrastructure project in the history of the United States and included unprecedented planning and engineering, as described in Luberoff and Altshuler's political history of the Big Dig (1996), and reflected in the many awards for recognized excellence the project received (listed in the appendix to this book).

The Big Dig was originally projected to cost $2.5 billion and was to be completed by 1998. Instead, the project cost $14.8 billion and was not completed until 2006. Truly a massive project, the Big Dig involved 5000 workers, 130 major contractors, an army of construction equipment including more than 150 cranes, excavation of enough dirt to fill a football stadium to the rim 16 times, enough reinforcing steel to make a 1-inch steel bar long enough to wrap around the planet, and enough concrete to build a sidewalk 3 feet wide and 4 inches thick from Boston to San Francisco and back three times.

Unfortunately, the important lessons learned from this project have never been formally developed or disseminated, and limited information about the project's numerous processes, policies, and procedures is available. As we likely will never see a project of this size and complexity again in the United States, it is important to preserve now the important lessons of this monumental project for students, project leaders, and government policy makers.

The need for knowledge about megaprojects is apparent from every corner of the globe. Cities and towns across the United States are spending hundreds of billions of dollars annually to preserve the nation's infrastructure and construct the next generation of roads, bridges, tunnels, energy resources, and water supply, as are countries around the world. The Big Dig's two decades of experience provide valuable lessons for students, scholars, urban planners, engineering and construction professionals, project sponsors and investors, regulators, and government transportation officials interested in infrastructure and urban development. Better ways must be found to manage infrastructure projects and reduce the cost overruns, schedule delays, injuries and property damage, and the overall cost of risk that plague so many megaprojects.

Significantly, the Organization for Economic Co-operation and Development (OECD) is forecasting that global investment in infrastructure alone will cost as much as $70 trillion through 2030.[1] Procurement under World Bank–financed projects alone results in the awarding of about 25,000 contracts with a total value of about $20 billion each year. Thus, the need for development expertise is extensive and incorporates a broad range of disciplines such as project and program management, competitive strategy, risk management, privatization, corporate responsibility, social and economic policy development, project finance, investment policy, business-government relations, sustainability, negotiations, contract law, and ethics, to name a few.

KEY CONCEPTS AND OBJECTIVES

This book provides an analysis of the difficulties in managing megaprojects during each phase and throughout the life span of the project. Despite the huge volume of news articles, papers, and reports that have been published on the Big Dig, very little has been written about the day-to-day reality of managing projects from a project manager's perspective as well as the management of the complex risks faced by the nation's largest megaproject. With the exception of several comprehensive political and historical writings on the Big Dig (Tobin 2001; Hughes 2000; Luberoff and Altshuler 1996), much of the writing about the project is anecdotal, and little is of research quality. More important, it has never been studied for its lessons in the management of megaproject risk, cost, and schedule, particularly in interrelation to technical, legal, political, and social factors. Significantly, there has been no systematic analysis to date of how project costs and risks can be managed across the megaproject life cycle. For example, the Transportation Research Board's *Final Report on Cost Estimation and Management for Highway Projects* concluded that most efforts to date have focused on cost estimation (tools to improve estimates) and have completely neglected the difficult problems of cost management during the project's execution (Anderson et al. 2006).

Students and practicing professionals will find useful lessons on why projects go wrong and what can be done to prevent project failure and gain a competitive advantage. The primary goal of this book is not just to reflect on current project management theory or practice but to stimulate new

---

[1]Organization for Economic Co-operation and Development (OECD) Infrastructure to 2030, Volume 2: Mapping Policy for Electricity, Water, and Transport. 2007. Paris, France.

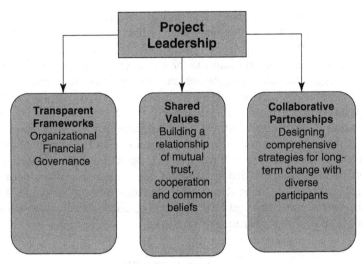

Figure 0.1   Course Themes

ideas to enhance project management performance and innovation in our global society. The lessons here are not just applicable to megaprojects, or to U.S. public projects, but are meant to develop dialogue across cultures and diverse projects and to generate new ways of looking at projects and improving practices through understanding both project imperfections and project advancements. Three key themes of this book are summarized here: transparent frameworks, shared values, and collaborative partnerships in project management (see Figure 0.1). Each of these subjects is described briefly here and elaborated upon in concepts, case studies, and ethical considerations throughout the book.

TRANSPARENT FRAMEWORKS

A key theme of this book is that transparent frameworks are critical to structural integrity and project success. Projects inherently have unique structures as compared to the more traditional structures of their parent organizations. Transparency in projects has become an essential requirement in all countries where economic development and financing are dependent upon public integrity, whether the project is in a war-torn country like Chad or Cameroon or in a cornfield in Kansas.

Linked with transparency is the framework for the project's (1) organizational structure, (2) financing structure, and (3) governance structure. Each of these structures is defined briefly here.

Organizational Structure

Organizational structure, as defined by *A Guide to the Project Management Body of Knowledge (PMBOK® Guide)*—Fifth Edition, published by the

Project Management Institute (PMI) and other project management bodies such as the Association for Project Management (APM) and the Australian Institute of Project Management (AIPM), is an enterprise environmental factor that can affect the availability of resources and the way projects are conducted. Organizational structures can range from functional to projectized, with a variety of matrix structures between them. Project integration is perhaps one of the most critical aspects of project organizational structure and should be planned at the earliest stages of project development. The importance of integrated processes, especially on long-term projects, has become a key requirement of all project management methodologies. A fully integrated project requires integration of the internal and external stakeholders, integration of all contracts, integration among multiple designers and contractors, integration of the project's controls, and integration of the project's financial and governance structures.

Financial Structure

Financial structure is the manner in which the project is funded, whether through public or private financing, equity, debt, or revenue streams. It also addresses the sequencing and core principles of project finance. The important aspect of project financial structure is not just the source of funding but also the transparency with which the funding is budgeted, allocated, and disbursed. As you will learn, financial structure matters and the financing of a megaproject should be transparent to all shareholders, stakeholders, local citizens, and all those impacted by the project's finances.

Governance Structure

Governance, simply defined, is an oversight and control function that can change to adapt to the emerging context of the project (Miller and Hobbs 2005). Megaprojects are unique in that traditional hierarchical structures are replaced by a unique blending of vertical and horizontal engagements that require coordination. The importance of the transparency and integrity of the governance structure is a major theme throughout this book.

SHARED VALUES

Building a relationship of shared values requires a commitment that begins at project conception and lasts throughout the life of the project. Shared values are those principles or beliefs that the project participants agree are the most important and will be given priority over all other principles that may arise as the project evolves. For example, the value of a sustainable, safe, and healthy project environment supersedes all other goals or objectives, including scope, budget, cost, and schedule constraints. Project values must be clearly understood and articulated in all project communications, and conflicts must be addressed. Key questions that must be asked include the following:

- Do project participants share a common vision of where the project will lead?
- Have all participants openly discussed and agreed to the same principles?
- Is there an environment of mutual trust?
- Is each side willing to communicate openly?

COLLABORATIVE PARTNERSHIPS

The purpose of this book is not to describe the various communication tools and techniques in the management literature, but rather to explain the unique processes and procedures utilized on the Big Dig to collaborate with stakeholders to make sure all voices were heard and represented in the daily life of the project. Project, program, and portfolio managers will be able to understand how to respond to the following key questions:

- What is my partnership philosophy and methodology?
- Have I fully identified all project stakeholders and possible interests and expectations?
- Do I continually monitor these alliances and relationships to ensure they are working effectively?
- What processes and procedures will be most effective in collaborating with all project participants?
- How will the project's goals and objectives be enforced?
- How will I measure the effectiveness of my collaborations?
- What impact is my partnership methodology having on the project deliverables?

PEDAGOGY

Since this book is designed to be used primarily as a textbook, it is structured to provide pedagogical tools to enhance the learning experience. Each chapter provides background on the major concepts as drawn from the extensive literature from the major project management standards organizations, including the PMI, the APM in the United Kingdom, and the International Project Management Association (IPMA); from actual megaproject case studies; from the Big Dig's numerous government reports, practices, and procedures; and, most important, from interviews with many of the project's major participants. Without the insights of the dedicated team of project managers, engineers, and construction workers, this book would not be possible. The goal of the book is to foster three important learning goals.

Knowledge Enrichment

Students will learn the importance of the alignment of projects with business strategy and the role that organizational, financial, and governance structure plays in project development and ultimate success. In today's global society, students must be prepared to deal with constant change, technological advancement, and uncertainty. The focus in each chapter is on actual issues as they arose on the Big Dig and the innovative and interdisciplinary thinking used to find solutions.

Cultural and Ethical Awareness

A major goal of the course is to assist students in recognizing the need to develop a framework for managing projects in a legal, ethical, and moral environment that enhances the probability of both economic and social returns for the organization. Moreover, students will develop an appreciation for working with people from varied backgrounds, with different values and ideological views, and will learn how to resolve problems from multiple perspectives.

Skill Building

Since projects require the ability to manage risk and complexity, cases and application of lessons learned will assist students in identifying, assessing, and responding to project risks. Many of the cases are in the form of lessons from practice and include problems faced by project managers on various subjects including cost estimation, schedule control, risk management, claims and changes, and best practices. Ideas, strategies, and an ability to deal with project complexities will be examined from an interdisciplinary perspective.

COURSE STRUCTURE

This book contains 12 chapters. As described here, the chapters correspond to different phases of the project and different aspects of project management. Each chapter highlights the most important practices and summarizes how these practices and strategies can be implemented to achieve the approval of the project stakeholders and project management and, ultimately, to ensure project success. Each chapter also discusses the important lessons learned and the use of best practices. Some of these practices are set forth in the project management literature and in the standards of the leading international project management organizations including the PMI's highly respected *PMBOK® Guide* and *Standard for Program Management* and the APM's guidelines.

Each chapter contains a similar framework and flow and includes the following elements:

1. Introduction: An overview of the topic covered and the goals of the chapter along with the role of the topic within the broader context of project and program management.
2. Concepts: An explanation of the fundamental elements that build upon the various disciplines and strategies, methodologies, and tools and techniques used in megaprojects generally and specifically on the Big Dig. Relevant theoretical and empirical studies are highlighted in each chapter.
3. Lessons Learned: Highlights of the most important lessons learned from the Big Dig to assist the reader in understanding how projects apply the concepts in real life.
4. Best Practices: Examples of strategies and tools and techniques to improve upon current practice.
5. Summary: A review of the key points raised in the chapter.
6. Ethical Considerations: At the end of each chapter, a problem is presented that requires students to address various ethical dilemmas faced by project managers and respond to the following questions:
   - Is the project based on an ethical foundation?
   - Has the project earned the trust of its stakeholders?
   - Do the project goals align with the strategic goals of the owner?
   - What are the long-term impacts of the project?
7. Discussion Questions: Discussion Questions incorporate case studies, critical thinking, and problem-solving exercises that afford students an opportunity to apply the concepts reviewed in each chapter.
8. References: A list of the author's research and the relevant literature on the chapter topic.

OVERVIEW OF COURSE CHAPTERS

Chapter 1: Introduction to Megaprojects and the Big Dig

The first chapter provides a general overview of megaprojects, including typical characteristics and the benefits and challenges of large-scale projects. While the primary goal of this chapter is to set forth a framework for understanding the importance and goals of megaprojects, it also analyzes what makes megaprojects unique and worthy of future analysis and research.

Chapter 2: History and Financing of the Big Dig

This chapter provides a brief overview and the historical background of the Big Dig, describes the pressing need for new infrastructure in the City of Boston, and explains the extensive preconstruction and environmental planning process that was undertaken, as well as the impact and benefits of this monumental endeavor. Innovation was utilized constantly on the Big Dig to solve problems, some of which may have prevented the project from moving forward. The Big Dig faced highly unusual challenges, including being executed in one of the most congested urban areas in the country. This chapter explores difficult decision points throughout the project and the important role that innovation played in managing these challenges. A comparison of the financing of public and private projects is introduced through an analysis of selected projects, including the advantages and disadvantages of various project finance structures.

Chapter 3: Stakeholders

Stakeholder management is a key component of project management, and poor communication is ranked as the most common cause of project failure. The Big Dig had an extensive communication process involving tens of thousands of stakeholders, both internal and external to the project. The important role that stakeholders played in the project and the collaborative relationships that were established between and among stakeholders are described in depth as critical factors in the project. These stakeholders include the community, the taxpayer, the media, local businesses, abutters, residents, the contactors and designers, the suppliers, the insurers, the consultants, and the interrelationships among local, state, and federal government agencies. This chapter provides insights into some unusual strategies utilized on the Big Dig to identify and manage stakeholder influence and expectations and discusses how to deal with unknown stakeholders.

Chapter 4: Governance

As the project management literature provides very little research on governance structures, this chapter introduces an important subject to the project management taxonomy from the perspective of the country's largest infrastructure project. Transparency as an essential element of governance is a focus of this chapter, and a comparative analysis of what happens in transparent and nontransparent projects is explored. The chapter examines the unique organizational and governance structure of the Big Dig and contrasts it with other megaprojects both in the United States and abroad. The importance of integration and public-private partnerships is emphasized, along with the essential elements of an effective partnership and the design and management of multiple governance structures.

Chapter 5: Megaproject Scope Management

The Big Dig had the most extensive construction bidding process ever implemented. With more than 110 general contractors, 132 contract packages, and more than 9000 processes and procedures, the project was in a constant cycle of preliminary design, final design, procurement, contracting, performance, testing, completion, and takeover. Each one of these phases is discussed in this chapter, including the most important lessons learned. The transition from a construction organization dominated by project management consultants to an operations organization that is composed largely of full-time staff was one of the most difficult transitions and important lessons gleaned from this process.

Chapter 6: Schedule

This chapter focuses on the impact of time on all aspects of managing large-scale projects, from the establishment of a timeline to the life cycle of complex projects and the problems encountered along the way. Solutions to these problems are discussed along with recommendations for accelerated project delivery, managing interfaces and multiple critical paths, and the essential tools to control and mitigate delay.

Chapter 7: Cost History

The Big Dig, as with most megaprojects, is well known for its numerous cost escalations and its rapidly increasing budget. The initial estimated cost of the Big Dig in 1985 was $2.56 billion, but in 2007 the project reached a final budget of approximately $14.8 billion, almost six times the original estimate.

This chapter traces the unusual cost history of the Big Dig, discusses the reported reasons for this cost increase, and contrasts these reasons with quantitative research. The Big Dig was an exception to the commonly asserted reasons for cost overruns. This chapter breaks down the project's cost elements, showing the substantial changes in the budget overtime and the reality behind those changes.

Chapter 8: Cost Management

This chapter examines the critical issues in cost estimation management and control for large-scale projects. Strategies, tools, and techniques for managing cost are analyzed. Extensive research on cost escalation for megaprojects in general and for the Big Dig in particular is examined, along with the importance of strategic planning to protect the process from internal and external pressures.

Chapter 9: Megaprojects and Megarisk

The Central Artery/Tunnel owner-controlled insurance program (OCIP) was the largest wrap-up program ever developed, according to one of the project's major insurers, Lloyds of London. This chapter focuses on the unique aspects of risk and risk financing for a megaproject, the benefits of an OCIP, how the process was formulated, and how the cost of risk was monitored. The project's risk management model is introduced, including risk identification, risk analysis, risk response, and allocation of known and unknown risks. This chapter also highlights how risk management and safety were integrated into every aspect of the project's operations and the important lessons learned from developing an incentivized safety program early in the project.

Chapter 10: Quality Management

The interface between quality and cost, schedule, and scope is one of the most challenging responsibilities of the megaproject manager. This chapter describes the critical elements of a quality program including quality planning, quality assurance and quality control, and the complex structures that were developed on the Big Dig to address the integration of quality across the project. Several case studies are examined to determine the root cause of quality mismanagement and various strategies to enhance quality governance.

Chapter 11: Building a Sustainable Project through Integration and Change

This chapter introduces the important concept of project integration management and its impact on managing change at both the corporate level and the project level. The utilization of integrated processes, especially on long-term projects, has become a key requirement of all project management methodologies. Integrated project management is commonly defined as the combining of all of the major dimensions of project management under one umbrella and involves applying a set of knowledge, skills, tools, and techniques to a collection of projects.

Chapter 12: Leadership

This chapter employs the lessons learned from all the preceding chapters and the leadership research and scholarship to explore the essential characteristics needed to take large-scale projects with technical complexity, a vast amount of uncertainty, and political and environmental risk from concept to reality, despite the difficult burdens, threats, and obstacles faced along the way.

REFERENCES

Anderson, S., K. Molenaar, and C. Schexnayder. 2006. *Final Report for NCHRP Report 574: Guidance for Cost Estimation and Management for Highway Projects During Planning, Programming and Preconstruction.* Web-Only Document 98 (September).

Hughes, T. P. 2000. *Rescuing Prometheus.* New York: Vintage Books.

Luberoff, D., and A. Altshuler. 1996. *Mega-Project: A Political History of Boston's Multibillion Dollar Artery/Tunnel Project.* Revised edition. Cambridge, MA: Harvard University.

Miller, R., and B. Hobbs. 2005. "Governance Regimes for Large Complex Projects." *Project Management Journal* 36(3):42–50 (Summer).

Tobin, J. 2001. *Great Projects: The Epic Story of the Building of America, from the Taming of the Mississippi to the Invention of the Internet.* New York: Free Press.

MEGAPROJECT MANAGEMENT

MEGAPROJECT
MANAGEMENT

Chapter 1

Introduction to Megaprojects
and the Big Dig

The difficult is what takes a little time; the impossible is
what takes a little longer.
—*Fridtjof Nansen, Nobel Peace Prize Winner, 1922*

INTRODUCTION

A veritable research and development laboratory of engineering and
construction, the Central Artery/Tunnel Project, famously known as
the Big Dig, was the largest infrastructure project ever undertaken
in the United States and the largest inner-city construction project
in the world. Its degree of difficulty was far greater than that of the
other megaprojects of the twentieth century, the Panama Canal, the
Hoover Dam, and the English Channel Tunnel. Those projects were
constructed in "greenfield" sites. There was nothing there. The Big
Dig, however, was constructed in the heart of a major, operating city.
In addition, the proposed roadways were to be built off of the Colonial
shoreline. That meant they would be built not on consolidated soil but
on filled land, which possessed undetermined strength characteristics.
Due to the proximity of the harbor, the water table throughout this
unconsolidated soil was between 5 and 8 feet below the level of the
streets. The deepest Big Dig tunnel would have a roadway surface
120 feet below the streets.

   The Big Dig turned out to be quite a dichotomy. Challenges that had
never before been faced were overcome not only in the design phase but
also during construction, and on a daily basis. Technologically, the Big Dig
is a resounding success, a marvel of ingenuity, engineering, design, and
construction. It did resolve the age-old vehicular gridlock problem in the City

1

of Boston. However, the road to its completion was paved with extraordinary challenges in its execution.

There is now an unparalleled example of what works and what doesn't work on megaprojects. Each chapter in this book offers a view of the Big Dig from the inside out and attempts to provide a perspective heretofore unavailable. The goal of this book is to convey an understanding of the systemic difficulties in managing large-scale projects and the need to develop better solutions for implementation of these projects, including controlling costs, schedule, scope, quality, and risk. The literature is filled with academic analysis and recommended practices, but, despite the complexity of megaprojects, there is scarce examination of the numerous processes and procedures that govern these projects and the knowledge and skills needed for managing large-scale projects around the world.

The objective of this chapter is for readers to learn the benefits of studying megaprojects, as well as to explore typical characteristics of megaprojects and how projects like the Big Dig are conceived and developed. This chapter provides a brief overview of the characteristics of megaprojects generally and the unique characteristics of a megaproject built through an inner-city as well as the impact and benefits of this monumental endeavor for future project managers. While the primary goal of this chapter is to set forth a framework for understanding the importance and goals of megaprojects, it also analyzes what makes megaprojects unique and worthy of future analysis and research.

WHY STUDY MEGAPROJECTS?

> In light of the magnitude and technological complexity of these projects—to say nothing of their intriguing historical and political stories—it is surprising that more has not been written about the phenomenon of megaprojects.
>
> —*Haynes 2002*

Megaprojects exhibit many interesting and unique characteristics, and many reasons have been advanced for studying megaprojects including understanding how projects create value (Esty 2004) and the concepts and strategies for success (Merrow 2011). There are additional compelling reasons to study megaprojects; a few of the most important are highlighted as follows.

1. Delivery of Lessons from Practice

> We cannot undo the past, but we are bound to pass it in review in order to draw from it such lessons as may be applicable to the future...
>
> —*Sir Winston Churchill*

One of the primary reasons for project management research is the development of a body of lessons learned that can be applied to future projects across industries and continents. The greatest teacher is experience, as evidenced in this popular quote from Will Rogers: "Good judgment comes from experience and a lot of that comes from bad judgment." The many lessons from the Big Dig and other megaprojects must be shared so that all projects can benefit from this experience, both the good and the bad.

In the National Academies' 2003 report *Completing the "Big Dig": Managing the Final Stages of Boston's Central Artery / Tunnel Project* (Board 2003), the committee that reviewed the project management practices employed on the Boston Central Artery/Tunnel (the Big Dig) Project recommended that other megaprojects "could benefit from the lessons learned from the Big Dig—the causes of the many problems . . . as well as the solutions developed by the management team, design engineers, and construction contractors. Participants in these new projects will need to learn how to develop realistic expectations and manage efforts to achieve them."

During the past decade, megaprojects have had an enormous impact on the global economy and the advancement of transition and developing countries. Research on megaprojects tends to focus on their failures, in terms of cost overruns, delays, and endemic stakeholder conflicts. However, there are also great benefits that are associated with project development and implementation processes that are rarely discussed. This book attempts to focus on both the lessons that are learned when things go wrong, but also the lessons to be gleaned from success, so that they may be systemically pursued.

2. Advancement of Knowledge and Innovation

Institutional learning is proposed as a process through which adaptations can be made to accommodate shortcomings in the prevailing institutional environment (Hall et al., 2001); (Greiman and Rwabizambuga 2009). The nature of megaprojects brings together significant tacit knowledge that is embedded within particular groups in the project (Bresnen 2003). In project-based activities, the flows of personnel, material, and information as social processes are important in the diffusion and transfer of technology and knowledge. Social processes play a great role in the transfer of knowledge and learning. Large projects demonstrate the relationship between knowledge, technology, and organization. This interrelationship emphasizes the importance of structuring the project right from the outset to maximize the flow of knowledge in and out of the project to the benefit of the broader organizational goals.

Advancement of knowledge and innovation at the Big Dig was at the heart of its mission. As noted by the U.S. Federal Highway Administration (FHWA), "[w]hile some aspects of the Central Artery/Tunnel Project (CA/T) in Boston, . . . have been controversial, this monumental undertaking has been responsible for improving the state-of-the-practice in transportation design and construction" (FHWA 2001). This knowledge includes innovations in managerial, operational, and technological tools and processes. Throughout this book many of these innovations and advancements are highlighted and are used to emphasize the importance of studying megaprojects to gain insights into methodologies and tools for improved practices in future projects. Sharing knowledge is not just a domestic goal but a worldwide strategy led by multinational development banks and country- and region-based knowledge-sharing alliances.

3. Projects as an Engine for Economic Development

Large-scale infrastructure has long been an essential factor in economic development. The U.S. Department of Transportation (USDOT), has recognized that "in rebuilding our roads, bridges, transit systems, and airports, we can spur the creation and growth of small businesses, America's economic engine" (USDOT 2011). In 2010, The U.S. Department of the Treasury issued *An Economic Analysis of Infrastructure Investments*, which described the merits of direct private investment in infrastructure as follows:

> Many studies have found evidence of large private sector productivity gains from public infrastructure investments, in many cases with higher returns than private capital investment. Research has shown that well designed infrastructure investments can raise economic growth, productivity, and land values, while also providing significant positive spillovers to areas such as economic development, energy efficiency, public health and manufacturing.
>
> **(Treasury 2010)**

Moreover, the Congressional Budget Office has determined that additional investment in infrastructure is among the most effective policy options for raising output and employment (CBO 2010). These positive benefits are a major reason why the lessons from megaprojects are so important in identifying greater opportunities for building efficiencies into our transportation and infrastructure systems and building national communities that can enhance global competitiveness.

4. Global Expansion and Improvement of Societal Benefits

Development projects have had a long history of improving societal benefits including environmental sustainability, quality of life, infrastructure development, and economic viability; however, there is a long way to go, considering that more than half the world—over 3 billion people—live on less than $2.50 a day (Chen and Martin 2008). In some countries, projects are the only way to deliver sustainable development; thus, understanding how

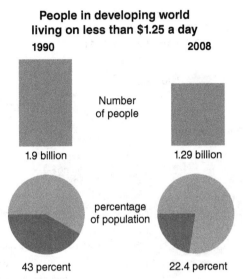

People in developing world living on less than $1.25 a day

Figure 1.1 Poverty Picture in the Developing World 1990–2008
Source: World Bank: Poverty and Equity Data Portal.

they can be used to greater effect is a key to solving major global problems including poverty alleviation, food security, global health, and the general welfare of local citizens. Figure 1.1 shows the poverty levels in the developing world in 1990 versus 2008. According to the World Bank, the focus on poverty alleviation has reduced by almost half, the percentage of people living on less than a $1.25 a day (WB 2012; 2011).

As of 2011, an estimated 880 million people in the world live without safe water, 1.4 billion lack electricity, 2.5 billion lack sanitation, and more than 1 billion lack access to telephone services. Total demand for infrastructure investment and maintenance from developing countries is estimated at more than $900 billion a year, with the greatest needs in Africa and Asia (WB 2011). Increasingly, the Bank Group is linking developing countries so they can share knowledge gained from their experiences. As a group, the bank continues to focus on infrastructure—its largest investment sector—as well as efforts to connect investment to private-sector financing, which includes supporting public-private partnerships. Figure 1.2 shows 53 percent of the lending by sector in Africa dedicated to infrastructure development in Agriculture and Forestry, Energy and Mining, Industry and Trade, Transportation and Water, Sanitation, and Food Protection.

The importance of infrastructure development is further emphasized by the World Bank's partnership with the Government of Singapore, in launching the first Infrastructure Finance Center of Excellence to provide customized services to governments in developed and developing countries as they develop mechanisms to finance infrastructure, including with more private capital.

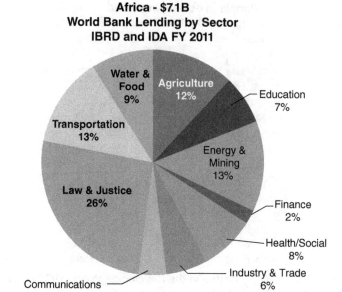

Figure 1.2   World Bank Lending by Sector (Africa) FY 2011
Source: World Bank: Annual Report 2011: The Year in Review: Africa.

5. Fulfilling the Growing Need for Major Investment in Transportation and Energy

Our global society now connects us in ways that we could never have imagined. Seven billion humans now have the opportunity to interact with each other and share knowledge and experience, and our technology enables us to pursue innovative pathways and incredible challenges. Major investments in capital-intensive projects are needed for projects around the globe to build pipelines for the supply of natural gas, to build alternative energy resources such as wind farms, to relieve urban traffic congestion, and to rebuild and modernize bridges, tunnels, and highways as they reach the end of their original design life. The growth in infrastructure investment funds is expected to continue both domestically and globally with billions available in equity to invest in projects that can produce a reliable revenue stream through tolls, tunnels, and cloud-based computer services. The World Bank reports that financing for infrastructure remains its core business, accounting for 46 percent of total assistance in 2011 (WB 2011).

6. Improving Transparency and Oversight

Another important reason to study megaprojects is to learn from the politics of large-scale investment to make sure that, through transparency and public scrutiny, better oversight of these projects is secured.

Megaprojects generate a tremendous amount of scrutiny and public concern. In 2009, the U.S. Department of Transportation (USDOT) Office of Inspector General (OIG) reported 278 indictments and 235 convictions, 191 years of jail time for offenders, and more than $737 million in fines based on OIG investigations related to highway, transit, and airport infrastructure projects contract and grant fraud (Barnet and Russell 2009).

Senator Fred Thompson's report, *Government at the Brink (2001)*, highlights the impact on the public: "These management problems exact a terrible toll on public trust and confidence in the Federal Government. A degree of public skepticism toward our government is a healthy thing. Rampant cynicism is not." He concluded that the combined effect of this cynicism and indifference creates a vicious cycle: "Our leaders can't really be effective if the public feels it can't trust them" (Thompson 2001).

To enhance transparency and streamline government operations, on June 13, 2011, the president used an Executive Order to establish the Governmental Accountability and Transparency Board (GATB) to provide strategic direction for enhancing the transparency of federal spending and advance efforts to detect and remediate fraud, waste, and abuse in federal programs (GATB 2011). In December 2011, the GATB issued a Report and Recommendations to the president recommending the following three actions: (1) the government should adopt a cohesive, centralized accountability framework to track and oversee spending; (2) the government must consolidate and streamline into a single automated electronic collection system that uses a limited but well-defined set of data elements to promote consistent reporting and data standardization; and (3) the government should migrate to a universal, standardized identification system of all federal awards.

These actions are quite common in reference to public projects, and they reflect the vital need to preserve the public's trust. We cannot preserve trust if we do not understand the reality of the complex and difficult-to-understand set of public dynamics (Capka 2004). All projects, whether funded publicly or privately, raise concerns of trust for the simple reason that all projects deliver services, products, or both to the ultimate consumer, the public citizen.

The challenges faced by every project, whether it is a mission to the moon, a nuclear power plant, product development, or a race in cyberspace, involve building trust with all stakeholders. If we fail to meet stakeholder expectations we have impacted our chances for success. Each chapter of this book builds upon the importance of public trust and the approaches and methods for succeeding in projects regardless of the size, complexity or adversity faced by the project promoters.

PROJECTS, PROGRAMS, AND PORTFOLIOS

A Guide to the Project Management Body of Knowledge (PMBOK® Guide)— Fifth Edition is a global standard from the Project Management Institute (PMI) that defines project management as "[the] application of knowledge, skills and techniques to project activities in order to meet the project require-ments." The *PMBOK® Guide* represents what is recognized as common practice in managing projects. Project managers should be skilled at adapt-ing their management methods for the unique qualities of each project. As you will learn throughout this book, in the context of a megaproject, no one size fits all. The project management approach in large scale projects has to take into consideration all of the unique characteristics of megaprojects and will require the use of project standards (*PMBOK® Guide*), program stan-dards (PMI Program Standard 2013) and other methodologies such as agile project management, improvisation, systems engineering and configuration management described in this book. These approaches are often managed concurrently and recognizing these various approaches for enhancing project management success, and when and how to apply each, is critical to effective management of large scale projects.

In the project management literature and in practice, the terms *project, program*, and *portfolio* are used interchangeably and can create confusion as to the real meaning of the terms (*PMBOK® Guide* 2013). Although these terms are related, they are not the same. Portfolios, programs and projects are aligned with or driven by organizational strategies (*PMBOK® Guide* 2013). PMI provides standards for managing projects, programs and portfolios and understanding the interfaces between these standards is critical to ensure successful organizational strategies.

The *PMBOK® Guide* describes a "program" as a group of projects managed in a coordinated way to obtain benefits not available from managing them individually, while a "project" is defined as a temporary endeavor undertaken to create a unique product, service or result. A program can also be a larger project that has been broken down into smaller projects. The integrative nature of program management processes involves coordinating the processes for each of the projects or programs, individually and also as a whole system (PMI Program Standard 2013). In this book and in practice we refer to the Big Dig as a project, even though it essentially contains elements of both projects and programs. The interface between PMI's *PMBOK® Guide* and PMI's Program Management Standard (2013) is particularly relevant to the Big Dig as each would apply to different elements of the project. For example, on the Big Dig, the multiple interrelated projects for design and construction were managed in a coordinated way as a program; however, within that program were the following individual projects:

- Complete 2 miles of underground highway within the city.
- Build a tunnel to connect the city with an airport.
- Develop a landfill to address environmental requirements.
- Construct an interchange to connect local roadways with an inner-state highway system.

To manage multiple projects, the concept of a *program management office* (PMO) has been established in the project management field. A PMO is defined by PMI as a management structure that standardizes the program-related governance processes and facilitates the sharing of resources, methodologies, tools and techniques (PMI Program Standard 2013). Program managers coordinate efforts between projects but typically do not directly manage the individual components. Researchers recommend that PMOs should be used only when they add value to the organization (Kendall and Rollins 2003)—that is, when a cost-benefit analysis reflects that there are more advantages to managing multiple projects under one centralized program rather than separately.

In many multinational companies and large organizations, projects and programs are grouped together under a *portfolio*. PMI has established its own Portfolio Management Standard and defines a portfolio as "a collection of components that are grouped together to facilitate the effective management of that work so as to meet strategic business objectives" (*PMBOK® Guide* 2013). Unlike a program, the projects or programs in a portfolio may not be related or interdependent. Portfolios are usually managed at the highest levels of an organization, and the portfolio manager is charged with managing the portfolios based on specific goals. The major goal of portfolio management is to align the portfolio to the strategic objectives of the company. The portfolio provides an overview of the organization's goals, mission, and strategic objectives. Most large companies and organizations such as NASA, Raytheon, Microsoft, Google, and IBM employ portfolio managers to recommend to the CEO the projects and programs that are most effective in meeting the organization's goals and to eliminate those that are not aligned with the strategic goals of the organization.

Megaprojects: The Literature

Megaprojects have been characterized by size, duration, uncertainty, ambiguity, complex interfaces and integration, and significant political and external influences. The Federal Highway Administration (FHWA) characterizes a megaproject as any project of $1 billion or more in size or a project of a significant cost that attracts a high level of public attention or political interest because of substantial direct and indirect impacts on the community, environment, and state budgets. *Mega* also connotes the skill level and attention required to manage the project successfully (Capka 2004). Megaprojects can also be defined as "initiatives that are physical, very expensive, and public" (Altshuler and Luberoff 2003).

The Big Dig was characterized as a megaproject not only by its cost, at more than $14.8 billion, but also by its construction duration of more than 15 years and its heavy dependence on specialized infrastructure and unique and complex technology. As J. Richard Capka, FHWA deputy administrator and former Big Dig CEO, explains:

> Before one embarks on a mega project whether as an owner, sponsor, lender or contractor, or in any capacity, it is imperative to understand what makes a mega project unique.
>
> **(Capka 2004)**

Allen Sykes, an international adviser on megaprojects, outlines nine characteristics that distinguish megaprojects from other large but less complicated projects (Sykes 1998): (1) size and the likelihood of multiple owners; (2) public opposition to the likely social, economic, political, and environmental impacts; (3) time—a decade or more to plan, design, finance, and build; (4) located in remote and/or inhospitable areas; (5) potential to destabilize markets because of the demand on labor and supplies; (6) unique risk, especially when the project spans economic cycles; (7) financing difficulties; (8) insufficient experience, especially in managing complex undertakings; and (9) career risks, because most of the undertakings do not advance past the planning stage and, therefore, pose an unpopular career course for senior managers. Although most megaprojects contain all nine characteristics, there are some exceptions.

According to Sykes, megaprojects fail not because of myriad design and engineering challenges but because leaders are unable to forge and hold together workable alliances with major stakeholders or to raise the necessary funds—problems that require significant political and organizational skills. He calls for an independent "project directorate" of experts to review each critical aspect of the project and report directly to the owner (Sykes 1998).

Megaprojects in the United States

The transportation sector accounts for more than 10 percent of the U.S. gross domestic product (GDP), behind only housing, food, and health care. Across the country, taxpayers are pumping billions of dollars into innovative transportation initiatives. As reported in the U.S. Department of Transportation's *Agency Financial Report*, three major transportation initiatives will take place in the upcoming years to address the infrastructure needs of America's future (USDOT 2010). These include:

1. The Next Generation Air Transportation System (NextGen) to replace World War II–era, ground-based radar technology with satellite operations, while ensuring the safe and efficient operation of the National Airspace System. As part of this long-term modernization project, in 2010 the Federal Aviation Administration (FAA) launched a full-scale, nationwide deployment of the satellite-based surveillance system called Automatic Dependent Surveillance-Broadcast (ADS-B), which tracks aircraft with greater accuracy, integrity, and reliability than the current radar-based system.
2. Through an initial $8 billion investment, the groundwork has been laid for development of an efficient, high-speed passenger rail network of 100- to 600-mile intercity corridors that represent an essential component of a modernized, nationwide system.
3. DOT's third major endeavor is the nation's first Livable Communities Initiative, which will measurably enhance the quality of life for families,

workers, and communities across America. The program offers more public transportation choices and more commercial and residential development around transportation hubs. Local cities and towns will use the funds to integrate planning and design for livable communities.

During the past decade, the U.S. Department of Transportation identified more than 33 federally funded megaprojects—that is, construction projects costing in excess of $1 billion—currently under way or completed in the United States. The list included such diverse endeavors as the $4.5 billion Los Angeles Red Line, Salt Lake City's $1.6 billion I-15 reconstruction project, the $5.0 billion Miami-Dade International Airport expansion, the $2.2 billion New St. Louis Mississippi River Bridge connecting Illinois and Missouri, the $2.5 billion Woodrow Wilson Bridge connecting Maryland, Virginia, and Washington, D.C., Boston's $14.8 billion Central Artery/Tunnel Project, and the $1.7 billion Miami Intermodal Center.

Megaprojects around the World

Megaprojects are growing at a fast pace, not only in the United States but in all corners of the world. China, Brazil, the Middle East, and other developing regions account for nearly half of the most costly projects in the world. Some recent projects under way include the $25 billion Crossrail Project in London, presently the largest rail network expansion project in Europe; the $8 billion Trans-Afghanistan pipeline, which reached agreement between Afghanistan and India in 2012; and the $40 billion Songdo Sustainable International Business District Project in Seoul, South Korea.

In both developed and developing countries, major megaprojects supported by the World Bank and other development banks have been completed or are under way. Remarkably, 90 percent of new-country assistance and partnership strategies at the World Bank emphasize climate action. Bank-funded low-carbon-growth studies in Brazil, China, Colombia, India, Indonesia, Mexico, Poland, and South Africa are supporting efforts to implement national climate change action plans.

The diversity of these major megaprojects and the benefits are demonstrated by the following examples:

- The World Bank has taken up a megaproject, touted as the first of its kind, for conserving the rich biodiversity and boosting socioeconomic development of the Sundarbans area in West Bengal.
- In China, by strengthening the Yangtze River Dikes, about 75 million people and more than 1.4 million hectares of farmland have been protected from flood damage.
- In Cameroon, 1.6 million people benefited directly from improved infrastructure, including more than 98,000 from improved access to educational facilities.

- In the Dominican Republic, electricity losses were cut by 14 percent during 2005–2008 under a regional Caribbean project on secure and clean energy.
- In Hungary, pollution in the Danube River Basin was reduced by more than 50 percent by expanding the wastewater treatment capacity of utilities during 2000–2007.
- In Malawi, there was a 12 percentage point decline in the poverty head count, from 52 percent in 2005 to 40 percent in 2008, attributed in part to infrastructure development.
- In the Philippines, about 5 million residents of Bicol, who had suffered power shortages because of typhoons, benefited from a stable power supply in 2008.
- The first Low-Carbon Development Policy Loan for Mexico ($401 million) was approved in November 2010.
- A development policy loan for Poland ($1.11 billion), approved in June 2011, supports the energy efficiency and renewable energy components of the Energy Policy of Poland until 2030 program.

CHARACTERISTICS OF MEGAPROJECTS

Megaprojects are not just characterized by their cost or complexity; there are many characteristics, as reflected in literature and practice, and for many developing countries a megaproject may be well under the FHWA characterization of $1 billion yet still be considered a megaproject as contrasted with the country's gross national product. Recognizing and understanding the dynamics of megaprojects is a critical first step in planning for the uncertainty and ambiguity that make managing megaprojects a tremendous challenge. Highlighted as follows are 25 common attributes of megaprojects, along with some less obvious characteristics that were unique to the Big Dig.

1. Long Duration

Megaprojects are often of long duration—between 3 and 15 years or longer for some oil and gas concessions, which can run as long as 20 to 40 years. One of the longest concessions in history was the D'Arcy Concession, a petroleum oil concession that was signed in 1901 and gave D'Arcy the exclusive rights to prospect for oil in Persia (now Iran) for 60 years.

The length of the project alone creates multiple unknowns, ambiguity, uncertainty, and risk that do not exist in projects of much shorter duration (Capka 2004; Haynes 1996, 2002; Merrow 1988). Long projects also require very large amounts of resources including labor, financing, supplies, and equipment (Hall et al. 2001). Calculating the cost and availability of steel 14 years into the future is difficult enough, let alone determining whether the soil conditions will be sufficient to build complex structures based on erosion over time.

According to a 2002 GAO report, *Preliminary Information on the Timely Completion of Highway Construction Projects*, the time required to complete an average highway project varies widely. The time required depends on the size of the project, its complexity, and the public interest in the project. Some projects may take as few as 3 years, while others may take more than 13 years. Because there was no gold standard on time to complete projects set by the FHWA, the Big Dig's completion date evolved over time. While original projections predicted the year 1998, in 1995 the finish date officially crept to 2001, with many observers anticipating further changes to the schedule at that time, resulting in a new estimated completion date of 2004 and a final completion date of 2007—almost ten years later than originally predicted.

2. Scale and Dimension

Though the FHWA has characterized a megaproject as costing more than $1 billion, the cost of a megaproject is relevant only as it is contrasted with the size of the location or country where it is built. For instance, the Mozal Project, an aluminum smelter plant project in Mozambique, pales in comparison to the size of the Big Dig and the English Chunnel, yet its earliest estimates at $1.4 billion approached Mozambique's GDP of $1.7 billion. Since 2001, Mozal has grown to a size of $2.5 billion and is one of the biggest aluminum foundries in Africa. Others define megaprojects broadly as projects that transform landscapes rapidly, intentionally, and profoundly in very visible ways and require coordination and application of capital and state power (Gellert and Lynch 2003).

3. Type of Industry and Purpose

Megaprojects have been categorized by type of industry and purpose. Most definitions are imprecise and tied to specific types of projects. For example, oil and gas projects are almost always characterized as megaprojects regardless of the size. The literature and research reflect five typical types of megaprojects that include the following:

1. Infrastructure projects such as roads, bridges, water security, tunnels, and dams
2. Extractive industries such as oil and minerals
3. Production industries such as agriculture, rubber plantations, and exports
4. Research and development including software design, biotechnology, and aerospace innovation
5. Consumption such as travel and tourism, film festivals, Olympic stadiums, and entertainment complexes

4. Design and Construction Complexity

Engineering is the art of modeling materials we do not
wholly understand, into shapes we cannot precisely analyze, so as to withstand forces we cannot properly assess,
in such a way that the public has no reason to suspect.

—*Dr. E.H. Brown 1967*

There are multiple definitions of project complexity, for all types of projects,
but for infrastructure the most common definitions include an analysis of
design and construction complexity. *Design complexity* is described in two
ways: First, it can be described by the number of steps it takes to complete
a final product. For example, the tunnel portion of the Big Dig contained a
number of phases including conceptual, environmental feasibility and sustainability, geotechnical, structural, tendering, supervision, operational, and
maintenance. The second way is through design criteria such as performance parameters, variability, vulnerability and ergonomics. The tunnels
also required a number of engineering specializations including civil, electrical, mechanical, and environmental. The tunneling portion was more complex
than the roadways and, thus, the degree of complexity can vary from one
contract to another in a megaproject.

Construction complexity is generally defined in terms of integration and
organizational complexity. For example, the first working definition of Integrated Project Delivery (IPD) was established in May 2007 by the AIA
California Council Integrated Project Delivery Task Force. In addition to
the design phases it includes the following phases: implementation documents phase (construction documents), buyout phase, agency review phase,
construction phase, closeout phase, and facilities management. Megaprojects
generally require complex construction integration and technical, resource,
and materials management characterized by a long time frame and numerous
interfaces among multiple contractors and third parties.

5. Sponsorship and Financing

Megaprojects generally have complex financing schemes that involve combi-
nations of debt, equity, grants, bonds, notes and in-kind contributions, and
multiple sponsors from both the public and the private sectors. Chapter 2
focuses on the financing of large-scale projects with diverse financing sources
that change over time. Generally, there is little time to look for new financing
when costs increase and budgets are underestimated, as is frequently the
case on megaprojects (Flyvbjerg et al., 2003). Walking away from a partially
built project is rarely an option. Lenders normally charge higher interest
rates for new debt, and equity sponsors are not always willing to contribute
after construction has commenced. In public projects, government funds may
impact the local business climate and the ability to fund other projects. Funding requirements can affect a state's bond rating and the ultimate cost of

borrowing. The dramatic increase in cost on the Big Dig and the payments for debt that continue until 2039 illustrate the unique funding issues in megaprojects and the challenges that projects face in remedying these problems.

6. Life Cycle

The project management literature characterizes projects by various phases known as the *project life cycle*. Complex projects are much more difficult to define in terms of the traditional project life cycle, as the processes are repetitive and recurring throughout the life of the project and it is difficult to define where one phase ends and the next begins. Initiation on some parts of the project may be occurring very late in the life of the project while closure has already been achieved on other parts of the project. The Big Dig closed on several major portions of the project early on, including the completion of the Ted Williams Tunnel in 1995, while the significant demolition, excavation, and construction had not yet begun on the I-93 underground tunnel through Boston.

7. Long, Complex, and Critical Front End

The long front end of the Central Artery Project was best described by Fred Salvucci, one of the project's chief visionaries and master planners of the Big Dig:

> ... It was a 15 year process from initial authorization to final approval. The Project was first authorized by Congress in 1976, but it took until 1991 when the Environmental Feasibility study was officially submitted to the Federal Highway Administration for the Project to be finally approved.
>
> **(Salvucci 2012)**

At the outset, the level of ambiguity of large complex projects tends to be extremely high. Most projects of this type go through a long "search" period during which both the problem and the solution are sorted out. During this period, some of the players are already known but many more are yet to be identified. In a significant number of cases, this period of preliminary search lasts for decades. For example, many transportation infrastructure projects and facility development projects are in the air for decades before the timing is right to move to some form of concrete proposal for action.

The search phase may be initiated by a perceived need or opportunity or by a signal from an important player that he or she is open to proposals for a particular project or type of project. Governments create opportunities and signal their interest through policy statements and through changes to the institutional framework. This phase is very entrepreneurial. Not only are the problem or opportunity and the solution being sorted out, but coalitions of players are also taking form. The pace is broken and sporadic. Projects often go into limbo after periods of considerable exploratory activity. Exploratory processes often lead to dead ends and are abandoned, at least temporarily.

In their research on projects, Miller and Hobbs (2005) learned that the long, complex, and critical front end of projects, sometimes called the *exploratory phase* or *formulation phase*, was essential to ensuing project success. Their research revealed that the front ends of projects were very long—seven years on average—and often very expensive (up to 33 percent of the total budget). Moreover, the management of this phase was critical and showed significantly more impact on project performance than the management of the engineering, procurement, and construction phases. This phase is often preceded by an extensive lobbying phase conducted by different interest groups. Projects can go through lengthy periods of time to vet both the problems and the various scenarios for solutions. The Big Dig had one of the longest exploratory phases in U.S. history, and the issues raised were technological capability, environmental feasibility, funding availability and political support, and risk, among other concerns (CA/T 1990).

During this exploratory phase, the problems facing major public investment projects can be interpreted in terms of deficiencies in the analytical or the political processes preceding the final decision to go ahead and the interaction between analysis and decision makers in this process (Samset et al. 2006). Such processes are often complex, disclosed, and unpredictable (Miller and Lessard 2000). During this phase, the environmental feasibility studies are completed and approved. Initial testing is commenced and financing is approved. Permitting, licensing, and fees are secured.

8. High Public Profile

Large projects have a high profile with the political subdivisions of the government and the public and are often the focus of government regulators, the media, and public and private audits. The active role of third parties, including local communities, may create conflict and disputes that must be addressed in a timely manner to avoid damage to the reputation of the project and its leaders. The ability to maintain the support of multiple and diverse stakeholders over a long period of time requires tremendous resources and an ability to address the ever-changing demands of stakeholders and the project environment. Researchers and practitioners have noted the public opposition to the likely social, economic, political, and environmental impacts of large-scale projects (Sykes 1998). Chapter 3 provides an overview of the political, technical, legal, economic, and environmental issues raised by stakeholders in megaprojects, as well as the necessity of developing a structure that is open to public participation and community involvement.

9. Public Scrutiny

In addition to a high public profile, high-performing projects are subject to intensive scrutiny. The project sponsor plays an important role in ensuring that projects are scrutinized. The involvement of other stakeholders with diverse interests and perspectives in a governance structure that encourages scrutiny also contributes to the development and delivery of feasible projects; examples include risk and financial evaluations by those providing funding and environmental and social acceptability evaluations through diverse mechanisms of public consultation. Often, the ownership structure creates a context in which stakeholders with both the ability and the incentive to scrutinize projects have decision-making power. Rigorous scrutiny provided through diverse mechanisms contributes significantly to the development, selection, and delivery of feasible projects.

Large infrastructure projects are visible and contestable (Miller and Hobbs 2005). They are never truly private endeavors. Because of their visibility and their environmental, social, and economic impacts, these types of projects are always subjected to considerable public scrutiny and are frequently contested very actively by groups with widely varying interests and perspectives. Public scrutiny and contestability are central to the promotion of the public good. However, these can lead to perverse effects such as constituents pressuring politicians to renege on their commitments and projects being captured by interest groups and held for ransom.

Scrutiny was provided throughout the life cycle of the Big Dig through various entities, structures, and reporting requirements including the legislatively established oversight and coordination commission, dispute review boards, extensive press coverage, numerous internal and external auditors, the local community and businesses, and the project's wrap-up insurance program and trust fund.

10. Pursuit of Large-Scale Policy Making

Megaprojects are often preceded by large-scale policy making to accomplish major infrastructure challenges across cities, states, and countries (Bosso 1994; Tobin 2001). Luberoff and Altshuler provide fascinating insights into the political history of the Big Dig and the muddled aspects of public policy making (Luberoff and Altshuler, 1993, revised 1994).

Paul Schulman, an authority in policy making, argues that large-scale public policy represents the pursuit of objectives that cannot be fulfilled by a series of individualized, partial, and disaggregated steps (Schulman 1980). The particular tactics by which flexibility can be achieved obviously vary greatly among policy contexts, and different partisans will find some tactics more advantageous to them than others.

Especially for political reasons but also to some extent because of the nature of space exploration, NASA is said to have had to work at a large scale, or not at all (Schulman 1980). It took several decades to find out that giant nuclear power plants would be politically and economically unacceptable in most nations, by which time hundreds had been constructed throughout the world for several hundred billion dollars. The error was irreversible, the learning slow, and the cost enormous. Policy makers could have pursued much smaller reactors, using different designs that would have been less expensive, more flexible, and apparently incapable of catastrophic meltdown (Morone and Woodhouse 1989). Nuclear power is presently supported by the federal government in the United States, and is described as one of the safest forms of energy production, despite the nuclear meltdown brought on by the 2011 tsunami and earthquake in Japan.

Large-scale policy making was essential on the Big Dig to accomplish the master plan to replace the aboveground highway with an underground tunnel and to connect the interstate with both the airport and the City of Boston, while at the same time addressing multiple environmental and community concerns.

11. Project Delivery and Procurement

Complex megaprojects require innovation in contracting and procurement to address the allocation of risk during the early planning stages. Megaprojects are known for varied and unique delivery methods. Project delivery is a description of the contracting methods and relationships between the owner, designer, and contractor required to design and build a construction project and includes planning, budgeting, financing, design, construction, and operations (Sanvido and Konchar 1999). In the United States, individual state departments of transportation (DOTs) typically manage and control the full cycle of project delivery, from inception through construction. They may elect to contract with engineering consultants or construction contractors to perform various services related to the project development process.

Some of the more common project delivery methods include design-bid-build (DBB), design-build (DB), construction manager/general contractor at risk (CMR/GC), and build-operate-transfer (BOT). It is contended that DB projects provide greater opportunities for small business (as subcontractors) to perform substantial portions of such projects (FHWA 2006).

On the Big Dig, the more traditional DBB delivery method was used to separate the procurement of designers from the procurement of the contractors. In this delivery method, the project owner or the selected designer furnishes to the constructor design documents, which the constructor is obligated to follow. Essentially, the designer warrants to the constructor that the design is in compliance with the contract documents. As discussed in later chapters, the mechanism chosen for project delivery on the Big Dig was a source of concern due to the constant tension between design and construction. By combining these two functions into a centralized management system, such as DB, the constructor is responsible for both design and construction, eliminating the potential for conflict and numerous disputes.

12. Continuity of Management

It is significant that there is less likelihood of maintaining continuity of management in long-duration projects, particularly in public projects during

Table 1.1   Massachusetts Governors Serving during Big Dig Life Span

Project Phase and Dates	Governors
Conceptual, 1970s–1980s	Sargent, Dukakis, King, Weld
Procurement and engineering/design, 1985–2004	Dukakis, Weld, Cellucci, Swift, Romney
Construction, 1991–2006 (substantial completion)	Weld, Cellucci, Swift, Romney
Operation and maintenance, 1995–2095 (100-year life span of cable-stayed bridge)	Weld, Cellucci, Swift, Romney, Patrick

which administrations change frequently and new policy and agendas develop over time. Realistically, there is also a burnout rate, as it is often difficult to manage the pressures, political realities, and obstacles that accompany the role of project management in a megaproject. As an example, eight governors served Massachusetts during the lifetime of the Big Dig, including the long conceptual phase of the project (Table 1.1). That in turn meant that several project directors and program managers were appointed, depending on the particular expertise viewed as essential by the appointing authority. The lack of continuity was raised as a concern at the Big Dig (Board 2003). Though the private-sector management consultant remained constant throughout the life of the project, the state government entity responsible for oversight changed in 1997, when the Massachusetts Highway Department (MHD) was replaced by the Massachusetts Turnpike Authority (MTA), the ultimate operator of the project. This created a major gap in institutional knowledge and expertise during the peak years of construction. There are some who contend that frequent change in high-level leadership is a good thing, as it can bring creative ideas and a fresh look at the project.

13. Technological and Procedural Complexity (Urban Design)

Large projects are famous for new technologies and the new risks these technologies bring. Projects without precedent can bring many challenges including safety, health and environmental risks, and the potential for increased costs and extended schedules during the testing and implementation phases of the project. Technologically complex projects require expertise that may not be readily available and the use of cutting-edge and emerging design and construction techniques and methodologies. The complexity of urban design and unknown subsurface conditions is well documented in numerous engineering reports, audits, and the project management literature (Hatem 1998).

The Big Dig was known not only for its technological innovation but also for the development of innovations in business organization, development, financing, design, execution, and operations. As a public entity, the Big Dig was subject to increased project scrutiny to ensure the project was represent-ing the public interest. Traditional models of project design and execution would not have worked due to the many complex processes and procedures, the need for shared risk and responsibility, and the difficulty of managing change and innovation in a structured environment.

14. Organizational Structure

Complex projects often have unique organizational structures with multiple levels of authority that require both vertical and horizontal coordination. On the Big Dig, the organization was originally managed on the public side by a project director and on the private construction side by a program manager, with the introduction of an integrated project organization during its peak years of construction. Typical of large-scale projects, the Big Dig was organized by area. The area managers were often assigned geographically and were responsible for administration of their area work as well as coordination among different area work groups. The lower-level or resident and field engineers were assigned to specific contracts and would maintain direct responsibility for design and construction decision making on those contracts.

15. High Degree of Regulation

Megaprojects tend to produce critical infrastructure that is highly regulated. The potential for catastrophic loss and breach of infrastructure security tends to be high on megaprojects as evidenced by the extensive regulation of nuclear power plants, bridge and tunnel projects, gas and oil pipelines, and energy resources. The Department of Homeland Security, the Nuclear Energy Regulatory Commission, the Environmental Protection Agency, the Department of Energy, and the U.S. Department of Transportation all play major roles in critical infrastructure oversight and enforcement. The U.S. Department of Homeland Security's National Infrastructure Protection Plan (NIPP) provides a unifying framework that integrates a range of efforts designed to enhance the safety of critical infrastructure in the United States. The overarching goal of the NIPP is to build a safer, more secure, and more resilient America by preventing, deterring, neutralizing, or mitigating the effects of a terrorist attack or natural disaster and to strengthen national preparedness, response, and recovery in the event of an emergency. The Big Dig had an extensive emergency response and critical infrastructure and security program that operated 24/7 to ensure the safety of all workers, project employees, and local society impacted by the project.

16. Multiple Stakeholders

Megaprojects are almost always embedded in a complex network of public interests due to the abundance of stakeholders with connections and influence in the project. Large numbers of stakeholders create management challenges that don't exist in smaller projects (Chinyio and Olomolaiye 2010; Altshuler and Luberoff 2003; Miller and Lessard 2000). Public and private interests often diverge in projects where the public interest can be compromised by the private-sector stakeholder's profit motivations. The impact of stakeholders on the Big Dig was enormous in terms of mitigation efforts required to protect the interests of local residents, businesses, the general public, and government agencies. Participation of stakeholders in the daily life of the project was essential, and there was a constant need to manage the balance between the shifting interests and influence of stakeholders both internal and external to the project (Goodijk 2003).

17. Dynamic Governance Structures

Governance of megaprojects has become an emerging issue with the expansion of globalization, and research is desperately needed to develop enhanced government frameworks and hybrid models for governance that involve greater local community participation and adherence to principles of distributive and procedural justice (Levitt et al. 2009).

As described in Chapter 4, the governance models used for megaprojects are very different from the traditional hierarchical structure of most corporations and nonprofit organizations such as schools, medical facilities, and government agencies. On megaprojects, all roads lead to governance because the root cause of most problems is weak governance, nonexistent governance, or the wrong governance structure. Multiple governance structures that coexist within the organization are common in large-scale projects, as are nontraditional modes of decision making and oversight. For instance, the Big Dig's governance structure included federal oversight, an owner's board of directors, an owner's project director, and a program manager led by the project's private joint venture consultant, among numerous other decision-making and approval authorities and several hundred project teams that needed to be integrated and coordinated.

On the Big Dig, governance was compounded by the fact that the government relied on the project's management consultant to complete the preliminary designs (which formed the basis for hiring the final design firms), monitor the work of the final design firms, oversee the soils testing and remediation work, prepare the construction bid packages, oversee the construction contracts, negotiate claims and changes, and manage construction in the field, among many other responsibilities.

18. Ethical Dilemmas and Challenges

In today's fast-growing global environment, development of a good ethical framework is part of the human condition. Ambition and the drive for greatness are a constant struggle against greed and self-promotion. As a result, there is an increasing need for project management professionals to learn more about the importance of ethics, particularly as they impact megaprojects. Ethical dilemmas can arise from poor governance structure, conflicting roles of project participants, a lack of transparency, failure to involve stakeholders, relationships with businesses and the community, and environmental conditions. To instill a confidence in the project management profession, PMI developed the PMI Code of Ethics and Professional Conduct, which all PMI members and credential holders must sign (PMI Ethics). Ethical conduct is at the heart of the operation of all megaprojects, and the success of a project depends upon high ethical standards.

19. Consistent Cost Underestimation and Poor Performance

Large, complex projects have characteristics that make them extremely challenging to estimate and which estimators should always consider when reviewing costs assumptions. These include the stretching of available resources to the limit—labor, material, management skill, and information systems, and the management of contingencies and inflation. Research bears out that large-scale projects are consistently underestimated (Anderson et al. 2007; Luberoff et al. 1993; 1994; Flyvbjerg et al. 2002). The Big Dig, the English Channel Tunnel, Germany's Inner-City Express, and the San Francisco Bay Bridge all were dramatically underestimated. The reasons behind these huge overruns vary from project to project; however, cost overruns tend to be a distinguishing characteristic of megaprojects.

The literature on megaprojects also reflects that these mammoth projects are plagued with poor results. Researchers have indicated a variety of factors that contribute to the high rate of failure of megaprojects. Extensive studies on the reasons for poor performance of large-scale projects have concluded that the following are significant factors: (1) political bias, (2) unrealistic original cost estimates, (3) changes in design, (4) low contingencies, (5) underestimation of geological risk, (6) quantity and price undervaluation, (7) political risk and expropriation, (8) technological risk, and (9) underestimation of the length and cost of delays (Flyvbjerg et al. 2003a; Flyvbjerg et al. 2003b).

20. Risk Management in Complex Projects

Complex megaprojects face emergent risks that are not usually present in traditional projects. Therefore, risk management requires a shared vision, partnering, and an integrated structure to mitigate and eliminate the enormous risk potential. The literature has shown that major risks in complex projects include (1) political risk that results in uncertain financing and a significant decline in potential revenues, (2) potential for catastrophic loss, (3) complex engineering and design risk, and (4) substantial unknowns that impact budgets and schedules. The Big Dig had one of the world's largest owner-controlled insurance programs to manage 132 major contracts at its peak and thousands of subcontracts. As described in Chapter 9, the centralized risk management, safety, and loss control program resulted in substantial benefits to the project due to its unique organizational and governance structure.

21. Socioeconomic Impacts

Megaprojects tend to produce significant socioeconomic effects that can have both positive and negative impacts. Diverse stakeholder interests create challenges for project owners that must be addressed before projects can be approved and initiated. The Big Dig created an unusual amount of public attention and criticism due to its sheer size, technological feats, environmental concerns, and visibility. Interest groups have held projects hostage throughout history, sometimes resulting in the abandonment of projects due to the difficulties in overcoming extreme public pressure caused by concerns over neighborhood disruption and safety, health, and environmental concerns. Rejected projects include cancellations by regulators, courts, or local authorities; abandonment by utilities; or projects placed on hold due to regulatory, financial, or other problems. Concerns about global warming played a major role in cancellation of five proposed Florida coal plants, seven proposals in Western states that have newly implemented strict carbon regulations on coal, and numerous highway projects in San Francisco, Atlanta, New York, and Philadelphia (USDOE 2012).

22. Cultural Dimension

Megaprojects are known for unique cultural environments. *Culture* is defined broadly in project management theory to include the "people" side of project management (Cooke-Davies 2002; Pinto 2009). Since megaprojects are made up of numerous participants including public officials, citizens, developers, designers, contractors, and community organizations with different values, perceptions, and needs that often cross countries and continents, it becomes a significant factor in the structure, organization, and governance of the project. Project culture has many dimensions and includes differing political, strategic, economic, and ethical backgrounds that must be harmonized. Cultural challenges on the Big Dig included integrating diverse project teams, philosophies, and practices through partnering and collaborative efforts.

23. Systems and Methodology Complexity

Megaprojects are not just unique because they cost more but because they require extensive amounts of financial, human, and material capital and are designed to address complex systems that involve many interrelationships and interdependencies, within multiple systems and multiple feedback loops (Haas 2008). As an example, schedule alone on large projects often involves multiple critical paths and numerous interfaces. This requires a special skill and expertise that cannot be easily found, as smaller project experience rarely can meet the capabilities required for large-scale projects. Project configuration with multiple activities, processes, and interfaces only adds to the systems complexity requiring the concurrent application of multiple management methodologies. Often, engineering talent can be hard to find, considering the unique and complex structure of megaproject decision making and organization.

24. Environmental Impact

Megaprojects are inundated with environmental challenges, as evidenced by the Big Dig's extensive Environmental Feasibility Study. Though much smaller projects face environmental issues, the sheer magnitude of these problems on a megaproject necessitates extensive up-front planning during the conceptual and preliminary engineering phases of the project and continuous monitoring through all project phases until transition of the project to the ultimate owner or operator. In accordance with state and federal law, the Big Dig required an extensive Environmental Assessment, which took years to complete before the project received final approval to proceed. The environmental assessment included the impact on the 1.5 million people that entered the city each day, along with the more than 600,000 residents of Boston and the numerous businesses that lined the artery. Issues involving air quality, noise and dust control, traffic congestion, rodent control, and health and safety were analyzed, with recommendations for mitigation. The environmental impact not only must be planned for many years in advance but also must be monitored and controlled through all phases of the project.

25. Collaborative Contracting, Integration, and Partnering

All organizations have moved toward a collaborative environment, but it is probably no more evident than in the management of large-scale projects. Examples of collaboration include concurrent engineering, which is a work methodology based on the parallelization of tasks and refers to an approach whereby all functions are integrated to reduce the time needed to bring a product to market. On the Big Dig, engineers utilized concurrent engineering in lighting, utility placement, and air and heating ducts. Other collaborative efforts included partnering as a dispute resolution technique, integrated risk management, safety, health and insurance programs, integrated change control, integration of the project's utilities program, and the establishment of an intergrated oversight coordination commission (CA/T/OCC 1998).

MEGAPROJECT FRAMEWORK

To describe a megaproject in isolation from the concepts, practices, and theory that gives it life would be a difficult task. Thus, throughout this book you will find examples of real-life case studies; application of project management strategy, policy, standards, processes and theory; and analysis of conflicts and problem-solving techniques used by the project's numerous stakeholders. The Big Dig's megaproject framework, illustrated in Figure 1.3 and defined in Table 1.2, best describes the context in which the project operated and the various elements that were critical in moving the project from the conception phase through to completion.

1. Project Management in Practice

In recent years there has been a marked surge in professionalism in project management through educational programs, the awarding of university degrees in project management, and recognized certifications by the pro-fessional organizations. Much of project management practice has developed from the processes and procedures developed by the professional standards organizations. The Project Management Institute (PMI), in the United States, is recognized worldwide for its project management standards. Other widely respected professional standards organizations include the U.K. Associa-tion for Project Management (APM), the International Project Management Association (IPMA), and the Australian Institute of Project Management (AIPM).

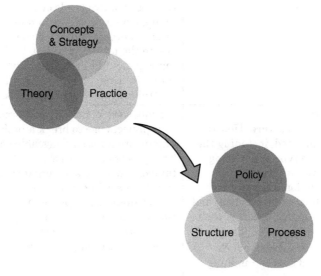

Figure 1.3   Megaproject Framework

Table 1.2   Megaproject Framework

Framework Elements	Definition
1. Concepts and Strategy	A direction in a project that contributes to the success and survival of the project in its environment and aligns with the goals of the project's parent organization.
2. Theory	A theory derives primarily from concepts and causal relationships that relate these concepts (Whetten 1989) and thus contributes to understanding as well as providing a prediction of future behavior (Koskela and Howell 2000).
3. Practice	Project management practice is a specific type of professional or management activity that may employ one or more techniques or tools. The practice of megaproject management is broken down into the following three categories: (a) policy, (b) process, and (c) structure.
a. Policy	A definite course or method of action selected from among alternatives and in light of given conditions to guide and determine present and future decisions.
b. Process	Establishes the total scope of the effort, defines and refines the objectives, and develops the course of action required to attain those objectives. The *PMBOK® Guide* (2013) states that projects are composed of two kinds of processes: project management processes and product-oriented processes (which specify and create the project product). Project management processes are further divided into initiating, planning, execution, controlling, and closing processes.
c. Structure (1) Financial structure: How the project is financed, including the sponsors, the type of financing, and the revenue stream (2) Organizational structure: Defines who reports to whom and what the responsibilities of each position are (3) Governance structure: An oversight and decision-making function	A framework of policies and procedures that projects use to break a project organization into manageable activities. This process involves establishing a financial structure, an organizational structure setting specific job responsibilities, a governance structure that creates a line of authority for managers, and a decision structure for major issues or opportunities.

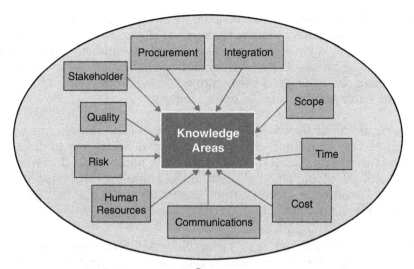

Figure 1.4   *PMBOK® Guide* Knowledge Areas
Source: Project Management Institute (PMI). 2013. *A Guide to the Project Management Body of Knowledge (PMBOK® Guide)*—Fifth Edition.

The *PMBOK® Guide* is a global standard from the Project Management Institute (PMI) that defines project management as "[the] application of knowledge, skills and techniques to project activities in order to meet the project requirements." The *PMBOK® Guide* represents what is recognized as common practice in managing projects, however, project managers must adjust their management method for the unique qualities of each project. The *PMBOK® Guide* defines ten areas of knowledge, shown in Figure 1.4, that contain the processes that need to be accomplished within its discipline in order to achieve an effective project management program. Seven chapters of the book are devoted to seven of the ten knowledge areas as they were applied on the Big Dig (stakeholder, scope, time, cost, risk, quality, and integration management). Three knowledge areas (communication, human resources, and procurement) are discussed in various chapter sections throughout the book. It is important to note that the application of the knowledge areas, and the tools and techniques used, can vary widely between large-scale projects, where there is more complexity, ambiguity, uncertainty, and greater risk, and smaller projects, where there is less uncertainty and thus less risk. Though the Big Dig recognized each of these knowledge areas, in applying these areas, the standards, processes, and procedures required were very different from smaller-scale projects, where there is less uncertainty, complexity, and risk.

2. Project Management Strategies

A strategy in the context of project management can be defined as the direction and scope of an organization over the long term that achieves advantages for the organization, through its alignment of resources within a challenging environment, to meet the goals of the organization and to fulfill stakeholder expectations. To be successful, projects must always be aligned with the strategic goals of its parent organization. Numerous strategies were used to accomplish the goals of the project's owner, but a few of the more important strategies are summarized as follows.

1. Develop a Project Vision   Key to the success of the project was a strategy aligned with the vision of the project owner, which was to develop an infrastructure that included a roadway, bridges, and tunnels that were safe, reliable, and affordable for the benefit of the public stakeholders. Reaching that vision required a strategy from the conceptual phase of the project through to project completion.

2. Determine a Political Strategy   From the outset of this mammoth project, concern was high that the ever-increasing cost of the project would impact public support and funding. A political strategy was also required to deal with the numerous stakeholders with diverse interests and influences that required numerous mitigation efforts.

3. Evaluate Project Management from a Benefits Realization and Entrepreneurial Approach   A cost-benefit analysis is critical in convincing the project owner and sponsors that the project is worth doing and will produce benefits beyond just the building of a physical structure. On the Big Dig, these benefits were realized in the form of dramatic reduction of traffic congestion; replacement of an aboveground highway with a more efficient, environmentally safe underground tunnel system; and improvement of air quality through the establishment of green space.

3. Project Management Theory

Projects have been embraced across many organizations and within many sectors as the dominant framework for carrying out unique, dynamic, and temporary actions (Dinsmore and Cooke-Davies 2005; Turner 1999a). Though projects have existed for centuries, it was in the 1950s that organizations started to systematically apply project management tools and techniques to complex engineering projects (Johnson 2002). There is now widespread agreement on the processes and tools for managing projects; however, there is still a lack of agreement on what constitutes project management theory (Shenhar and Dvir 2007; Morris 2004; Turner 1999b). Meanwhile, the field of project management, as a research and academic discipline, has seen a significant increase in trend analysis in recent years (Morris et al. 2011). Based on the growing literature, there has been pressure to better shape the theoretical basis of the subject and to make project management research more relevant to managers, sponsors, policy makers, and others concerned with the management of projects, without diminishing the standards of academic rigor (Morris et al. 2011).

This book examines the project management research to understand the context in which the Big Dig was conceived and executed. Though, typically, project managers look to the international standards bodies for guidance in managing projects, project managers also must consider new methodologies and theories based on the unique attributes of each project. These newer methodologies can be applied concurrently with traditional theory. In other words, both new approaches and traditional processes can integrate effectively within the same project. For example, there is an emerging view that uncertainty caused by environmental turbulence and changing requirements can be resolved by using creativity, intuition, and tacit knowledge built up over time and through experience (Leybourne 2009).

As experience shows, megaprojects can have tremendous impacts on local communities and even countries; however, there are limited opportunities to gain knowledge on best practices and lessons learned about these projects. As illustrated throughout this book, project managers, in the absence of experience in a particular matter or methodology, often have to draw upon intuition or project management theory. Both the desire to maintain control of the decision-making process and the lack of experience and know-how foster a situation in which improvisation is common (Miller and Hobbs 2005).

In recent years, a shift has taken place from the rigid, process-oriented approach to project management to a more behavioral (Jaafari 2003; Snider and Nissen 2003) and improvisational approach (Leybourne 2007). Improvisation has been defined as the practice of reacting and of making and creating. Improvisation is linked with aspects of time and, particularly, pressure to achieve to a demanding or compressed timetable, which is a typical attribute of most megaprojects (Leybourne 2008). Projects that are surrounded with uncertainty and complexity need to explore new ways of delivery outside of the hierarchical, structured approach of most project management regimes.

Improvisation as a developing theory of project management is not recognized universally by the professional bodies, including the U.S. Project Management Institute, the U.K. Association for Project Management, and the International Project Management Association.

In the software development field, a new methodology, known as *agile project management* (APM), has been developed to address the constraints of cost, time, and schedule. Similar to improvisation, APM is a shift from the traditional planning and reporting process approach of project management to a more flexible, informal approach that evolves over time. Both improvisation and APM draw on an intuitive feel for what will work in a given situation. *Intuition* is generally defined as the ability to acquire knowledge without inference or the use of reason. Thus, it is suggested that both experience and the buildup of tacit knowledge over time will assist the project manager or team members in assessing how to meet undocumented requirements of a given situation (Leybourne 2008). Further research is needed on the use of both improvisation and APM outside the software development field to determine the role of these emerging project management methodologies in large-scale infrastructure development.

LESSONS LEARNED

The lessons from megaprojects can provide valuable tools and innovative ideas for the improvement of all projects. Some of the most important lessons learned about megaprojects from the Big Dig include the following:

1. Megaprojects can provide frameworks for structural decision making, risk analysis, managerial incentives, and investment choices that can be beneficial to all projects.
2. Megaprojects provide solutions to agency conflicts that exist in traditional corporate organizations through organizational, capital, contractual, and governance structure.
3. Knowledge enhancement, attitudinal development, and skill building are all major benefits of examining the unique characteristics of megaprojects.
4. Involving the public at the conceptual stage of the project and throughout the life of the project is essential to project success.
5. Lessons learned from megaprojects must be shared to assist in the development of global best practices for project management.
6. Complex megaprojects face emergent risks that are not usually present in traditional projects. Therefore, risk management requires a shared vision, partnering, and an integrated structure to mitigate and eliminate the enormous risk potential.
7. Megaprojects require collaborative contracting, integration, and partnering as a framework for success.
8. Megaprojects are critical to economic growth and prosperity in both developed and developing countries.

SUMMARY

There are many lessons to be learned from large-scale projects, and as you read the remaining chapters in this book you will see some commonalities among projects regardless of size, duration, industry, geographic location, sponsorship, or mission, as well as some unique aspects of megaprojects that cannot be easily duplicated. Research on megaprojects is desperately needed in the field of project management, and thus filling this need is an explicit goal of this book.

ETHICAL CONSIDERATIONS

In a report released in January 2008, the nonprofit Ethics Resource Center (ERC) revealed that 52 percent of federal, 57 percent of state, and 63 percent of local government respondents witnessed violations of ethical standards, policies, or laws in their workplaces (ERC 2008). From the perspective of the USDOT's Office of Inspector General (OIG), having a strong culture of ethics in the workplace is central to promoting program effectiveness and preventing or stopping fraud, waste, abuse, and other irregularities. Effective internal controls and oversight mechanisms must be in place to detect and reduce instances of fraud that prohibit the transportation community from accomplishing its goals (Crumpacker 2009).

Ethics Violation: Boeing Case Study—Conflict-of-Interest Conviction

In 2003, the media reported that a Department of Defense (DoD) official had helped negotiate a plan to lease Boeing 767 commercial jets to the Air Force for use as aerial refueling tankers. The DoD official and Boeing's former chief financial officer were fired after internal investigations found they had violated DoD and company policies, respectively. The Boeing executive had communicated with the DoD official about possible employment with Boeing while the official still worked for the Air Force and before she recused herself from involvement with Boeing contracts. Both tried to conceal their misconduct (Crumpacker 2009).

Based on these facts, respond to the following questions:

1. Why does the conduct of both the federal official and the Boeing executive raise major ethical concerns? Whom do their actions impact, and what is the damage that could result if this conduct were permitted to continue unpunished?
2. In addition to ethical violations, does their conduct also constitute violations of the law? What is the difference between a legal and an ethical violation? Should the penalties be the same for both?
3. Should the government and Boeing also be penalized for the actions of their employees? If so, in what way?
4. Why is the cover-up of wrongful conduct often worse than the conduct itself? What are the benefits of full disclosure of unethical behavior?
5. What could Boeing have done to better educate its employees about ethical and legal violations?

DISCUSSION QUESTIONS

1. How can infrastructure development be used to advance and improve societal interests? As a project manager in a developing country where half the population lives on a dollar a day, what strategies would you implement to address poverty alleviation and social improvement?
2. Assume you are appointed by the U.S. Department of Transportation (USDOT) to serve as the project manager on one of the largest infrastructure projects in the history of the United States. What recommendations would you make to ensure transparency and oversight of this project?

List five questions you would need to ask of the USDOT before you could develop your recommendations.

3. Of the three major megaprojects to be implemented in the United States reported in the USDOT's *2010 Financial Report*, which do you think has the greatest risks and why? Be sure to include a brief analysis of technological, financial, construction, and operational risks. The megaprojects are (a) The Next Generation Air Transportation System (NextGen), (b) the high-speed passenger rail network, and (c) the first Livable Communities Initiative.

4. What are the types of risk that are inherent in long-duration projects similar to the Big Dig? How can these risks be mitigated at the inception of the Project? Give three examples.

5. How does the life cycle of a megaproject differ from that of a smaller-scale project?

6. Why does Paul Schulman, an authority in policy making, argue that large-scale project policy represents the pursuit of objectives that cannot be fulfilled by a series of individualized, partial, and disaggregated steps?

7. What is meant by project delivery? What makes it a unique characteristic of megaprojects?

8. Why is continuity of management important in megaprojects such as the Big Dig? Keep in mind that the Big Dig spanned the terms of eight governors of the state of Massachusetts.

9. Why do projects without precedent create greater risk? Projects are defined as unique and one of a kind. Does that mean that all projects are without precedent?

10. Describe three socioeconomic impacts that were produced by the Big Dig.

11. What are the essential elements in a megaproject framework? Distinguish between project management (a) practice, (b) strategy, and (c) theory by giving an example of each.

12. What is the role of the professional organizations such as PMI, APM, IPMA, and AIPM in the management of megaprojects?

13. Define *improvisation* and *agile project management*, and explain how they are alike and how they are different.

14. Why are public projects highly scrutinized? Give an example of how public scrutiny can be managed on a megaproject.

15. This chapter includes 25 common and not-so-common attributes of megaprojects. Can you think of two or three additional characteristics of megaprojects and, in particular, of the Big Dig that were not included in this long list?

REFERENCES

Altshuler, A., and D. Luberoff. 2003. *Mega-Projects: The Changing Politics of Urban Public Investment*. Washington, DC: Brookings Institution.

Anderson, S., K. Molenaar, C. Schexnayder 2007. *NCHRP Report 574: Guidance for Cost Estimation and Management for Highway Projects*

During Planning, Programming, and Preconstruction, National Cooperative Highway Research Program, Washington, DC: Transportation
Research Board.

Barnet, B., and M. E. Russell. 2009. "Maximizing Transportation Invest-
ments: Collaborative Fraud Prevention and Outreach," *Public Roads* 72(5).
Washington, DC: U.S. Department of Transportation, Federal Highway
Administration.

Board on Infrastructure and Constructed Environment. 2003. *Completing
the Big Dig: Managing the Final Stages of Boston's Central Artery/Tunnel
Project*. National Academy of Engineering, National Research Council,
Transportation Research Board of the National Academies. Committee
for Review of the Project Management Practices Employed on the Boston
Central Artery/Tunnel ("Big Dig"). Washington, DC: National Academies
Press.

Bosso, C. J. 1994. "The Contextual Bases of Problem Definition." In *The
Politics of Problem Definition: Shaping the Policy Agenda*, edited by David
A. Rochefort and Roger W. Cobb, Chapter 9. Lawrence: University of
Kansas Press.

Bresnen, M., B. L. Edelman, B. S. Newell, A. H. Scarbrough, and J. Swan.
2003. "Social Practices and the Management of Knowledge in Project
Environments." *International Journal of Project Management* 21:157–166.

Brown, E.H. 1967, Structural Analysis, Volume One, Chichester, West Sussex, UK: John Wiley & Sons, Ltd.

Capka, R. J. 2004. "Megaprojects: They Are a Different Breed." *Public Roads*
68(1). Washington, DC: Federal Highway Administration.

CA/T 1990. *(FEIS/R) Final Supplement Environmental Impact Report*,
Central Artery (I-93)/Tunnel (I-90) Project. Boston: Commonwealth of
Massachusetts, Department of Public Works. November.

CA/T/OCC 1998. *Central Artery/Third Harbor Tunnel Project Oversight Coordination Commission (OCC) Summary*. Commonwealth of Massachusetts.
July.

Chen, S., and R. Martin. 2008. *The Developing World Is Poorer than We
Thought, but No Less Successful in the Fight against Poverty*. Development
Research Group. Washington, DC: World Bank.

Chinyio, E., and P. Olomolaiye, eds. 2010. *Construction Stakeholder Management*. Chichester, West Sussex, UK: John Wiley & Sons, Ltd.

CBO (Congressional Budget Office). 2010. *Policies for Increasing Economic
Growth and Employment in the Short Term*. Washington, DC: Congressional Budget Office. January.

Cooke-Davies, T. 2002. "The Real Success Factors on Projects." *International
Journal of Project Management* 20:185–190.

Crumpacker, J. H. 2009. "Fostering a Culture of Ethics." *Public Roads* 72(4).
Washington, DC: U.S. Department of Transportation, Federal Highway
Administration.

Dinsmore, P. C., and T. J. Cooke-Davies. 2005. The *Right* Projects *Done
Right*! Hoboken, NJ: John Wiley & Sons, Inc.

Esty, B. 2004. *Modern Project Finance*. Hoboken, NJ: John Wiley & Sons, Inc.

ERC (Ethics Resource Center). 2008. *National Government Ethics Survey: An Inside View of Public Sector Ethics*. Washington, DC: Ethics Resource Center.

FHWA (Federal Highway Administration). 2001. *Big Lessons from the Big Dig*. Focus: Accelerating Infrastructure Innovations. Pub. No. FHWA-RD-01-065. Washington, DC: U.S. Department of Transportation, Federal Highway Administration.

FHWA (Federal Highway Administration). 2006. *Report to Congress on the Effectiveness of Design-Build*. Washington, DC: U. S. Department of Transportation, Federal Highway Administration.

Flyvbjerg, B., N. Bruzelius, and W. Rothengatter. 2003a. *Megaprojects and Risk: An Anatomy of Ambition*. Cambridge, UK: Cambridge University Press.

Flyvbjerg, B., M. K. S. Holm, and S. L. Buhl. 2002. "Cost Underestimation in Public Works Projects: Error or Lie?" *Journal of the American Planning Association*, 68(3):279–295.

Flyvbjerg, B., M. K. S. Holm, and S. L. Buhl. 2003b. "How Common and How Large Are Cost Overruns in Transport Infrastructure Projects?" *Transport Reviews* 23(1):71–88.

GAO (General Accounting Office). 2002. "Highway Infrastructure: Preliminary Information on the Timely Completion of Highway Construction Projects." Testimony before the Committee on Environment and Public Works, U.S. Senate, Statement of Katherine Siggerud, Acting Director, Physical Infrastructure Issues. GAO-0201067T. Washington, DC: General Accounting Office.

GATB (Government Accountability and Transparency Board). 2011. *Delivering an Efficient, Effective and Accountable Government*. Established under Executive Order 13576. June 12.

Gellert, P. K., and B. D. Lynch. 2003. *ISSJ 175 UNESCO*. Oxford, UK: Blackwell Publishing, Ltd.

Goodijk, R. 2003. "Partnership at Corporate Level: The Meaning of the Stakeholder Model." *Journal of Change Management* 3(3):225–241.

Greiman, V., and A. Rwabizambuga. 2009. "Maximizing the Benefits from Mega Infrastructure Projects: An Institutional Perspective." *Boston University Project Management in Practice Proceedings*. Boston, MA.

Haas, K. B. 2008. *Managing Complex Projects: A New Model*. Tysons Corner, VA: Management Concepts.

Hatem, D., ed. 1998. *Subsurface Conditions: Risk Management for Design and Construction Management Professionals*. Hoboken, NJ: John Wiley & Sons, Inc.

Hall, A., N. Clark, S. Taylor, and R. Sulaiman, 2001 (January). *Institutional learning through technical projects: Horticulture Technology R&D Systems in India*. Agricultural Research & Extension Network, Network Paper No. 111.

Haynes, W. 1996. Constructing an Oversight Plan for the Central Artery/ Tunnel Project: The Long and Winding Road. Presented at the American Society for Public Administration National Conference, Atlanta, GA.

Haynes, W. 2002. "Transportation at the Millenium." *The Review of Policy Research* 19(2):69–72 (Summer).

Jaafari, A. 2003. "Project Management in the Age of Complexity and Change." *Project Management Journal* 34(4):47–57.

Johnson, S. B. 2002. *The Secret of Apollo: Systems Management in American and European Space Programs*. Baltimore: Johns Hopkins University Press.

Kendall, G. I., and S. C. Rollins. 2003. *Advanced Project Portfolio Management and the PMO, Multiplying ROI at Warp Speed*. Boca Raton, FL: J. Ross Publishing.

Koskela, L., and G. A. Howell. 2002. *The Theory of Project Management— Problem and Opportunity*. Working paper. VTT Technical Research Centre of Finland and Lean Construction Institute.

Levitt, R. E., W. J. Henisz, and D. Settel. 2009. "Defining and Mitigating the Governance Challenges of Infrastructure Project Development and Delivery." Submitted to the Conference on Leadership and Management of Construction, Lake Tahoe, CA.

Leybourne, S. 2008. "Improvisation and Agile Project Management: A Merging of Two Ideals?" PMI Research Conference, Warsaw, Poland. July 16–19.

Leybourne, S. 2009. "Improvisation and Agile Project Management: A Comparative Consideration." *International Journal of Managing Projects in Business* 2(4):520.

Leybourne, S. A. 2007. The Changing Bias of Project Management Research: A Consideration of the Literatures and an Application of Extant Theory." *Project Management Journal*, 38(1):61–73.

Luberoff, D., A. Altshuler, and C. Baxter. 1993. *Mega-project: A Political History of Boston's Multibillion Dollar Artery / Tunnel Project*. Alfred Taubman Center for State and Local Government, John F. Kennedy School of Government. Cambridge, MA: Harvard University. Revised June 1994.

Merrow, E. 2011. *Industrial Megaprojects—Concepts, Strategies, and Practices for Success*. Hoboken, NJ: John Wiley & Sons, Inc.

Merrow, Edward W. 1988. *Understanding the Outcomes of Megaprojects: A Quantitative Analysis of Very Large Civilian Projects*. Santa Monica, CA: Rand Corporation.

Miller, R., and B. Hobbs. 2005. "Governance Regimes for Large Complex Projects." *Project Management Journal* 36(3):42–50.

Miller, R., and D. R. Lessard. 2000. *The Strategic Management of Large Engineering Projects: Shaping Institutions, Risk and Governance*. Cambridge, MA: MIT Press.

Morone, J. G., and E. J. Woodhouse. 1989. *The Demise of Nuclear Energy? Lessons for Democratic Control of Technology*. New Haven, CT: Yale University Press.

Morris, P. 2004. "Current Trends in Project and Programme Management." In *Association for Project Management Yearbook*. High Wycombe, UK: Association for Project Management.

Morris, P. W. G., J. K. Pinto, and J. Soderlund, eds. 2011. *The Oxford Handbook of Project Management*. Oxford, UK: Oxford University Press.

Pinto, J. K. 2009. *Project Management Achieving Competitive Advantage*. 2nd ed. Upper Saddle River, NJ: Pearson.

PMI (Project Management Institute). 2006. *PMI Code of Ethics and Professional Conduct*. Newtown Square, PA: Project Management Institute.

PMI (Project Management Institute). 2013. *A Guide to the Project Management Body of Knowledge (PMBOK® Guide)*—Fifth Edition. Newtown Square, PA: Project Management Institute.

PMI (Project Management Institute). 2013. *The Standard for Portfolio Management. 2013*. 3rd ed. Newtown Square, PA: Project Management Institute.

PMI (Project Management Institute). 2013. *The Standard for Program Management. 2013*. 3rd ed. Newtown Square, PA: Project Management Institute.

Salvucci, F. 2012. Author's personal interview with Frederick P. Salvucci, former Massachusetts secretary of transportation. May 25.

Samset, K., P. Berg, and O. J. Klakegg. 2006. "Front End Governance of Major Public Projects." Paper presented at the EURAM Conference, Oslo, Norway. May 18, 3.

Sanvido, V., and M. Konchar. 1999. *Selecting Project Delivery Systems: Comparing Design-Bid-Build, Design-Build, and Construction Management at Risk*. State College, PA: Project Delivery Institute.

Schulman, Paul R. 1980. *Large-Scale Policy Making*. New York: Elsevier North Holland, Inc., 132.

Shenhar, A., and D. Dvir. 2007. *Reinventing Project Management: The Diamond Approach to Successful Growth and Innovation*. Boston: Harvard Business School Press.

Snider, K. F., and M. E. Nissen. 2003. "Beyond the Body of Knowledge: A Knowledge-Flow Approach to Project Management Theory and Practice." *Project Management Journal* 34(2):4–12.

Sykes, A. 1998. "Megaprojects: Grand Schemes Need Oversight, Ample Funding." *Forum for Applied Research and Public Policy* 13(1):6–47.

Thompson, F. 2001. *Government at the Brink: Volume II, An Agency by Agency Examination of Federal Government Management Problems Facing the Bush Administration*. Washington, DC: U.S. Senate, Committee on Governmental Affairs.

Tobin, J. 2001. *Great Projects: The Epic Story of the Building of America, from the Taming of the Mississippi to the Invention of the Internet*. New York: Free Press.

Turner, J. R. (1999a). *The Handbook of Project Based Management: Improving the Processes for Achieving Strategic Objectives*. New York: McGraw-Hill.

Turner, J. R. 1999b. "Project Management: A profession based on knowledge or faith?" Editorial. *International Journal of Project Management* 17(6):329–330.

U.S. Department of Energy (USDOE), National Energy Technology Laboratory. 2012. *Tracking New Coal-Fired Power Plants*. Data update 1/13/2012. Washington, DC: U.S. Department of Energy, Office of Strategic Energy Analysis and Planning.

U.S. Department of Transportation (USDOT). 2010. *Agency Financial Report (FY 2010)*. Washington, DC: Office of the Secretary of Transportation, Assistant Secretary for Budget and Program Performance.

U.S. Department of Transportation (USDOT). 2011. *Agency Financial Report (FY 2011)*. Washington, DC: Office of the Secretary of Transportation, Assistant Secretary for Budget and Program Performance.

U.S. Department of the Treasury. 2010. *An Economic Analysis of Infrastructure Investment: A Report Prepared by the Department of the Treasury with the Council of Economic Advisers*. Washington, DC: U.S. Department of the Treasury.

Whetten, D. A. 1989. "What Constitutes a Theoretical Contribution?" *Academy of Management Review* 14(4):490–495.

World Bank. 2011. *2011 Annual Report: The Year in Review*. Washington, DC: World Bank.

World Bank. 2012. "World Bank Sees Progress Against Extreme Poverty, But Flags Vulnerabilities." Press Release No: 2012/297/DEC. Washington, DC: World Bank News and Broadcast.

Chapter 2

History and Financing of the Big Dig

The Planning for a megaproject must be different if a highway agency expects to achieve success. Project leaders and the management team must do more than just manage a project; they must manage a "public journey."

Richard Capka, former federal highway administrator and CEO/executive director of the Massachusetts Turnpike Authority (Capka 2004)

INTRODUCTION

The Big Dig has been depicted as one of the great projects of the twenty-first century (Tobin 2001). Because of its scale and impacts, the project has been a major issue in national and local politics for more than three decades. This chapter provides a brief overview and the historic background of the Big Dig, explains the pressing need for new infrastructure in the City of Boston and the extensive preconstruction and environmental planning process that was undertaken, as well as discussing the impact and benefits of this monumental endeavor. Finally, the concept of project finance is introduced along with the challenges of financing a megaproject with numerous political, technological, economic, and legal risks. Key features of megaproject finance are highlighted along with discussion of the various challenges in funding megaprojects where there are dramatic changes in budgets and schedule during long-duration projects.

THE VISION

If history were taught in the form of stories, it would never be forgotten.
    —*Rudyard Kipling*

The Central Artery/Tunnel Project—famously known as the Big Dig—like most megaprojects, grew from a vision of a small group of people who saw an opportunity for a city in desperate need of revitalization. Boston is a city rich in history and beauty and is known for such historic events as the Boston Tea Party, the famous battle of Bunker Hill, and the historic ride of Paul Revere. In 1634, Boston built the first public park in America, the Boston Common. It was also in Boston, in the late nineteenth century, that Frederick Law Olmsted designed the park and drainage masterpiece known as the Emerald Necklace, and the fourth-oldest subway system in the world was built in 1897. Boston is often called "the Athens of America," having the largest concentration of colleges and universities in the country, and proudly is home to such cultural achievements as the Boston Symphony Orchestra and the Museum of Fine Arts. In recent history, Boston is perhaps best known for its great sports teams, including baseball's Red Sox, hockey's Bruins, basketball's Celtics, and football's New England Patriots. The city is also host to the first Annual Marathon in the United States.

The Big Dig was also a record for the United States—it was the first and largest inner-city construction project ever conceived. It was the most complex urban infrastructure project in the history of this country and included unprecedented planning and engineering. Its list of engineering marvels includes the deepest underwater connection and the largest slurry wall application in North America, unprecedented ground freezing and tunnel jacking, extensive deep-soil mixing programs to stabilize Boston's soils, the widest cable-stayed bridge, and the largest tunnel ventilation system in the world. Unfortunately, the important lessons learned from this project have never been formally developed or disseminated.

The Big Dig faced highly unusual challenges, including the necessity of working in one of the most congested urban areas in the country. Coordinating more than 132 major work projects added complexity to the tasks of the project constructors and engineers, and moving 29 miles of gas, electric, telephone, sewer, and water lines maintained by 31 separate companies added extraordinary challenges to the project's utility relocation program.

The Pressing Need for the Big Dig

The Big Dig was built to address many urgent issues, including inner-city congestion, the deterioration of a 1952-vintage elevated highway system, and the need for green space. The original Central Artery was built in Boston in the late 1950s, the period characterized by the urban redevelopment movement (Klemeck 2011; Krieger 1999; Tajima 2003) and the era of great megaprojects. The Artery was built to handle 75,000 vehicles per day, but by the 1980s it was jammed with over 190,000 vehicles daily. Supported by federal financing, the Artery cut through old neighborhoods occupied mostly by Italian and Asian immigrants and divided the City of Boston in two with

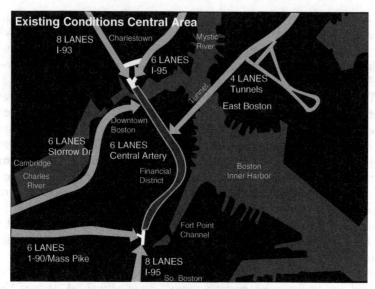

Figure 2.1   Traffic Lanes Feeding into the Central Artery
Source: Central Artery/Tunnel Project.

an ugly green highway in the sky. The creation of new open spaces knit together the urban fabric that had been torn apart by the construction of the Central Artery in the 1950s but also added a new character to central Boston (Altshuler and Luberoff, 2003).

The greatest need for the Big Dig is depicted in Figure 2.1, which shows 38 lanes all connecting with the Central Artery. The Central Artery traverses the Financial District to downtown Boston, one of the most densely developed areas in New England. The major reason for the all-day congestion was that the Central Artery had 38 lanes of traffic that fed into the 6 lanes of the main corridor that carried not only north–south traffic but much east–west traffic as well. Boston's Logan Airport lies across Boston Harbor in East Boston, and before the Big Dig the only access from downtown was through the paired Callahan and Sumner tunnels. Traffic on the major highways from west of Boston—the Massachusetts Turnpike and Storrow Drive—mostly traveled on portions of the Central Artery to reach these tunnels. Getting between the Central Artery and the tunnels involved short diversions onto city streets, increasing local congestion.

The congestion caused numerous problems including air quality, noise, and environmental concerns, and it was an economic drain on the City of Boston, as commuters sat for hours trying to get in and out of the city on a daily basis. Traffic crawled for more than 10 hours each day. The accident rate on the deteriorating elevated highway was four times the national average for urban interstates. The same problem plagued the two tunnels under Boston Harbor between downtown Boston and East Boston/Logan Airport. Without major improvements to the Central Artery and the harbor crossings, Boston anticipated a stop-and-go traffic jam for up to 16 hours a day—every waking hour—by 2010. The annual cost to motorists from this congestion in terms of an elevated accident rate, wasted fuel from idling installed traffic, and late delivery charges was estimated at $500 million.

As bad as these problems were, perhaps the biggest problem was the fact that the structure carrying 190,000 cars a day was built in the 1950s to hold only 75,000 cars. The former route of the aboveground Artery was known locally by many names including "the highway in the sky," "the world's largest parking lot," the "distressway," and "the other Green Monster," a reference to the Boston Red Sox baseball team because of the paint color of its girders and its disruption of previously uninterrupted passage between Boston neighborhoods. The highway itself was planned as early as the 1920s. The aboveground Artery was built in two sections. First was the part north of High Street and Broad Street to the Tobin Bridge, built in the 1950s. Soon after it was built, the residents began to abhor the new highway and the way it towered over and separated neighborhoods, dividing the city in two. As a result of this opposition, the southern end of the Central Artery, through the South Station area, was built underground, through what became known as the Dewey Square Tunnel. Eventually, the entire highway was moved underground as part of the Big Dig Project.

Planning the Big Dig

With public sentiment, nothing can fail. Without it, nothing can succeed.

—Abraham Lincoln

There are many stories of the Big Dig's long up-front planning process and the cobbling together of local coalitions from Boston's neighborhoods— working with Congress and U.S. Speaker of the House Tip O'Neill, legendary for operating in smoke-filled rooms and convincing President Ronald Reagan and his resistant secretary of transportation that this project was the right thing to do. This was no easy task. The mastermind behind this effort, Fred Salvucci, former secretary of transportation and an MIT engineer, credits another MIT engineer, Bill Reynolds, with providing the inspiration for his thinking about the Big Dig (Aloisi 2004). Remarkably, after ten years of planning and perseverance, the funding was obtained. It would be another 15 years before the project was completed. During this time the project leadership needed to inspire and motivate thousands of workers and project teams to do things they had never done before, in order to finally make the vision a reality.

During the long planning period, there were many community organizations and advocates involved in the consultation process. These included the

Bridge Design Review Committee, the Sierra Club, a National Environmental Review Organization, the Artery Business Committee representing the business interests in the planning and construction of the Big Dig, the Boston Chamber of Commerce, and the North End Central Artery Advisory Committee, a neighborhood group that represented the interests of the residents in the design, construction, safety, and environmental concerns surrounding the Big Dig (FEIS/R 1990). Key milestones in the history of the Interstate Highway System and Boston's Central Artery/Tunnel (CA/T) Project are highlighted in Table 2.1.

Engineering of the Big Dig

Although commonly referred to as a single project, the Central Artery/Tunnel Project was actually composed of three related but distinct design and construction activities in the heart of Boston and included (1) depressing the Central Artery (I-93); (2) extending the turnpike (I-90) through South Boston across Boston Harbor to Logan International Airport by way of a newly constructed third harbor tunnel, named the Ted Williams Tunnel, after the legendary baseball star; and (3) building the Leonard P. Zakim Bunker Hill Bridge over the Charles River. The massive project was designed to improve traffic flow and safety in one of the nation's oldest and most congested cities, and it promised to promote economic development in the region. In all, the CA/T Project called for building or rebuilding 161 lane miles of urban highway (about half of which would be in tunnels) in a 7.5-mile corridor of tunnels, bridges, viaducts, and surface streets, as well as project-related buildings.

INNOVATION AND PROBLEM SOLVING

> Opportunity is missed by most people because it comes dressed in overalls and looks like work.
>
> —*Thomas Alva Edison*

The challenges facing the planners of the Big Dig were manifold and, at times, daunting. The urban excavation had unearthed a slew of geotechnical and logistical problems, not the least of which were what to do with existing utility lines, where to put the excavated soil, and how to handle noise, dust, traffic, and rodent problems. These and a plethora of related questions had, not surprisingly, generated concerns from a host of groups voicing their particular interests—neighborhood residents, environmentalists, elected officials, government agencies, businesses, engineers, unions, historic preservationists, the Coast Guard, advocates of improved public

Table 2.1   Timeline for the Central Artery/Tunnel Project

Year	Milestone
1956	Both houses of Congress voted to proceed with construction of America's Interstate Highway System.
1959	The Elevated Central Artery in Boston is open for traffic.
1960s to 1970s	The growth of anti-highway sentiment was fueled in part by rising environmental consciousness.
Early 1970s	The concept for replacing the elevated Artery with a depressed Artery emerged and was attributed to engineer and constructor Bill Reynolds by Fred Salvucci, former MA secretary of transportation.
1975	The Federal Highway Administration and the House and Senate Public Works Committee approved the inclusion of the Central Artery/Tunnel Project in the 1975 interstate cost estimate (ICE).
1982	Planning for the Big Dig as a project officially began in 1982, with environmental impact studies starting in 1983.
1985	The original Environmental Impact Statement (FSEIS/R) was issued by the Massachusetts Department of Public Works (DPW) and a very conceptual design completed.
1986–1990	Many visions and plans were discussed for the Big Dig including "Scheme Z," a controversial bridge proposal for the Charles River Crossing.
1987	Federal grant approved for the Big Dig and ICE was developed.
1991	Construction started on the Central Artery/Tunnel Project.
1991	A new stakeholders group was formed by the secretary of transportation to find an alternative to "Scheme Z."
1994	The Massachusetts Highway Department (MHD) approved a new cable-stayed bridge design and related FSEIS/R for the Charles River Crossing.
1995	The first major construction milestone was reached: the opening of the Ted Williams Tunnel.
1997	State legislation created the Metropolitan Highway System (MHS) and transferred responsibility for the CA/T Project from the MHD to the Massachusetts Turnpike Authority (MTA).
2000	Federal law was enacted to limit federal funding for the project to $8.459 billion (including $1.5 billion to pay the principal of the federal grant anticipation notes (GANs).
2003	Three major milestones were reached: (1) I-90 connector from South Boston to Route 1A opened in January; (2) I-93 Northbound opened in March; (3) I-93 Southbound opened in December.
2006	Major components of the Central Artery/Tunnel Project were substantially complete.
2008	Rose Kennedy Greenway opens to the public.

Sources: A. Altshuler and D. Luberoff. 2003. *Mega-Projects: The Changing Politics of Urban Public Investment*. Massachusetts Transportation Authority, Project Finance Plans 2000–2007.

transportation, and many others. As described by former Big Dig consultant Ted Weigle:

[m]anaging this project is like trying to crowd liquid mercury into a corner. Every time you think you have it contained, you realize it's leaking out the other side. Whereas most people in business like to think that 70 percent of their day is predictable, on a job like this only 30 percent of the day is predictable. It's a process of nonstop, hands-on management and of constantly trying to anticipate where and when the next challenge will occur.

(Rigoglioso et al. 1993)

The Central Artery/Tunnel Project has had many noteworthy technological accomplishments and many firsts in urban construction. Tobin, in his book *Great Projects*, sets forth an excellent overview of the political and technological challenges of the Big Dig, providing a framework for understanding why the project's budget grew so dramatically and the early efforts that were undertaken to address the public's concern (Tobin 2001). It would take volumes to describe all of the project's major technological advances; therefore, this chapter focuses on a few of the most important advances that provide lessons for future urban construction as described in the project's finance reports and detailed descriptions by former FHWA structural engineer Dan Wood (Wood 2001) and popular Big Dig author Dan McNichol (McNichol 2000).

1. Immersed Tubes

The first major challenge of the Big Dig, was building the Ted Williams Tunnel, which connects Logan Airport to South Boston. The 12 binocular-shaped steel tunnel sections, each longer than a football field and each costing $1.5 million, were built in the Bethlehem (Beth) Shipyard in Maryland and sent by barge to the harbor (see Figure 2.2). The tubes came to rest temporarily at Black Falcon Pier along the South Boston waterfront, where they were outfitted with steel-reinforced concrete walls and roadbed. Meanwhile, a huge dredging machine was digging a three-quarter-mile-long trench in the harbor between the South Boston waterfront and the airport. When the preliminary work on the tubes was completed, they were moved by barge into the harbor, lowered into the trench, and connected. The tunnel was then completed with tile, lighting, ceiling panels, emergency systems, and other features.

After they had been connected, the bulkheads were removed, thereby lengthening the tunnel another 325 feet. A combination of blasted rock and natural rock called *riprap* was then placed over the concrete to finish off the bottom of the harbor floor, restoring it to its natural state.

Figure 2.2   Two of the Binocular-Shaped Tube Sections
Source: Central Artery/Tunnel Project.

2. The Fort Point Channel

Problem: This method of floating in the tubes from Maryland could not be used under the Fort Point Channel because the four existing bridges across the channel were too low for a tube to float underneath.

Solution: Project planners turned to a European technique and decided to build a concrete immersed tube tunnel. The six tubes were manufactured in a casting basin—a hole 305 meters (1000 feet) long, 91 meters (300 feet) wide, and 18 meters (60 feet) deep (see Figure 2.3). The basin was sealed off from the water by a series of steel cofferdams filled with crushed stone. When the sections were completed, the basin was flooded and the tunnel boxes—the largest weighing 45,350 metric tons (50,000 short tons)—were floated out of the basin and put in position to be lowered into a trench dug in the channel bottom. Positioning the tubes was done precisely (13-millimeter [1/2-inch] tolerance) because they cannot be moved once they're in place.

But exact positioning wasn't the only issue. The Red Line Subway sits 60 feet below the floor of the channel. It is the oldest subway system in America and the fourth-oldest in the world—London, Athens, Budapest, Boston. To mitigate any loss, 110 concrete shafts were drilled as much as 145 feet into bedrock on both sides of the subway tunnel. These tunnel tubes and caissons fit together like Legos and match up within 1/16 inch of perfection. Two of the tunnel tubes permanently rest exactly 4 feet above the Red Line. To add to this engineering feat, the westernmost portion of

Figure 2.3   Casting Basin
Source: Central Artery/Tunnel Project.

the concrete immersed tube tunnel serves as the foundation for a ventilation building. These were both first-of-their-kind engineering solutions.

3. The Casting Basin

As shown in Figure 2.4, once the tunnel boxes were completed in the dry basin, the cofferdams were removed and the casting basin was flooded. The tunnel boxes were then floated out of the casting basin. The coffer cells were then rebuilt. The basin was dewatered a second time, and the final two tunnel tubes were constructed.

Problem: In order to do the cut and cover work in the "liquid area," it was first necessary to turn the water into land, and then turn the land back into water to float out the completed tunnel box.
Solution: Utilizing a technique called *soil mixing*, the problem was resolved. This process, imported from Japan, entails mixing various types of sand, rock, and soil with a cementitious grout in order to create a permanent and stable plot of earth. After the soil mixing process was complete, cut and cover work connected the jacked tunnel boxes with the immersed tunnel tubes.

The Central Artery/Tunnel Project Casting Basin: Tunnel Box Float Out

Figure 2.4   Tunnel Box Float-Out
Source: Central Artery/Tunnel Project.

4. The Slurry Walls:

Problem: Planners of the Big Dig promised the local Boston community that the mammoth construction project could be accomplished without bringing the life of the city to a halt. Traffic would continue to flow, and business would continue with little or no disruption. As former Big Dig project director Peter Zuk was known to say, "Constructing the Big Dig was like having open-heart surgery while playing tennis."
Solution: Slurry walls were the solution to the problem. In fact, the Big Dig represents the largest single use of the slurry-wall technique in North America. Slurry walls, which are similar to drilled shafts, are concrete walls that run from the surface of the ground down to bedrock, defining the area to be excavated for underground highway construction. A clamshell bucket excavates the ground down to the bedrock, while simultaneously pumping in a mixture of bentonite and water. Once the desired depth is achieved, concrete is pumped from the bottom up, which displaces the bentonite mixture. The wall's immediate purpose was to keep construction trenches from collapsing while the soil was being removed. In the final stages, the walls were incorporated into the permanent tunnel structure.

5. Cable-Stayed Bridge

Problem: Designing a bridge over the Charles River that connects the City of Boston with the Northern Expressway to New Hampshire was a subject of much controversy after several attempts to design the bridge failed. In 1987, with the entire Big Dig threatened, then State Transportation Secretary Fred Salvucci offered "Scheme Z," an all-bridge design that featured 18 travel lanes on six levels. While it was the most environmentally friendly to the Charles River, it was so aesthetically unfriendly that it received poor marks from not only the U.S. Environmental Protection Agency (EPA) but also Salvucci's own design team. Most commentators suggested the bridge design was too massive and would overwhelm the river and adjacent parklands and impair future open space (FEIS/R 1990). In a recent interview with the master designer of the Central Artery/Tunnel Project concerning things he would have done differently, he responded:

> Yes, I often ponder...Is there anything I could have done to make the Z scheme come out differently so you would not have to cross the River twice? Though another scheme would have saved $500 million, I still thought it cost too much.

(Fred Salvucci, former Massachusetts secretary of transportation)

Solution: In 1994, after six years of hearings, the ten-lane asymmetrical Zakim Bunker Hill Memorial Bridge (Zakim Bridge) was conceived by world-renowned Swiss bridge designer Christian Menn (see Figure 2.5). This bridge, which replaced an aging and unsightly double-decked six-lane span, created a new northern gateway into the City of Boston over the Charles River. At 183 feet, it is the widest cable-stayed bridge in the world. The Rusky Bridge in Russia with a span of 1104 meters (3622 ft.) is the longest cable-stayed bridge in the world as of 2012. Prior to that the Sutong Yangtze River Bridge in China, with a span of 1088 meters (3570 feet) was the longest cable-stayed bridge in the world.

In many ways, the 1457-foot-long cable-stayed Zakim Bridge is the public face, the most visible element of the Central Artery/Tunnel Project. Notably, while the bridge was under construction, then Governor Paul Cellucci issued a proclamation declaring November 30, 2000, Christian Menn Day to honor the designer's vision and engineering prowess as part of New England's future.

With its thick, carefully placed cables swooping dramatically from roadbed to twin concrete towers, the bridge looks more like a magnificent piece of sculpture than a structure designed to carry thousands of vehicles daily between Boston and Charlestown. On October 14, 2002, elephants from the Ringling Brothers and Barnum & Bailey Circus crossed the new Zakim Bridge in Boston to demonstrate the bridge's structural integrity (Zakim 2002). The 14 elephants proved that the bridge supports 112,000 pounds (CA/T 2002). The Boston elephant march resembled tests of the 1800s, when

Figure 2.5   Cable-Stayed Bridge Elephant Walk
Source: Photo taken by V. A. Greiman, October 14, 2002.

the engineering of bridges was more questionable and elephants were used to test their integrity.

THE MOST IMPORTANT BENEFITS OF THE BIG DIG

Though many stories have been written about what went wrong on this mammoth project, there are many stories describing what went right. In addition to the many technological advancements described in this chapter, there were also many quality-of-life advantages for the local citizens and businesses in Boston as well as the commuting public. A few of the benefits of the Big Dig are described here based on economic and environmental research undertaken before, during, and after completion of the project and in the following:

> The Big Dig gave us cleaner air and the Boston Harbor project gave us cleaner water, but these two remarkable projects did much more than that.

Together they set the stage for the redevelopment and the revitalization of our waterfront neighborhoods and beachfront communities from Nahant to Nantasket, and provide proof that government can work.

(Bruce Berman, Director of Strategy,
Communications and Programs Save
the Harbor/Save the Bay)

1. Environmental Mitigation

Critical to the acceptance of the Big Dig was the support of the numerous stakeholders, especially the local community of citizens, the local businesses, the local and state politicians, and all government agencies. The first step in the process was approval of the project's Environmental Assessment.

Despite all its challenges, the environmental record of the Big Dig is a particularly notable success story. Managing mitigation on the project had a fairly broad meaning. It included the categories of traffic, community outreach, and the environment. Environmental planning for the Big Dig began in 1982, almost ten years before construction began (FEIS/R 1990). Thousands of federal, state, and local environmental permits, licenses, and approvals were required for the project, and environmental reviews continued throughout the project's construction. The innovative ways that planners found to mitigate the environmental effects of the Big Dig will continue to benefit the region for decades after the project is completed.

The two long decades in which the Big Dig's future infrastructure was examined produced tens of thousands of documents including feasibility studies, design procedures and policy, engineering drawings, geotechnical analysis, soil testing, research, data, financial analysis, and commentary from around the country and the world. In neighborhoods surrounding the old elevated artery, the new underground traffic pattern reduced noise levels by 25 to 33 percent, depending on the time of day, and also created 320 acres of new parks (EDRG 2006).

2. Expansion of the Shellfish Population

The Big Dig was certainly good news for the local shellfish population because of the construction of an artificial reef in Boston Harbor's Sculpin Ledge Channel between Spectacle Island and Long Island. Created in collaboration with the National Marine Fisheries Service and the U.S. Army Corp of Engineers, the reef is designed to compensate for filling in 1.6 acres of blue mussel habitat in the harbor during the closing and capping of the former municipal landfill on Spectacle Island. As the northernmost artificial reef system in the United States, the complex has become home to lobsters, crabs, and finfish, as well as the displaced blue mussels (Wood 2001).

3. Creation of Open Space

Excavating the 3.8 million cubic yards of dirt and material from the Big Dig to build a highway underground through Boston created a problem and an opportunity. Spectacle Island is situated in Boston Harbor, some 4 miles (6.4 kilometers) offshore from downtown Boston. The island has been a huge beneficiary of the Big Dig's mitigation program. Before the project began, Spectacle Island was little more than a mountain of decaying garbage, much of which was leaching into Boston Harbor. Project planners, working with local and state officials, came up with a plan that would benefit the project by providing a cost-effective place to put 3.8 million cubic yards of excavated material and help enhance the city by creating a new island park. Besides Spectacle Island, other cities and towns in Massachusetts, Rhode Island, and Connecticut have also been assisted in efforts to close and redevelop landfills and restore marshes for vegetation and wildlife by receiving clay and other excavated materials from the Big Dig. In addition, the Big Dig created 365 acres of open space, parks, and landscape from Charlestown to South Bay to East Boston to the Boston Harbor Islands.

4. Reduced Traffic Congestion

The goal of the Big Dig project was to relieve the chronic congestion affecting Boston toward the end of the twentieth century, by replacing the six-lane elevated Central Artery (Interstate 93), which was deteriorating rapidly. The first major report since completion of the Big Dig to analyze and link driving benefits to its economic impacts was released in 2006 (EDRG 2006). The report relied on data obtained once the project's milestones were completed in 2003. The report issued several findings:

1. The Central Artery and the Ted Williams Tunnel are now providing approximately $168 million annually in time and cost savings for travelers. This includes $25 million of savings in vehicle operating costs plus a value of $143 million of time savings. Slightly over half of that time savings value ($73 million) is for work-related trips and can be viewed as a reduction in the costs of doing business in Boston.

2. Before the project was built, the average traffic speed on I-93 Northbound was 10 miles per hour (mph). Today it is 43 mph, dropping the average peak travel time from 19.5 minutes to 2.8 minutes, and it has increased by 800,000 the number of people in eastern Massachusetts who can now get to Logan International Airport in 40 minutes or less. Speed for all harbor tunnels increased from 13 mph to 36 mph; Storrow Drive Eastbound to I-93 North improved from 4 mph to 21 mph, dropping afternoon peak hour travel times from 16 minutes to 3.1 minutes.

3. The project reduced by 62 percent the number of daily vehicle hours traveled on the Central Artery, the airport tunnels, and Storrow Drive eastbound.

4. Highway improvements will attract $7 billion in private investment, adding more than 43,000 jobs along the I-93 corridor and in the South Boston Seaport District.

5. Property tax revenues from Big Dig development on the South Boston Waterfront, where large parcels remain undeveloped, will equal 9 to 11 percent of the city's 2005 tax base of $1.13 billion when the waterfront is fully developed as planned, around 2030.

6. The wages paid to construction workers along the South Boston Waterfront are predicted to yield $5 million to $6 million annually in state income tax and sales tax revenue, as long as development continues.

5. Technology Transfer Program

In an effort to expand the knowledge gained from the Big Dig, the U.S. Department of Transportation's Federal Highway Administration (FHWA) developed a technology transfer program to share project management lessons with audiences throughout the United States and the international transportation community. The FHWA Research and Technology Partnerships Program covers many subjects, including project management lessons, operations lessons, and technology lessons. The specific knowledge areas include project director management issues, financial planning, cost and schedule tracking systems, wrap-up insurance, innovative contracting, cost containment programs, environmental and construction mitigation activities, urban slurry wall technology, soil improvement techniques, and tunnel fireproofing and ventilation systems.

6. Growth of Small, Women-, and Minority-Owned Businesses

In addition to technological and operational advancements, the Big Dig became a training ground for small and medium-sized business enterprises throughout the region.

According to Yoke Wong, senior affirmative market inspector for the Central Artery/Tunnel Project:

> One of the Big Dig's major accomplishments was the development and advancement of hundreds of minority and women owned businesses known as disadvantaged business enterprises (DBEs). Since completion of the Big Dig these businesses continue to thrive based on the knowledge and expertise gained from involvement in the Big Dig, considering the magnitude of the project and the technological innovations that were developed over the life of the project.
>
> **(Wong 2012)**

The program exceeded the goals established by the federal government throughout the project life, and it provided many opportunities for minorities and women to work in this complex project (CA/T Project 2007a).

7. Worker and Safety Innovations

The Big Dig is notable for innovations in worker health and safety protection that saved lives, health, and money. Financial statements and safety records reflect that Boston's Big Dig was one of the safest heavy construction projects for workers on record (CA/T Project 2007b). Among its innovations were site-specific safety plans, electronic worker tracking, innovative incentive programs, and full-time safety personnel. Collaboration with local universities and hospitals reduced work-related musculoskeletal disorders, noise-induced hearing loss, and respiratory health effects for dust, diesel, and silica. As noted by Charlie Rountree, Bechtel Parson's safety and health program manager on the Big Dig:

> Good safety depends upon four prongs: process, programs, training and partnering.
>
> **(Hollmer 2002)**

These important lessons must be shared with projects worldwide, particularly in developing countries, where prevention of health and safety risk is essential to the successful outcome of major infrastructure development. In addition to innovative risk and safety programs, the Big Dig introduced many innovative policies, procedures, and processes for partnering and dispute resolution that saved the project millions of dollars and have been adopted by projects throughout the country.

8. National and International Recognition for Technological Advancement

Despite many setbacks and a history of schedule delays and cost overruns, the Big Dig has been recognized worldwide for its technological advancements and marvels. A few examples are:

1. The American Society of Civil Engineers (ASCE) awarded the Zakim Bunker Hill Bridge its Outstanding Civil Engineering Achievement Award in 2004, credited to Swiss bridge designer Christian Menn, who designed the widest cable-stayed bridge in the world, a design that ties cables from the roadbed directly to the support towers. A year earlier, the National Steel Bridge Alliance (NSBA) recognized the bridge as the winner of the Major Span Category, noting its visually striking, well-executed three-dimensional detailing.

2. In 2004, Bechtel's joint-venture program management team, and AIG Consultants, Inc., was awarded the Risk and Insurance Management Society's Arthur Quern Quality Award. The award cites the venture's development, on the Big Dig, of an electronic personnel-tracking system for use in emergency tunnel evacuations.

3. The successful execution and completion of the *Boston jacked tunnels* set a new precedent in the world, as they became the largest and most complex set of tunnels ever installed using this method. These jacked tunnels were actually 10 times the size of any jacked tunnels ever attempted within the United States before. The project, through its team of engineers from Mott MacDonald, the company responsible for overseeing this phase, was awarded the prestigious NOVA Award from the Construction Innovation Forum in 2004. The award "recognizes innovations that have proven to be significant advances that have positive important effects on construction to improve quality and reduce cost." The team also received numerous accolades and industry awards, including the 2003 Quality in Construction Awards, the International Achievement prize in the 2003 Building Awards, the 2002 British Construction Industry International Award, and ASCE's Charles Pankow Award, its highest recognition for innovation.

THE FINANCING OF MEGAPROJECTS

> The light at the end of the tunnel has been turned off due to budget cuts.
>
>   —*Anonymous*

The financing of megaprojects is one of the most important aspects of project management, yet surprisingly little research has been conducted on the subject. The breadth of the types of projects included under the general rubric of "project finance" is staggering, since it is broadly defined to include "the financing of long-term assets through cash flows." Complex projects like the Big Dig, the English Channel Tunnel (the Chunnel), and the Hoover Dam often require multiple sources of finance including funding from both the public and the private sector and multiple entities may be involved.

In the literature and in project management, there is no single agreed-upon definition of project finance. Some examples include:

> ... the raising of funds to finance an economically separable capital investment project in which the providers of the funds look primarily to the cash flow from the project as the source of funds to service their loans and provide the return of and a return on their equity invested in the project.
>
>   **(Finnerty 1996, 2)**

> The financing of long-term infrastructure, industrial projects and *public services* based upon a non-recourse or limited recourse financial structure where project debt and equity used to finance the project are paid back from the cash flow generated by the project.
>
>   **(International Project Finance Association)**

Project finance involves the creation of a legally independent project company financed with nonrecourse debt (and equity from one or more corporate entities known as sponsoring firms) for the purpose of financing investment in a single-purpose capital asset, usually with a limited life.

(Esty 2004)

Each of these definitions reflects the important fact that projects depend upon both private and public sponsors that often lend or extend equity to the project with the expectation that their profits and returns will be secured through cash flow. These cash flows, commonly called *revenues*, are generated in a variety of ways, including tolls, taxes, asset sales, leases, and fees. Unless one is a project owner, sponsor, or lender, too often there is an assumption that financing will be available once a project is approved.

Credit rating agencies are an important source of information about project finance. In the United States, three major agencies—Standard & Poor's, Moody's Investor Service, and Fitch Ratings—play an important role in evaluating the likelihood of success of a public financing undertaking (Rigby and Penrose 2003). Although there is tremendous demand for private financing (through project finance or other techniques) of basic public infrastructure in developing markets, Fitch's offers a distinction between what it views as successful project finance to develop private "industrial capacity and energy" and what it views as less successful efforts involving project finance of basic public infrastructure systems such as water, sewer, or transportation (Fitch 2001).

The Fitch analysts conclude that the basic difference between the two types of projects is "the political nature of these basic infrastructure services," emphasizing the necessity that the basic infrastructure project gain "broad public acceptance for a corporate role in public service." In addition to garnering public support, it might also be assumed that an important role for the government is to conduct a cost-benefit analysis that justifies the project as advancing the welfare of the public. This analysis should include the impact of negative externalities of the project. For instance, a government is peculiarly situated to evaluate the effects of the projects on all that will be affected by it, whether or not it is an explicit stakeholder in the project (Fitch 2001).

PUBLIC-PRIVATE PARTNERSHIPS

Public-private partnerships (PPPs) are a much-misunderstood and still-evolving innovation in transportation infrastructure (Miller 2008). The USDOT defines a PPP as

A contractual agreement formed between public and private sector partners, which allows more private sector participation than is traditional. The agreements usually involve a government agency contracting with a private company to renovate, construct, operate, maintain, and/or manage a facility or system. While the public sector usually retains ownership in the facility or system, the private party will be given additional decision rights in determining how the project or task will be completed.

(USDOT 2004)

PPPs cover as many as a dozen types of innovative contracting, project delivery, and financing arrangements between public- and private-sector partners. These more integrated approaches are sometimes described as design-build (DB), design-build-finance-operate (DBFO), or build-operate-transfer (BOT). The Big Dig was a design-bid-build (DBB) project, in which, essentially, delivery was made in the traditional fashion whereby design is completed first, followed by competitive lump-sum bidding for construction.

There is a wide spectrum of reasons why governments are seeking to develop such partnerships. However, the main goal is to deliver better quality of services for the same amount spent by the public sector. The first and most common reason is to obtain private financing when public financing is unavailable. The second reason is to transfer risk from the government or public owner to parties better able to manage the risk. However, in recent years, a third and arguably the most important rationale for partnerships has emerged to promote and enhance technological innovation and to improve the lives of citizens in the local communities where these projects are constructed.

PPPs can potentially allow cities, states, and countries to develop infrastructure faster and at lower cost, but PPPs are not a panacea, bringing with them higher risk of failure if project details, quality management, and risk allocation are not extremely well planned, defined, and agreed-upon. Governments need to create specialized units to handle the process and often hire specialized consultants. The numerous policies, guidelines, codes, and rules that have been written and implemented governing public-private partnerships incorporate some common objectives but vary significantly when it comes to defining the financial, technical, legal, economic, and managerial risks that should be shared or allocated under a "true" public-private partnership.

As noted by the FHWA, "the challenge has been to develop public-private partnerships that are genuinely partnerships and have benefits for both sides" (Capka 2006). Recent public-private partnerships in the United States include the Massachusetts Route 2 North Project, The Chicago Region Environmental and Transportation Efficiency Program (CREATE), and the Dulles Greenway. In all these projects there were obstacles to be overcome and funding shortfalls that needed to be resolved through innovative solutions. Overall, 43 states (plus the District of Columbia, Puerto Rico, and the Virgin Islands) have legislation authorizing the use of PPPs commonly referred to as P3s, and/or design-build by state transportation agencies (Capka 2006).

In addition to the Big Dig during the past decade, the U.S. Department of Transportation funded more than 33 megaprojects—that is, construction projects costing in excess of $1 billion. The list includes such diverse endeavors as the $4.5 billion Los Angeles Red Line; Salt Lake City's $1.6 billion I-15 reconstruction project; the $5.0 billion Miami-Dade International Airport expansion; the $2.2 billion New St. Louis Mississippi River Bridge, connecting Illinois and Missouri; the 2.5 billion Woodrow Wilson Bridge, connecting Maryland, Virginia, and Washington, D.C.; and the $1.7 billion Miami Intermodal Center. The list does not include completed transportation megaprojects such as the $5.3 billion Denver International Airport; The $1.6 billion I-25/I-225 Southeast Corridor (T-REX) in Denver, Colorado, designed by Parsons; and nontransportation megaprojects such as the $4 billion Boston Harbor Cleanup Project (USDOT 2010).

The use of public-private partnerships to develop transportation infrastructure is more widespread in other parts of the world than in the United States. A European Investment Bank report (EIB 2006) compared the cost of PPP road projects across Europe with conventionally procured road projects and found that PPPs were on average 24 percent more expensive than the public-sector roads. This 24 percent premium is about the same as estimates of cost overruns on public projects, so the extra cost reflects the cost to the contractor to accept construction risk. A review of EIB-funded PPPs across Europe also found that the projects evaluated were completed on schedule and budget and to specification (EIB 2005). Successful international PPPs include the Australia-Sydney Harbor Tunnel, the M5 Toll Motorway in Hungary, and the Hong Kong County Park Motorway.

1. Structuring a Public-Private Partnership

For the purpose of understanding the financing of large-scale megaprojects, it is useful to compare three such projects, the Big Dig, the Eurotunnel, and the Mozal Project in Mozambique—in the following three categories:

1. Financed and managed totally by the public sector
2. Financed and managed totally by the private sector
3. Some combination of the two

Since a PPP is generally defined as a government agency and a private-sector partner contracting to construct, operate, maintain, and/or manage a facility, most PPPs fall under category 3. Contrasting the structure and funding of the Big Dig, the English Channel Tunnel (Eurotunnel), and the Mozal project in Table 2.2 indicates that each of these projects was managed and financed in a very different way. These examples are used not to draw statistical conclusions but to demonstrate the basic structures of public-private partnerships based on the typical categories listed here. They also represent PPPs across three continents and three countries.

2. The Big Dig: Public Finance

The Big Dig was 100 percent funded by the public sector; however, the design and construction of the project were delegated to a private-sector management consultant. Figure 2.6 shows the basic structure of the Big Dig with 48 percent of the financing coming from the federal government and 52 percent from the state government. The structure shown in Figure 2.6 is typical of many megaprojects and highlights the project company, which is often a separate legal entity. In the case of the Big Dig, the designer and constructor formed a joint venture to manage the project under 15 separate contracts known as *work programs*, while the government owner served as the primary funder, oversight authority, and guardian of the public interest.

All parties were united through a series of contractual agreements and commitments. These agreements numbered in the thousands and included labor agreements; work program agreements; contractual requirements with the designers, the contractors, and subcontractors; and agreements with numerous third parties to provide various services such as utility services, professional services, geotechnical inspections, emergency response and traffic control, and audit and oversight functions. The project included internal and external stakeholders who had both an interest in the project and influence over its decisions. Throughout its long life, the media, the local community, and the government regulators were major participants in the daily life of the project.

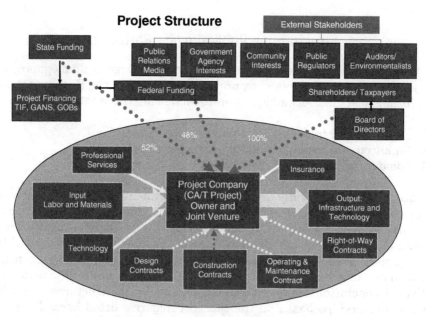

Figure 2.6   The Big Dig Financing and Stakeholder Structure

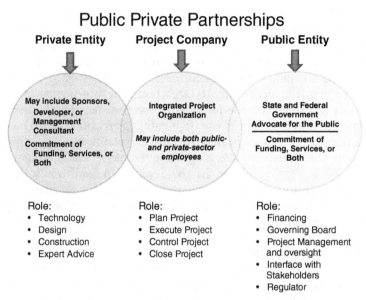

Public Private Partnerships

Private Entity   **Project Company**   **Public Entity**

May include Sponsors, Developer, or Management Consultant

Commitment of Funding, Services, or Both

Integrated Project Organization

May include both public- and private-sector employees

State and Federal Government Advocate for the Public

Commitment of Funding, Services, or Both

Role:
- Technology
- Design
- Construction
- Expert Advice

Role:
- Plan Project
- Execute Project
- Control Project
- Close Project

Role:
- Financing
- Governing Board
- Project Management and oversight
- Interface with Stakeholders
- Regulator

Figure 2.7   The Central Artery/Tunnel Project Public-Private Partnership Structure

As shown in Figure 2.7, the primary goal of the Big Dig project was to allocate the risk of construction and engineering to a private joint-venture firm while retaining public oversight and governance of the project with the state and federal government. Thus, the Big Dig falls into the third category because it combines public finance and private-sector management. Though the Big Dig is often described as a public-private partnership, the Pioneer Institute, an independent research institute in Boston, contends that the Big Dig project was structured not as a PPP but as a collection of traditional design-bid-build projects, with many interconnected pieces and interfaces, in which design is completed first, followed by a competitive bidding process for construction (Miller 2008). In 1999, the Big Dig became an integrated project organization (IPO), in which state employees were integrated with employees of the management consultant, Bechtel/Parsons/Brinckerhoff, with the goal of creating a more collaborative and seamless project management structure, similar to the structure of some PPPs (FHWA 2000).

3. Eurotunnel: Private Finance

By way of contrast, the English Channel Tunnel (Eurotunnel) project exemplifies a basic public infrastructure project that is both managed and financed privately. British prime minister Margaret Thatcher agreed to approve the project only if no government funds or government guarantees were involved; thus, making the Eurotunnel the largest privately financed transportation project in history.

Much has been written about the Eurotunnel, both the largest project financing and one of the largest private infrastructure financings between two countries, England and France, in history. To benefit local personnel from a relatively poor region of France, a unique training and tutorial program was established with the help of the national and regional government authorities. The program involved providing 183,000 hours of site access training and 560,000 hours of further on-the-job training so that people who initially had little experience and training in the applicable professions could be qualified to work on the project (Vandebrouck 1995). The results speak for themselves: 95 percent of the manual labor and 68 percent of the management and supervisory staff were recruited in the region. In addition to good labor relations, the Eurotunnel project cleared away many uncertainties about undersea construction of megaprojects. The experience gained has permitted the vision, throughout the world, of other ambitious projects, not only in terms of excavating tunnels but also in the construction of complex railway systems (Vandebrouck 1995).

The project is also known for its costly overruns, more than 80 percent over budget, and its massive debt (Flyvbjerg et al. 2003). The major failure of the Eurotunnel project has been attributed primarily to the wrong governance structure set up at the inception of the project (Grant 1997). Long-term contracts led to major conflicts between the company's sponsors. A significant part of the financial risk was held by individual shareholders without the knowledge or ability to manage the structure. Groupe Eurotunnel S.A. ("the Company") was formed on August 13, 1986, for the purpose of financing, building, and operating the Channel Tunnel ("the Tunnel") between Britain and France. In May 2007, a restructuring plan was approved by shareholders to address the enormous project debt. Deutsche Bank, Goldman Sachs, and Citigroup agreed to provide 2.9 billion pounds sterling of long-term funding, the balance of the debt was exchanged for equity, and the shareholders agreed to waive their generous perks such as unlimited free travel. The restructuring process was similar to Chapter 11 bankruptcy protection in the United States (BBC 2007). The Company's debt was restructured entirely with private funds, and the restructuring was one of the most complex and difficult European restructurings of recent times (Mallon and Pilkington 2009). The Eurotunnel debt is not expected to be paid off before 2086, three-quarters of a century away. Figure 2.8 provides an overview of the Eurotunnel financing and the structure of the project's concession agreement.

4. The Mozal Project: Public and Private Finance

Another approach to project structure and finance is the Mozal project, which involved the construction of a 250,000-ton-per-annum primary aluminum smelter plant in the war-torn county of Mozambique. Though on an order

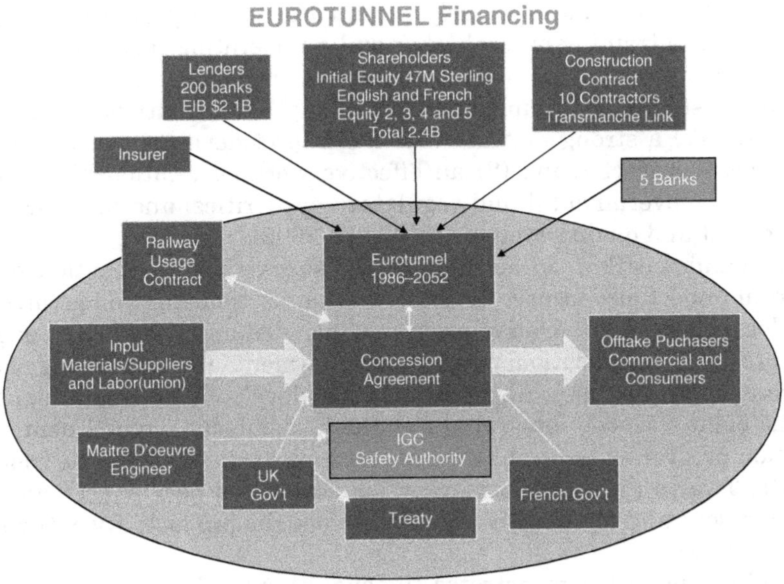

EUROTUNNEL Financing

Figure 2.8 Eurotunnel Financing
Source: Eurotunnel Financial Restructuring Documents, European Investment Bank Documents.

of magnitude it is small in comparison to Eurotunnel and the Big Dig, at $1.4 billion, it is large relative to Mozambique's gross domestic product (GDP) of $1.7 billion.

The project illustrates the combination of public and private financing and was managed by an international consortium. Despite its location in a poverty-stricken country, with poorly developed industrial infrastructure and civil engineering capacity—not to mention swarms of mosquitoes and the worst floods imaginable—the project was completed six months ahead of schedule and $110 million under budget. Its benefits were recognized when it was declared by Project Finance International as the Industrial Deal of the Year (PFI 1999) and by the Project Management Institute as the 2001 Project of the Year. The Mozal smelter was owned by an international consortium led by London-based Billiton (47 percent) and included South Africa's Industrial Development Corporation (24 percent), Mitsubishi of Japan (25 percent), and the government of Mozambique (4 percent) (Esty 2004).

Megaprojects generally succeed only if there is broad public acceptance, which was a major contributing factor in this case. Ian Dryden, area manager of casting and harbor facilities for the Mozal smelter project, attributed the overall success of the project to the following factors: (1) incentives provided by the Mozambique government; (2) an experienced owners team and contractor who had previously executed a nearby project (the Hillside project); (3) the training of local labor and an operating team for the plant; (4) the establishment of a project labor agreement; (5) a highly developed and rigorously tested project implementation plan; (6) international financing of the project; (7) a strong matrix, with the project developer clearly aligned to the Mozal project team; (8) an effective working relationship with the Mozambican governmental and regulatory authorities; and (9) proven risk management and quality systems (Williams 2002).

It is significant that, in addition to the success factors mentioned here, the Mozal project also focused on local community concerns and involvement of the local citizens. Innovative programs included an HIV/AIDS task group formed to focus on education, prevention, treatment, and monitoring of sexually transmitted diseases. Also a community development program ensured that the plant was well integrated into the Mozambican environment, and a relocation program was established for persons displaced from the construction site. Twelve thousand farmers were moved to a nearby area and then trained in seed and fertilizer supply to improve the productivity of the farms (Williams 2002).

The Mozal project demonstrates the significance of a true public-private partnership in which the project owners, sponsors, contractors, developers, and local community came together for the benefit of the greater good to create not only a project but a quality of life that continues to yield benefits in the form of future projects, employment, and an improved standard of living for the household poor of Mozambique. Though in order of magnitude it is much smaller than the Eurotunnel or the Big Dig and conceptually simpler, this case nonetheless demonstrates that even in war-torn, poverty-stricken countries, projects that are well conceived, with good governance and organizational structures, can be successful.

5. Lessons Learned

As the three cases demonstrate, a universal solution to project financing doesn't exist. Though some projects may benefit more from public funding and oversight, other projects may benefit from a combination of public and private financing and management. In analyzing these three cases, neither the 100 percent publicly funded Big Dig nor the 100 percent privately funded Eurotunnel were successful in keeping schedule or costs under control, yet the Mozal project in the besieged country of Mozambique came in six months ahead of schedule and $100 million under budget. There are important lessons to be taken from these cases and analyzed in order to fully understand the impacts of project structure and the real meaning of public-private partnerships. Research is desperately needed to assist project managers in properly assessing the advantages and challenges to structuring project finance and public-private partnerships to ensure more successful project outcomes.

6. Key Features of Megaproject Finance

Table 2.2   Financing Comparison

Characteristics	Central Artery/ Tunnel	Eurotunnel	The Mozal Project
Authority	Statutory	Treaty	Contractual
Asset type	Interstate highway, bridge, and tunneling system	Three undersea rail tunnels	Aluminum smelter
Structure	Joint venture/ contract	Contractual	Consortium
Governance	Governor-appointed board of directors	Bank-controlled board of directors	Public-private governance structure
Management/ employees	Government employees and seconded	Seconded	Seconded
Project owner	State government	Transfer from private to public ownership upon tunnel completion	International consortium
Project sponsors/ founders	Federal/state government	5 banks/10 contractors	Consortium
Category of financing	100% public	100% private	28% public 72% private
Primary sources of financing	Government direct funding, debt (grant anticipation notes), public bonds	Loan syndication: junior and senior debt (12 tranches) and 5 rounds of equity	Consortium of public and private partners
Leverage	Medium 38% average	High 80% average	High 60% average
Availability of loans	Bonds issued as required and grant anticipation notes issued	Bank funds available only after all equity depleted	World Bank IFC loan and Export Credit Agency loans of $680 million
Multilateral institutions	N/A	European investment bank (EIB)	International Finance Corp. (IFC)
Cost estimation and overruns	*10% of 1994 estimate, 275% of original 1985 estimate	140% of original estimates	Six months ahead of schedule and $100 million under budget

(*continued*)

Table 2.2   (*Continued*)

Characteristics	Central Artery/ Tunnel	Eurotunnel	The Mozal Project
Total cost of construction	$14.789B (2008)	$13.5B (1994)	$1.4B
Restructuring plan	N/A	2006 Safeguard Procedure (conversion of junior debt to bonds) reduced debt by 54%, created new parent company Groupe Eurotunnel SA (GET SA)	N/A
Infrastructure	7.5 miles of inner-city and underwater tunnel, first tunnel jacking, largest slurry wall, largest vent system, deepest cofferdam, first asymmetrical and widest cable-stayed bridge	Three tunnels 38 km under the sea connecting Britain to Calais in northern France; longest undersea tunnel in the world	250,000-ton-per-annum primary aluminum smelter representing the largest single foreign direct investment in Mozambique
Term of construction	14 years to build	7 years to build	2 years to build
Major unforeseen events	Subsurface conditions, engineering challenges	Tunnel fire, imprecise specification of tunnel boring equipment, changes in work, rolling stock costs underestimated	Massive storm and flooding, 6000 cases of malaria/ HIV AIDS
Revenues	Public tolls increased 20% just prior to project closure	Revenues seriously underestimated	Revenues at full capacity

Sources: Information adapted from Central Artery/Tunnel Project Finance Plans, Eurotunnel Financial Restructuring Documents, and Esty (2004).

7. The Big Dig Funding Plan

On April 2, 1987, funding for the Big Dig was confirmed by Congress in the Surface Transportation and Uniform Relocation and Assistance Act of 1987. The purpose of the act was to complete the interstate route through Boston and provide access to an international airport, Boston Logan. Under this act, all portions of the Central Artery/Tunnel Project were eligible for federal funds at a ratio of up to 90/10, which meant the federal government would fund 90 percent of the project and the state would pay the balance of 10 percent (FHWA 1956). The 90 percent federal funding that existed for interstate highway projects in the 1950s was eventually overturned when the federal government, due to the rising cost of the Big Dig, ultimately capped the project. As of the year 2000, federal aid represented approximately 50 percent of revenues, but that percentage fell to 48 percent by 2005, in part because federal funding contributions were capped at $8.549 billion. The remaining 50 percent of the revenues were from state and other sources, including general obligation bonds, license and registry fee bonds, federal grant anticipation notes (GANs), the Turnpike Authority, and Massport (see Figure 2.9).

Tolls or Taxes   Given the limited sources of revenue, toward the end of 2008, the state of Massachusetts was facing increasing costs from the $2.2 billion debt on the project, and this stirred a widely publicized debate over options to pay for this debt—mostly a discussion about either tolls or taxes. In

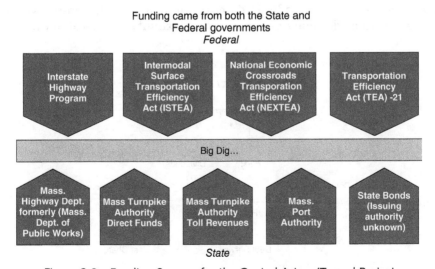

Figure 2.9   Funding Sources for the Central Artery/Tunnel Project
Source: Adapted from "Transportation Infrastructure: Progress on and Challenges to Central Artery/Tunnel Project's Costs and Financing" (GAO 1997).

November 2008, the Turnpike Authority voted to double the $3.50 toll at the Sumner and Ted Williams tunnels under Boston Harbor and introduced a 75-cent increase at both the Route 128 exit in Weston and Boston's Allston-Cambridge tollbooths. Earlier toll hikes that went into effect early in 2008 had raised tolls by 50 cents and 25 cents, respectively. Not surprisingly, the expected toll hike was met with a strong reaction from the public, in particular those relying on the tunnels to connect with the rest of the city. Moreover, in May 2009, a group of motorists organized as a trust approved by the Middlesex Probate Court filed a class-action lawsuit claiming tolls collected on the Massachusetts Turnpike are an illegal tax (Universal Hub 2009).

In the interim, Massachusetts taxpayers must pay on Big Dig bonds until 2039. Figure 2.10 highlights the various funding sources and expenditures that flow between participants in a project finance structure. Some projects are "pay as you go" through tolls or other sources of revenue, while other projects, like the Big Dig, are funded heavily through debt service from bond and grant obligations that may extend years beyond the project's life. Whatever the source of funding, transparency is essential to ensure that all stakeholders, both internal and external to the project, understand the realities and the impact of projects that have cost overruns and underfunded project commitments.

Innovative Financing Resources on the Big Dig To address the challenges of financing megaprojects, transportation agencies worldwide are looking at new financing tools and techniques but are also forming partnerships to bring private-sector dollars into public projects to deliver the maximum infrastructure at the lowest cost to taxpayers and users. The term *innovative finance* has been used broadly to describe an array of policy initiatives and finance programs designed to enhance the flexibility of federal-aid funding,

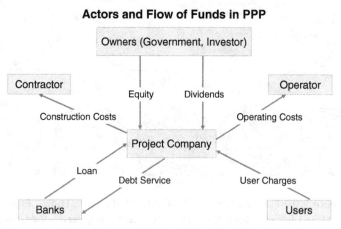

Figure 2.10   PPP Fund Flow Participants

facilitate access to the capital markets, and encourage increased private-sector participation in project delivery (NCHRP 2009).

Megaprojects, defined by the FHWA as $1 billion-plus projects, are critical to increasing the capacity of the transportation infrastructure and improving mobility. Unfortunately, the associated megacosts of the projects make it a challenge to finance these mammoth projects with public dollars. New and innovative delivery methods and sources of capital are desperately needed to fund these projects. In reality, financing a megaproject not only involves funding the construction costs but, in addition, requires financing for operating, maintaining, and rehabilitating existing systems—known as *life cycle costs*—and also paying down the debt service once funding sources are obligated.

MAJOR SOURCES OF BIG DIG FUNDING

The Big Dig was financed solely by public funds that came from both the state and the federal government, as shown in Figure 2.9. Many of the projects of the 2000s relied exclusively on conventional public financing. For instance, the Woodrow Wilson Bridge near Washington, D.C., which was designed to alleviate significant congestion on the I-95 corridor, was funded approximately 85 percent with federal dollars and the balance with state funding. Innovative financing on the Big Dig included new forms of borrowing as described in this section. The Major funding sources for the Big Dig as of May 2007 are shown in Table 2.3.

1. Federal Grant Anticipation Notes (GANs)

As shown in Figure 2.6 approximately 48 percent of the Central Artery/Tunnel Project's funding came from the federal government's Interstate Highway Program. However, with all foreseeable federal and general obligation bond funding committed to the project, new financing mechanisms had to be identified to alleviate the funding shortfall without increasing the overall general obligation debt of the Commonwealth of Massachusetts and adversely affecting its bond ratings.

The GANs program was one of these "new financing mechanisms." It was an innovative financing program that leveraged future federal highway funds to provide current cash for project costs without a general obligation pledge from the Commonwealth. Its purpose was to reduce the funding variance between immediate construction cost needs and future federal highway reimbursements without creating any adverse cost or schedule impacts and without impacting the Commonwealth's credit ratings.

GANs differ from other notes in that they are longer term than typical notes. In addition, the GANs are secured by a pledge of future federal highway reimbursements. Thus, once federal grants are received, the funds go into a grant anticipation note trust fund and are used first to pay debt service

Table 2.3   Major Funding Sources as of May 2007 Cost Schedule Update

Sources by Funding	Total
Federal (non GANS)	7,049 billion
GANs	1,500 billion
State Bond	1,710 billion
Transportation Infrastructure Fund (TIF)	2,482 billion
Massport (Fund 0182)	302 million
Mass Turnpike Authority (MTA) (Fund 0182)	1,451 billion
State Interest on MTA Funds	24 million
MTA Direct Payments	140 million
Insurance Trust Revenue	140 million
Other Revenue	0
Total	14,798 billion

Table 2.4   GANs Repayment Schedule ($ in Millions)

	05	06	07	08	09	10	11	12	13	14	Total
CA/T	$118	$104	$110	$117	$127	$151	$159	$166	$177	$184	$1,413
SWRB		$20	$20	$20	$16						
Total	$118	$124	$130	$137	$143	$151	$159	$166	$177	$184	$1,489

on GANs. The term *debt service* refers to required payments on borrowings, including state bonds and notes. Debt service consists of repayments of the principal amount of the bonds plus accrued interest.

The GANs were to be repaid by the project and the Statewide Road and Bridge (SWRB) Program over a nine-year period (2005–2014). Table 2.4 shows the repayment schedule.

2. General Obligation Bonds (GOBs)

General obligation bonds (GOBs) were issued by the Commonwealth to finance a significant portion of the Project. General obligation bonds are debt instruments issued by state and local governments to fund highway and infrastructure projects, and are the principal non-federal source of financing for most of the Commonwealth's capital infrastructure invest-ment. General Obligation Bonds totaling $1.7 billion were issued in 2000, and Commonwealth General Obligation Bonds totaling $675 million in variable rate debt and $325 million in fixed rate debt were issued in

November and December 2000. The Massachusetts Department of Transportation (MADOT), the Commonwealth's transportation agency, spends approximately $155 million, or about 21 percent of its operating budget, annually in debt service payments. Such debt levels are manageable only because of the Commonwealth's commitment to provide $100 million per year to support the debt obligations associated with the Central Artery/Tunnel Project (Mullan 2011). In accordance with the Commonwealth's financial reports, the debt service will not be paid off until 2039 (HC 2011).

3. Transportation Infrastructure Fund (TIF)

The Central Artery and Statewide Road and Bridge Transportation Infrastructure Fund (TIF) was created within the Commonwealth of Massachusetts and relied on a variety of revenue sources to fund project costs, including the following:

- Massachusetts Turnpike Authority revenues
- Massport Authority contributions
- General obligation bonds funded by license and registration fees
- Commonwealth debt service savings achieved through the defeasance of Commonwealth debt
- Interest earnings from MTA funds

4. Massachusetts Port Authority Bond Anticipation Notes (BANs)

Massachusetts Port Authority (Massport) originally agreed to provide a total of $300 million (not including an additional $65 million in roadway transfers) to acquire MHS roadway assets that exclusively serve to provide enhanced access to the airport. However, due to the events of September 11, 2001, Massport had difficulty meeting this payment schedule. To cover these expenditures, the Commonwealth issued $180 million in bond anticipation notes (BANs) in March 2002. By issuing BANs, the Commonwealth ensured that project funding would not be affected by the timing of the Massport contributions.

5. Massachusetts Turnpike Authority (MTA)

The Massachusetts Turnpike Authority contributed approximately $1.6 billion toward financing the project. Additional MTA contributions were made as needed both under the Commonwealth's plan to cover the additional funding needs for the Project and in an ongoing manner consistent with the spirit and intent of the Metropolitan Highway System legislation.

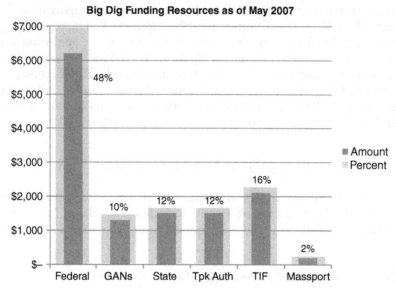

Figure 2.11   Big Dig Funding Resources as of May 2007
Source: Central Artery/Tunnel Project. Cost Schedule Update. May 2007.

BIG DIG REVENUES BY SOURCE, DOLLAR AMOUNT, AND PERCENTAGE OF TOTAL FUNDING

Overall, the budget and funding estimates did not change drastically between 2000 and the project's completion in 2007, once the real cost of the project was recognized. The difference between the total revenues by source is depicted in Figure 2.11, which shows the percentage breakdown by revenue source.

THE REAL COST OF A MEGAPROJECT

Because megaprojects are long-duration projects that can last years and, often, decades, research has shown that the cost of financing a megaproject is too often overlooked due to the desire of politicians to have their projects approved (Flyvbjerg et al. 2003). Budget shortfalls, coupled with dramatic increases in cost, have been accepted as the rule rather than the exception. Consequently, taxpayers are asked to pay inordinate amounts of money to ensure that once a project is started, it is completed regardless of the cost. Though the project management research often expresses the cost of a project, rarely included in that number is the financing required to pay for the project.

In March 2001, when the Big Dig project cost had reached about $14.1 billion, the Massachusetts inspector general reported that the final cost of the Big Dig would likely total $18 billion, including interest on debt, interim borrowing, principal repayment, and possible future growth of the bottom line for construction and support contracts (OIG 2001). This approximately $18 billion consists of the $14.1 billion cost estimate, $3 billion in revenue bond interest, and $750 million in interest on grant anticipation notes. That number was increased in 2008 to $22 billion, based on an extensive analysis of hundreds of documents by the *Boston Globe* (Murphy 2008). The authority's annual payments on its Big Dig debt are presently close to $100 million. According to the Massachusetts Department of Transportation Annual Report, those payments will increase to $110 million annually by 2020 and continue for another 19 years, until 2039 (MADOT 2010).

Of the major projects under construction at the time of completion of the Big Dig, four were financed under a federal funding ratio of 80 to 95 percent, with states and localities providing the remainder. The four projects under this funding structure included the Washington, D.C.–area Woodrow Wilson Bridge, the Springfield Interchange in Virginia, the Tampa Interstate System in Florida, and the New Haven Harbor Crossing Corridor Improvement Program in Connecticut (Capka 2006).

The Federal Highway Administration reports that projects with less-than-traditional federal funding participation include Boston's Central Artery/Tunnel, at 48 percent; California's Foothill Freeway, at 55 percent; the Miami Intermodal Center, at 5 percent; Denver's Southeast Corridor (T-REX) project, at 53 percent; the San Francisco–Oakland Bay Bridge, at 5 percent; the Central Texas Turnpike, at 28 percent; Houston's Katy Freeway, at 61 percent; and Milwaukee's Marquette Interchange, at 54 percent. Projects with lower levels of federal funding usually depend on larger contributions from state and private sponsors (Capka 2006).

State transportation agencies have compelling reasons to look to sources other than federal funds to pay for megaprojects. Federal dollars apportioned to the states do not cover all the projects eligible for federal funding, so states must make hard decisions on how they will use the funds they do receive. In many cases, smaller projects that have captured the interest of local or political stakeholders use up the available federal funding in a given fiscal year.

In addition, many megaprojects are so large and the need for them is so critical that pay-as-you-go through toll or tax revenues is not a viable option. Instead, states are stepping up with higher contributions and using innovative financing techniques—including federal loans and state bonding initiatives.

Regardless of how they are financially structured, major infrastructure projects (for example, new roads, ports, dams, power plants) typically have significant environmental and social impacts that are causing project costs to continue to rise dramatically.

LESSONS LEARNED

1. Educate the public and encourage participation in the project from the first moment. The public must understand the very high levels of complexity involved and be given a stake in the ownership of the project to ensure a more positive outcome.
2. Obtain political buy-in and public acceptance and clarity regarding costs to ensure approval, financing, implementation and success of a public project.
3. Conduct a cost-benefit analysis on megaprojects with well-substantiated data on environmental impact and mitigation, rigorous independent technical and engineering analysis, and extensive input from the local community, government agencies, and project advocates as well as project detractors.
4. Analyze public-private partnerships for their benefits and risk allocation. If the public-sector sponsor is bearing all the financial risk, the private-sector consultant should be incentivized to maintain cost, schedule, scope, and quality, and held accountable for its obligations
5. Review funding techniques such as debt, equity, and grants for their long-term impact on project financing and ultimate cost to the project shareholders or taxpayers.
6. Publicly justify all costs of mitigation, including the cost of movement of utility lines and backup systems, in the project's original budget.
7. Identify and secure reliable sources of revenue before approving project budgets.
8. Exercise transparency throughout the project life cycle to earn and maintain public confidence in the project. Transparency includes acknowledgment and correction of mistakes, no matter how small or large the impact on the project.
9. The project owner must maintain an independent role in order to effectively oversee the performance of the management consultant. This may mean that an integrated project organization is not always in the best interests of the public.
10. When calculating the total cost of ownership, remember to include the capital cost of money.

BEST PRACTICES

1. The real meaning of *public-private partnership* is often overlooked in megaprojects. As a result, these projects are often not properly structured so that all stakeholders have sufficient incentives to consider the long-term implications of decision making. First, the host government, upon the surrender of responsibility to the private parties to construct the project, should have the managerial expertise and technological capability to effectively control and monitor the construction and ultimately to operate

the project. Second, the contracts should create incentives for the private sponsor to ensure that the project, at the time of transfer, will be capable of being operated economically and efficiently for its expected remaining useful life.

2. Ensure that the owner or sponsor retains decision-making responsibility throughout the life of the project, since the owner owns both the project budget and the business case for the project. This is particularly important where projects are funded entirely by the government owner but managed through external consultants.

3. In reality, financing a megaproject not only involves funding the design and construction costs but, in addition, requires financing for operating, maintaining, and rehabilitating existing systems and also for paying down the debt service once funding sources are obligated. Full life cycle costs should be determined prior to project start-up to ensure that the project is properly conceived and structured.

SUMMARY

For the majority of the last century, infrastructure development and management have focused primarily upon capital construction. In addition, a substantial amount of the financing for infrastructure, particularly within the United States, has come from federal sources, as evidenced by the Interstate Highway System Program and the Environmental Protection Agency Construction Grants Program. The proclivity to focus upon the capital development cycle and the reliance upon federal funding have generally limited innovation in approaches to infrastructure development and minimized the importance of life cycle management. However, new methods for both delivering and financing infrastructure have experienced a rebirth over roughly the past two decades. Integrated delivery strategies such as design-build-operate (DBO) and design-build-finance-operate (DBFO) have increased the emphasis upon viewing constructed facilities as systems and have forced the recognition that sustaining these facilities requires more than just the initial capital investment.

Megaprojects require long up-front planning to clarify political, community, and governmental concerns. Projects must demonstrate benefits that are clear to the decision makers, and all environmental impacts must be addressed in the planning process. Project finance should provide the appropriate balance and incentives between the roles of the public sector and the private sector in terms of both management and funding of the project. At the outset of a project, the obligations of the government and the private sector should be clearly understood, and risks should be allocated accordingly. Agencies are looking beyond public dollars and exploring public-private partnerships to help share the costs of major projects. These partnerships if properly conceived enable transportation agencies to tap private-sector financial, technical, and management resources to achieve public objectives such as greater cost and schedule certainty, innovative technology applications, specialized expertise, and access to private capital.

ETHICAL CONSIDERATIONS

Merriam-Webster's Online Dictionary defines ethics as "the discipline dealing with what is good and bad and with moral duty and obligation" and "the principles of conduct governing an individual or a group."

In the federal government, employees swear an oath to the American people to conduct themselves in an ethical manner. The first sentence of Title 5 of the Code of Federal Regulations, Part 2635, reads, "Public service is a public trust. Each employee has a responsibility to the United States Government and its citizens to place loyalty to the Constitution, laws, and ethical principles above private gain." State and local governments, and even private organizations, have similar requirements.

The Office of Inspector General (OIG) of the U.S. Department of Transportation (USDOT) views trust as the cornerstone of public service. From the perspective of the OIG, having a strong culture of ethics in the workplace is central to promoting program effectiveness and preventing or stopping fraud, waste, abuse, and other irregularities.

Applying the standards of ethics as defined by the federal government and the U.S. Department of Transportation, assume you are a federal employee assigned as project director to manage an existing $10 billion megaproject in a major U.S. city. Pursuant to your responsibilities you discover there has been a practice of approving cost overruns to keep the project on schedule, and financing the increased cost through issuance of general obligation bonds backed by the state's assets. The value of the bonds has deteriorated based on the state's credit rating and thus bondholders are impacted by a potential default on the bonds. Moreover, the project's cost has increased dramatically to $16 billion due to the high interest payments that must be made on the bonds over a twenty year period. None of this has been disclosed to the public or the project's stakeholders in the project's financial statements. The project director is responsible for delivering the defined scope of the project within time scale and budget, and ensuring that sufficient funding is available to pay all project costs.

Based on these facts, respond to the following questions:

1. As the new project director what ethical concerns would you have with the project's cost escalation and borrowing practices?
2. Should project managers be responsible for disclosing cost overruns funded by the public through interest payments on public bonds? Does it matter if the project is $5 million over budget or $500 million over budget? Is failure to disclose this practice an ethical violation? Why or why not? If you consider the violation to be an ethical violation what should the penalty be?

3. Is the project director responsible for notifying the public of the real cost of the project including any interest or debt payments that arise from future borrowings due to cost escalation? Does it matter if it is a public or a privately funded project?
4. Describe the policies, processes, and procedures you would implement to build more ethical awareness into the project culture relating to project practices and public disclosure.

DISCUSSION QUESTIONS

1. Is there a difference between project finance for public works projects like the Big Dig and purely private project finance? If so, what guidelines should be used to help distinguish the two?
2. Is a project that is fully funded by public sources but managed by a private consultant a good example of a public-private partnership? Why or why not? Does it meet the U.S. Department of Transportation's definition of a PPP?
3. What is meant by innovative financing? Describe three examples of innovative financing used on the Big Dig.
4. What are the impacts to project finance when a public project has spiraling cost overruns? What are the project's options when costs increase and funding is unavailable from public sources?
5. Explain what is meant by project uncertainty and describe how uncertainty impacts project finance and how uncertainty can be mitigated at the conceptual stage of the project.
6. Explain the meaning of cost-benefit analysis? Why is a cost-benefit analysis critical to obtaining commitment of project funding? How would you go about gathering data on the costs and benefits of a megaproject like the Big Dig?
7. Contrast the Eurotunnel project with the Big Dig and describe what you believe to be the major root cause of runaway costs on each of these projects. Dig deep into the research and think critically before responding to this question.
8. There are many benefits described in this chapter for the building of the Big Dig. Of all the benefits listed what is the most important benefit and why? What is the least important benefit and why?

REFERENCES

Aloisi, J. 2004. *The Big Dig: New England Remembers*. Beverly, MA: Commonwealth Editions.

Altshuler, A., and D. Luberoff. 2003. *Mega-Projects: The Changing Politics of Urban Public Investment*. Washington, DC: Brookings Institution.

BBC (British Broadcasting Company). 2007. *Eurotunnel "Saved" by Investors*. May 25.

Berman, Bruce. 2012. Interview with Bruce Berman, director of strategy, communications and programs, Save the Harbor/Save the Bay, Boston, MA. September 27.

Capka, J.R., (2004). "Megaprojects: Managing a Public Journey." Public Roads 68 (1) (January/February). Washington, DC: Federal Highway Administration.

Capka, R. (2006). "Financing Megaprojects." *Public Roads* 69(4) (January/February). Washington, DC: Federal Highway Administration.

CA/T (Central Artery/Tunnel Project). 2002. "14 Elephants Cross Zakim Bridge." Press release, Massachusetts Turnpike Authority. October 14.

CA/T (Central Artery/Tunnel Project). 2007a. Disadvantaged business report (DBE). Boston: Massachusetts Turnpike Authority.

CA/T (Central Artery/Tunnel Project). 2007b. Finance plan. Boston: Massachusetts Turnpike Authority.

EDRG (Economic Development Research Group, Inc.). 2006. *Economic Impact of the Massachusetts Turnpike Authority and Related Projects, Volume I: The Turnpike Authority as a Transportation Provider.* Prepared for Massachusetts Turnpike Authority, Boston, MA.

EDRG (Economic Development Research Group, Inc.). 2006. *Economic Impact of the Massachusetts Turnpike Authority and Related Projects, Volume II: Real Estate Impacts of the Massachusetts Turnpike Authority and the Central Artery / Third Harbor Tunnel Project.* Prepared for Massachusetts Turnpike Authority, Boston, MA.

EIB (European Investment Bank). 2005. *Evaluation of PPP Projects Financed by the EIB: Synthesis Report.* Operations Evaluation by Campbell Thomson and Judith Goodwin and External Consultant E. R. Yescombe, Yescombe Consulting Ltd. March.

EIB (European Investment Bank). 2006. *Ex Ante Construction Costs in the European Road Sector: A Comparison of Public-Private Partnerships and Traditional Public Procurement.* Economic and financial report by Frederic Blanc-Brude, Hugh Godsmith, and Timo Valila.

Esty, B. 2004. *Modern Project Finance.* Hoboken, NJ: John Wiley & Sons, Inc.

Federal-Aid Highway Act (National Interstate and Defense Highways Act). 1956. Public Law 84–627. Enacted June 29.

Federal-Aid Highway Program Obligation Authority—Fiscal Years (FY) 2004–2011. Washington, DC: U.S. Department of Transportation, Federal Highway Administration.

FEIS/R (Federal Environmental Impact Report). Central Artery (I-93)/Tunnel (I-90) Project Final Supplement (November 1990). Boston: Massachusetts Department of Public Works.

FHWA (Federal Highway Administration). 2000. *Review of Project Oversight and Costs.* Federal Task Force on the Boston Central Artery/Tunnel Project. Washington, DC: Federal Highway Administration.

Finnerty, J. D. 1996. *Project Financing: Asset-Based Financial Engineering.* New York: John Wiley & Sons, Inc.

Fitch Ratings. 2001. *Reemergence of Infrastructure Finance in Emerging Market*. New York: Fitch, Inc. June 12.

Flyvbjerg, B., N. Bruzelius, and W. Rothengatter. 2003. *Megaprojects and Risk: An Anatomy of Ambition*. Cambridge, UK: Cambridge University Press.

GAO (General Accounting Office). 1997. *Transportation Infrastructure: Progress on and Challenges to Central Artery / Tunnel Projects' Costs and Financing*. Report to the Chairman, Subcommittee on Transportation and Related Agencies, Committee on Appropriations, House of Representatives. GAO/RCED-97-170. Washington, DC: General Accounting Office. July.

Grant, M. 1997. "Financing Eurotunnel." *Japan Railway and Transport Review* (April).

HC (House Committee on Bonding). 2011. *Capital Expenditures and State Assets, Report on Capital Planning and Spending in the Commonwealth of Massachusetts (2011–2012)*. Representative Antonio F. D. Cabral, Chairman. Boston: Massachusetts State Legislature.

Hollmer, M. 2002. "The Big Risk—Insuring the Big Dig." *Insurance Times* XXI (19) (September 17).

Klemek, C. 2011. *The Transatlantic Collapse of Urban Renewal: Postwar Urbanism from New York to Berlin*. Chicago: University of Chicago Press.

Krieger, A. 1999. "Experiencing Boston: Encounters with the Places on the Maps." In *Mapping Boston*, edited by A. Krieger, D. Cobb, and A. Turner. Cambridge, MA: MIT Press, 146–172.

Mallon, C., and C. Pilkington. 2009. "Eurotunnel: A Landmark Restructuring." *Norton Annual Review of International Insolvency* 6. Nashville, TN: Norton Institutes.

MassDOT (Massachusetts Department of Transportation). 2010. *Official Statement Relating to Metropolitan Highway System Revenue Bonds (Senior) $207,665,000 Variable Rate Demand Obligations 2010 Series A-1 and A-2 and $893,865,000 2010 Series B*. Boston: Commonwealth of Massachusetts.

McNichol, D. 2000. *The Big Dig*. New York: Silver Linings.

Miller, J. B. 2008. "An Assessment of Select Public-Private Partnerships in Massachusetts." *Pioneer Institute Public Policy Research*, No. 45 (December). Boston: Pioneer Institute.

Mullan, J. (Secretary and CEO of MassDOT). 2011. *Testimony before the Committee on Bonding, Capital Expenditures and State Assets*. July 27.

Murphy, S. 2008. "Big Dig's Red Ink Engulfs State." *Boston Globe*, July 17.

NCHRP (National Cooperative Highway Research Program). 2009. *Synthesis 395, Debt Finance Practices for Surface Transportation*. T. Henkin, Transportation Research Board of the National Academies. Washington, DC: National Academy of Sciences.

OIG (Office of the Inspector General). 2001. *History of Big Dig Finances 1994–2001*. Boston: Massachusetts Office of the Inspector General, March.

PFI (Project Finance International). 1999. Yearbook, 113.

Rigby, P., and J. Penrose. 2003. Project Finance Summary Debt Rating Criteria. In Standard & Poor's 2003–2004 *Project & Infrastructure Finance Review: Criteria and Commentary*. October.

Rigoglioso, M., G. Emmons, and C. Hogg, 1993. *By Land and by Sea, Boston Rebuilds for Tomorrow Harvard Business School Bulletin*. Cambridge, MA: Harvard Publishing. June.

Tajima, K. 2003. "New Estimates of the Demand for Urban Green Space: Implications for Valuing the Environmental Benefits of Boston's Big Dig Project." *Journal of Urban Affairs* 25(5):641–655. Oxford, UK: Blackwell Science Ltd.

Tobin, J. 2001. *Great Projects: The Epic Story of the Building of America, from the Taming of the Mississippi to the Invention of the Internet*. New York: Free Press. 230–235.

Universal Hub. 2009. Class Action, Massachusetts Superior Court.

USDOT (U.S. Department of Transportation). 2004. *Report to Congress on Public-Private Partnerships*. Washington, DC: U.S. Department of Transportation. December.

USDOT (U.S. Department of Transportation). 2010. *Agency Financial Report (FY 2010)*. Washington, DC: Office of the Secretary of Transportation, Assistant Secretary for Budget and Program Performance.

Vandebrouck, P. 1995. "The Channel Tunnel: The Dream Becomes Reality." *Tunneling and Underground Space Technology* 10(1):17–21.

Williams, E. 2002. "River of Aluminum." *PM Network* (January). Newtown Square, PA:Project Management Institute.

Wong, Y. 2012. Interview with Yoke Wong, senior affirmative market inspector for the Central Artery/Tunnel Project, May 25 and June 26.

Wood, D. C. 2001. "Learning From the Big Dig." *Public Roads* 65(1) (July/August). Washington, DC: Federal Highway Administration.

Zakim Bunker Hill Bridge. 2002. "Elephant Crossing." In "14 Elephants Cross Zakim Bridge." Press release, Massachusetts Turnpike Authority. October 14.

Chapter 3

Stakeholders

There is no substitute for active public participation. The openness of the process that allows citizens to directly participate and ask embarrassing questions... forces you to confront those questions that it might be convenient at the moment to duck.

> —*Fred Salvucci, former Massachusetts secretary of transportation (Salvucci 2004)*

As we proceed with this project, we constantly come up against problems that could not have been anticipated, and these cause delay. In the end, this is good, because it means that we're allowing some or all of the various constituencies to have input; we're allowing for compromise. No one is strong-arming. Ultimately, we're doing what's best for the community.

> —*Ted Weigle, former Bechtel / Parsons Brinckerhoff program manager for the Big Dig (Rigoglioso et al. 1993)*

INTRODUCTION

The importance of the stakeholder in managing megaprojects is evidenced in the two introductory quotes to this chapter. Though one represents the viewpoint of the former Massachusetts transportation secretary and the other the experience of the former private-sector management consultant on the Big Dig, both agree that "the local community" as a key stakeholder would be given a major voice in the project. When the concept of the project was first introduced in the early 1980s, the recognition that the role of the citizen would be central to the development of this monumental project was rarely subject to question. However, as the project evolved and the number of stakeholders rapidly increased, managing the stakeholder process became a time-consuming and costly project unto itself. Project management recognized early on that mitigation efforts would cause project costs to rise by nearly 30 percent to meet important demands of local businesses and residents.

The focus of this chapter is not only understanding the role of the stakeholder in large projects but, more significantly, analyzing how stakeholders add value to a project and enhance project governance, which is the key to project success.

DEFINING THE STAKEHOLDER

The concept of the stakeholder was first introduced to project management theory in 1984 when Freeman defined a *stakeholder* as "any group or individual who can affect or is affected by the achievement of the organization's objectives." Cleland later defined stakeholders as having an "interest in" the project, and introduced stakeholder identification, classification, and analysis as important stakeholder management processes (Cleland 1986). In recent literature, stakeholder management has been incorporated as an essential soft skill in project management (Crawford 2005; Morris et al. 2006).

PMI defines *stakeholder* as an individual, group, or organization who may affect, be affected by, or perceive itself to be affected by a decision, activity, or outcome of a project (PMI 2013, 562). PMI's Standard for Program Management defines the following three processes in stakeholder management (PMI Standard 2013):

1. *Identify program stakeholders.* The systematic identification and analysis of program stakeholders.
2. *Stakeholder engagement planning.* The involvement of stakeholders in the program and the measurement of stakeholder impact based on issue and prioritization tracking. An analysis of stakeholder culture, influence, attitudes and expectations and a detailed strategy and guidelines.
3. *Stakeholder engagement.* The process of managing stakeholder communications to satisfy the requirements of, and resolve issues with, program stakeholders and to gain and maintain stakeholder buy-in for the program's objectives, benefits, and outcomes.

Stakeholders are recognized worldwide as an important participant in development projects. They attract a high level of public attention and interest because of the substantial impact they can have on social and environmental reform. Partners and stakeholders are often defined similarly. The International Finance Corporation (IFC) of the World Bank Group defines partners and stakeholders to include "a wide range of groups that have a stake in their projects, are affected by their work, or help strengthen impact on sustainable private sector development." They have been identified by the IFC as civil societies (nonprofits often involved in representing the interests of local citizens), development institutions, local communities, foundations and companies, professional organizations and academic institutions, donors, and the media.

STAKEHOLDER PRINCIPLES

In every project, it is critical to identify the guiding principles concerning the responsibility of the project for its stakeholders and the role that each stakeholder or stakeholder group will play in the project. These principles are usually based on a shared vision in collaboration with the project's stakeholders and senior management. Table 3.1 lists some important principles recommended for implementation on large-scale projects.

Table 3.1   Principles of Stakeholder Responsibility

Ten Principles of Stakeholder Responsibility
1. Identify your stakeholder(s) or stakeholder groups during the conceptual stage of the project and involve them at the earliest possible date.
2. Recognize the stakeholder as a valuable contributor to the project.
3. Prioritize stakeholder interests, but remember that these interests may change over time.
4. Never ignore a stakeholder's concerns, or these will become your biggest problem.
5. Don't forget to include stakeholder concerns in your budget, and provide an allowance for stakeholder exposures as you would for any other potential claim.
6. Strive to bring stakeholder interests together over time.
7. Recognize that stakeholders' values are important to an inclusive and ethical process.
8. Seek solutions to issues that satisfy multiple stakeholders simultaneously.
9. Engage in intensive communication and discourse with stakeholders, particularly those with whom you disagree—and not just those whose interests you support.
10. Proactively manage stakeholder relationships and understand the impact of their concerns on scope, schedule, and cost.
11. Constantly monitor and redesign policies, processes, procedures, and practices to better serve stakeholders.
12. Fulfill your commitments to stakeholders, and develop a relationship of trust and respect.

PROJECT STAKEHOLDER FRAMEWORK

Stakeholders have been identified as individuals, groups, or organizations and include both internal and external parties. Internal stakeholders in infrastructure projects are generally comprised of the project owner, sponsors, management consultant, contractors, subcontractors, and suppliers. External stakeholders include community groups, the public, regulatory bodies, the media, and special interest groups. All project stakeholders, whether internal or external to the project, with considerable influence or no influence, with high interest or low interest, must have a role in the project. Determining that role is not easy, and many approaches have been offered in the project management literature. Figure 3.1 presents eight steps to the development of a stakeholder framework that will assist project managers in managing stakeholder expectations and their often conflicting agendas.

Steps in Stakeholder Framework Development

Step 1: Identify stakeholders and analyze their interests; where there are common interests group them together into categories such as local community, business and economic, environmental, right-of-way, regulatory and oversight, media, and public relations interests.

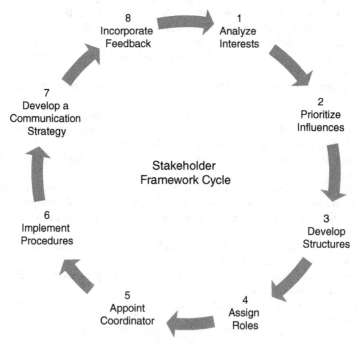

Figure 3.1   Stakeholder Framework Cycle

Step 2: Identify the various influences that each stakeholder may have including political, legal, expert, advocate, coercive, and authoritative.

Step 3: Determine the types of structures that need to be developed to integrate stakeholders into the project, including committees, advisory board, task force, program management office (PMO), or partnership.

Step 4: Assign roles for each stakeholder or group, such as monitor, decision maker, oversight authority, auditor, responder, developer, group leader, or community organizer.

Step 5: Appoint a coordinator who will integrate the various individuals and groups and develop processes and procedures for managing stakeholder responses, questions, and feedback. On large megaprojects, there may be two coordinators—one for internal and one for external stakeholders.

Step 6: Implement the processes and procedures developed in Step 5.

Step 7: Establish a sophisticated communication process with all stakeholders, including the dissemination of project information and the conduct of regular meetings with stakeholders to assess satisfaction with roles and responsibilities, to obtain feedback on project concerns, and to resolve outstanding issues.

Step 8: Respond to and incorporate feedback into the project's processes, procedures, best practices, and standards.

Stakeholder Analysis As shown in Figure 3.1, strategies and tactics for managing stakeholders begin with a stakeholder analysis. There are several important outcomes that can be achieved as a result of a good stakeholder analysis:

- A better understanding of the organizational and wider context within which a project initiative sits, such as the organizational challenges, senior management priorities, or changes in the external environment
- An understanding of the power base within an organization—who has a strong influence on how others behave and perform?
- Identification of those stakeholders who can help and those who can hinder the implementation of a project
- Providing insights that help focus additional data collection on those project areas or types of knowledge that are critical to success

Stakeholder Influence/Interest Matrix

> Your most unhappy customers are your greatest source of learning.
>
> —*Bill Gates*

Because much of the knowledge that key stakeholders have is pertinent to wider organizational issues, interviews with key stakeholders, and examining relevant documentation, should be done as early as possible in the project planning stage and long before stakeholder prioritization or risk assessment is completed.

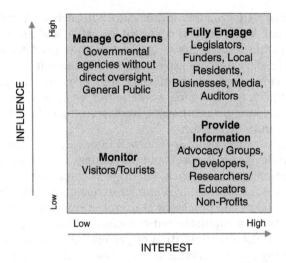

Figure 3.2   Stakeholder Influence/Interest Matrix

A stakeholder analysis involves the building of a stakeholder qualitative assessment similar to the matrix utilized for risk management, as shown in Figure 3.2. The key axes on the matrix are as follows:

Interest (vertical axis)—Indicates how the stakeholders are affected by the success of what is being defined or done. It reflects the stakeholder's technical and social concerns and perceptions of the project and its desired outcome.

Influence (horizontal axis—The degree of influence a stakeholder has over what is being defined or done within the project, often called the stakeholder's *power base*. Power is the stakeholder's ability to contribute or withhold resources and/or to accept or reject outcomes.

An interesting outcome generated by this analysis is that interest can sometimes matter more than influence in determining the value of interactions between the project owner and stakeholders. High-interest, low-influence stakeholders can give you the support and contextual information needed to make your case with the high-influence stakeholders. However, this may not always be the case, as some high-interest stakeholders may be very critical of the project and provide obstacles for moving forward. Low-interest, high-influence stakeholders, in contrast, require attention and will need to be satisfied that their concerns are being recognized; however, they will play a much more passive role. Projects will succeed or fail primarily based on the actions of people who care enough to defend or oppose them.

The results of a stakeholder analysis should be discussed with senior management in the organization and senior internal stakeholders, and it should help to prioritize work in the various project phases. As the project evolves, this analysis will be continually refined. The knowledge you have gathered about your stakeholders should be organized and managed in accordance with best practices.

Classification of Stakeholders   *High-influence, high-interest quadrant:* Some stakeholders may have a lot of influence over the project, and they also may be very interested in the project. It is vital to understand the viewpoints of such stakeholders—specifically, what potential objections they might raise. Spend the most time with these stakeholders, and consider giving them a role in the project governance such as (1) reporting information on project risks, (2) serving in an advisory capacity, or (3) leading a stakeholder committee or support group.

Low-influence, high-interest quadrant: Other stakeholders may have a lot of interest but little real influence. These stakeholders may include technical experts, consultants, researchers, nonprofits, nongovernmental organizations, or advocacy groups. Such stakeholders (if they support the project) can be valuable sources of information: They can get access to documents relevant to your project, fill you in on the institutional history of past efforts in your project domain, and help you identify what the organizational challenges to the project will be. These are good stakeholders to meet with first, since each interaction is relatively low risk.

High-influence, low-interest quadrant: Stakeholders with high power but low interest need to be broadly satisfied. They won't pay attention to the details of your project, since they perceive the project as not affecting them. However, they have influence on whether the project will be a success. For example, they may have a vote during the approval process of a project, or they may be involved in regulatory oversight. The goal of your interactions with this type of stakeholder should be to give them enough information about the project that they will not create obstacles for your project. These stakeholders may include governmental organizations not directly overseeing the project or permitting organizations that view the project as just another customer.

Low-influence, low-interest quadrant: You should spend less time with stakeholders who have little influence and little interest in the project. They aren't interested in what you are doing and are not in a position to help you do it. These individuals or organizations may include local visitors or tourists or those temporarily involved in the project but with no vested interest.

Building the Relationship with Stakeholders

Building relationships and seeking input from stakeholders is just as important within the project team as it is outside (see Table 3.2). Good relationships can mean the difference between outstanding success and failure. Good relationships with stakeholders are essential to determining needs and meeting stakeholders' expectations. Stakeholders are valuable advocates for projects and can assist in all stages of the project's development, from initiation through closure. Some of the key information that should be derived from stakeholder interviews and open forums are listed in Table 3.2.

Table 3.2   Stakeholder Relationships and Input

Categories for Input from Stakeholders	Questions Concerning Stakeholders
Role	What is their role with respect to the project and the wider organizational context? What are the implications for the project?
Expectations	What are their expectations of the project organization? What benefits do they receive as stakeholders?
Knowledge	What knowledge do they need in order to perform their role for the organization? Where do they source this knowledge?
Contribution	How do they contribute to better outcomes? What knowledge do they possess that the project organization can exploit?
Relationships and Networks	What is their relationship with the organization; is it one-way, two-way, single-focus, multifaceted? How do they relate to the organization's competitors, clients, suppliers; what networks are they part of; what knowledge do they gain through these relationships?
Influence	What role might they play in advancing the project? What are their own perspectives on the value of the project and how it should be managed?

Stakeholder Structures

Project governance is described in detail in Chapter 4, including various forms of stakeholder governance and decision-making structures that include stakeholder advisory committees and boards, partnerships, working groups, and collaborative teams. The project stakeholder governance structure must be clear in its goals, it must provide a framework for decision making, and stakeholders must be held accountable for assigned responsibilities.

As an example of effective stakeholder collaboration on the Big Dig, in 1996, the Artery Business Committee Transportation Management Association (ABC TMA), formerly known as the Artery Business Committee (ABC), was established in partnership with the Central Artery/Tunnel (CA/T) project and the City of Boston in order to address employer concerns about Big Dig construction. ABC worked with private and public partners to ensure that the City of Boston remained open for business during construction of the project, while also solving problems and building consensus on design, funding, and operational issues critical to success of the project. The ABC Board of Directors is comprised of leaders from almost 90 businesses and institutions in Greater Boston. After the Big Dig was completed, ABC continued to work with local and state officials to achieve tangible results on transportation, land development, city parks, and public realm infrastructure in the City of Boston and to work on investments important to the city's future economy and quality of life. One important aspect of the collaboration was the support the ABC lent to the initial approval of the project. Without that support, project approval might have been much more difficult.

Role of the Stakeholder

It is a basic principle of stakeholder process that all stakeholders are not equally important (Hobley and Shields 2000; Ostrom et al. 1994; North 1990). The priority given a particular stakeholder and the role that stakeholder will assume in the project may change over time depending on the importance of that role to the overall objectives of the project. There is a need to differentiate (1) the stakeholders who are relevant at the different stages of development of the project, (2) the organizational structure or process that is required to best represent the interests of the stakeholders, and (3) the appropriate number of stakeholders who will take part in the process.

Stakeholders may not have an official role in the project; nevertheless, they may have interests that must be managed. Stakeholders also must be able to communicate their concerns in an orderly process to project management. There are many tools used to formalize the stakeholder's role, including matrices and mapping (Freeman 1984; Elias et al. 2002; Winch and Bonke 2002). Key questions that arise regarding the role of the stakeholder in megaprojects are:

- Who will determine whether and how stakeholders should participate in a project?
- How will stakeholders be identified and classified?
- What is the primary role of the stakeholders?
- What are the different stakeholders groups that are critical to project performance?
- Who will represent these groups?
- Will they have legitimate decision making authority?
- How will they be held accountable?
- When should stakeholder participation be changed or terminated?
- Will the stakeholders have a role in project governance?

STAKEHOLDER MANAGEMENT ON THE BIG DIG

From the earliest stages of the Big Dig project, stakeholder involvement was key. For the project to ultimately succeed, it needed a strong foundation of public participation and consensus building to help secure the support of Boston's diverse community of public and private stakeholders. Scholars, government officials, and practitioners have focused on the need to increase public participation so that the public trust and confidence in major megaprojects can be improved (Altschuler and Luberoff, 2003; Capka 2004).

The Big Dig's environmental assessments set forth in great detail the concerns of the project and its stakeholders. These included extensive meetings with the local residents and businesses, resulting in numerous mitigation requirements. During the long history of the Big Dig, thousands of meetings were held with the stakeholders, which resulted in agreements and policy that addressed mitigation of noise, dirt removal, rat and odor control, traffic congestion, groundwater movement, access to homes and businesses, environmental pollution, asbestos from the demolition of a 50-year-old elevated highway, preservation of the shellfish through construction of an artificial reef, and numerous other ecological impacts. Building and maintaining trust with the local community was a number one concern, and continuous outreach was essential to ensuring not only that the stakeholders were satisfied, but that they bought into the benefits of the project and the ultimate improvement of their lives as long-term residents of the City of Boston.

An excellent example of stakeholder collaboration in the early years on the Big Dig occurred in 1991, when Richard Taylor, secretary of transportation under the governor of Massachusetts at the time, William F. Weld, brought together various business and community interest groups and established the Bridge Design Review Committee. The 42-member committee made up of representatives from national and local environmental and transportation groups, the Artery Business Committee, and neighborhood coalitions exemplified the open, participatory, multidisciplinary model to build a consensus. Secretary Taylor charged the committee with finding the means to reduce the negative environmental and aesthetic impacts of the Charles River Crossing. The committee's open style and collaborative efforts resulted in a new bridge design by Swiss bridge architect, Christian Menn (Hughes 1998). Years later, the design continues to be proclaimed one of the most elegant bridge structures in the world.

The Big Dig's Key Stakeholders

Every project and organization, whether large or small, is comprised of internal and external stakeholders. Internal stakeholders typically include the owner, the management consultant, the project contractors, and the project team. External stakeholders are usually defined as those who influence or have an interest in the project but are not normally engaged with the project business and may not be critical to the completion of the project.

The Big Dig was no different, except the stakeholders numbered in the thousands and represented diverse interests, motivations, influence, and positions both inside and outside the project. Conflicts among these stakeholders arose frequently, as described in the next section. The Big Dig, like all projects, had key internal and external stakeholder groups; however, the line between these stakeholders was often blurred due to the multiple government agencies involved at the federal and state levels and the relationship between the public interests and private management objectives. Some stakeholders were both internal and external to the project, depending on the role they might play at any particular time.

To provide a framework for understanding stakeholder structure and participation on the Big Dig, we begin with the key stakeholders in the project, constituting five major groups of owners, sponsors, consultants, contractors, and operators, as defined in Table 3.3.

Table 3.3   The Big Dig's Key Stakeholders

Stakeholder	Role/Objectives	Risks
Owner/sponsor— 1. Massachusetts Highway Department (MHD) (inception to 1997) 2. Massachusetts Turnpike Authority (1997 to project end)	Guardian of the public interest, funder, regulator, project director, publicist, monitor (see Figure 3.4)	Conflicts between roles, inability to shift all risk, lack of control over design and construction, unallocated or unknown risk falls to project owner
Federal Highway Administration (FHWA)—sponsor/ oversight	Primary funder and responsible for oversight of the project budget and finance plan	Owner fails to complete project, cost escalation, and shortfall of financing from the federal government
Management consultant—Bechtel/ Parsons Brinckerhoff (joint venture)	Maintain control over project company, build integrated teams, shift risk to other parties, set strategic corporate objectives, extract a profit	Conflict between corporate and project objectives, share in unknown risk, responsible for faulty work of contractors if not properly allocated
Construction management	Maintain control over contract site, shift risk, extract a profit, split loyalties to project company and project owner	Insurance insufficient to cover risk, responsible for faulty work of subcontractors, assumption of unknown risk
Project teams	Meet performance requirements, keep on schedule and budget, manage risk and safety, and ensure quality	Responsible for failure to meet performance requirements and manage project risk and quality
Operator— Massachusetts Turnpike Authority (MTA)	Earn sufficient revenue to cover debt and operating expenses, represent the public interest, and repair budget	Inherit faulty design or workmanship, insurance, performance bonds and warranties expire, and revenue shortfall

CONFLICTS OF INTEREST AMONG INTERNAL STAKEHOLDERS

> You cannot rely on the [Consultant's] desire to maintain a good reputation as a control mechanism—there have to be specific controls in place and accountability from the entity monitoring those controls.
>
> —*Mary Connaughton, former Massachusetts Turnpike Authority board member*

Construction of major public infrastructure in the United States and globally has become a notorious cauldron for conflict (Anderson and Polkinghorn 2008). The quote from former Massachusetts Turnpike Authority board member Mary Connaughton highlights the concern about the owner's role in oversight of the project's private management consultant. Conflicts among stakeholders frequently arise in large, complex projects, and a careful analysis must be made of potential conflicts early in the process.

There are many examples of conflicts that arise from multiple roles. For instance, Figure 3.3 highlights the multiple roles of the project owner. If the owner is the project funder but is also involved in oversight, the potential for these two roles to conflict is high. Table 3.3 further highlights the potential for conflict among the project owner, the management consultant, the contractors, and the operator based on conflicting roles, objectives, and motivations. For instance, how does one reconcile a profit motivation with an obligation to protect the public interest? If the public interest becomes paramount and it means the project costs will escalate to accommodate these interests, the management consultant and the contractors may

Figure 3.3   Multiple Roles of the Government Owner

suffer a reduced profit if cost escalation was not provided for in the project contracts.

A perceived conflict occurred in 1998 on the Big Dig when project officials created a so-called integrated project organization (IPO) combining government employees and private-sector employees under one umbrella. Interestingly, the integrated organization was created to do just the opposite—reduce conflict and create a project with one voice and shared goals. The Massachusetts inspector general noted in 2000 that "intertwining of the Project oversight function with the private management consulting function raises serious questions about conflicts of interest, risk allocation, and accountability to the public for cost and quality" (OIG 2003). This assertion was strongly refuted by the project's management consultant in a lengthy response (Bechtel 2006). Integration of public and private teams is an important consideration in all projects, and the relationship must be thoroughly understood and managed if the oversight function is to remain with the government owner. Developing an appropriate balance between the project owner, who provides the strategic guidance of the project, and the project consultant, who leads and manages the implementation, is a critical factor if the project is to be successful.

Partnering between public and private organizations is required for megaprojects to succeed. With partnering come relationships that can blur the distinction between the partners' differing roles and missions. Building a trusting relationship with project partners while at the same time maintaining independent oversight of the project is a balancing act that requires careful planning, constant vigilance, and ethical fortitude, even when faced with economic, personal, or political pressure. In some projects, it may even require an independent oversight board separate and apart from the government owner.

MULTIPLE ROLES OF PROJECT OWNERS AND SPONSORS

Governments play diverse roles, including promoter, provider of funds and other resources, facilitator, and protector. Scholars have maintained that government officials refuse to accept this reality in defense of their role as independent guardian of the public good (Miller and Hobbs 2005). This leads to contradictions, delays, and misunderstanding. In their extensive research on public projects, Miller and Hobbs stressed that the challenges of governance for these complex projects is not being adequately addressed by current practice or prior research on public management, as evidenced by their dismal success rates (Miller and Hobbs 2005).

The project owner is usually the owner of the project's assets, and the project sponsor usually provides financing for the project in the form of equity or debt. Sometimes an owner or sponsor can serve in a dual role as developer or management consultant and as an investor or funder of the project. Typically, privately funded projects have separate owners and sponsors; however, as described in Chapter 2, the responsibility for funding and oversight on the Big Dig resided solely with the following three government agencies:

1. The U.S. Department of Transportation, Federal Highway Administration (FHWA). Shared commitment with Massachusetts for financing the Big Dig, as well as statutory oversight responsibilities.
2. The Massachusetts Highway Department (MHD). Shared commitment with the federal government for financing the Big Dig, as well as responsibility for management of the Big Dig through 1997.
3. The Massachusetts Turnpike Authority (MTA). Under the 1997 Enabling Act, the CA/T Project Management Agreement between the Authority and MHD transferred all of the remaining management responsibility to the MTA. The act gave the MTA broad powers, including the power to "own, construct, maintain, repair, reconstruct, improve, rehabilitate, finance, refinance, use, police, administer, control and operate" the Massachusetts Highway System (MHS).

Because the government served in multiple roles on the Big Dig, including project manager, sponsor, funder, organizer, publicist, regulator, and guardian of the public interest, the balancing of control over the project was by far its biggest challenge. The project organizational structure required that some managers reported directly up to the governmental owner and sponsor, while other managers reported directly to the project's joint-venture design and construction program manager.

Developer. The project was conceived over a long period of time with input from multiple stakeholders including federal and state government agencies, environmental organizations, and the local community, which encompassed the business and residential communities. Ultimately, the leaders of that process were not involved in the initial design, construction, or operations of the Big Dig due to changes in administration over the course of its long life.

Funder. The Big Dig was 100 percent funded by the federal and state government, requiring active participation in the review of the project scope, timeline, costs, risk, quality, finance plans, and project budget. Finance plans and cost commitments and forecasts had to be coordinated to ensure that sufficient funds were available to meet unexpected events and changes to the budget over time.

Project director. The owner's project director was responsible for oversight of the project's management consultant as well as being directly responsible for oversight of the owner's management team and staff, and was accountable to the owner's CEO and board of directors.

Promoter. The government was the ultimate promoter of the project with the community, legislators, stakeholders, and the various government agencies and auditors involved in the project. The state government agencies involved often served as their own lobbyists in influencing Congress and the executive branch of the continuous need for additional funding of the project.

Regulator and enforcer. The project's obligations as regulator and over-seer of compliance with state and federal law were extensive, including coordination on various aspects of the project with more than 50 federal, state, and local agencies including transportation agencies, the U.S. and Massachusetts Departments of Environmental Protection, the Occupational Safety and Health Administration, the Executive Office of Labor and Work-force Development, the Federal Reserve, the Massachusetts attorney general, the U.S. attorney general, numerous federal and state audit agencies, Health and Human Services, the Federal Bureau of Investigation, the Department of Homeland Security, the local police and fire departments, Boston City Hall, and the Massachusetts State Police.

Governing board. The owner's board of directors was responsible for execu-tive decisions on major issues including changes in scope, significant claims, major litigation, high-level management and personnel decisions, labor agree-ments, and general oversight of the project's finance plan, budget, schedule, quality, and risk management.

MULTIPLE ROLES OF THE MANAGEMENT CONSULTANT (CONSULTANT)

Founded in 1898 and considered one of the world's master builders, Bechtel, the San Francisco–based construction and engineering companies, has man-aged an impressive list of projects including the Washington, D.C., Metro, the creation of the Saudi Arabian city of Jubail, the Hoover Dam and the Chan-nel Tunnel between France and England. The New York–based firm Parsons Brinckerhoff, also a world leader in transportation infrastructure projects, including the New York City Subway System, the Taiwan high-speed rail project, and the Woodrow Wilson Bridge, has collaborated in joint ventures with Bechtel many times. The two firms' combined expertise in planning, engineering, project controls, and construction management provided the full range of skills necessary to manage large and complex public works projects.

The joint-venture Bechtel/Parsons Brinckerhoff (B/PB), as management consultant (consultant) to the government owner on the Big Dig project, was responsible for preliminary design, management of the final design process and construction by other consultants and contractors, and reporting on the project's overall cost and schedule. The consultant also prepared the semiannual finance plans and a myriad of other reports.

To carry out these responsibilities, the management consultant contracted with the state through a series of 15 work programs. These work programs included initial planning and mitigation, construction management, the Vir-ginia Fire Testing Program, construction management services, the project wrap-up insurance program, right-of-way, design, and design management. Some programs lasted one or two years, while other programs lasted three or more years. For each work program, a scope of work was established with a preapproved cost and schedule. The owner evaluated the agreed-upon cost

Figure 3.4   Roles of the Management Consultant
Source: *The Big Dig: Key Facts about Cost, Scope, Schedule, and Management.*
Bechtel/Parsons Brinckerhoff. December 2006.

and schedule monthly. Each work program included a plan, scope-of-work statement, and a staffing plan (CA/T 1996).

Throughout the project, the state always maintained authority and responsibility for policy-level decision making, direction of the project, and oversight of the management consultant. The state hired other engineering and construction firms to take responsibility for final design and actual construction. As shown in Figure 3.4, the management consultant had multiple roles in the project that created enormous opportunity for conflict, often raised in audit reports and oversight reviews (OIG 2001). However, contrary to the assertions of potential conflict, in 2003, in its independent review of the final stages of the Big Dig, the National Academies stated, "The integrated project organization (IPO) structure currently utilized by the MTA to direct the design and construction of the CA/T project appears to be functioning reasonably well" (Board 2003, 5). Moreover, the report stated, "The existing management tools and metrics currently in use are sufficient for overseeing the management consultant" (Board 2003).

STAKEHOLDER CONCERNS AND MITIGATION TOOLS

Table 3.4 highlights the various stakeholders, the common concerns, and the stakeholder communication and mitigation tools used on the Big Dig. Some stakeholders actually had decision-making authority, and communication was regularly exchanged concerning project incidents, impacts, new issues, complaints, reporting requirements, lessons learned and actions implemented, and results or outcome of various project actions.

Table 3.4   Project Stakeholder Concerns and Mitigation Tools

External Stakeholders and Influence Level	Common Concerns	Communication Tools and Mitigation
Federal government sponsor (FHWA)	Cost/schedule/budget Financing Getting the job done safely Oversight	Transmittal of all project financial data FHWA project review response
Designers/contractors	Interfaces between projects Schedule impact Financing Claims handling	Contractor daily meetings Project management monthly reports Performance progress reports
Residential community	Project status (schedule) Preservation of property Access to property Mitigation of risk Scheduled construction Environmental	Weekly community forums with project updates Mitigation of risk claims procedures Insurance and safety program Emergency response Community liaisons and project partnership
Labor	Compliance with labor regulations Safety and health of all workers Drug-free worksites	Labor representatives meetings Detailed labor agreement permitting all union shop and requiring no-strike policy
Business community/abutters (those along the project alignment)	Impact on business Business access Business interruption Lost profits Environmental	Weekly meetings Partnering with the Artery Business Committee Geological testing Traffic monitoring Emergency response
Auditors	Project status Cost, schedule, scope, quality, and risk Financial status	Document request and response Implementation of recommendations

(continued)

Table 3.4   (*Continued*)

External Stakeholders and Influence Level	Common Concerns	Communication Tools and Mitigation
Public relations and news media	Project status Financial status Safety and health Catastrophic potential Claims Community concerns Environmental Public corruption/ criminal conduct	Weekly press briefings Monthly cost, schedule, and financing updates Annual report reviews Press releases and briefings Exchange of information Investigations
Government agencies	Meeting contractual commitments Planned improvements Regulatory oversight	Quarterly meeting Financial documentation Document requests
Fire and police	Traffic incidents Worker safety and health Protection of the public	Weekly traffic, health, and safety reports Emergency response
Utilities	As-builts (the design drawings showing the actual placement of the project utilities as constructed) Construction schedules	Monthly meetings on issue resolution of all utility companies (numbering more than 30 at the project's peak) Monthly claims reporting Submittal of updated as-builts by utility companies
Suppliers	Schedule updates Material testing results	Quality assurance review Quality testing Quality control
Insurers	Safety and health Mitigation Resolving claims and disputes Catastrophic potential	Weekly loss control and claims meetings Safety walk-downs OSHA partnering Emergency response Safety reports
Historical society	Removal and preservation of artifacts	Notification of archeological sites Participation in removal and preservation of artifacts

Source: Annual Financial Reports 2000–2006.

Table 3.5   Dimensions of Corporate Social Responsibility

Dimension	Definition
Environmental	The natural environment
Social	The relationships between business and society
Economic	Socioeconomic aspects describing corporate social responsibility (CSR) in terms of a business operation
Voluntariness	Actions not prescribed by law

Adapted from A. Dahlsrud. 2006. *How Corporate Social Responsibility is Defined: An Analysis of 37 Definitions.* New York: Wiley Interscience.

CORPORATE RESPONSIBILITY INITIATIVES

Projects continue to face challenges concerning environmental, social, and economic demands from stakeholders. Projects must rise up and meet these challenges in the early conceptual phase of the project by incorporating stakeholders' concerns into project scope, budgets, and timelines. Throughout the project life cycle, management must continuously focus on stakeholder concerns (see Table 3.5).

STAKEHOLDER PARTICIPATION

As the ramifications of an infrastructure project can extend far beyond the tenure of the public decision makers, transparency measures must be instituted that will enable the public to be informed and engaged throughout the term of the infrastructure project. Project management research reveals that the most successful projects are those that have strong stakeholder participation programs. Ironically, several of the most successful projects have been delivered in the developing world. Lessons from these projects should be shared so that the benefits of stakeholder participation can be realized through the establishment of independent, accountable, hybrid institutions that encourage public participation and mechanisms for dispute resolution (Greiman 2011). Important lessons from the Kecamatan Development Project (KDP) in Indonesia are highlighted in Table 3.6. The KDP project focused on a model of participatory development designed on social rather than economic theory. The goal was to deliver development resources to rural communities "using local representative community forums ... wherein villagers, not government officials or external experts, determine the form and location of small-scale development projects via a competitive bidding process." The major mission of KDP was to provide "a more efficient and effective mechanism of getting valued development resources to a designated target group (in this case, the rural poor)." A major study suggests that such processes have been effective in this regard with respect to enhancing the capacity of KDP participants, specifically participants in other development

Table 3.6   The Kecamatan Project in Indonesia

Feature	Implementation
Interim Institution	Design a structure where community members not government officials or external entities decide form and location of small scale development projects.
Participatory	Focus on interests of community as opposed to rights-based negotiation strategies
Transparent	Decision making done in the open and subject to scrutiny of general public and media
Accountable	Design explicit and accessible procedures for managing disputes and provide for evaluation and reform of the process
Enforceable	Require enforceable commitments from all stakeholders

Source: D. Adler, C. Sage, and M. Woolcock. 2009. *Interim Institutions and the Development Process: Opening Spaces for Reform in Cambodia and Indonesia*, 4. University of Manchester: Brooks World Poverty Institute.

projects, to constructively manage everyday disputes. The key challenge is the changing of the mindset of both government and World Bank officials from a focus on the necessities of agency supply to one in which projects respond to community demand. Projects that have explicit and accessible procedures for managing disputes arising from the development process are less likely to cause conflict (Adler et al. 2009; Barron et al. 2007; Guggenheim et al. 2006).

Communicating with Stakeholders

The key to project success in managing stakeholders is not only identifying the stakeholders and defining their role but determining the project stakeholder information needs and defining a communication approach. The following questions must be asked at the outset of the project:

- Who has influence on, an interest in, or an expectation for the project?
- What information needs to be provided to the stakeholders, and to whom should it be distributed? What information does the project need from stakeholders?
- When do they need it?
- How will it be communicated?
- Who will deliver the information?

Communication assumptions, constraints, methodologies, and strategies must be clearly planned out, not only at the inception of the project but continually throughout the life of the project. If you don't find your stakeholders, they will find you—and often at difficult or inconvenient times. Developing a project communications plan is the first step in identifying the stakeholders and determining the interests, expectations, and influence of the stakeholders and how to manage and mitigate their concerns. Stakeholder communication analysis can help identify important alliances to build support throughout the project life cycle.

Important reasons to have a good communication strategy include the development of trust, social responsibility, fiscal transparency, and professional ethics, all of which support the overall goal of reducing risk and protecting the public interest.

Communication Model

A communication model that supports multiple communication mechanisms for both receiving and disseminating information is essential in complex megaprojects. Communication methods are strategically linked to the particular stakeholder group. Whatever method is chosen, it must facilitate two-way communication. The following are some of the most successful methods for stakeholder communication on the Big Dig:

- Frequent and extensive dissemination of financial information on the project's cost, scope, timeline, budget, risk and quality management and safety and health programs, including the project monthly report (PMM) and semiannual financial reports
- Warnings and alerts on safety and health risks disseminated through the project early warning system, contract site notifications, and the project's emergency response team
- 24/7 emergency response center linked to fire, police, airport, and other government agencies
- High-technology cable optics and central nervous system with 400 video cameras to alert drivers, fire, and police of traffic flow and impending dangers
- Critical infrastructure and security program
- Daily contractor meetings and utility response program
- North end residential risk identification and mitigation program
- Legislative and governmental hearings
- Letters/e-mails/publications to stakeholders
- Freedom of Information Act (FOIA) requests
- Community updates and educational programs
- Audits and government reports
- Public relations, press releases, and press briefings
- Interactive project website and information portal
- Surveys and requests for information
- Workshops and training
- Questionnaires

- Ombudsman
- Radio, television, and print media
- Research and environmental feasibility studies
- Meetings, forums, educational programs and formal and informal dialogue
- Project library and archeological museum

Table 3.7   Stakeholder Communication Reporting Process

Reporting Requirements	Communication Format
In addition to total project cash requirements, to-go cash requirements were added.	Project management monthly (PMM)
Planned versus actual progress information on a contract-by-contact basis.	PMM
Information on construction change orders, both actuals and projections.	PMM and finance plans
Status against budget at a detailed level for change orders and by major to-go cost area.	PMM
Definitive and speculative cost exposures and reductions (rough order-of-magnitude assessments).	PMM
More detailed information on project management expenses (labor and staffing levels).	PMM
Key project safety statistics.	PMM
Planned versus actual cash flow and federal obligation financial information and progress on all revenue generation activities.	PMM
Six-month bottom-to-top assessment of to-go project costs including allowances for potential but unknown issues.	PMM and future finance plans
Updated project finance and progress information.	Available on the project's website and finance plan
Quarterly review sessions with senior executive division and national FHWA officials to focus on the project's vital signs.	Quarterly review meetings
Retention of national consulting firm to validate project cost and schedule assessments.	Available to interested federal and state agencies

Source: Central Artery/Tunnel Project. 2000. Finance Plan. March, p. 19, and June 16.

Communication of Financial Information on the Big Dig

To increase public confidence and ensure openness and trust between the public and private sectors, information on the project's finances and contractor's performance must be readily available and subject to scrutiny. Financial information on the Big Dig was communicated to the federal government and all stakeholders through a semiannual finance plan and a project management monthly (PMM). The plan identified the cash flow requirements of the existing budget and the available funding sources to support this cash need.

Transparent information and communication was essential to the maintenance of the project's relationship with its thousands of stakeholders. In March 2000, the finance plan update recommended several mechanisms to improve communication with the project's many stakeholders, and these mechanisms were implemented shortly thereafter (CA/T 2000a).

In order to provide timely and current information, the PMM was issued within four weeks of the close of each month and reviewed at the project's monthly open meetings. Table 3.7 highlights some of the enhancements to the reports that would be essential information for all large-scale projects to communicate to its stakeholders.

KEY LESSONS LEARNED ABOUT STAKEHOLDER MANAGEMENT ON THE BIG DIG

The lessons learned on the Big Dig about stakeholder management would fill several volumes if all project stakeholders were to participate in that endeavor. Though much has been written about the mistakes, problems, and tragedies of the Big Dig, very little has been written about the best practices for stakeholder management on megaprojects or large-scale programs. Some of the more important stakeholder management lessons can be gleaned from the extensive interviews with project management, the political and economic history of the Big Dig, reports, reviews, audits, and the print and news media, as described here.

1. Be proactive in the management of stakeholder expectations.

    All stakeholders, no matter how small or large their influence or interest, have concerns, claims, legal rights, and expectations that must be managed. Develop a stakeholder matrix that incorporates these influences and interests, and monitor each of these throughout the life of the project. Look for early warning signs of problems and concerns, and take action at the earliest possible date to prevent or resolve these matters by seeking input from all involved stakeholder groups, implementing an action plan, and then evaluating the outcome of any action taken. As stakeholder coalitions begin to form, seize the opportunity to develop a relationship with that group, and find ways to benefit the group at large as well as the needs of the project. Early stakeholder groups can be enormously beneficial in working with the local press, the media, and the community at large.

2. Develop stakeholder partnerships.

Developing partnerships with all stakeholders is a critical first step in building good relationships. Strong relationships with stakeholders are linked to project success (Chinyio 2010). Forming partnerships can help to identify shared concerns and ways to collaborate in resolving them. On the Big Dig, stakeholder partnerships were used to improve environmental conditions and safety, health, and quality-of-life issues; enhance business viability; as well as to resolve claims, disputes, and conflicts. Examples of these partnerships are collaborating with government agencies to develop more streamlined and focused procedures; partnering with contractors to resolve disputes; establishing residential pilot programs; and partnering with the local business community through an official representative to track air quality, noise, traffic congestion, and access to buildings and homes and to assess risk prevention and mitigation opportunities.

3. Communication is a two-way street.

In today's global and technologically advanced environment, many stakeholders may have information about the project before internal stakeholders have received notice. Never assume you have access to all the information about your project, and as you keep stakeholders informed about the project, also encourage them to keep the project informed on important matters of which they become aware. Make sure there are sufficient feedback mechanisms so that both internal and external stakeholders have various options to provide information, recommendations, anonymous reports, and threats as well as opportunities.

4. Build honesty and trust with your stakeholders.

Project success requires transparency and accountability measures. Always provide a transparent and open environment with your stakeholders with open forums and frequent meetings. If you cannot provide information on a particular matter, explain why. It may be as simple as "the matter is still in deliberation" or "the matter cannot be disclosed because of confidentiality requirements," but, whatever the reason, be sure you have notified the stakeholders and given them the opportunity to respond. When a trusting and honest relationship is built with the stakeholders in your project, they will respect you for your actions and appreciate the fact they were fairly treated. All project managers should be trained in state and local disclosure requirements and the federal government's Freedom of Information Act (FOIA) so that public matters can be disclosed promptly and there are proper channels to address confidential matters within the project organization.

5. Plan stakeholder management into your project budget.

Stakeholder management should not be an afterthought but should be analyzed at the conceptual stage to determine the cost of establishing stakeholder groups and the cost of administering these groups. Communication is expensive and sometimes requires the hiring of additional resources as the expectations and demands of stakeholders increase during the active years of the project. On the Big Dig, additional funds were allotted to increase the size of the Mitigation Program and the Public Information Office, particularly during the peak years of construction, when communication with the local media, businesses, residents, commuters, and taxpayers was most intense. Additional funds were requested to increase the size of the project's claims and changes operation to address contractor, designer, and subcontractor complaints and demands.

6. Acknowledge when mistakes are made and apologize for those mistakes.

   To gain the trust and support of all stakeholders including shareholders and taxpayers, be the first to admit that a mistake was made and apologize openly for the mistake to avoid later embarrassments and possible allegations of dishonesty or lack of transparency. The numerous public reports that were issued by the many oversight agencies, including the State and Federal Office of the Inspector General, the Massachusetts State Auditor's Office, and the daily news media and publications, highlighted not only mistakes that were made but concerns about transparency, engagement, and failures to respond. The openness on many aspects of the Big Dig was beneficial to stakeholders; however, the understanding of cost increases and financing concerns required greater vigilance throughout the project. Public owners and private consultants need to be prepared for 24/7 responsiveness to the concerns of the public on all aspects of a megaproject.

7. Use stakeholders to identify risks and opportunities.

   Develop programs to train stakeholders to identify both risks and opportunities that will impact their interests and objectives. Assist the stakeholders in creating control strategies to prevent and mitigate negative risks and maximize positive risks. This process will enable the stakeholders to learn from other stakeholders and may lead to the harmonization of conflicting interests. Stakeholders on the Big Dig assisted in identifying potential problems and solutions, including environmental recommendations, worker health and safety medical advancements, and quality-of-life improvements during the 15 years of heavy construction and demolition in the inner city.

8. Reward stakeholders for their contributions.

   Too often, stakeholders are told what they cannot do and, thus, are not encouraged to be creative or innovative in improving their stake in the project. Stakeholders should be looked upon as potential participants in the success of the project and should be motivated to contribute to that success. The rewards do not have to be monetary but can be recognized through public announcements, letters of acknowledgment, presentations at project or public events, or increased involvement in project decision making, monitoring, oversight, or assessment. Some examples of stakeholder recognition on the Big Dig project included the Contractor Quality Awards Program, the Safety and Health Awards Program for

Recognized Excellence (SHARE), the state minority- and women-owned business (M/WBE) and the federal disadvantaged business enterprise (DBE) purchasing programs, the Innovations and Advancement Program, the Artery Business Committee Excellence Awards, and the Artery Arts Program.

9. Be a good corporate citizen.

One of the important responsibilities that project owners and corporate sponsors share is demonstrating good citizenship by respecting local rules, laws, culture, and customs. Corporate citizenship can be implemented in many ways through training programs for local labor, sustainability programs, and a commitment to social responsibility, transparency, and legal and ethical behavior. Through the project's actions, community support will be realized, leaving a lasting positive impression on local citizens, the host government, and the general public.

10. Involve stakeholders in creative solutions to major urban problems.

Megaprojects can provide great benefits if they can be used to develop creative thinking to solve major urban problems. Both internal and external stakeholders can contribute to the process of building institutional learning by the development of better processes and procedures, best practices, and innovative technological solutions to infrastructure development. Stakeholders are key sources of knowledge and innovative ideas. There were several key programs and research projects that grew out of the Big Dig. The project's benefits, however, extended far beyond the city of Boston. The Big Dig's Innovations and Advancements Program helped planners and urban officials in the United States and throughout the world develop better and more efficient transportation solutions (Wood 2001).

BEST PRACTICES

1. Use multiple processes such as public participation, expert advice, organizational and stakeholder analysis surveys, and impact analysis to identify the organizations and key individual stakeholders likely to have an interest in or influence over the project.

2. Once all the stakeholders are identified, a stakeholder analysis should be conducted to determine the priority and role that a stakeholder should be given based on the interest that the stakeholder has in the project and that stakeholder's influence on the project and build a stakeholder assessment diagram, as shown in Figure 3.2.

3. Recognize that there are many opinions about the role of the stakeholders—the stakeholders' assessment of their own role, project management's assessment of their role, and the project owner and sponsor's evaluation of the stakeholders' role. These perspectives may

not always be the same. Assign roles based on a critical analysis of all the varying factors.

4. Develop a stakeholder communication strategy that provides for both inputs from the stakeholder and the methods and frequency of the project's communication with the stakeholder.

5. Establish a governance structure for all stakeholder groups and identify the authority of each group including oversight, decision making, and monitoring responsibilities.

6. Provide processes for managing stakeholder expectations, such as conflict resolution, feedback, consultation, information sharing, and accountability.

7. Provide organization and governance structures to manage project stakeholders. Recognize that stakeholders must be managed separately from the project's core decision-making structure. Stakeholder involvement in every aspect of the project can slow down project decision making and have an impact on both project cost and budget. Stakeholders' needs must be addressed in a consistent forum. Project management should not be spending an inordinate amount of time working with different interest groups such as community advocates, suppliers, environmentalists, technical specialists, consultants, and other stakeholder organizations.

8. Establish an independent board of directors consisting of sponsor representatives and outside experts, to oversee the project that is not compromised by other goals of the larger organization and has sufficient time to devote to the multiple and complex issues faced by the project.

9. Develop positive and mutually supportive stakeholder relationships that encourage trust and stimulate collaboration by addressing conflict in the early planning stages.

10. Concerns about governance, ethics, and the environment need to be a top priority and central to the stakeholder management process.

11. Develop an appropriate balance between the project owner, who provides the strategic guidance for the project, and the project consultant, who leads and manages the implementation.

12. Clearly define communication protocols and infrastructure among the numerous stakeholder groups and encourage feedback from the stakeholders through all project phases.

13. Determine ownership and management of internal and external stakeholders and allocate responsibility contractually.

14. Establish a framework to manage dependencies, including interfaces between contractors, government agencies, project teams, and community groups.

15. Integrate political, environmental, and community concerns into the project's plans; encourage stakeholder participation; and remain committed to the stakeholders' needs and concerns throughout the project life cycle.

SUMMARY

This chapter highlights a strategic framework for the management of multiple project stakeholders in a megaproject. Projects fail when stakeholders are not properly integrated into the project environment (Bourne and Walker 2005). Understanding stakeholder power and influence is essential to ensuring success on a long-term project with a complex political, technological, and legal environment. Most important, manage the interdependencies, interfaces and the conflicts among stakeholder groups and remain continuously aware of changing stakeholder expectations and goals.

ETHICAL CONSIDERATIONS

As described in this chapter, the government owner can have multiple roles in a project. The owner may have the role of regulator, oversight authority, protector of the public interest, and project director. Assume in its role as project director that it is obligated to keep the project on schedule, but in its role of protecting the public interest it is better if the project is delayed to ensure quality control.

Based on these facts, respond to the following questions:
1. What ethical considerations are raised by these conflicts?
2. How can an owner manage these conflicting roles on a project?
3. When there is a conflict among roles, should certain responsibilities take priority over other responsibilities? If so, why?
4. How do these conflicts impact project stakeholders and the project generally? Give three examples.

DISCUSSION QUESTIONS

1. Explain the difference between stakeholder influence and stakeholder interest in a project. Is a stakeholder who has high influence on a project more important than a stakeholder who has a high interest in the project but no influence? Why or why not? Would you manage stakeholders with high influence and low interest differently than those with a high interest but a low influence? If so, how?
2. Describe two project management tools that can be used to measure the influence and interest of stakeholders.
3. Define the difference between internal and external stakeholders. Should these stakeholders be treated differently? Should internal stakeholders be given greater authority in the governance of the project than external stakeholders? Why or why not?
4. Why is it critical to keep the project stakeholders informed? What transparency mechanisms can you use to enhance communication with your stakeholders?

5. How can the trust of your stakeholders be developed on a large-scale project, and how can a trusting relationship be maintained?
6. Explain the concept of corporate social responsibility and how it can be applied for the benefit of all stakeholders on megaprojects.
7. What measures can you use to increase public confidence in the project?

REFERENCES

Adler, D., C. Sage, and M. Woolcock. 2009. *Interim Institutions and the Development Process: Opening Spaces for Reform in Cambodia and Indonesia, 4.* University of Manchester: Brooks World Poverty Institute. See also John Voss, *Impact Evaluation of the Second Phase of the Kecamatan Development Program in Indonesia,* www.pnpm-mandiri.org/elibrary/files/disk1/1/pnpm--theworldba-21-1-kdp_impa-l.pdf. June 2008.

A Guide to the Project Management Body of Knowledge (PMBOK® Guide)— Fifth Edition. Newtown Square, PA: Project Management Institute.

Altschuler, A., and D. Luberoff, D. 2003. *Mega-projects: The Changing Politics of Urban Public Investment.* Washington, DC/Cambridge, MA: Brookings Institution Press, Lincoln Institute of Land Policy.

Anderson, L. L., and B. Polkinghorn. 2008. "Managing Conflict in Construction Megaprojects: Leadership and Third-Party Principles." Conflict Resolution Quarterly, 26(2) (Winter). Wiley Periodicals, Inc., and the Association for Conflict Resolution. doi: 10.1002/crq.229.

Barron, P., R. Diprose, and M. Woolcock, M. 2007. *Local Conflict and Development Projects in Indonesia: Part of the Problem or Part of a Solution?,* 13. World Bank Policy Research Working Paper no. 4212.

Bechtel/Parsons Brinckerhoff. 2006. *The Big Dig: Key Facts about Cost, Scope, Schedule, and Management.* Bechtel/Parsons Brinckerhoff. December.

Board on Infrastructure and the Constructed Environment. 2003. *Completing the Big Dig: Managing the Final Stages of Boston's Central Artery / Tunnel Project.* National Academy of Engineering, National Research Council, Transportation Research Board of the National Academies. Washington, DC: Committee for Review of the Project Management Practices Employed on the Boston Central Artery/Tunnel ("Big Dig"). National Academies Press.

Bourne, L., and D.H. T. Walker. 2005. "Visualizing and Mapping Stakeholder Influence." *Management Decision.* 43(5):649–660, Bingley, West Yorkshire, UK: Emerald Group Publishing Limited.

Capka, R. 2004. "Megaprojects: Managing a Public Journey." *Public Roads* 68(1):1. U.S. Washington, DC: Department of Transportation, Federal Highway Administration.

CA/T (Central Artery/Tunnel Project). 2000a. Finance Plan, (March 15, p. 19). Boston: Massachusetts Turnpike Authority.

CA/T (Central Artery/Tunnel Project). 2000b. Finance Plan. (June 16.) Boston: Massachusetts Turnpike Authority.CA/T (Central Artery Tunnel

Project). 1996. Work Program Plan and Amendments. Boston: Massachusetts Turnpike Authority.

Chinyio, E., and P. Olomolaiye. 2010. *Construction Stakeholder Management.* West Sussex, UK: Wiley-Blackwell, John Wiley & Sons, Ltd.

Cleland, D. I. 1986. "Project Stakeholder Management." *Project Management Journal* 17(4):36–44.

Connaughton, M. 2007. "The Big Dig Uncovered—Lessons Learned." Comments by Mary Connaughton, member, Massachusetts Turnpike Authority Board of Directors, Audit Committee Chairperson, National Conference of State Legislatures. Annual Conference, Boston, MA. August 8.

Connaughton, M. 2012. Interview with Mary Connaughton, former member of the Massachusetts Department of Transportation, Board of Directors responsible for oversight of the Central Artery/Tunnel Project. Boston, MA. October 13.

Crawford, L. 2005. "Senior Management Perceptions of Project Management Competence." *International Journal of Project Management* 23(1):7–16.

Dahlsrud, A. 2006. *How Corporate Social Responsibility is Defined: an Analysis of 37 Definitions.* Wiley Interscience. www.interscience.wiley.com DOI:10.1002/csr.132.

Elias, A. A., R. Y. Cavana, and L. S. Jackson., 2002. "Towards a Shared Mental Model of Stakeholders in Environmental Conflict." *Proceedings of the Institute of Australian Geographers' Conference* Canberra, Australia. Canberra, Australia.

Freeman, R. E. 1984. *Strategic Management: A Stakeholder Approach.* Boston: Pitman.

Greiman, V. 2011. "The Public/Private Conundrum in International Investment Disputes: Advancing Investor Community Partnerships." *Whittier Law Review* 32(3). Costa Mesa, CA.

Hughes, T. 1998. *Rescuing Prometheus: Four Monumental Projects that Changed the Modern World,* New York: Vintage Books.

Guggenheim, S. 2006. "Crisis and Contradictions: Understanding the Origins of a Community Development Project in Indonesia." In *The Search for Empowerment: Social Capital as Idea and Practice at the World Bank* 127, edited by A. Bebbington, M. Woolcock, S. Guggenheim, E. Olson, Bloomfield, Ct: Kumarian Press.

Hobley, M., and D. Shields. 2000. *The Reality of Trying to Transform Structures and Process: Forestry in Rural Livelihoods.* Working Paper, 132. London: Overseas Development Institute (ODI).

Metropolitan Highway System (MHS). General Laws of Massachusetts, Chapter 81A (MGL, c. 81A). Massachusetts Turnpike Authority and Metropolitan Highway System. Section 1, Massachusetts Turnpike Authority.

Miller, R., and B. Hobbs. 2005. "Governance Regimes for Large Complex Projects." *Project Management Journal* 36(3):42–50.

Morris, P. W. G., H. A. Jamieson, and M. M. Shepherd. 2006. "Research Updating the APM Body of Knowledge." 4th ed. *International Journal of Project Management* 24(6):461–473.

North, Douglass C. 1990. *Institutions, Institutional Change and Economic Performance*. Cambridge, UK: Cambridge University Press.

OIG (Office of the Inspector General). 2003. *Analysis of Bechtel/Parsons Brinckerhoff's Reply to the* Boston Globe's *Investigative News Series Concerning the Big Dig*. Commonwealth of Massachusetts, 23.

OIG (Office of the Inspector General). 2001. *Cost History of the Central Artery/Tunnel Project, 1994–2001*. Commonwealth of Massachusetts.

OIG (Office of the Inspector General).2000. *A Review of the Central Artery/Tunnel Project Cost Recovery Program*. (December.) Commonwealth of Massachusetts.

Ostrom, E., R. Gardener, and J. Walker. 1994. *Rules, Games, and Common-Pool Resources*. Ann Arbor: University of Michigan Press.

PMI (Project Management Institute). 2013. *Standard for Program Management*. 3rd ed. Newtown Square, PA: Project Management Institute.

Rigoglioso, M., G. Emmons, and C. Hogg. 1993. *By Land and by Sea, Boston Rebuilds for Tomorrow*. Harvard Business School Bulletin. Cambridge, MA: Harvard Publishing, June.

Salvucci, G. 2004. *Reflections on the Big Dig*. Speech. Cambridge: Massachusetts Institute of Technology, School of Engineering Professional Education Program. http://video.mit.edu.

Winch, G. M., and S. Bonke. 2002. "Project Stakeholder Mapping: Analyzing the Interests of Project Stakeholders." In *The Frontiers of Project Management Research*, ed. D P Slevin, D I Cleland & J K Pinto, 385–403. Newtown Sq., PA: Project Management Institute.

Wood, D. C. 2001. "Learning from the Big Dig." *Public Roads* 65(1) (July/August). Washington, DC: U.S. Department of Transportation, Federal Highway Administration.

Chapter 4

Governance

On Decision Making—Rien n'est plus difficile, et donc plus précieux, que d'être capable de décider. [Nothing is more difficult, and therefore more precious, than being able to decide.]

—*Napolean Buonaparte*

INTRODUCTION

Governance can mean many things in the project management context, and developing a governance framework requires an understanding of the organization of institutions, programs, projects, and procedures. This chapter focuses on the meaning and process of governance in large projects and, in particular, the lessons learned about governance at the Big Dig. In light of the magnitude and technological challenges of megaprojects—and their complex organizational structures—it is remarkable that more has not been written about the governance structure of large-scale projects. Project management has generally focused on the tools and techniques essential to managing projects rather than the underlying systemic framework that is required to make sure that a project's goals and objectives are met. Importantly, in recent years there has been a new focus on governance, with the adoption of international standards by multilateral organizations such as the Organization for Economic Co-operation and Development (OECD) and the World Bank, and the development of project governance standards by the Project Management Institute (PMI) and the Association for Project Management (APM).

Fundamental to the success of megaprojects is the building of an active public-private partnership that aligns with the goals of the owner to deliver a project in the public interest. As demonstrated throughout this book when projects fail, all roads lead to governance. Weak governance has been the root cause of many project failures, yet remarkably it is often overlooked when evaluating essential change needed to prevent future loss or failure (Grant 1997). In this chapter, we explore the important issue of multiple governances and finding the right balance for the project to succeed. The chapter provides a framework and perspectives on governance structures essential to megaproject management, which requires coordination and alignment to achieve the megaproject's strategic objectives and benefits. Key questions that will be explored are:

- What is governance?
- What are the current governance structures being utilized in public and private megaprojects?
- Which structures have been most effective?
- Why is the involvement of all stakeholders in governance vital to project success?
- How do you improve megaprojects through a carefully constructed governance framework?
- How do you hold all participants accountable?
- How do you maintain a transparent and ethical environment in a megaproject?

WHAT IS GOVERNANCE?

The term *governance* originated from the Greek word *kyberman*, meaning "to steer or guide." From its Greek origins it moved to Latin, where it was known as *gubernare* and then migrated to France as *governer*. There are many definitions of *governance* in the corporate governance literature, and one of the most frequently used is from the OECD.

Corporate governance, as defined by the OECD (2004), involves:

A set of relationships between a company's management, its board, its shareholders and other stakeholders. Corporate governance also provides the structure through which the objectives of the company are set, and the means of attaining those objectives and monitoring performance are determined.

Corporate governance is generally defined as "the system by which organizations are directed and controlled." As shown in Figure 4.1, it involves a set of relationships between an organization's management, its board of directors (board), and its shareholders. The responsibility of the board is to protect the shareholders' or, in the case of a public project, the taxpayers' assets and to ensure they receive a return on their investment.

When we use the term *corporate governance* in this chapter, we refer to the project's parent organization, which in the case of the Big Dig was a public

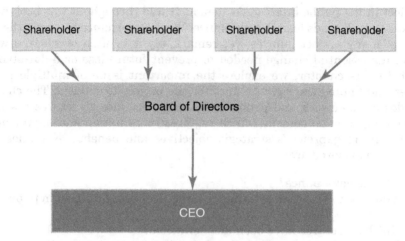

Figure 4.1   Corporate Governance Structure

agency, the Massachusetts Turnpike Authority (MTA). However, the Big Dig was also subject to oversight by the U.S. Federal Highway Administration (FHWA) as a primary funder of the project.

The corporate governance literature addresses the issue of what structures should be set up to govern an organization and is most often presented as a hierarchical, binary relationship between a principal and an agent (Williamson, 1996). The role of the board of directors in corporations has been defined as the "link between the people who provided capital (the shareholders) and the people who use the capital to create value (the managers)..." (Monks and Minow 1995, 178).

Those writing on corporate governance make an assumption that the governance structure will remain in place for some time. There is a sharp contrast between the hierarchical and static nature of corporate governance relations and the innovative, team-based structure found in the network relations typical of the governance of megaprojects. Since projects are of a "temporary" rather than a permanent nature, it is this contrast that attracts and creates different approaches, structures, and behaviors.

Purpose of Governance

In recent years, several high-level corporate collapses have brought to light shareholder demands that organizations strengthen their governance systems and pay closer attention to concerns of the stakeholders. In response to Enron, Tyco, WorldCom, and Europe's Enron (Parmalat), there have been more rigid oversight and regulatory requirements and a broadening corporate governance agenda to include stakeholders' concerns as well as shareholder accountability. Governance structures have been used on projects for the following primary purposes:

- To ensure the organization receives a maximum return on investment
- To direct and control its operations and strategic activities
- To respond to the legitimate rights, expectations, and desires of its shareholders and stakeholders
- To formalize organizational learning
- To monitor the delivery of benefits through
  - Progress reports and audits
  - Reviews at various phases in the project's life cycle
- To evaluate performance before permitting the project to progress

Governance as a Factor of Success

When undertaking a very large project without an adequate governance regime, most organizations are exposed to a high probability of failure and the resulting significant negative impacts (Miller and Hobbs 2005). Because megaprojects are more complex and riskier, they require governance frameworks that are different from those of more routine and less risky endeavors. Governance frameworks, including government roles, policies, regulations, and standards, have been described in the research as vitally important to project success and essential to the planning and management of projects (Morris and Hough 1987; Miller & Lessard 2000; Flyvbjerg et al. 2003; Garland 2009; Klakegg 2008). Though the numerous awards and technological advancements on the Big Dig were certainly factors indicating successful governance, as listed in the appendix to this book, there were also examples of governance failure that caused schedule delays, cost overruns, and financing shortfalls.

Much can be learned from international models of good governance. The World Bank has benchmarked a country's corporate governance framework and company practices against the OECD principles of good governance. Table 4.1 highlights the six OECD Principles of Good Governance with recommended oversight tools based on best practices and lessons learned at the Big Dig.

PROJECT GOVERNANCE

As distinct from corporate governance, which involves the relationship of the shareholders, the board, and the CEO, project governance structure can look very different. Governance, as it applies to portfolios, programs, projects, and project management, "coexists within the corporate governance framework" (Müller 2009). The PMI Standard for Program Management (2013) provides a broad definition of *program governance* as:

> The process of developing, communicating, implementing, monitoring and assuring the policies, procedures, organizational structures, and practices associated with a given program. Governance is oversight and control.

Table 4.1   OECD Principles of Good Governance

Principle	Responsibility	Big Dig Oversight
Accountability	Government actions consistent with objectives	Independent Government Oversight Coordination Commission and external audit committees, performance evaluations, individual and team responsibility, contractual commitments, market pressure, completion agreements, enforceability, termination, and incentive/disincentive programs
Transparency	Decisions open to scrutiny by the general public	Stakeholder participation, public meetings, and detailed financial reports
Efficiency	Quality outputs and services meeting original intent	Independent quality review, integrated monitoring across the organization, community participation, and extensive testing and evaluation
Responsiveness	Capacity and flexibility to respond rapidly to change	Change-order response timeliness evaluation, feedback, audits, and integrative processes
Forward vision	Anticipate future problems based on current trends	Performance indicators, earned value and trend analysis, tracking processes, root-cause analysis, and implementation of lessons learned and best practices
Rule of law	Enforcement of contracts, statutes, and regulations	Sustainability review committee, dispute resolution through partnering and collaboration, incentives and penalties for noncompliance, aggressive cost recovery for design errors or omissions, and value engineering

Source: Office of Economic Co-operation and Development, (OECD), Paris, France.

This standard presents the role of the program board as providing the overarching governance and quality assurance of the program. The composition of the board is typically a cross-functional group of senior stakeholders responsible for initiation of the program, approval of plans, review of the program's progress, compliance, and establishment of frameworks and limits for decision making on program investments.

Scholars have described governance regimes for major investment projects as comprising "the processes and systems that need to be in place on behalf of the financing party to ensure successful investments" (Samset et al. 2006) and as "an organized structure established as authoritative within the institution, comprising processes and rules established to ensure projects meet their purpose" (Klakegg 2008).

The term *governance* has been used broadly in project management to describe contractual structure, process and procedures, strategies, managerial charter, global infrastructure, systems integration, project delivery, organizational framework, and the authority of the project's governing board. In its simplest terms, project governance is the framework that ensures that the project has been correctly conceived and is being executed in accordance with best project management practice and in alignment with the governance processes established by the project's corporate or institutional framework.

MULTIPLE GOVERNANCE STRUCTURES AS A DYNAMIC REGIME

Governance is conceptualized in the literature as an oversight and control function. The structures are stable, but the activities being overseen are dynamic and changing. Governance scholars contend that governance regimes themselves must be dynamic—that they can change to adapt to the emerging context (Miller and Hobbs 2005, 48).

Significantly, public infrastructure projects do not always meet the expectations of its stakeholders. Most are delivered too late and above budget, and do not meet agreed quality standards. The subject of governance is rarely discussed in the public discourse, yet it is essential to understand how governance may contribute to the success or failure of projects and how more effective governance frameworks can better meet stakeholder expectations and an improved return on investment to society. An important part of understanding governance is recognizing that projects must continually change to meet the demands of its stakeholders and the needs of its customers. For instance, an organization may start out with a strong centralized governance framework but may become more decentralized as the organization evolves, requiring decision making to be delegated to a lower level of the organization, where the technical knowledge and expertise can be applied firsthand.

In accordance with PMI taxonomy, megaprojects are in reality "Programs" consisting of hundreds of related projects and other work that require alignment with the strategic goals of the parent organization. On the Big Dig, this required collaboration and coordination between state and federal governmental executives, a private joint venture, internal and external agencies and stakeholders, and hundreds of project teams. The governance framework was constantly progressing at the Big Dig due to the numerous stakeholders and the sheer scope and size of the project. New processes and procedures were constantly introduced because of innovative technical requirements

GOVERNANCE

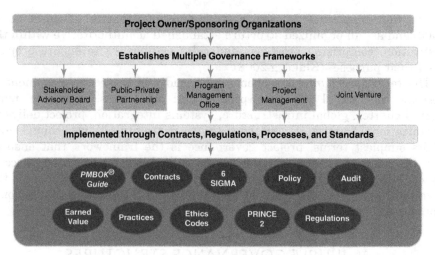

Figure 4.2   Multiple Governance Framework

that had not been attempted on previous projects. Because of the many risks and potential catastrophic loss that the project faced, process became all the more important. Throughout each phase of the project, procedures were reviewed and sometimes amended based on lessons learned or changes in owners' requirements. Critical to the implementation of a process was the importance of integration and collaboration among the participants to ensure that these innovative processes were properly delivered. Thus, project governance regimes must remain open to change based on the evolving mission and goals of the project.

To coordinate the complex organizational strategies, goals, requirements, and processes and procedures, multiple governance structures were established. Figure 4.2 illustrates the complexity of governance in a large megaproject. The interaction and coordination of each of these governance structures is essential to enhanced project performance and delivery of benefits. As noted by project management scholars in recognizing the benefits of multiple regimes:

> ...project governance regimes could be analyzed not with the goal of identifying the single best structure to put in place, but for the rich mix of governance regimes to be put in place to manage different issues and different stages of the life cycle and the variation in their usage as the project and its context evolve.

(Miller and Hobbs 2005)

Project organizations as illustrated in Figure 4.2 are primarily designed to fulfill the project's objectives within a limited period of time. These organizations therefore require a very dynamic environment.

DEVELOPING A MEGAPROJECT GOVERNANCE FRAMEWORK

Miller and Hobbs (2005) have highlighted the need for design criteria when developing a governance regime for a megaproject that would permit transformation of the governance structure as the project unfolds over a long period of time. In their study of large engineering projects, they argue that since the governance structure will undoubtedly change, there is a need for flexibility in project structures rather than a single megaproject governance structure.

In *Megaprojects and Risk: An Anatomy of Ambition*, the authors conclude that the problem of governance in megaprojects is one of risk negligence and lack of accountability on behalf of project promoters whose main ambition is to build projects for private gain, economic or political, and not for the public benefit. Their suggested remedy for what is termed the *megaproject paradox* is: (1) that risk and accountability should be much more centrally placed in megaproject decision making than is currently the case, (2) that regulations should be in place to ensure that risk analysis and risk management are carried out, (3) that the role of government should be shifted from involvement in project promotion to keeping an arm's-length distance and restricting its involvement to the formulation and auditing of public interest objectives to be met by the megaproject, and (4) that four basic instruments be employed to ensure accountability in decision making by (a) ensuring transparency, (b) specifying performance requirements, (c) making explicit rules regulating the construction and operations of the project, and, finally, (d) involving risk capital from private investors, the assumption being that their willingness to invest would be a sound test of the viability of the project up front (Flyvbjerg et al. 2003).

PROJECTS AS TEMPORARY INSTITUTIONAL STRUCTURES

Megaprojects face choices over what type of governance structure will best serve the goals and demands of the project. Megaprojects are usually governed by temporary institutional governance structures that borrow resources and technical capacity from their parent organizations through a secondment process. In the case of a public project, the government agency with authority for infrastructure development typically appoints members to a governing board, while in private infrastructure projects, the governing board is often represented by the project's sponsors.

In private infrastructure projects, consortiums are formed such as that of Bechtel, Arup, Systra, and Halcrow, established to run the $10.4 billion Channel Tunnel Rail Link project linking the United Kingdom to Europe's high-speed rail network (Davies et al. 2009). A consortium is essentially a contract, between the government owner and the private-sector management consultant, that allocates risk, accountability, and decision making among the participants.

The Big Dig was unique in that the management of construction was carried out by a temporary joint venture, Bechtel/Parsons Brinckerhoff (B/PB), represented by the project's designer, Parsons Brinckerhoff, and the project's contractor, Bechtel Corporation, while the major supporting functions reported directly to the public owner. The joint venture was overseen by a board of control made up of representatives of each joint-venture partner.

GOVERNANCE FRAMEWORK DEVELOPMENT: FIVE-STEP PROCESS

Guidance on the development of governance frameworks can be found in various sources, including the World Bank (2000), PMI Program Management and Portfolio Management Standards (2013), and the APM Standard, "Directing Change: A Guide to Governance of Project Management" (APM Governance SIG, 2011). Defining a governance structure for a megaproject can be difficult and time consuming, and requires considerable commitment from the project owner at the inception of the project. The following sections highlight five key steps in developing an effective framework. These steps are iterative and will repeat themselves continuously as new structures are established or as existing structures are modified or abolished. This framework is based on lessons learned from megaprojects including the Big Dig, project management research, and a comprehensive analysis from numerous projects both public and private in various countries around the world. It is important to note that each project is unique and may require additional or alternative steps at any time in its life cycle.

Step 1: Defining the Project's Governance Structures

> No man is good enough to govern another man without that other's consent.
>
> —*Abraham Lincoln*

The first step in developing a governance framework for any organization is deciding the structures that will best enable the organization to implement its strategy and accomplish its goals and objectives. There is no one model that fits the needs of every organization, and multinational enterprises tend to rely on various governance structures to meet the needs of its complex organization. For organizations with a broad portfolio of projects and programs, different governance structures may be used at different times in the life of the particular project or program.

The need for alternative governance structures arises from the difficulties of hierarchical coordination and the competing interests and values that must

Table 4.2   Project Governance Structures

1. **Enterprise governance**—The entire accountability framework of the organization.
2. **Corporate governance**—The system by which an organization is overseen and controlled by its shareholders.
3. **Joint venture (JV)**—The cooperation of two or more entities for a finite period in which each agrees to *share* profit, loss, and control in a specific enterprise. The parties to the JV can be private or public entities.
4. **Program governance**—The structure by which related projects and other work are integrated, coordinated, and managed among all stakeholders in alignment with the strategic goals of the parent organization.
5. **Project governance**—The system by which projects are managed to ensure benefits are received and requirements are met in alignment with the organization and/or program's goals.
6. **Stakeholder governance**—The process by which stakeholders or external groups or committees are involved in the project's decision making or oversight.
7. **Architecture governance**—The principles, standards, guidelines, contractual obligations, and regulatory framework within which goals are met at an enterprise-wide level.

coexist under the same organizational umbrella. Before one can understand how governance works, it is important to distinguish among the various governance structures that can exist in an organization (see Table 4.2). Multiple structures are essential in large-scale projects that require complex coordination, numerous interfaces, and internal and external integration. The structures defined in Table 4.2 are examples of governance structures used in the Big Dig to manage the relationships between the organization's board and the project's board, shareholders and stakeholders, regulatory authorities and auditors, and projects and programs. The umbrella over all of these structures is known as *enterprise governance*, which represents the entire governance framework for the organization. Each of these structures tends to follow a different approach to governance, including oversight, advocacy, support, consensus building, compliance monitoring, control, and delivery of projects, programs, and services.

1. Organizational Structure at the Big Dig   Figure 4.3 provides the organizational structure of the Big Dig after project integration of both the management consultant's employees and the owner's employees in 1998. At the beginning of the CA/T project, the relationship between the state and the consultant reflected the usual owner/consultant relationship. However, as the project moved from design to construction, the structure was modified to address performance problems, enhance communications, reduce the number of management layers, and moderate conflicts between owner and consultant (Board 2003).

The organization structure represents both vertical and horizontal coordination of the various governance structures as they are defined in Table 4.2.

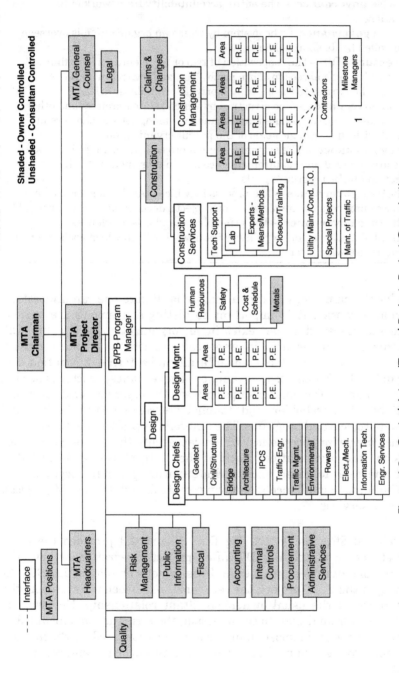

Figure 4.3   Central Artery/Tunnel Project: Project Organization
Source: Central Artery/Tunnel Project. 1998. Integrated Project Organization.

The shaded boxes represent the owner's employees, while the unshaded boxes represent the management consultant's employees. The government owner (MTA) represented the highest level of governance at the corporate level, and the owner's representative, the MTA project director, represented the highest level of governance at the project level. The horizontal coordination was much more challenging, as it depended upon a high degree of teamwork and on the goals and methodologies such teams formulated and continually improved.

During the transition to the integrated project organization (IPO) structure in 1997–1998, the best-qualified person available for a particular managerial position was selected regardless of organizational affiliation. This arrangement does not resemble the usual owner/consultant relationship, in which public-sector employees and the consultant's employees operate independently, as was the case at the Big Dig before the integration. Some of the reasons for this integrated, more traditional structure were to establish clear lines of responsibility and accountability, to create a system of checks and balances, to eliminate perceived conflicts of interest, and to have a clear understanding of owner/consultant risk allocations (Board 2003). The organizational structure was not without its critics, who contended that this type of arrangement rendered the CA/T Project vulnerable to divided loyalties and conflicting interests (OIG 2000). For example, the MTA's director of construction reported both to the consultant's top program manager and to the MTA's project director.

2. Projectized, Functional, and Matrix Organizations   Since many organizations derive most of their revenue from projects, the way the project is organized can be a major factor in its success or failure, assuming that the project gets the necessary priority, support, and focus from its parent organization. Generally, projects are organized in one of three ways (PMI 2013):

As illustrated in Table 4.3, the Central Artery/Tunnel Project was structured as a projectized organization, which is typical of most megaprojects and most building and infrastructure projects. This meant that the project director had access to its own resources, had substantial authority to make day-to-day decisions, and reported directly to the government owner's CEO. However, unlike privately funded projects, the Big Dig was not independently financed and was highly dependent on both the state and federal government for its funding.

3. Program Management Offices (PMOs)   Where projects or contracts are organized systematically under a program, as was the case at the Big Dig, the program sets the framework for governance. A program management office (PMO) is an organizational unit designed to centralize and coordinate the management of projects. The PMO can oversee the management of projects, programs, or a combination of both, and should be used only when

Table 4.3   Projectized, Functional, and Matrix Organizations

1. Projectized organization Project manager has high to almost total authority.	Project manager has full authority to assign priorities, apply resources, and direct the work. Typically, they also have separate financing and budgets from the parent organization.
2. Functional organization Project Manager has little or no authority.	A hierarchical structure where the entire organizational activities are divided into specific functions such as operations, finance, marketing, and personnel relations and staff is grouped by areas of specialization and managed by a person with expertise in that area.
3. Matrix organization Weak: Project manager has limited authority. Project manager reports to functional manager, and staff reports to functional managers. Balanced: Project manager has low to moderate authority. Project manager reports to functional manager or to a manager of project managers, and staff reports to project manager on a dotted-line basis. Strong: Project manager has moderate to high authority. Project manager reports directly to CEO or to manager of project managers, and project staff reports to project manager directly or on a dotted-line basis.	A structure in which the project manager shares responsibility with the functional managers for assigning priorities and for directing the work of persons assigned to the project. A matrix can take various forms, such as weak, balanced, or strong.

Source: PMI (Project Management Institute). 2013. *A Guide to the Project Management Body of Knowledge (PMBOK® Guide)*—Fifth Edition. Newtown Square, PA: Project Management Institute.

it can add value to an organization through the coordination of projects and subprojects tied to the parent organization's or sponsors' overall business objectives (Kendall and Rollins 2003), or when it can serve as a change agent, or improve current results through standardization (Pellegrinelli and Garagna 2009).

The government owner at the Big Dig gave responsibility to the management consultant for coordination of thousands of contracts as well as for developing and implementing the project's standards and procedures and monitoring and controlling project performance of all contractors. This was a monumental task that could not have been managed other than through a centralized program management structure.

4. Project Board of Directors   Another mechanism for governing projects is through a project board. Project board members are usually chosen by the political governing authority and are not elected by the shareholders, nor are they chosen by the corporate board members. Many of the project's decisions have already been made before the board is formed. The role of the board in hiring, firing, and monitoring the management team is usually heavily exercised in public projects by the owner; however, the degree of control over the project depends upon whether the project has private sponsors or has assigned the control of the project to a private management team.

The Big Dig did not have a separate project board; instead, it was overseen by the owners' board of directors. This was problematic, as the owners board, in addition to overseeing the project, had responsibility for the design, construction, and maintenance of the Commonwealth of Massachusetts' state highways and bridges and for overseeing traffic safety and engineering activities, including the Highway Operations Control Center, to ensure safe road and travel conditions. The owner's board of directors was represented by politically appointed individuals who worked on behalf of the shareholders/taxpayers to ensure that the best interests of the citizen taxpayers were addressed. The board originally consisted of three members and was expanded to five members during the peak years of construction (MTA By-Laws 1997). The criteria for selection of the board members is an important aspect of governance and should be set forth in legislation or policy at the organizational level. Before structuring a project board, the important questions set forth in Table 4.4 should be analyzed and a framework developed for organizing, structuring, and monitoring the board and its members.

The Role of the Board of Directors   Project boards have tremendous responsibilities for overseeing projects. The roles of these boards vary in accordance

Table 4.4   Key Questions for Structuring and Maintaining a Project Board

1. Is the purpose of the governance structure communicated to the stakeholders?
2. What are the values that guide the board and the organization?
3. Has there been a cost-benefit analysis of the project?
4. How much trust does the board have in the ability of the director of project management and in the CEO?
5. How are board members held accountable?
6. Is the governance model up to date and meeting the goals of the organization and the project?
7. How much of a commitment is there to increasing the knowledge and skills of the board members?
8. How is conflict of interest resolved among board members? Is there a policy on conflicts, and is it enforced?
9. How are disagreements and disputes handled? Are the voting procedures sufficient?
10. How effective is the board's recruitment methodology in getting new board members?

with their charter and by-laws. Project boards have been utilized on a number
of projects to provide oversight and accountability. For example, the English
Channel Tunnel, or Chunnel (Eurotunnel), a privately financed project, established a project board in 1986 to finance, build, and operate a tunnel between
Great Britain and France. The board's responsibilities over the many years of
the project's development included setting strategic goals, considering major
strategic transactions, and hiring, firing, and setting annual performance
objectives for Eurotunnel's CEO and CFO (GET SA 2011).

In contrast, on the Big Dig, a publicly funded project, the board's authority
was extensive and included oversight for both the Massachusetts Turnpike
System (the interchange stretching from Boston to the New York border)
and the $14.9 billion Central Artery/Tunnel Project. In accordance with its
by-laws, the board had authority to set policy and to approve all financial
agreements, construction contracts, the purchase of goods and services, and
agreements with other political authorities. Significantly, they also had the
power to approve the hiring of the Big Dig's project director, chief counsel,
chief of staff, chief financial officer, and spokespersons on the recommendation
of the MTA's executive director/CEO (MTA By-Laws 1997).

Key Questions for Board Members   Board practices can vary widely among
industries from IT development to infrastructure development; the larger the
project, the higher risk the board faces (Nolan and McFarlan 2005). Once the
board is selected, other important questions arise, such as:

1. Does the board have access to reliable information on the project's
   progress, budget forecasts, contingencies, risks, and quality control?
2. Are there criteria that allow for the elevation of significant issues to the
   board, and are significant issues presented in a timely fashion for board
   review?
3. Does the board obtain independent evaluation of the project's reported
   progress, costs, forecasts, change allowance, and key documentation?
4. Does the board have approval authority over significant issues, including legal settlements, claims and changes, expanded scope, budget
   increases, and other matters above a minimum threshold?

5. Project Oversight Committees, Steering Groups, and Advisory Boards

> To provide institutional knowledge I appointed a Second
> Opinion Committee consisting of three experts on the Com-
> monwealth's transportation systems.
>
> —*Fred Salvucci, former Massachusetts secretary of
> transportation and master planner of the Big Dig*

As an alternative to project or program boards, project steering groups and
advisory boards have been effective monitoring structures. These structures
may play various roles, including serving as advisers to a project or as

audit or oversight committees on various matters such as technology, cost, schedule, quality, risk, or financing. The IT industry, as an example, has hired experts to address the company's short-term business needs with long-term IT investments. Steering groups can typically serve broad roles and execute both governance and support functions. These functions can include appointing project managers, setting limits on budgets and schedule criteria, and defining the goals to be achieved by the project (Crawford et al. 2008).

To coordinate oversight on the Big Dig, an executive Oversight and Coordination Commission (OCC) was established by legislation to oversee the extensive number of projects and contracts and to ensure transparency and control for the citizens of the Commonwealth of Massachusetts.

6. Stakeholder Governance   Stakeholders play a visible role in the project governance framework, and their involvement comprises many activities that include residential pilot programs, business advisory groups, networked alliances, labor partnerships, and environmental sustainability processes and procedures. From recent initiatives by the World Bank, the International Institute for Sustainable Development (2012), and the United Nations Conference on Trade and Development, multi-stakeholder processes have gained recognition as valid mechanisms to develop and implement social and environmentally responsible management practices toward sustainable development. As a result, the issue of stakeholder governance is becoming a central focal point for the initiation of new institutional structures to deal with these matters of great public concern. Key questions that arise concerning stakeholder governance on projects are:

   a. How will the identification of the relevant stakeholders be determined? (social, economic, political, environmental concerns)
   b. What structures should be established to address stakeholder concerns and at what phase of the project? (board, advisory council, support group, partnerships, networks, alliances, community liaison)
   c. What roles or decisions will be delegated to stakeholders? (development of standards and processes, policy formulation, dispute resolution)
   d. How will decisions be made by stakeholder groups? (majority vote, consensus, through representatives)
   e. What mechanisms will be available to support disadvantaged stakeholder groups? (financial support, information sharing, capacity building)

Step 2: Planning and Defining Roles and Responsibilities

Once the project governance structures are established, the second step in developing a governance framework is to identify the roles and responsibilities of the people participating in oversight and decision making at the project. Figure 4.4 illustrates the various participants in project governance at the

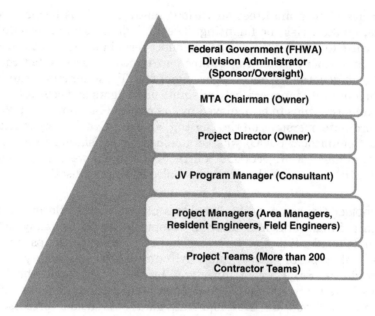

Figure 4.4   Project's Key Decision Makers
Source: Central Artery/Tunnel Project.

Big Dig, ranging from the federal government's division administrator, the project's main sponsor to the project teams who carry out the daily work of the project. Defining these roles and allocating decision making and oversight responsibility is no easy task on a complex project. Because a megaproject is an evolving institution, the initially assigned responsibilities may change over time. The sections that follow define the various responsibilities of the project's key decision makers. Don't be misled by the simplicity of Figure 4.4, as many different configurations of governance exist. Getting to just the right one for a given project requires an understanding of the strategic goals of project organizational design. Similar to governance structures, governance roles and responsibilities may need to change and adapt throughout the project life cycle based on the needs of the owner, the sponsors, and the public at large.

Federal Administrator's Role: Project Sponsor   Figure 4.4 illustrates the hierarchical organizational relationships at the Big Dig. However, this hierarchical structure can be understood only in relation to the multiple governance structures shown in Table 4.2. Organizational structures and governance structures on complex projects represent two very different dynamics of project management, yet they require linkage throughout the life cycle of the project to ensure that all governance structures are coordinated to maintain alliance with the organization's overall strategy. As shown in Figure 4.4, the federal government had top-level responsibility for oversight of the Big Dig project as a whole because of the contribution of federal funding. The federal government's governance role included:

- Ensuring adherence to federal regulations and standards
- Critical evaluation of the state's funding and cash flow program structure
- Approval of certain project contracts, including major changes
- Providing technical assistance as necessary
- Ensuring that adequate controls were in place to safeguard spending to prevent the misuse of federal funds

The Massachusetts Turnpike Authority Chair's Role: The Owner/Sponsor   On the Big Dig, there were two major sponsors providing the financial resources for the project: the federal government and the state government. In addition to the two sponsors, the ultimate owner of the project was not determined until 1997, well after most of the engineering work was complete. Initially, the Massachusetts Highway Department (MHD) was charged with responsibility for the Big Dig. In 1997, the Massachusetts legislature created the Metropolitan Highway System (MHS) and transferred responsibility for the Big Dig from the MHD to the Massachusetts Turnpike Authority (MTA). There was constant concern that uncertainty in ultimate ownership could naturally lead to less-than-tight controls.

In Massachusetts, the governor named the Turnpike Authority chair, who also served as the chief executive officer and was responsible for oversight of both the Central Artery/Tunnel Project and the massive turnpike operations. In addition to the turnpike chair, from 1997 through 2001 the Central Artery/Tunnel Project was overseen by a three-member board of the MTA appointed by the governor (MG.L. c. 81A). In 2002, the board was increased from three to five members. The only criterion for board membership, other than residency, was that no more than three of the five members would be from the same political party. In 2009, the MTA and the MHD were merged under a new mega transportation agency known as the Massachusetts Department of Transportation (MassDOT). This new agency is responsible for oversight of roads, public transit, aeronautics, and transportation licensing and registration in the Commonwealth of Massachusetts as well as winding up the final stages of the Big Dig and managing its ongoing debt service.

The Project Owner's Role in Governance   A key role in project governance is that of the project owner. The project owner has three main areas of responsibility: to the board, to the project manager, and to the project stakeholders. These responsibilities include:

1. For the board, the owner provides leadership on culture and values, owns the business case, keeps the project aligned with the organization's strategy and portfolio direction, governs project risk, works with other

sponsors, focuses on realization of benefits, coordinates stakeholders, recommends opportunities to optimize cost/benefits, ensures continuity of sponsorship, and provides assurance, feedback, and lessons learned.

2. For the project manager, the owner provides timely decisions, clarifies the decision-making framework, clarifies business priorities and strategy, communicates business issues, provides resources, engenders trust, manages relationships, supports the project manager's role, and promotes ethical conduct.

3. For other project stakeholders, the project owner engages stakeholders, governs stakeholder communications, directs client relationships, directs governance of users and suppliers and arbitrates between stakeholders.

Owner's Oversight of the Big Dig   Governance of a public project is in some ways similar to corporate governance in a large organization. Rather than responsibility to the shareholders, the public owner has responsibility to the taxpayers to ensure not only that the public interest is properly represented but that benefits accrue to the intended parties. On the Big Dig, the placement of responsibility for oversight was with the government agency that was also responsible for the fiscal management of the project. This structure can be problematic, as noted by one former Big Dig official:

Efficiency won over oversight and that had a consequence, some of which we are seeing now. I'd have the oversight function and the financial management system report to agency boards separately from the people running the project. You need to put restrictions on who can be on those boards which too often consist of former legislators or political appointees (Primack 2006).

(Andrew Natsios, CEO and chairman of MTA 2000–2001)

Oversight was an issue at the Big Dig. A Federal Task Force Report issued by the Federal Highway Administration in 2000, shortly after $1.4 billion in cost overruns were uncovered, stated, "The FHWA failed to maintain an independent enough relationship with the State to adequately fulfill its oversight" (FHWA 2000).

As expressed by a former member of the Massachusetts Turnpike Authority board in her appearance before the National Conference of State Legislators in 2007:

Perhaps an owner's board should have been established with professionals in the field of engineering, finance, construction and transportation with the sole purpose of providing checks and balances and reporting to the public. The board would challenge engineering decisions in the very early and most critical stages of the project. It would certainly be expensive to compensate this board, but, no doubt, well worth it.

(Connaughton 2007)

Project Director's Role   As shown in Figure 4.3, the project director generally reports to the organization's CEO or the project or owner's board. The project director is responsible for the day-to-day management of the project and makes decisions on behalf of the project owner. Essentially, the project director is the CEO of the project organization. As the representative of the owner, the director must work closely with the program manager and the project's core managers to ensure delivery of the project's requirements. The project director must also work closely with the stakeholders and may establish with the board's approval a stakeholder advisory committee or stakeholder working groups. Early on, the Big Dig established a resident's pilot program in Boston's North End neighborhood and worked with the Artery Business Committee to address the concerns of local residents and local businesses. The project director serves in an important interface role between the owner and internal and external stakeholders, including other government agencies. The program manager responsible for managing all of the project's contractors reports directly to the project director, who serves as the interface with the project owner.

Program Manager's Role   In 1985, the Massachusetts Highway Department hired Bechtel/Parsons Brinckerhoff (B/PB) to act as management consultant. B/PB was responsible for supervising day-to-day operations, estimating costs, and managing the designs. B/PB prepared preliminary design documents, managed final design contracts and construction, provided administrative and technical support, and prepared cost estimates and budget forecasts. B/PB also prepared the semiannual finance plans and a myriad of other reports.

B/PB was hired for two main purposes:
- It was necessary for design and construction expertise.
- To provide continuity for administration changes—the Big Dig spanned eight state governors, from initial approval of the Central Artery/Tunnel Project in the Interstate Cost Estimate in 1975 to completion of the project's Parks and Greenway in 2007.

Due to the large number of contracts, the joint venture was led by a program manager, who was responsible for management and oversight of all design, construction management, and construction services. In addition, the joint venture was overseen by a board of control made up of representatives of the two joint-venture partners (OIG 2001). However, the overall responsibility for the project remained with the project owner.

Project Managers' Roles: Area Managers and Resident Engineers   As shown in Figure 4.3, there were several levels of reporting and decision making below the program manager on both the design and the construction sides of the project. As an example, construction, oversight, and decision making were coordinated at several levels, from the area manager to the resident engineers to the contractors in coordination with the milestone managers for each area. Claims and Changes had a dotted-line reporting relationship with construction. The technical complexity and scale of the Big Dig added extensive oversight and decision-making requirements that normally do not exist on midsized or smaller projects. Thus, cost, scope, schedule, risk, and quality decision making and oversight were complicated by the numerous unknowns, internal and external interfaces, integrated project teams, multiple critical paths, technological challenges, design-bid-build structure, and extensive internal and external oversight.

Project Team's Role   Megaprojects require not only the integration of numerous processes and people but also the integration of communities of knowledge, including business process innovation, strategic management, socioeconomic impact, public policy, and quantitative and qualitative analysis across disciplines. Partnership alliances are critical to successful megaproject management, both internal and external to the project organization, and engagement between the public and private sector is essential. Since many decisions were delegated to the project teams, they played a significant role in oversight of the workers and in daily decision making. Thus, development of a team approach to problem resolution was critical to prevent the escalation of numerous decisions to those with less capacity to understand what was happening on the ground.

GOVERNANCE AS DECISION MAKING

In addition to establishing governance principles and goals, governance means setting up a structure—a set of decision-making processes and methods for accumulation of knowledge to ensure that creativity and discipline are brought to bear. Within the governance structure, decision-making frameworks should be set up to make sure that (1) the right questions are being asked, (2) responses can be evaluated and verified, and (3) parties are held accountable. Large multinational firms have often put in place complex frameworks, composed of five or six decision gates, in which most issues are addressed. Governmental frameworks have been described as less complex, with fewer decision points (Miller and Lessard 2000). Organizational governance in practice is the placement of decision-making authority within the organization.

Four questions are critical to developing a framework for governance:

1. What decisions should be made to ensure effective progress toward the target goals of the organization.
2. Who should have input into these decisions?
3. Who should make these decisions?
4. How will these decisions be monitored, controlled, and enforced?

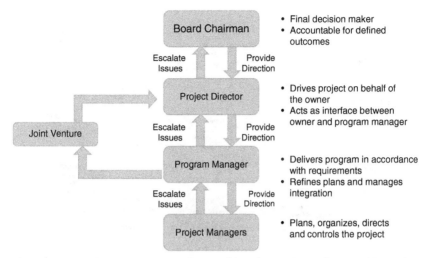

Figure 4.5   Governance Direction and Escalation Central Artery/Tunnel Project

Governance Escalation at the Big Dig

To thoroughly comprehend the benefits of a good governance structure one must analyze the decision-making process. At what levels are decisions made, and who has the ultimate decision-making authority in the organization? Figure 4.5 illustrates how certain decisions were escalated in a hierarchical structure and how direction was deescalated within the same structure at the Big Dig. Deciding which decisions will be escalated is a major part of developing the project governance framework.

Governance Issues for Decision

The decision-making authority between owner's boards and project boards must be clearly allocated based on a strategic analysis of the purpose of each governing structure. The types of decisions that will be made by these two types of governing bodies vary based on the need to delegate some decisions to the project level, where expertise on technical matters is more readily available, while retaining key decisions that have an impact on the project funding or budget with the owner's board. For example, the project board, or steering committee as it is called in some organizations, is responsible for milestone changes, program evaluations, and shareholder requests, while the owner's board is responsible for high-level policy and strategy, the hiring and firing of senior managers, the finance agreement, and major scope changes. Figure 4.6 shows a typical decision made by owner's boards versus project boards in megaprojects generally and specifically at the Big Dig. Though the owner's board at the Big Dig made decisions similar to those shown in Figure 4.6, at the project level major decisions such as milestone changes,

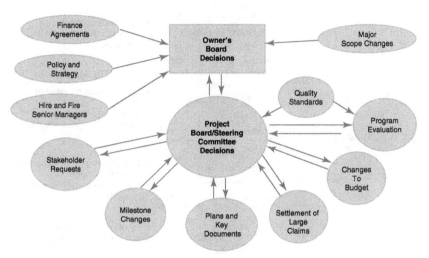

Figure 4.6   Governance Issues for Decision: Comparison of Owner's Board
and Project Board

settlement of large claims, and changes to the budget were recommended by the director in consultation with the management consultant, but in the absence of a project level board, they required approval from the Federal Highway Administration and the owner's CEO.

Step 3: Implementing the Governance Architecture

Architecture governance consists of the practices and procedures by which the governance framework is implemented at the enterprise level, as shown in Figure 4.2. Architecture governance typically does not operate in isolation but within a hierarchy of governance structures, which include boards of directors, project directors, and program managers. Architecture governance has been widely used in the information technology (IT) industry to enable businesses to achieve their goals and objectives. Conceptually, it is an approach, a set of principles, standards, and a regulatory framework within which goals are met at an enterprise-wide level. Weill and Ross (2004) researched more than 116 enterprises in 20 countries and concluded that firms with above-average IT governance effectiveness had 20 percent higher profits as measured by three-year industry-adjusted returns on assets.

Governance structures are implemented by project participants through the governance architecture. The architecture varies from project to project and may include models, standards, strategies, regulations, processes, procedures, guidelines, principles, and policies. As an example, the Big Dig was managed through several thousand project and program management processes and procedures and through the interfaces between the numerous contracts. Developing and implementing standardized procedures for its designers and contractors was critical to the delivery process. The goal of these tools and techniques was to keep the project on budget and schedule, reduce risks, control waste, improve safety, and provide quality assurance.

The primary governing documents for projects are the contracts entered into between the owner and the project management consultant, designers, and contractors. These documents are the primary tool for enforcing scope, schedule, cost, budget, quality, and risk. As previously described, the Big Dig's management consultant entered into 15 work programs or agreements with the Big Dig regarding the responsibilities for oversight of the design and construction process, including procurement, development of specifications, training, compliance monitoring, and general oversight and enforcement of all design and construction contracts.

An important aspect of architecture governance in projects is the use of standards. Among several project management standards that are applied internationally are those developed by the world's leading project management professional organizations. These organizations include the Project Management Institute (PMI), the International Project Management Association (IPMA), the Australian Institute of Project Management, and the UK Association for Project Management (APM).

As an example of a governance standard, the APM Specific Interest Group (SIG) has published a standard on project governance titled *Directing Change: A Guide to Governance of Project Management* (APM 2011). This standard specifically addresses the bridge between corporate governance and corporate strategy on the one hand and project management on the other. The standard does not provide the specific structures and processes that should be put in place but outlines guidelines largely in the form of key questions to be addressed. The standard is not directly applicable to megaprojects; however, both the general approach of specifying design criteria and issues that must be resolved and some of the specific key questions can be drawn upon in the design or analysis of governance regimes for megaprojects. Moreover, it identifies lack of clear senior management ownership and leadership as one of seven common causes of program and project failure.

Step 4: Measuring Performance of the Governance Framework

Projects must establish clear and measurable performance goals and then monitor and enforce those goals to protect the public interest. When a project is over budget and behind schedule, we often look for reasons within the project organization but rarely point to project governance as the cause of the project's problems. Governance is often the root cause of all kinds of problems, including escalating budgets and failed baselines, as illustrated in the National Aeronautics and Space Administration's JWST Project, the subject of the following case study.

JAMES WEBB SPACE TELESCOPE (JWST) NASA CASE STUDY

An excellent example of governance gone wrong is an independent review team actually blaming the governance structure for a project failure at the National Aeronautics Space Administration (NASA) project James Webb Space Telescope (JWST). The JWST Project was widely recognized as the next great observatory to replace the Hubble Space Telescope (HST). In this project, the budget was flawed because of a failure to conduct a bottoms-up estimate and account for known threats. The review team asserted that leadership at Goddard Space Flight Center (GSFC) and NASA Headquarters failed to independently analyze the project's performance and recognize the flawed baseline; thus, as costs on the project increased, so did the funding.

The project was ultimately confirmed with the flawed budget, and the failure to meet the launch schedule was interpreted by NASA leadership as a cost-control issue on the part of the contractor rather than a fundamentally broken estimate. The lack of an operational and effective cost and programmatic analysis capability at HQ was a contributing factor. Such a capability is required as a forcing function to define for senior NASA leadership what the current project status is and what resources would be required to execute the project.

Among the findings of the Independent Review Panel in assessing the problem in this case were the following (JWST 2010): Lack of clear lines of authority and accountability contributed to a lack of executive leadership in resolving the broken JWST life cycle cost baseline. The flawed budget should have been discovered as part of the center's execution responsibility, but the interpretation of the agency governance policy on the center's role in this regard is ambiguous and not uniformly interpreted within the agency. Ongoing, regular independent assessment and oversight processes at the agency were missing.

To fix the problems in the JWST Project, NASA actually changed the governance structure by moving the JWST management and accountability from the Astrophysics Division to a new organizational entity at HQ that would have responsibility only for the management and execution of JWST. Various managers were reassigned to other jobs, and new managers took over the leadership roles.

Source: James Webb Space Telescope (JWST) Independent Comprehensive Review Panel (ICRP). October 9, 2010. The Aerospace Corporation.

Mechanisms for Measuring Governance Performance   Good governance is driven by benchmarks and processes that are measurable and can be evaluated. Three mechanisms for measuring governance performance are summarized here; however, in reality, projects generally measure performance on all aspects of the project on a daily basis through such tools as milestone management, root-cause analysis, and earned value. If projects are substantially behind schedule, or costs are escalating out of control, it is most likely the result of a weakness or failing in the governance framework that needs to be evaluated through the following analytical tools:

1. Auditing, as an analytical tool, is a good device for measuring governance performance and infrastructure quality. Governance on the Big Dig was measured through more than a dozen external government agencies that conducted regular audits, as well as independent auditors hired by the owner and the Commonwealth of Massachusetts. Changes were implemented based on these recommendations, including the restructuring of the project to better address governance and the dismissal of several Big Dig project managers.
2. External regulation is another tool that drives good governance. As an example, the Sarbanes-Oxley Act was implemented in 2002 to set new or enhanced standards for all U.S. public company boards, management, and public accounting firms (SOX 2002). The bill was enacted as a reaction to a number of major corporate and accounting scandals including those affecting Enron, Tyco Peregrine Systems, and WorldCom.
3. A third way to measure governance performance is through focused reviews at key decision points in the project life cycle known as staged development described in the next section (OGC 2009).

Staged Development as a Governance Measurement Tool   In 2001, the Office of Government Commerce (OGC) in the United Kingdom developed the Gateway Project Review Process and introduced it across Central Civil Government as part of the Modernization Agenda, to support the delivery of improved public services. The process as used in the United Kingdom consists of a series of short, focused, independent peer reviews at key stages of a project or program. The reviews highlight risks and issues, which, if not addressed, would threaten successful delivery.

The Gateway Process, sometimes called the Stage Gate Process, has been used on large projects in the United States. NASA practiced the concept of staged development in the 1960s with its phased project planning or what is often called *phased review process*. The phased review process was intended to break up the development of any project into a series of phases that could be individually reviewed in sequence. Review points at the end of each phase required that a number of criteria be met before the project could progress to the next phase. The phased review process consisted of five phases (Preliminary Analysis, Definition, Design, Development, Operations) with periodic development reviews between phases. NASA's phased review process is considered a first-generation process because it did not take into consideration the analysis of external markets in new product development.

Similarly, PMI's *PMBOK® Guide* and the project management literature describe how projects move through various phases described as the project life cycle. Complex projects are much more difficult to define in terms of the traditional project life cycle, as the processes are repetitive and recurring throughout the life cycle of the project and it is difficult to define where one phase ends and the next begins. Initiation on some parts of the project may be occurring very late in the life of the project, while closure has already been achieved on other parts of the project. The Big Dig had an extensive process of performance review at several levels prior to the acceptance and payment of any contract. This included overall technical compliance with scope and schedule specifications, start-up, testing, and test data approval activities. Failure to comply could result in withholding of payments, denial of incentive pay, or termination of the contract.

Step 5: Optimizing the Governance Structure

An important part of understanding governance is recognizing that projects must continually change to meet the demands of its stakeholders and the needs of its customers. To ensure that a governance framework is functioning at the highest level, constant evaluation is needed to make sure that safeguards are in place to prevent projects from spiraling out of control. As Miller and Hobbs (2005) have reflected in their extensive research on project governance, not only must projects be adaptable to change, but the governance frameworks in which they operate must be adaptable to the changing needs of the organization and the innovative projects that coexist within the organization, yet move the organization forward. The structure necessary at the planning stage of a project may look very different from the structure at the implementation stage. For example, at the beginning of the project it is critical to have expertise in strategy and infrastructure policy planning and financing, while at the implementation stage critical governance skills include technical expertise and extensive experience in how the plans and policy will be carried out. Some important questions that arise in assessing the need for governance optimization include the following:

1. Is the governance structure transparent, and does it instill an ethical culture?
2. Can performance be measured in a timely way, and is it effectively managed?
3. Is project oversight too narrowly focused?
4. Have expected project behaviors been effectively communicated?
5. Is the requisite expertise available through the project employees, or is additional independent oversight required?
6. Are inconsistent decisions emanating from the project's governance structures?
7. Are project incentives delivering the expected results?
8. Are responsible participants being held accountable?

THE CHALLENGES OF IMPLEMENTING PROJECT GOVERNANCE FRAMEWORKS

1. Reconciling Project Authority with Corporate Power

The comparison between the more specialized project governance structure and the hierarchical structure of the project's corporate parent means that project authority becomes based more on interdependence of the team members than on hierarchical status. Hierarchical power tends to depend on bureaucratic legitimacy embedded in policies and rules, while project authority typically requires creativity, teamwork, and innovation in the accomplishment of objectives, rather than adherence to strict rules. As experienced project managers know, such strict rules are merely resources for creativity and innovation in their interpretation and negotiation (Clegg 1975). Thus, project management governance can be considered a hybrid between the centralized enactment of rules and procedures and a capacity to create the future through problem solving.

Success can be measured in the ability to increase autonomy and efficiency. Many of the problems facing major public investment projects can be interpreted in terms of deficiencies in the analytic or the political processes preceding the final decision to go ahead and the interaction between technicians and decision makers in this process.

The more fundamental differences between concept and the final outcome can typically be traced back to the earliest conceptual phases of the project, while the more day-to-day problems of cost efficiency, delays, and cost overrun are management issues that arise during the project's implementation and are solved through creative and sound decision making.

2. Problems of Multiple Governance Regimes

One of the more difficult problems facing projects is the aspect of multiple governance systems that need to coexist within the same framework—essentially, the conflict between centralization and decentralization. Centralized authority gives greater control over standards and realizes economy of scale, while decentralized authority can result in more customized, innovative solutions to problems for the project owner. These issues have been involved in many decisions during the last decade, from politics to corporate organizations, to the way in which projects are controlled within the larger organization. The IT industry has been dealing with the problems of multiple governance systems—or, as they are commonly referred to, bipolar systems—for decades (Golub 1975).

3. Symptoms of Ineffective Project Governance: Root-Cause Analysis

There are many symptoms of ineffective project governance including (1) owner and sponsor conflicts, (2) cost overruns and schedule delays, (3) quality control and assurance issues, (4) increased project incidents, and (4) escalating claims and risk problems. Often, these symptoms are accepted as the problem rather than investigating the underlying root causes of these symptoms. Root-cause analysis is critical at the project level, and if properly implemented through accountable and transparent governance systems, it could eliminate a significant number of project failures. For example, if costs continue to rise on a megaproject across contracts, this is a signal that either the scope is too vague or the project owner or manager is not enforcing the agreed terms of the contract. Either way, this is a governance problem that calls for strong leadership to prevent costs from escalating out of control.

4. Trust and Governance

Projects are increasingly the means by which business value is delivered. Understanding the mechanics of trust behavior enhances the delivery of projects and helps project managers to be more effective in balancing the conflicting issues that normally arise on projects. Despite a clear awareness of the importance of interpersonal or interorganizational trust and a growing body of evidence that trust alters transactional governance and performance (Puranam and Vanneste 2009), the field of project management still lacks a clear understanding of the mechanisms by which trust is developed and sustained in project networks (Levitt et al. 2009).

As Frankel powerfully concludes in her scholarly book, *Trust and Honesty: America's Business Culture at a Crossroad*, "too many people and too many leaders have abandoned trust and honesty as a goal," creating a disarming trend. To inspire trust and honesty, Frankel contends that "changing particular rules and actions may not make much difference unless there is an attempt to change the culture" (Frankel 2006).

Questions of trust often arise in relationships between and among the project owner and project sponsors, consultants, and project team. Steven Covey, author of *The Seven Habits of Highly Effective People*, has written that trust is built on three behaviors:

1. Transparency: Tell the truth in ways people can verify and validate for themselves.
2. Keeping commitments: Do what you say you will do.
3. Trusting others: Extend trust to your team, and they will trust you in return.

Determining how trust is developed and maintained is well beyond the scope of this book; however, recognizing when a problem of trust exists and being willing to acknowledge the problem and attempt to resolve trust issues will go a long way toward enhancing project performance and improving project governance.

The former managing director of Eurotunnel (the Channel Tunnel) highlights the importance of trust in the negotiation of the construction contract for the largest private-sector project of the twentieth century:

> ... the circumstances within which the construction contract was negotiated resulted in a complete breakdown in trust between the contractors and the owner. This lack of trust perpetuated even when the owner became fully independent, resulting in near disaster. Under pressure from the lending banks a joint accord between the owner (Eurotunnel) and the contractors (TML) was reached ...
>
> **(Stannard 1990)**

5. Ethics and Governance

Megaprojects face enormous ethical challenges today dealing with globalization, greater complexity, and cross-cultural relations. Often, managers of projects, programs, and portfolios face the same crucial questions (IPMA 2008):

Is the project based on an ethical foundation?
Will initial position, objectives, and constraints of the project be accepted within and outside the project team?
Can I myself fully align with the project goals?
What are the long-term effects of the project?

From a project management perspective, ethical considerations impact every aspect of a project's operations and are a critical component of the successful completion of most projects. Ethics is also important to the well-being of the many stakeholders in the project, including the performing organization, project managers and employees, customers, suppliers, sponsors, and members of society impacted by the project's operations.

Project ethics won't ensure you are a successful project manager; however, not acting ethically will almost always ensure your project will fail. As stated in the PMI Code of Ethics and Professional Conduct, "a project manager must accept responsibility for his or her actions." This means acknowledging when you are wrong, learning from your mistakes, and putting actions into place that will help you to prevent or mitigate problems in the future. Project managers are responsible for all activities that occur or fail to occur on their projects. Is the project and its consequences economically, ecologically, legally, and socially sustainable and in line with the expectations of the stakeholder?

Not unlike other large-scale projects, the Big Dig had to constantly assess its ethical standards and code of conduct to make sure all practices and procedures were in compliance with project management professional standards, as well as meeting the high standards expected of a public project. Ethics research consistently shows that a strong ethical tone at the top of the organization is a key to ethical performance (ERC 2011). This requires a constant assessment of stakeholder perceptions, communications, and training, and leaders that are effective and aggressive advocates for a strong ethical environment. Chapter 12 explores the essential characteristic of leaders who set the high ethical tone and instill a culture of transparency that permeates the entire organization.

6. Whistle-blowers

Though subject to much controversy, whistle-blower laws play an important role in ensuring the utmost integrity and transparency on a megaproject, particularly where managing a massive number of contracts, contractors, subcontractors, and workers becomes a challenge to any governance system. Essentially, these laws contribute to maintaining good governance. *Whistle-blowing* is generally defined as the disclosure by a person, usually an employee in a government agency or private enterprise, to the public or to those in authority, of mismanagement, corruption, illegality, or some other wrongdoing. Since the 1960s, the public value of whistle-blowing has been increasingly recognized. For example, federal and state statutes and regulations have been enacted to protect whistle-blowers from various forms of retaliation. Even without a statute, numerous decisions encourage and protect whistle-blowing on grounds of public policy.

In addition, the federal False Claims Act (31 U.S.C.A. § 3729) will reward a whistle-blower who brings a lawsuit against a company that makes a false claim or commits fraud against the government. Important to construction projects, the Occupational Safety and Health Administration's (OSHA) Whistleblower Protection Program enforces the whistle-blower provisions of 21 whistleblower statutes, including protecting employees who report violations of various workplace safety, airline, environmental, nuclear, pipeline, public transportation agency, railroad, maritime, and securities laws.

In 2011, in accordance with a survey by the Ethics Resource Center (ERC), an alarming 45 percent of U.S. employees said they had observed misconduct in the previous 12 months, and roughly two-thirds of those who observed wrongdoing reported it. The findings also confirmed that employees are more likely to report when they feel confident in their job security and are not worried about retaliation (ERC 2011). It is essential that projects provide an environment where wrongdoing can be reported to an anonymous source without fear of reprisal or lack of acceptance.

The Big Dig provided several channels for those concerned about possible ethical or legal violations to report those concerns free of fear of retaliation through the use of an anonymous reporting channel and an ombudsman. Though, generally, statistics are not available on the number of cases reported, it is important to make all stakeholders and employees aware that whistle-blowers will be treated fairly and that concerns will be handled confidentially and expediently without fear of retaliation.

One whistle-blower suit at the Big Dig alleged, among other things, that the defendant supplied out-of-specification or nonconforming concrete to the Big Dig. In 2007 and 2008, his claims (and those of other whistle-blowers) were settled with the federal and state government for more than $42 million. The defendant also pled guilty to false or fraudulent claims to the government and paid a criminal fine (US 2007).

7. Corporate Social Responsibility

Social responsibility is critical to the governance of major projects and requires that the owner and sponsors be engaged in local community outreach and that they work closely with local citizens and other stakeholders. *Corporate social responsibility* (CSR) is defined by the World Bank as the commitment of business to contribute to sustainable economic development, working with employees, their families, the local community, and society at large to improve quality of life, in ways that are both good for business and good for development.

In July 2011, the United Nations Human Rights Council endorsed a set of principles designed "to ensure that companies do not violate human rights in the course of their transactions and that they provide redress when infringements occur." The groundbreaking Guiding Principles on Business and Human Rights outline how nation-states and businesses should implement the UN's "Protect, Respect and Remedy" framework in order to better manage business and human rights challenges (UN 2011).

The National Institute of Standards and Technology (NIST) under the U.S. Department of Commerce has established governance and social responsibility standards known as the Baldrige Performance Excellence Program, which provides exceptional guidance to projects in analyzing the project's governance system. As described in Table 4.5, the program includes guidance on accountability, legal and ethical behavior, and social responsibility and community support.

The Baldrige Performance Excellence Program (NIST) provides some key elements in analyzing an organization's governance system, as listed in Table 4.5.

Table 4.5   The Baldridge Performance Excellence Program

A. Organizational Governance
   1. How does your organization review and achieve the following key aspects of your system:
      • Accountability for the management's actions?
      • Fiscal accountability?
      • Transparency in operations and selection and disclosure policies for governance board members?
      • Independence in internal and external audits?
      • Protection of stakeholders' interests as appropriate?
B. Legal and Ethical Behavior
   1. How do you address any adverse impacts on society of your products and operations, and how do you anticipate public concerns and prepare for these concerns?
   2. What are your key compliance processes, measures, and goals for addressing risks and achieving compliance?
   3. How does your organization promote and ensure ethical behavior? What are your key processes and measures or indicators of ethical behavior? How do you respond to breaches of ethical behavior?
C. Societal Responsibilities and Community Support
   1. How does your organization actively support and strengthen your key communities? How do your senior leaders, in concert with your workforce, contribute to improving these communities?

Source: National Institute of Standards and Technology, U.S. Department of Commerce.

LESSONS FROM PRACTICE: THE UNITED KINGDOM'S T5 NEW PRODUCT DELIVERY PROJECT

Though there are many examples of failed projects due to weak governance structures, it is important to look to projects that have achieved success by recognizing that good governance matters. The BAA, formerly the British Airports Authority, is a highly regulated independent airport operator that owns and operates London's Heathrow Airport. The BAA also managed the Terminal 5 (T5) Project to design and build a new terminal that increased Heathrow's annual capacity from 67 million to 95 million passengers. The project was unusual in that it achieved its goals of delivering a high-quality project within schedule and a budget of $8.5 billion, and the project maintained an exemplary safety record.

David Hancock, the former head of risk for the T5 Project, attributes this success in large part to "the collaborative efforts of the managing director, the experience, pragmatism and delivery focus of the construction director, and BAA's ultimate acceptance that they held 'all of the risk' all of the time" (Hancock 2012).

The research summarized here, sponsored by the United Kingdom's Engineering and Physical Sciences Research Council, highlights the significance of the focus on delivery strategy and the benefits of a systematic benchmark study in developing an effective, collaborative governance structure.

LESSONS LEARNED

1. Strategically Plan Governance

Governance requires strategic planning from the inception of the project. The five-step process described in this chapter provides a framework for determining the structures, the roles of the participants, the architecture, the monitoring and control processes, and the optimization of the governance structure on a continual basis. Strategic planning requires a determination as to the responsible parties for decision making and oversight. The accountability of each of the major actors in the megaproject must be defined, including the owner, sponsors, the management consultant, program manager, project managers, and project teams. The governance structure must be continually monitored, since a defective governance structure will surely doom the project, as evidenced by the large number of projects that fail due to huge cost overruns and failure of quality assurance.

2. Appoint an Independent Advisory Board

An essential consideration in technically complex and large-scale projects is the need for an independent advisory board of technical experts. To the extent a government-appointed board does not have the expertise to manage a one-off megaproject, an advisory board made up of experts from various disciplines including design, construction, quality control, and risk management is critical to advise the owner's or sponsor's board of directors on various decisions that come before them. To expect all board members to be competent in the complex technology and processes and procedures of a one-of-a-kind project is unrealistic. Thus, advisory boards can fill the gap between the expertise of the project company and the lack of knowledge about project management at the board level. The role of the advisory board can vary from an audit function to performance measurement, to direct oversight of projects. The independent board also addresses the problem of close owner and consultant relationships and conflicts that inhibit the ability to serve as an independent voice for the people, particularly on a public project.

3. Manage the Interfaces between Governance Structures

Complex large-scale projects have multiple interfaces between internal and external project stakeholders. These interfaces exist between government agencies and project owners and sponsors, and among project designers and contractors, and community organizations and local businesses. The assignment of responsibility for interface management must occur at the inception of the project so there is a clear demarcation for accountability and decision making. On the Big Dig, the numerous interfaces involving scope, cost, schedule, quality, and risk decisions required additional resources during all phases of the project, but particularly during the peak years of construction. Numerous interfaces increase the likelihood that the project will be over budget and behind schedule, particularly if the contingency budget is insufficient to cover these unexpected events.

4. Measure Performance of the Governance Framework

The performance criteria in a long-term project will only have meaning if they are clear and measurable and reflect the project's goals, mission and the key performance requirements of the contract. To ensure the public interest is protected the performance of all project participants must be monitored and controlled and all contract requirements must be enforced. Contract provisions must provide for incentives and disincentives and they must be applied in accordance with the contract. When schedules slip and costs rise, these are indications that the governance is weak, nonexistent or has impaired accountability. To ensure that a governance framework is functioning at the highest level, constant evaluation is needed to make sure that safeguards are in place to prevent projects from spiraling out of control. For projects to succeed, they must be adaptable to change, and the governance frameworks in which they operate must be adaptable to the changing needs of the organization

5. Ensure a Mechanism to Maintain Institutional Memory

On large-scale projects, it is important to retain institutional memory about the project during transitions from one phase to the next. It is important, however, to distinguish between institutional memory at the project level and institutional memory at the corporate level. It is generally less important at the corporate level, as new leadership at the top level can also mean a new vision and an opportunity to reassess both corporate and project needs. Continuity, as described in this chapter, is much more important at the project level, where institutional knowledge can be used to solve problems, correct deficiencies, and identify responsible parties. As an example, those involved in the environmental feasibility studies of the project should remain involved through basic design. Those involved in the preliminary design must remain involved through construction. Finally, and most important, those key players involved in project construction should continue on until the project is safely transitioned to the new owner or operator, which sometimes can take years. Institutional memory is a key aspect of project governance that should always be planned for from the earliest phases of the project.

BEST PRACTICES

1. A megaproject must maintain a clear statement of strategy and vision of governance that is planned during the conception stage.
2. Comprehensive information on the project's corporate responsibility policies, including the policy objectives for each CSR area with quantified progress toward their achievement, is critical for effective program management.
3. Scrutinize the performance of management in meeting agreed goals and objectives.
4. Ensure the integrity of the financial information and that financial controls and risk management systems are robust and defensible.
5. Governance and strategy should be discussed with key stakeholders to determine the appropriate roles and responsibilities and decision-making authority of all project participants.
6. Structure accountability on an organizational level with a single point of contact to provide leadership and drive the project forward.
7. Ensure that the owner or project sponsor retains decision-making responsibility throughout the life of the project, since the sponsor owns both the project budget and the business case for the project. This is particularly important where projects are funded entirely by the government owner.
8. Understand the important distinction between project governance and organizational governance, and clearly separate the decision making of each structure. If the project governance structure is not given clear direction, the authority of both the project and the organizational governance structure is compromised, resulting in decisions that may not be enforceable.
9. Engage project stakeholders at a level that is commensurate with their importance to the organization and in a manner that fosters trust. Provide organization structure to manage project stakeholders in a consistent forum.
10. Establish an independent board of directors consisting of sponsor representatives and outside experts to oversee the project that is not compromised by other goals of the larger organization and has sufficient time to devote to the multiple and complex issues faced by the project.

SUMMARY

As evidenced in this chapter, technologically complex projects require multiple governance structures that are brought together through a centralized governing board of directors responsible for the overall budget and financing of the project. The important first step is the identification of benchmarks that must be brought to bear when developing a governance framework. Traditional hierarchical structures will fail in projects that require innovative solutions with multiple stakeholder interests, as risk must be balanced with the need for technological advancement. This is a balance that few projects have ever achieved. The Big Dig has led to the momentous question of multiple governances and the alignment of corporate, project, and political structures to achieve success. Alignment becomes all the more important on megaprojects where there may be an absence of tools or structures that fit within every scenario, thus requiring the need to look to higher authorities for strategic guidance.

Given the increasing internal pressures of project alignment and return on investment, as well as the external pressures of government compliance, stakeholder demands, and the continued pursuit of enhanced shareholder value, corporate entities are increasingly searching for the ideal project governance framework for their organizations. The importance of good governance is increasingly recognized, but CEOs are less sure of what form to employ. In an effort to improve upon traditional approaches to organizational governance, we need to explore the various options for project governance and build upon hybrid, multiple governance structures and the alignment of these various models.

ETHICAL CONSIDERATIONS

Henry was manager of construction on the new Super Star Energy Project in Colorado and reported up to the director of project management. He was assigned to this project through the Big Moon Company, the corporation he worked for. One of his responsibilities at the Super Star Energy Project was to work with all internal and external auditors who were reviewing the project. In accordance with this responsibility, he was asked by his boss, the project director, to prepare the project core management team for a meeting with the government auditors, which the team was having the next morning. He was not sure what the auditors might be looking for, so he advised his project team not to raise any controversial issues with the auditors and to only answer the questions asked. His quality assurance manager asked Henry if he should mention to the auditors that one of the buildings they constructed would not pass inspection because it did not meet environmental standards and the building as constructed raised both safety and health threats to the general public. Henry responded that it was his understanding that you should only respond to questions asked by auditors and never raise new matters, especially since the building met the project's contract specifications that had been approved by the government. The quality assurance manager was not happy with Henry's answer but understood the importance of loyalty to the project. Henry adjourned the meeting with his team so he could get some rest. He knew that tomorrow would bring new challenges, as that is what projects are all about.

Based on these facts, respond to the following questions::

1. Based on the problem described here, what are Henry's ethical responsibilities as the project manager:
   To the auditors?
   To the project?
   To the government agency that is funding the project?
   To the citizens who will use the infrastructure?
   To his boss, the project director?
   To the Big Moon Company?
   To the CEO at the Big Moon Company?
   To himself?
2. What are the governance problems raised by Henry's conduct? If you were the director of project management, what changes in governance would you recommend for the Super Star Energy Project, keeping in mind that governance is a dynamic regime in megaprojects?

DISCUSSION QUESTIONS

1. What does governance structure mean on a public project? Why is it important?
2. How can you measure performance of a governance framework?
3. What should be the role of a governance board?
4. What is the critical role of the project sponsor/owner (and the relative roles of sponsor, portfolio manager, and program manager in governing and managing projects)?
5. What are the critical success factors that should be measured by a project board?
6. Who owns the benefits on a project, and who has strategic responsibility for realizing these benefits?
7. What is the role of the strategic plan on a project, and who should have responsibility for the strategic plan?
8. Define the effective role of a governance structure, including systems and tools.
9. Who are the providers of funding for the Big Dig and what was there role in the project?
10. How is return on investment measured in a public versus a private project?

11. What potential problems can arise on public projects to prevent them from earning a return on the investment?

12. In the JWST NASA case study described in this chapter, the Independent Review Panel issued several findings concerning the failure of governance in the NASA organization and in the JWST program specifically. What are the lessons learned from this case study for future projects? If you were senior manager at this organization, what controls and structures would you put in place to make sure these problems did not occur again?

13. In the book *Megaprojects and Risk: An Anatomy of Ambition*, the authors suggest a cure for what is termed the "megaproject paradox." Two important recommendations they have are (1) that the role of government should be shifted from involvement in project promotion to keeping an arm's-length distance and restricting its involvement to the formulation and auditing of public interest objectives to be met by the megaproject and (2) involving risk capital from the private investor as a sound test on the viability of the project up front. Do you agree with these suggestions? Why or why not? If these suggestions had been implemented on the Big Dig, might the outcome have been different? Do you agree that the public owner should maintain an arm's-length distance?

14. How would you have structured the owner's board of directors on the Big Dig to ensure the best possible expertise? As noted by a former Big Dig Board Member: "perhaps an owner's board should have been established with professionals in the field of engineering, finance, construction and transportation with the sole purpose of providing checks and balances and reporting to the public. The board would challenge engineering decisions in the very early and most critical stages of the project. It would certainly be expensive to compensate this board, but, no doubt, well worth it." How would you assess the value of such a board?

15. a. What should be the composition of the board? Who should serve on a public board? Insiders? Outsiders? Contractors? Sponsors?
    b. What are the types of decisions a board should make?
    c. How should they be compensated?

16. What are the three most important lessons you learned in this chapter about the governance of megaprojects generally, and the Big Dig specifically, for future projects?

REFERENCES

APM (Association for Project Management). 2011. *Directing Change: A Guide to Governance of Project Management*.2nd ed. Buckinghamshire, England: Association for Project Management.

Board on Infrastructure and the Constructed Environment (BICE). 2003. *Completing the Big Dig: Managing the Final Stages of Boston's Central Artery/Tunnel Project*. National Academy of Engineering, National Research Council, Transportation Research Board of the National

Academies, Committee for Review of the Project Management Practices Employed on the Boston Central Artery/Tunnel ("Big Dig"). Washington, DC: National Academies Press.

Clegg, S.R. 1975. *Power, Rule and Domination*. London: Routledge and Degan Paul.

Connaughton, M. 2007. The Big Dig Uncovered—Lessons Learned. Comments by Mary Connaughton, Member, Massachusetts Turnpike Authority Board of Directors, Audit Committee Chairperson, National Conference of State Legislatures, Annual Conference, Boston, MA. August 8.

Connaughton, M. 2011. Author's interview with Mary Connaughton, former member of the Massachusetts Turnpike Authority Board of Directors overseeing the Central Artery/Tunnel Project. *October* 13, 2011.

Crawford, L., T. Cooke-Davies, B. Hobbs, L. Labuschagne, K. Remington, and P. Cen. 2008. "Governance and Support in the Sponsoring of Projects and Programs." *Project Management Journal* 39(Supplement):S43–S55.

Davies, A., D. Gann, and T. Douglas. 2009. "Innovation in Megaprojects: Systems Integration at London Heathrow Terminal 5." *California Management Review* 51(2):111.

ERC (Ethics Resource Center). 2011. *Inside the Mind of a Whistleblower: A Supplemental Report from the 2011 National Business Ethics Survey*. Arlington, VA: Ethics Resource Center.

FHA (Federal Highway Administration). 2000. *Federal Task Force on the Boston Central Artery/Tunnel Project Review of Project Oversight and Costs*. Washington, DC: Federal Highway Administration.

Flyvbjerg, B., N. Bruzelius, and W. Rothengatter. 2003. *Megaprojects and Risk: An Anatomy of Ambition*. Cambridge, UK: Cambridge University Press.

Frankel, T. 2006. *Trust and Honesty: America's Business Culture at a Crossroad*. New York: Oxford University Press, 197, 205.

Garland, R. 2009. *Project Governance: A Practical Guide to Effective Project Decision Making*. London: Kogan Page Lmtd.

GET SA (Groupe Eurotunnel). Registration Document 2011. Filed 1 March, 2012 with the French Market Authority (AMF).

Golub, H. 1975. *Organizing information system resources: Centralization vs. Decentralization*. The Information Systems Handbook, F. Warren McFarlan, and Richard L. Nolan,, Eds., Homewood, IL: Dow-Jones Irwin, 65–91.

Grant, M. 1997. "Financing Eurotunnel." *Japan Railway & Transport Review (JRTR)*. Tokyo: East Japan Railway Culture Foundation, 46–52.

Hancock, David (former head of risk for Heathrow's Terminal 5 Project). 2012. Communications. August 14–15.

International Institute for Sustainable Development (IISD). 2012. *Developing Social Capital in Networked Governance Initiatives: A lock-step approach, Paper: Gabriel A.* Huppé, Heather Creech, Manitoba, Canada: International Institute for Sustainable Development.

IPMA International Project Management Association. 2008. *Values and Ethics in Project Management*, Proceedings International Expert Seminar. Zurich: International Project Management Association.

JWST (James Webb Space Telescope Independent Comprehensive Review Panel [IRP]). Final Report. October 29, 2010. Aerospace Corporation.

Kendall, G. I., and S. C. Rollins. 2003. *Advanced Project Portfolio Management and the PMO: Multiplying ROI at Warp Speed*. Boca Raton, FL: J. Ross Publishing, Inc.

Klakegg, O. J. 2008. "Governance Frameworks for Public Project Development and Estimation," *Project Management Journal* 39:S27–S24.

Levitt, R.E., W. J. Henisz, and D. Settel. 2009. "Defining and Mitigating the Governance Challenges of Infrastructure Project Development and Delivery." Conference on Leadership and Management of Construction, Lake Tahoe, California, November 5–8.

Miller, R., and B. Hobbs. 2005. "Governance Regimes for Large Complex Projects." *Project Management Journal* 36(3):42–50 (Summer).

Miller, R., and D. R. Lessard. 2000. *The Strategic Management of Large Engineering Projects: Shaping Institutions, Risk and Governance*. Cambridge, MA: MIT Press, 25–26.

Monks, R., and N. Minow. 1995. *Corporate Governance*. Oxford, UK: Blackwell Business, 178.

Morris, P. W. G., and G. H. Hough. 1987. *The Anatomy of Major Projects: A Study of the Reality of Project Management*. Chichester, UK: John Wiley & Sons.

MTA (Massachusetts Turnpike Authority). By-Laws (Revised to October 20, 1997). Boston: Massachusetts Turnpike Authority.

Müller, R. 2009. *Project Governance*. Aldershot, UK: Gower Publishing.

Nolan, R., and W. F. McFarlan. 2005. "Information Technology and the Board of Directors." *Harvard Business Review*. Boston: Harvard Business School Publishing.

OECD. 2004. Office of Economic Cooperation and Development, OECD Principles of Corporate Governance, Paris: Office of Economic Cooperation and Development.

OGC (Office of Government Commerce). 2009. Prince 2. Accessed at www.ogc.gov.uk/methods_prince_2.asp, March 21.

Pellegrinelli, S., and L. Garagna. 2009. "Towards a Conceptualisation of PMOs as Agents and Subjects of Change and Renewal." *International Journal of Project Management* 27(7):649–656.

PMI (Project Management Institute). 2013. *The Standard for Portfolio Management*. 3rd ed. Newtown Square, PA: Project Management Institute.

PMI (Project Management Institute). 2013. *The Standard for Program Management*. 3rd ed. Newtown Square, PA: Project Management Institute.

PMI (Project Management Institute). 2007. *PMI Code of Ethics and Professional Conduct*. Appendix B 2. Newtown Square, PA: Project Management Institute.

PMI (Project Management Institute). 2013. *A Guide to the Project Management Body of Knowledge (PMBOK® Guide)*—Fifth Edition. Newtown Square, PA: Project Management Institute.

Primack, P. 2006. "Learning from the Big Dig." *Commonwealth Magazine*. Boston: Massachusetts Institute for a New Commonwealth (MassINC).

Puranam, P., and B. S. Vanneste. 2009. "Trust and Governance: Untangling a Tangled Web." *The Academy of Management Review* 34(1):11–31.

Salvucci, F. 2012. Author's interview with Frederick P. Salvucci, former Massachusetts secretary of transportation. June 22. Salvucci served from 1970 to 1974 as transportation advisor to Boston mayor Kevin White and then from 1975 to 1978 and 1983 to 1990 as secretary of transportation for the Commonwealth of Massachusetts under Governor Michael Dukakis. In those roles, he participated in much of the transportation planning and policy formulation in the Boston urban area and the Commonwealth of Massachusetts over the past 20 years. Commonly known as the mastermind of the Big Dig, Salvucci is credited with expansion of the transit system and for the development of the financial and political support for the Central Artery/Tunnel Project, and the design of implementation strategies consistent with economic growth in compliance with the Clean Air Act.

Samset, K., P. Berg, O. J. Klakegg,. 2006. "Front End Governance of Major Public Projects". Paper presented at the EURAM Conference, Oslo, Norway. May 18.

SOX (Sarbanes-Oxley Act). 2002. Pub. L. 107–204, 116 Stat. 745. (This law is also known as the Public Company Accounting Reform and Investor Protection Act of 2002.)

Stannard, C. 1990. "Managing a Mega-project—The Channel Tunnel." *Long Range Planning* 23(5):49–62.

UN (United Nations General Assembly, Human Rights Council). 2011. *Report of the Special Representative of the Secretary-General on the Issue of Human Rights and Transnational Corporations and Other Business Enterprises, John Ruggie Guiding Principles on Business and Human Rights: Implementing theUnited Nations "Protect, Respect and Remedy" Framework.* Washington, DC: United Nations.

US (United States and Commonwealth of Massachusetts). 2007. Ex rel. *Johnston v. Aggregate Industries*. PLC, et al., Civil Action No. 06-11379-GAO (D. Mass.) (criminal and civil settlements 2007 and 2008; a/k/a the "Big Dig" settlements).

Weill, P., and J. W. Ross. 2004. *IT Governance: How Top Performers Manage IT Decision Rights for Superior Results*. Cambridge, MA: Harvard Business School Press, 14.

Williamson, O. E. 1996. *The Mechanisms of Governance*. Oxford, UK: Oxford University Press.

World Bank. 2000. *Reforming Public Institutions and Strengthening Governance Bank Strategy*. Washington, DC: World Bank.

World Bank. 2008. *Annual Report*. Washington, DC: World Bank.

Chapter 5

Megaproject Scope Management

> The single best payoff in terms of project success comes from having good project definition early.
>
> —*RAND Corporation*

INTRODUCTION

Though much has been written about what went wrong on the Big Dig, it is amazing how much went right, considering its massive and technically challenging requirements. During the 14 years of Big Dig construction, seven and a half miles of highway, more than half in tunnels, were built along the old Colonial shoreline, above and below Boston's subway system and within feet of the city's tallest buildings, rearranging centuries-old gas, water, and electric lines, all while more than 1.2 million workers, visitors, and residents went about their business each day (BRA 1996). In addition to the extensive tunneling through the City of Boston, the landmark Zakim Bunker Hill cable-stayed bridge was completed by Swiss designer Christian Menn, and the interstate highway that starts in Seattle and crosses the United States was connected with Boston's Logan Airport. Many innovations were used along the way, including the largest application of slurry wall construction and ground freezing and the first cable-stayed asymmetrical bridge design. All of this can be defined in one word: *scope*.

This chapter addresses the complex relationships among scope, quality, cost, and schedule and all the influences that impact these project knowledge areas. For public megaprojects, the scope is magnified by the project's long duration, multiple stakeholders with diverse interests, and technological complexity. To aid in understanding the challenges faced by megaprojects, this chapter examines the interconnected strategies, processes, and procedures, as well as the tools and techniques, that were critical to effective scope management on the Big Dig.

1. SCOPE AND THE "TRIPLE CONSTRAINT"

Every project operates under the triple constraint, but on megaprojects the problem is magnified by the reality of the massive scope, scale, and duration of the project. The concept of triple constraint is based on the premise that if any one of the project elements changes (cost, scope, time), this may have an impact on the other two. Careful analysis of these three factors must be done on every project and every contract within the project to identify the solution that has the least undesirable impact. Quality, which is defined in *A Guide to the Project Management Body of Knowledge (PMBOK® Guide)*—Fifth Edition as "conformance to requirements," is often impacted by the triple constraint (PMI 2013). So quality, which is placed in the center of the figure, is in reality a part of the scope—that is, it is included in the specification. Quality is sometimes referred to as the fourth constraint, since it is an important factor in project success and can be compromised with an increase in scope or a decrease in budget or time.

Figure 5.1 highlights the interrelationship between these three elements and the influences on these elements. The influences on scope were considerable on the Big Dig due to the impact of construction in an urban environment. Thus, traffic, abutters, archeological sites, environmental hazards, safety, and risk had a huge impact on the ultimate project scope. To realize the goals of the Big Dig, these elements had to be effectively managed.

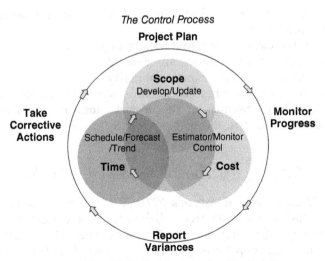

Figure 5.1   The Triple Constraint: The Control Process
Source: Central Artery/Tunnel Project, Project Controls Plan.

2. DEFINING THE SCOPE ON A MEGAPROJECT

Nothing is particularly hard if you divide it into small jobs.
—*Henry Ford*

The process of determining stakeholder expectations is a difficult mission on any project, but it was an especially long and tedious process on the Big Dig. As the project history reflects, scope definition was an iterative process and involved a multitude of stakeholders, including numerous federal and state agencies, transportation authorities, private industry, the local businesses, and residents and the citizens of the Commonwealth of Massachusetts. Adding to stakeholder demands was the technological complexity of designing a project that intersected with major rail systems, buildings, homes, and public streets.

Establishing the scope on the Big Dig involved the following steps:

1. Packaging the final design
2. Specifying the deliverables to be produced by each section design consultant (SDC)
3. Preparing the technical scope statements and the construction contracts
4. Defining in detail the special tasks or assignments that required unique expertise

On the Big Dig, scope was complicated by the following characteristics of large infrastructure projects:

- Involvement of multiple stakeholders with diverse needs and expectations
- Technological challenges that were not foreseen or understood when the project commenced
- Impact on the local citizens and society in general
- Complex networks, interfaces, and dependencies
- Colossal risks, uncertainty, and ambiguity
- Political realities that created demands, surprises, instability, and distress, specifically because of the project's long length, the change in political parties in power, and the evolving stakeholder needs

Scope in Relation to the *PMBOK® Guide*

The Project Management Institute's *PMBOK® Guide* defines *project scope* as "the work that needs to be accomplished to deliver a product, service or result with the specified features and functions" (PMI 2013). Simply stated, the scope is the road map for project management. It is the embodiment of the final deliverables that results in either the project's success or failure. If the scope is incomplete or inadequate or lacks clarity, then everything that follows will be impacted. Projects often seem to grow naturally as they progress from inception through development to construction. On highway projects, these changes can often be attributed to the changing needs of the stakeholders or environmental compliance in the area being served.

The elements of scope definition can vary from project to project, and in large-scale projects the scope evolves over a long period of time. The *PMBOK® Guide* focuses on the six processes described in the first two columns of Table 5.1 as essential to scope management. The Big Dig challenges listed in column three of the table reflect the difficulties of defining, verifying, and controlling scope where there were more than 9000 activities, thousands of policies and procedures, and numerous diverse stakeholder interests and requirements.

Table 5.1   Comparison of Scope Processes and Procedures

Process	The *PMBOK® Guide*	The Big Dig Unique Challenges
Plan scope management	Documenting how the scope will be defined, validated and controlled	Developing numerous processes and procedures to define how scope will be managed and how contractors will be held accountable.
Collect requirements	Defining and documenting stakeholders' needs to meet the project objectives	Multiple stakeholders needs with diverse expectations identified through open forums and governance structures
Define scope	The development of a detailed description of the process, project, and product	Complex process involving the coordination of hundreds of design and construction packages with numerous interfaces
Create WBS	Subdividing project deliverables and project work into smaller, more manageable components	Ten-level hierarchy with top management holding several levels
Validate scope	Formalizing acceptance of the completed project deliverables	Multifaceted process with multiple levels of input, inspection, and approval
Control scope	Monitoring the status of the project and managing changes to the scope baseline	Managed through project controls, the claims and changes process, and performance measurements

Sources: (1) The Project Management Institute (PMI) *A Guide to the Project Management Body of Knowledge (PMBOK® Guide)*—Fifth Edition. 2013. (2) The Central Artery/Tunnel Project Procedures and Division I Specifications of the Massachusetts Highway Department.

Scope Elements

An important determination that must be made at the inception of any project is the question of what to include in the project's scope. On the Big Dig, the scope for each of the 132 major contracts had to be developed and negotiated separately, and each contractor in turn had to develop the scope for numerous subcontractors and consultants in conformity with project standards and requirements. To simplify the concept of scope, we will look at the components of one of the project's engineering marvels, the Casting Basin. This mammoth dry dock, shown in Figure 5.2, was a huge hole in the ground used to build tunnel sections. At 1000 feet (305m) long, 300 feet (91m) wide, and 60 feet (18m) deep, it could accommodate three *Titanics* side by side. Once the tunnel boxes were built in this dry dock, it was flooded and the tunnel boxes were floated out and positioned to be lowered into a trench at the bottom of the channel with some extremely narrow tolerances, only a few feet above a subway tunnel. When looking at scope, it should be analyzed not only for the contract objectives it fulfilled but also for the larger project goals it fulfilled, as described here. The scope for the project's casting basin included the following elements.

- Project description: Construct casting basin in Fort Point Channel.
- Project goals and objectives: Connect the I-90 Interstate Highway with Boston Logan Airport.

Figure 5.2   Casting Basin
Source: Central Artery/Tunnel Project.

- Contract goals and objectives: Provide a dry work area in which the fabrication of tunnel tubes may take place.
- Cost-benefit analysis: The cost of building the basin with the benefits of the basin becoming part of the permanent cut and cover tunnel trajectory leading into the Ted Williams Tunnel.
- Technical Scope Statement: Comprises all the elements shown in Figure 5.2.
- Deliverables: Construct casting basin in an area 1000 feet long, 300 feet wide, and 60 feet deep, sealed off from the water by a series of steel cofferdams filled with crushed stone.
- Milestones: Complete casting basin by January 2003.
- Design package(s): DO1, DO2, DO3.
- Contract package(s): CO9A4, C11A1, C17A1, C17A2, C17A9.
- Interfaces with other contractors and stakeholders: South Boston residents and businesses, Gillette World Headquarters, Federal Reserve Building, Federal Postal Center.
- Force accounts: Third-party requirements include utility installation, Massachusetts Bay Transportation Authority additional security.
- Project boundaries, constraints, and assumptions: Additional project resources will be available to assist in the dewatering of the basin at the rate of approximately 180 gallons per minute.
- Risks and exposures: Increased risk of catastrophic potential due to dewatering and contract interfaces.
- Mitigation: (1) Purchase additional insurance; (2) construct dam to prevent water from flowing into land-based adjacent contract.

3. THE PROJECT ORGANIZATION: SCOPE CONTROLS PROGRAM

To better understand the various responsibilities of the participants in controlling scope, cost, and time, Figure 5.3 graphically displays the flow of obligations among the various participants as it was structured at project start-up. The project owner, the Commonwealth of Massachusetts, was represented during the early years by the Department of Public Works (DPW), followed by the Massachusetts Highway Department (MHD) and, ultimately, the Massachusetts Turnpike Authority (MTA). Within the management consultant structure pictured in the center of the chart in Figure 5.3, these four departments were involved with project scope: (1) the engineering department was responsible for preliminary design, reviewing the final designs from the section design consultants and providing technical support during construction; (2) the environmental department was responsible primarily for issues raised in the Environmental Impact Statement, including transportation planning, mitigation, and right-of-way; (3) the services department housed project controls, which also handled procurement, construction administration, human resources, and financial services; and (4), the construction

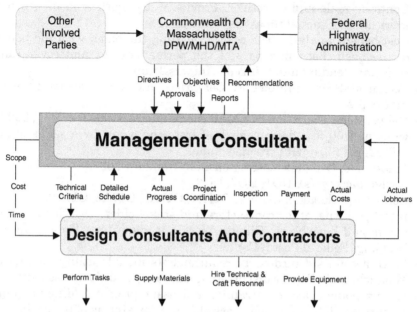

Figure 5.3   Flow of Responsibility among Project Participants
Source: Central Artery/Tunnel Project Control Plan.

department was divided into geographical areas, each managed by an area manager. Figure 5.3 shows the flow of obligations among the major project participants, with the owner providing the project direction and approvals and the management consultant responsible for design and construction management and oversight of the design consultants and contractors.

Contract Procurement and Administration

A major role of the Management Consultant was the development of a well-planned and transparent selection process for the section design contracts and the section construction contracts. The scope of services for all sections contracts was developed by the Management Consultant and approved by the owner and the project's major sponsor, the Federal Highway Administration (FHWA). Qualified design consultants were ranked according to qualification criteria and evaluations, and the highest ranked were invited to submit a fee proposal. The proposals were compared with estimates prepared by the management consultant to negotiate a contract value. Construction contract awards were based on prequalification criteria, certification under various regulations, completeness, and the low-bid process in accordance with Federal-Aid Requirements and the Massachusetts Highway Department, Standard Specifications for Highways and Bridges (CA/T Bid Documents).

The traditional means of procuring contractors on public projects in the United States has been the low-bid methodology, though this methodology has been widely criticized. On the Big Dig, due to the federal procurement requirements, alternatives to the low-bid methodology, such as best value, were not an option. Thus, the likelihood that contractors would apply for frequent claims and changes was a real concern, and, as reflected in the project's financial reports, claims and changes remained high throughout the life of the project.

As recognized by the Federal Highway Administration (FHWA), best-value procurement techniques have been successfully applied in recent years for highway and other public-sector construction to attain more qualified contractors, more innovative solutions, and shorter construction times (FHWA 2011). Best-value techniques may include:

1. The bidder's specific plan for how it will achieve or exceed the performance goals in the categories of safety, construction congestion, quality, time, cost effectiveness, customer satisfaction, environmental criteria, and innovation
2. The techniques and practices that will be used to conduct the work, including any innovative techniques and practices, that may be used over the life of the contract
3. Any assumptions, deviations, or exceptions to the bidding documents
4. Any technical uncertainties and specific proposals for resolving those uncertainties

Using the best-value approach can save time and reduce costs that may well exceed any initial benefits to be gained from the low-bid process. If this process had been allowed by the government agencies at the time of the Big Dig procurement, it might well have reduced the cost and scope of the project and returned additional benefits that were not possible under the low-bid methodology.

The Project Controls Programs

The heartbeat of the Big Dig was the project's Controls Center.

It was here that the Management Consultant team created a seamless working relation with the Project Owner, sub-consultants, and contractors and embraced the cohesiveness of the overall project objective.

(Nicole Hunter, former CA/T project cost engineer 2012)

In recognition of the project control objectives, the Central Artery/Tunnel Project implemented several control programs to monitor the critical control elements—scope, cost, and time. These programs were developed for the unique aspects of the Big Dig but retained the basic control concepts, which have proven effective on other major projects. A former Bechtel program manager described the process of managing the massive scope and coordinating 132 major prime construction contracts with numerous interfaces in the following way:

> The Central Artery Tunnel Project is really a series of self-contained projects. Each has a focus, a set of designers and contractors who were independent of the designers and contractors on other sections. The Management Consultant has to control the interface between these sections to ensure the completion of the project as a coherently functioning whole. Don Marshall, former Bechtel program manager
>
> **(Luberoff et al. 1993)**

The project plan served as the cornerstone to the successful execution of design and construction. Scope control was achieved through adherence to the project plan, which limited unnecessary overlapping of work scope between participants. The project's scope control program had seven key procedures for scope management as highlighted in Table 5.2. Each of these procedures was necessary to provide comprehensive contract packaging, to plan and manage interfaces, and to avoid scope redundancy for all design and construction packages.

Project Scope Controls Plan

> Plans are of little importance, but planning is essential
> —*Sir Winston Churchill*

There were four primary functions of the Big dig project scope controls plan:

1. Construct a means by which the Project scope can be organized, monitored and reported in relation to cost and time;
2. Provide a dynamic and flexible environment to meet the changing requirements of a complex engineering/construction project;
3. Ensure an effective, efficient coordination of the Project Owner, the federal government, consultants and contractors; and
4. Design so that critical areas are highlighted and potential problem areas are identified early in order to initiate proactive solutions.

The traditional control process is structured to enable the primary control elements—scope, cost, and time—to be effectively monitored and evaluated throughout the life cycle of the project. The project plan establishes overall criteria for each element, from which actual and forecast performance is evaluated. All variances from the plan are identified and corrective actions implemented. Subsequently, the project plan is either reconciled accordingly or updated to reflect current conditions.

Table 5.2   The Big Dig Scope Control Program

Scope Controls Program	What	Why	How	When	Who
1. Project controls plan	Definition of scope of services to be provided by the various project participants	Establish overall project responsibilities for the various project participants	Project guide	Continuous	Consultant
2. Technical scope statement	Definition of scope, limits, and interfaces of all project packages	Establishes bases of contract packaging and cost/time; ensures scope consistency	Itemized scope limits for each package	Continuous	Consultant
3. Work breakdown structure	Identifies and defines the project work	Basis of cost/time control	Project procedure defines the various levels of the WBS	Continuous	Consultant/ contractor
4. Contract services	Definition of required scope of deliverables and services	Establish commercial basis for performance	Negotiated contract	Per project schedule	Owner/consultant/ contractor
5. Change control program	Formal identification and approval of changes to contract scope	Identifies, authorizes, and tracks changes to each contract package	Form of processing amendments	As required	Owner/consultant/ contractor
6. Early identification and trend programs	Identify potential scope variances for management action	Provide client with early notice of potential scope variances and establish subsequent action	Continuous evaluation of scope/early warning and regular trend reports	Continuous	Owner and consultant
7. Quarterly assessment	Review of management consultant's work program deliverables	Provide project management with status of work program deliverables	Identify actions versus current planned deliverable scope	Each quarter	Owner and Consultant

Source: Central Artery/Tunnel Project, Project Scope Controls Program.

Levels of Scope Control   The five levels of scope control ranged from a general description of the project to specific work assignments, defined as follows:

- Level 1 defines the project in broad terms (7 miles of an interstate highway system serving Central Boston).
- Level 2 defines, in the general sense, the services to be provided in the preliminary design, final design, and construction phases of the project. The program management services are defined by the project owner in consultation with the project consultant.
- Level 3 provides more definitive scope for preliminary design, final design, and construction by individual work package or project segments.
- Level 4 elaborates on Level 3 information by specifying the deliverables and services that will be produced as a result of the various design and construction contracts.
- Level 5 identifies the tasks that need to be accomplished to produce the required deliverables or services.

4. THE TECHNICAL SCOPE STATEMENT (TSS)

According to the *PMBOK® Guide*, the *statement of work* (SOW), as it is commonly known, is a narrative description of products or services to be delivered by the project. On the Big Dig, the basis of scope control for the project was defined in the technical scope statement (TSS), as shown in Table 5.3. The TSS was much more comprehensive than a typical SOW and included a narrative description containing the official name of the scope of work, a brief description of the geographic location of the work, and an itemized listing of significant scope items, construction packages, design packages, and force accounts (third-party requirements). On the Big Dig, the TSS steered the project and provided the basis for the development of the project's contracts, work program, baseline, and budget.

5. PROJECT WORK BREAKDOWN STRUCTURE (WBS)

After defining the project scope, which includes all of the owner's requirements, the next step is to divide the scope into activities through a hierarchical process called the work breakdown structure (WBS). The WBS technique is the preferred management tool for identifying and defining project work, and it was a significant management tool used in managing the Big Dig. Since a WBS shows the relationship of all elements supporting the project, it provides a sound basis for cost and schedule control. As shown in Figure 5.4, the level of the structure is closely related to a management sphere within the project, providing the framework for relating time and cost summaries to appropriate levels of contractor and project management.

Table 5.3   Technical Scope Statement, D017A—I-93 Central Artery Congress
Street to North Street

Project Area

The D017A Design Package includes final design, contract plans and
specifications, and construction cost estimates for mainline tunnel structures and
auxiliary entrance/exit ramps and connectors. It also includes final design (from
the MBTA), contract plans and specifications, and construction cost estimates for
the MBTA Aquarium Station modernization.

Scope of Work

- Mainline tunnel structures (varies 8–10 lanes); cut-and-cover construction
- Ramp tunnel (1–2 lanes); cut-and-cover construction
- Transition sections (boat sections) (1–2 lanes)
- At-grade roadways (varies 1–4 lanes)
- MBTA Blue line at state street—Aquarium Station. The tunnel structure will
  accommodate southbound, northbound, and ramp alignments; the overall
  width of the tunnel box is approximately 230 feet; cut-and-cover tunnel
  structure associated with the MBTA Aquarium Station.
- Underpinning and support systems for the existing Central Artery Viaduct
- Vent Building #3 architecture and operations and maintenance of facilities
- Underpinning and support systems for the existing Central Artery Viaduct
- Utility relocations
- Site preparation and development
- Drainage including pump station
- Temporary facilities for traffic maintenance
- Demolition of the existing Central Artery Viaduct
- Highway architecture
- Tunnel finishes
- Embedded electrical conduit
- Embedded firefighting equipment requirements
- Signage and related sign supports

Contract Packaging

The D017A Design Package will be divided into nine construction packages as
follows: C17Al, C17A2, C17A3, C17A6, C17A8, C17A9, C17AA, C17AB, C14C4

Design Package Interfaces: D009B, D011A, D014C, D015A, D015C, D017D,
D018A, D020B, D021A, D022A

Related force accounts: City of Boston, Massachusetts Bay Transit Authority,
Boston Edison Company, Boston Water and Sewer Commission, Cablevision

---

Source: Central Artery/Tunnel Project.

The project's procedures define the various levels of the WBS and were
uniformly required throughout the project for every contract package. By
dividing the overall project into successively smaller components at defined
levels—a process called *decomposition*—all the project work elements are
identified. By using consistent levels and clearly defined elements, the WBS

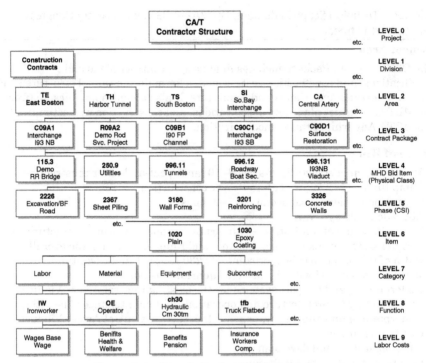

Figure 5.4   Sample Project Work Breakdown
Source: Central Artery Tunnel Project WBS Procedures.

provides a framework to unify the planning, design, estimating, scheduling, cost, management, and other project functions. The number of WBS levels can vary from project to project, anywhere from 2 to 10 or more levels. The project prepared a WBS for both the project and for each contract package.

The Work Breakdown Structure

As shown in Figure 5.4, the project breakdown structure consisted of the following 10 levels:

Level 0: Project cost centers—construction, engineering/design, program management, right-of-way, force accounts, insurance, and contingency
Level 1: Construction division of the project—construction contracts
Level 2: Geographic areas of the project—East Boston, Harbor Tunnel, South Boston, South Bay Interchange, Central Artery
Level 3: Contract packages for each construction area, sometimes consisting of as many as 20 to 30 packages
Level 4: Physical class of each bid item for the package, such as tunnels, viaducts, or utilities

Level 5: Specific phase of the construction, which may include excavation, sheet piling, reinforcing, or concrete roads

Level 6: Type of material used for the construction, such as epoxy coating or steel reinforcing

Level 7: Category of the work—labor, materials, equipment, or subcontract

Level 8: Function classification—ironworker, operator, or truck flatbed

Level 9: Labor costs—wages, overtime, benefits, pension, insurance

The WBS was prepared by the project's consultant and contractors. It allowed categorization and summarization of the various control elements of the Central Artery/Tunnel Project, at the level of detail required to ensure adequate control. It also provided timely and accurate data to evaluate project performance.

Hierarchical Levels of Control and Reporting

> The success of the Project is essentially determined by the proper execution of the planning activities,
>
> *—Nicole Hunter, CA/T cost engineer,*
> *Construction Controls Group*

To properly execute the planning activities, in addition to the work breakdown structure for construction, the project developed a hierarchy of project reporting levels so that the appropriate information was available based on need and level of responsibility, as shown in Figure 5.5. Major project objectives were established by the project owner (MHD) and represent the uppermost level in the control hierarchy. More detailed control points are in turn established to support the overall control objectives and further delineate scope, budget, or activities necessary to achieve the desired results. Information is received and monitored at these more detailed levels. The level of

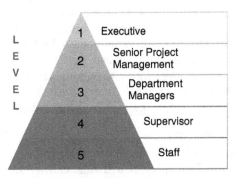

Project Controls Reporting Levels

Figure 5.5   Project Controls Reporting Levels
Source: Central Artery/Tunnel Project, Project Controls Plan.

detail is predicated on the entity, deliverable, or activity being controlled. This control information is structured to allow for more progressive or summary information.

The top or executive level of the WBS reporting structure provides overall or summary control information. This information is directed toward federal and state officials as well as senior project management. The next level of information is targeted for core managers who have oversight roles on the project. Further levels provide more detailed information depending on the needs of the various department managers, supervisors, and staff.

6. SCOPE EVOLUTION AND SCOPE CREEP

Scope change is a reality on all projects and continues to be a major issue for project managers. The *PMBOK® Guide* recognizes the impact of change in its processes and procedures. Project management research documents some of the reasons why project scope is almost certain to change, particularly in the early stages of the project. Many of the same reasons were evident on the Big Dig, and they include the following:

1. Technological uncertainty or advances in technology during the course of the project
2. Cost increases or schedule delays that force the project owner to reconsider some of the project's goals, based on the public interest and available funding
3. Changes in the legal, political, or economic landscape that mandate scope revisions, whether or not they are in the best interests of the project

Developing the scope of the Big Dig was an iterative process, and some of the major reasons for scope change are well documented in the project's history of scope and cost (CA/T 2007). Substantial changes in scope, totaling more than $2.3 billion including design development, environmental concerns, and right-of-way acquisitions, occurred from 1991 through 2000. Some of the major changes made in the early years included the shifting of the tunnels under the Fort Point Channel in response to historic preservation rules, redesign of the airport interchange based on the concerns of the residents of East Boston, and the change in concept and design of the Charles River Crossing that connected the Central Artery with four other roadways. The costs for some of these major changes are highlighted as follows (CA/T 2007):

1991 Added $554 million for Dewey Square Tunnel, East Boston tunnel covers, landscaping, railroad relocation, material disposal program, West Virginia Fire Tunnel Test, project utilities, change in steel and underpinning designs, and miscellaneous other items

1992 Added $324 million in scope elements related to the New Charles River Crossing and miscellaneous other items

1997 Added $400 million due to bid results, noise mitigation, dust mitigation, traffic mitigation, and deletion of future air rights credit

2000 Added $1.1 billion for design development, design during construction, additional construction costs, and force account work

Design Development

The Big Dig was subject to substantial uncertainty; thus, it was essential that processes and procedures were in place to analyze and respond to requests for scope change. The extensive report from the National Cooperative Highway Research Program (NCHRP) on cost estimation highlights that scope creep and scope changes are two of the 18 top reasons for cost escalation (Anderson 2006). Scope, which should be controllable, can lead to underestimation of project cost escalation. Such changes may include modifications in project construction limits; alterations in design and/or dimensions of key project items such as roadways, bridges, or tunnels; adjustments in type, size, or location of intersections; as well as other increases in project elements (Harbuck 2004; Board 2003; Chang 2002; GAO 1999; Callahan 1998; Mackie and Preston 1998; Booz-Allen 1995; Semple et al. 1994; Touran and Bolster 1994; Merrow 1988; Merrow 1986; Merrow et al. 1981; Hufschmidt and Gerin 1970).

There are many potential reasons for design changes. Design professionals must balance process and structural considerations with regulatory, maintainability, and human factors. On the Big Dig, multiple designers with different disciplines on each contract and the numerous interfaces increased the probability of change.

Scope and schedule strategies are also important at the operation level. The loss of scope control, particularly during engineering, ranks as a leading factor driving divergence of estimated project cost. This can be the result of a few major changes to the scope or of successive minor changes, often referred to as *scope creep*. The relationship between poor scope definition and scope changes is clear. A poorly defined project scope early in project development does not provide a clear baseline for estimating cost and then managing the project. There must be clear guidelines as to scope change authority and for notification of management about the impacts of scope changes.

Scope changes during the later stages of engineering design and construction can have ripple effects and can increase the project cost exponentially. A change in scope can lead to lower productivity, additional work hours, increased cost, and/or increased project duration.

Proactive methods should be used for engaging external participants and assessing the macro-environmental conditions that can influence project costs. In the case of most projects, engineers focus on technical solutions with little attention to community interests, and often fail to recognize market concerns. Highlighted in Table 5.4 are some of the important design development considerations for highway projects that had a significant impact on cost and schedule on the Big Dig.

Table 5.4　Design Development Considerations, The Central Artery/Tunnel Project

Historic Preservation Requirements	Shifting of tunnels under the Fort Point Channel in response to historic preservation rules
Community Concerns	Change in concept and design of the Charles River Crossing (Scheme Z)
Right-of-Way Acquisition and Valuation Problems	Property owner relocation, sudden growth, and area development, cost, and schedule impacts.
Geotechnical and Unknown Subsurface Conditions	Inadequate geotechnical investigations during the conceptual and alignment selection phases cause unforeseen conditions during excavation and construction of tunnels, bridges, and walls. This could be compounded by inadequate characterization of groundwater conditions and the uncertainty of the location of utilities
Bridge Foundations	The foundation type for bridges in the project may need to be adapted to new information that becomes available as the project progresses.
Local Arterial Improvements and Access	Local agencies and communities demand additional improvements to local arterials as a condition for support of the project. These include sustainable development mandates, transportation enhancements, airport access, and facilities.
Traffic Demand	Traffic demands are not accurate in some areas (e.g., inconsistent growth patterns, age of traffic projections). Traffic alleviated in the Central Arterial area may still cause backups in other areas.
Contaminated Soil	It is possible that even after thorough due diligence and the identification of contaminated sources during design of the project, new contaminated soils or groundwater may result in discovery of new or unknown conditions that need to be taken care of during construction.
Seasonal Restrictions	Restrictions on conducting some activities (e.g., earthwork) during some parts of the year (i.e., winter).
Natural Hazards	Storms, floods, earthquakes, etc., can cause damage to work under construction and may result in shutdown during construction. Such conditions damage the temporary water pollution controls, temporary structures, and earthwork, which must then be repaired.

Source: Central Artery/Tunnel Project, 1996 to 2004 Budget and Financial Reports.

Scope Creep

Scope creep is the tendency of the requirements to grow over time, and, as the literature reflects, it is a common affliction on all projects but particularly on large and complex projects that often require rework. A scope statement that is broad and imprecise is an invitation for scope creep. Most of the time, scope creep results in cost overruns and delays. A clear specification statement enables the project team to immediately realize when extra work is added and is a beneficial tool for controlling scope creep. However, a clear specification does not always work if the project manager ignores the process, or if specific requirements or stakeholders' concerns are not solicited or addressed at the conceptual or early stage of the project to help properly define such specification. Scope creep on the Big Dig resulted primarily from the first two considerations in Table 5.4: (1) historic preservation requirements and (2) community concerns about the original design of the Charles River Crossing.

7. THE SPECIFICATION MANAGEMENT PLAN

If you can't explain it simply, you don't understand it well enough.

—*Albert Einstein*

The Big Dig's fast-track approach, which permitted construction to begin on some contracts before design was complete on other contracts, had an impact on cost due to the continuous addition of scope as the project evolved. A way to prevent scope creep is to follow a specification management plan, which is a step-by-step process for managing changes to the project scope. This plan indicates (1) how scope changes will be identified, (2) how they will be integrated into the project, and (3) what approval requirements are needed and from whom. Specification management controls may also include progress performance requirements so stakeholders understand how frequently the specification might change and by how much.

Specification Problems and Solutions

PMI's the *PMBOK® Guide* defines *specifications* as "[a] document that specifies, in a complete, precise, verifiable manner, the requirements, design, behavior, or other characteristics of a system, component, product, result or service and, often, the procedures for determining whether these provisions have been satisfied."

On the Big Dig, the specification was essentially defined as the legal agreement between the project owner and the designers and contractors. Because of the nature of the project—excavating through a major city with businesses and residents nearby—the provisions had to address many concerns of the project's stakeholders and the local community. These included environmental conditions, traffic congestion, access to buildings, public safety and noise, and dust and rodent control. Poor specifications can cause delay, add millions of dollars in cost to a project, and have an effect on quality or benefits of the project.

All contracts had a standard set of specifications known as the Division 1—General Requirements and Covenants, and the Division 1 Special Provisions. It was important to have these general specifications in place early in the project, so that there was consistency among contracts. The Standard Specifications existed in every contract and included provisions such as bidding requirements, source of supply and quality, responsibility to the public, and payment methods. In addition to the Division 1 Specifications, each contract had a separate set of special provisions known as Division II Specifications. These special provisions were developed to address the unique requirements of a contract, including construction means and methods, the topography, and special environmental concerns.

Specifications are used to allocate risk among the various project participants. Serious problems can arise when these clauses contain errors, omissions, or inconsistencies. A review of the extensive case law that has arisen in construction contracting shows three areas of potential conflict that can seriously impact construction cost, schedule, quality and risk. These clauses fall under the following three categories: excusable performance (force majeure); claims and changes; and project control and responsibility.

- Force majeure clauses define the types of risks that will excuse performance such as severe weather, unforeseen conditions that were not contemplated at the time the contract was entered into, or a change in the law that impacts the investment. These risks must be carefully defined so the owner is protected from a risk that is within the control of the contractor, and the contractor is protected from a risk that is within the control of the owner. For instance, in a public construction project, the risk of differing site conditions is typically allocated to the contractor, while regulatory risk is allocated to the owner. These clauses should also define the obligations for mitigating an event once it occurs, as well as the time frame during which performance will be excused.
- *Claims and changes* provisions detail the procedures that are to be followed when there is a change to the project scope, the process that will be followed to resolve the changes, as well as any dispute resolution process that is required of the involved parties.
- *Project control* clauses generally define responsibilities of the parties and procedures for various aspects of the design and construction process. For example, the Spearin Doctrine, a landmark U.S. Supreme Court decision, is a legal principle that holds that when a contractor follows

the plans and specifications furnished by the owner, and those plans and specifications turn out to be defective or insufficient, the contractor is not liable to the owner for any loss or damage resulting from the defective plans and specifications due to an implied warranty given by the owner to the contractor (*United States v. Spearin* 1918). Thus, efforts must be made to ensure that project participants understand their differing roles and responsibilities that are assigned in the contract clauses and to comply with these provisions.

Prior to determining which law will govern the project contracts, it is important to have a complete legal analysis of the possible applicable laws by the organization's general counsel. To the extent the contract does address all issues, the local statutory and common law will govern the contract. Owners need to include in all contracts indemnity, liquidated damages, consequential damages, and differing site condition clauses to shift liability to the contractor for increased costs and delays in the event of the breach of the contract by the contractor.

A few selected provisions and the problems and risks these specifications presented at the Big Dig are highlighted in the three examples that follow.

EXAMPLE 1: SPECIFICATION

Section 4.04 Differing Site Conditions: If during the progress of the Work, the Contractor discovers that the actual subsurface conditions encountered at the site differ substantially or materially from those shown on the Plans or indicated in the Contract Documents, ... the contractor ... may request an Equitable Adjustment in the Contract Price ...

Problem: Disputes arising from this specification were quite common due to the differing interpretations of "substantially or materially" and whether the designer should be liable for not identifying the subsurface conditions in the drawing or the owner should be liable because the contractor was not at fault.

Solution: (1) the designer and the owner should work together to resolve any differences; (2) the meaning of "differ substantially or materially" should be defined to a greater extent in the specification; (3) the method of calculating the equitable adjustment should be included in the contract documents; and (4) the risks and exposures should be identified and included in the contractor's baseline, or through a construction contingency.

EXAMPLE 2: SPECIFICATION

Section 7.23 Archaeological and Paleontological Discoveries

All Articles of historical or scientific value, including coins, fossils, and articles of antiquity, that may be uncovered by the Contractor during progress of Work shall become the property of the Commonwealth of Massachusetts. Such findings shall be reported immediately to the Engineer who will determine the method of removal, where necessary, and the final disposition thereof. All Work in that area will be temporarily delayed while the State Archaeologist... inspects the site.

Problem: The project failed to include a sufficient contingency in the budget for artifact removal. Consequently, the owner absorbed the cost of frequent delays, sometimes lasting up to half a day or longer.

EXAMPLE 3: SPECIFICATION

Section 8.10 Excusable Delays or Force Majeure

An Excusable Delay is a delay, suspension or time extension which results from an event, ... which is due to some cause beyond the control and without the fault or negligence of the Contractor. Excusable delays include... abnormal tides (not including Spring tides), severe Coastal storms accompanied by high winds or abnormal tides, and freezing of streams and harbors. Provided, however, a rain, windstorm, or other natural phenomenon of normal intensity, based on United States Weather Bureau reports, for the particular locality and season of the year, shall not be construed as an "Act of God" and no extension in Contract Time(s) or Contract Milestone(s) will be granted for the delay resulting therefrom.

Problem: Should a contractor be excused from work if there is one foot of snow? Four feet of snow? What if the previous winter there were three snowstorms all under two feet deep? Is a four-foot snowfall normal intensity?
Solution: Be specific about when weather conditions will excuse performance and for how long, and what the obligations of the owner and the contractor are for delay costs and any resulting damage to the contract works.

8. SCOPE CHANGE AND VERIFICATION

A fundamental requirement for scope changes on projects is that any change has to be estimated and the impact on the project assessed for cost, schedule, quality, and technical sustainability. On the Big Dig, changes in specifications were controlled through an elaborate five-step approval process, as shown in Figure 5.6. Importantly, on the Big Dig it was the responsibility of all project personnel to identify changes to the project contract scope and communicate these changes to Project Controls. As described in this chapter, there were many ways for scope change to evolve, such as design development, regulatory changes, environmental mandates, and technical improvements. Figure 5.6 highlights the various levels of responsibility in the scope change process. Project Controls was responsible for coordinating communication of these changes via the technical scope statement to the owner and to project personnel. The technical scope coordinator then reviewed the feasibility of the proposed changes and, if required, coordinated with other project entities to confirm the cost-schedule benefit of such changes and prepared a recommendation. Final approvals had to be obtained from the program manager and the project owner before implementing the recommendations. It is important to distinguish scope change and verification from contractor-initiated claims and changes, which generally arose due to a dispute between the project manager and the contractor. The claims and changes process and dispute resolution are described in Chapter 11.

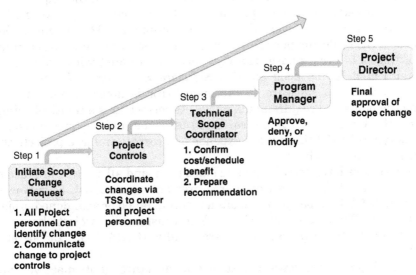

Figure 5.6   Project Scope Change Process
Source: Central Artery/Tunnel Project Scope Change Procedures.

9. THE TOP TEN SCOPE CONTROL TOOLS

The Big Dig used many tools to control scope as it required monitoring throughout the project life cycle. As design changed, so did construction means and methods, which often triggered a construction claim for an "equitable adjustment" or a design claim for changes during construction. The following sections examine a few of the more significant tools and techniques utilized to control scope on the Big Dig.

A. Controlling Requirements Errors

Requirements errors may result in the necessity of doing over an activity that was incorrectly done the first time. Many studies have shown that requirements errors are very costly. The primary sources of errors in construction consist of the design and drawings on which the construction is based including design changes and design errors and omissions (Burati et al. 1992). Design errors may include the failure to properly identify a sewer pipe, for example, or the omission of an important element of a design. In one case, the Big Dig's section designer consultant's failure to properly identify the need for a drainage system required a cost increase of $456,447 (OIG 2004).

According to various studies, the cost to fix a software defect varies according to how far along you are in the cycle. One NASA study of systems cost factors revealed that costs escalate in an exponential fashion and that early detection of errors is highly important to the success of any project (NASA 2010). Academics and practitioners in the software field have been collecting data for decades on the impact of errors made in the requirements stage of a project, yet it is perplexing how little progress we have made in understanding how to prevent these errors (Rothman 2002; Firesmith 2002).

In 1981, Barry Boehm performed some of the first cost studies to determine, by software life cycle phase, the cost factor associated with fixing errors (Boehm 1981). In his book entitled *Software Engineering Economics*, he concluded that if a software requirement error is detected and corrected during the plans and requirements phase, its correction is a relatively simple matter. If the same error is not corrected until the maintenance phase, the error is typically 100 times more expensive to correct on large projects than in the requirements phase.

Many studies have been conducted since then, and all seem to produce the same basic result. By one estimate, requirement errors cost U.S. businesses more than $59 billion per year and often result in failed or abandoned projects (NIST 2002). The direct costs of rework in construction projects have been found to be 10 to 15 percent of contract value (CIDA 1995; Burati et al. 1992).

The Big Dig required rework on some contracts through its massive claims and changes process. Without extensive research, it is impossible to determine the exact cost of rework. Each claim involved an analysis of design documents and drawings, construction means and methods, and risk allocation, scope, and contract analysis. Further research is needed on the cost of construction rework and redesign to determine the underlying causes and how rework can be prevented on challenging large-scale technology projects like the Big Dig.

B. Design to Budget

In order to ensure that designers are aware of how scope changes will affect project cost, it is advantageous to require inclusion of a cost estimate along with each design submittal. This process requiring designers to provide construction cost estimates is known as *design to budget*. The design-to-budget methodology assists in developing the baseline and also defines and estimates the basic construction components necessary to meet the project's requirements plus any nonproject costs.

On the Big Dig, when large differences between the conceptual estimate and the design estimate were reported (greater than 10 percent), approval was required from the supervisory level or higher before design could proceed, in order to ensure that sufficient funds were available for construction. If estimated project cost exceeds the existing budget, then changes will have to be made to reduce the overall project cost. In general when this happens on large projects, it may require project scope reduction. Design to budget forces designers to be constantly aware of the cost implications of their design decisions.

C. Cost Recovery

Cost recovery was an important tool used by the Big Dig project to address design development and scope change and transfer issues. Cost recovery is the process by which public and private owners file claims against design and construction management professionals for the costs claimed to be attributable to errors, omissions, or other "deficient" or unsatisfactory performance ("cost recovery claims") (OIG 2004). Cost recovery is a way to identify overruns and attribute responsibility to either the designer or the contractor who is at fault. Potential recovery costs may include (1) premium costs for omitted work (technical expert standard premium percentage to be applied), (2) cost changes associated with rework due to design error or deficient construction work, (3) additional costs associated with schedule impacts and delay due to design error or omission or deficient construction, and (4) costs of additional design work due to faulty original design or contractor failing to fulfill design obligations.

As soon as a potential cost recovery issue was identified from the list in Table 5.5, the reason was documented to ensure an auditable record of issue determination. Cost recovery must be understood in relation to the triple constraint and effective scope management.

Table 5.5   Cost Recovery Issues

Design Development: Preparation of drawings to shape design concept in terms of architectural, electrical, mechanical, and structural systems (rarely recoverable).
Schedule Adjustment: Excusable delay due to force majeure (rarely recoverable unless insurance) or delay due to failure of contractor to correctly estimate schedule risk (usually recoverable).
General Administration: Cost for salaries, equipment, and materials (usually recoverable).
Third Party: Business property is damaged due to negligence of contractor (usually recoverable through contractor directly or insurance).
Differing Site Conditions: Sewer pipes are struck by contractor, causing flooding of work site (not recoverable from contractor if contractor gives notice and mitigates damage and the cause is faulty design). If the sewer pipes were identified on the design drawings or contract documents and were foreseeable by the contractor, the costs were recoverable.
Regulatory: Cost of additional environmental compliance (recoverable if change in law during course of project).
Scope Transfers: Responsibility for access road is transferred between contractors (rarely recoverable).
Scope Changes: Additional work added to contract by owner (usually recoverable).
Value Engineering (VE) Proposal: Recommendation by engineer to redesign work to save cost (usually not recoverable if accepted by owner).
Other: Miscellaneous category for changes not included in a specific category.

Source: Central Artery/Tunnel Project Cost Recovery Procedures.

Best Practices for Cost Recovery:

1. Once a cost recovery issue is identified, each potential recovery must be reviewed and evaluated to determine whether there is responsibility and the amount of costs or damages the designer or contractor will be responsible for paying back to the project if there is liability.

2. Liability should be assessed based on the terms of the contract, construction plans, and specifications, and the professional standard of care to which the contractor/consultant is required to adhere under the contract. A designer's normal standard of care is exercising that standard of reasonable care required of members of his or her profession.

3. A cost-benefit analysis should be conducted to ensure that the cost of pursuing a matter does not exceed the amount that can reasonably be expected to be recovered.

D. Cost and Schedule Containment Programs

The Big Dig project encouraged the application of cost and schedule containment initiatives. Over the years, many scope-specific cost and schedule containment ideas had been implemented by the project, the results of which were included in the contemporaneous estimates.

The cost and schedule containment programs facilitated cost and schedule reduction ideas through various channels, including a formal employee suggestion program, day-to-day work activities of project staff, and monthly management review meetings. These ideas were analyzed for technical, commercial, and political feasibility and then implemented if appropriate. Savings from cost containment ideas over the life of the project were substantial. Since the base project estimate, the cost containment program resulted in tens of millions of dollars in cost reduction. Schedule containment initiatives provided benefits up to completion of the major roadway milestones (CA/T 2004).

E. Early Identification and Project Trend Analysis

These programs identified potential and real cost and schedule changes on the Big Dig project. The early identification program identified items while they were still in the conceptual stage. The trend program captured actual and pending scope and schedule changes on a monthly basis. These programs allowed management to focus on current and developing cost and schedule issues and provided lead time for the project to mitigate and contain the impacts.

F. Claims Avoidance Program

The claims avoidance program was designed to mitigate construction changes, claims, and disputes that often arise with subterranean construction and with multiple prime contractors operating on a fast-track schedule in close proximity to each other. The program identified design ambiguities and inconsistencies prior to bid, eliminated obvious areas of potential claims and disputes, and recommended corrective measures to prevent or mitigate exposures. The program reviewed design status, construction staging, contract documents, plans and specifications, unit cost pricing structure, and contemporaneous schedule needs. This program continually incorporated applicable lessons-learned items and experiences gained from other contracts as the overall Big Dig project progressed.

G. Partnering and Alternative Disputes Resolution Program

The partnering and alternative disputes resolution (ADR) programs were implemented to provide the most productive and nondisruptive environment possible for the various participants in the Big Dig. All parties involved in the design, construction, and management of the project were involved in the partnering program and were encouraged to interact in a mutually respectful manner and work as a team to achieve the goals of the project. This program was successful in reducing the often-adversarial relationships that develop on construction projects and keeping the project schedule progressing while disputes were settled. The ADR program was invaluable in settling contract disputes without proceeding to litigation, which would have been both expensive and time consuming.

H. Value Engineering (VE)

Value engineering is recognized on projects worldwide as a key to containing life cycle cost through identifying new or different ways of designing and constructing scope items during the concept and design phases that lead to cost and, often, schedule savings. In general, the goal of VE is to focus on performing a function or project activity at a similar or improved level, while reducing the overall costs, which ultimately enhances the value of a specific function or a project. This may be accomplished by continually monitoring the function-to-cost or project-to-cost ratio against a predetermined cost threshold (Johnson et al. 2011). The Federal Highway Administration (FHWA), recognizing the importance of VE, issued a directive in 2010 that mandated a VE analysis on all federal-aid projects with an estimated cost of $25 million or more (USDOT 2010). FHWA requires that any federal-aid project submit a VE analysis conducted by an independent, multidisciplinary team that provides recommendations for:

1. Developing the needed functions safely, reliably, efficiently, and at the lowest overall cost
2. Improving the value and quality of the project
3. Reducing the time to complete the project

On the Big Dig, value engineering and value engineering change proposal (VECP) programs reduced project costs through design and constructability reviews by engineers, consultants, and contractors. The project's VECP program solicited value engineering proposals from contractors, and, if implemented, the contractor and project shared the cost savings evenly.

I. VE Program—Proposals from Design Consultants

The section design consultant VE program solicited value engineering proposals from design consultants for inclusion in the final design of the Big Dig. The project's internal preliminary design VE program was extremely successful, avoiding over $480 million in project costs. This initial VE effort accounts for the majority of the cost benefit realized through VE (C/AT 2005). The section design consultant (SDC) VE program, the first in the nation for a designer on a federal-aid project, received over $27 million in proposed improvements (C/AT 2004, 48). The project was proud of the achievements of this program, recognizing that it was not approved for implementation until late in the project's design process.

J. Value Engineering Change Proposal Program (VECP)—Proposals from Contractors

The *Federal-Aid Policy Guide*, FAPG GO11.9, defines VECPs as:

A construction contract provision which encourages the contractor to propose changes in the contract requirements which will accomplish the project's functional requirements at a less cost or improve value or service at no increase or a minor increase in cost.

(FHWA 2010)

The net savings of each proposal is usually shared with the contractor at a stated reasonable rate. On the Big Dig, the VECP program with the construction contractors saved the project $24 million. The first VECP involved substituting ground freezing for other types of in situ soil stabilization techniques prior to tunnel jacking and for changes to the jacking system. The second was for the substitution of top-down tunnel construction (using slurry walls for support of excavation and permanent tunnel walls) for the more conventional cut-and-cover tunnel construction that would have required large amounts of soil stabilization. An important lesson for all projects is to implement VE and VECP programs at the conception stage to take advantage of all possible reductions in schedule and cost savings during the life of the project. Because the VECP program was implemented much later than the VE program, many of the potential benefits had already been secured.

LESSONS LEARNED

1. Containing scope on a public project requires boldness and the will to say no—regardless of the political cost.
2. All projects must have a shared vision of technical competence. Technical scope accuracy is not about the lowest bid but is solely about competence.
3. Scope control must be integrated with quality control, quality assurance, risk management, and safety and health.
4. All scope assumptions, constraints, limits and exclusions are interrelated and must be carefully reviewed to avoid ambiguity and conflicting requirements.
5. Scope should include not only what will be done, but also what will not be done.
6. To maintain megaprojects within cost and budget, early analysis of the cost of rework and design defects must be identified and measured and

processes and procedures must be put in place to prevent escalation resulting from failure of scope control.

7. If deficiencies are significant, corrective actions will be needed to bring the project back in line with the plan. In some cases, conditions or scope can change, which will require a change in the baseline plan to recognize the impact on cost and schedule.

8. Innovative risk and scope management programs such as Value engineering (VE), and value engineering change proposals (VECP), should be implemented early in the project at the conceptual stage and not after design and construction have commenced.

BEST PRACTICES

1. Develop a strategy for scope control that integrates quality, risk, and safety and health at the conceptual stage of the life cycle.
2. Scope should always answer the questions—what, how, where and who.
3. Access to historical data on project scope, cost, and schedule will ensure more accurate and complete specifications.
4. Consider alternative procurement methods to low bid, such as best value, that have been employed successfully on public and private projects.
5. Allow changes to scope only through a mature scope change control process.
6. If change control is not supported from the top of the organization by the owner, there is little potential for successful control. A cooperative atmosphere among the owner, management consultant, design professionals, and contractors will increase the effectiveness of the change control program.
7. Develop and implement cost containment, cost recovery, and value engineering programs during project inception to address the specific needs and structure of the project.

SUMMARY

This chapter emphasizes the critical mechanisms for addressing the complex relationships among scope, cost, and schedule and all the influences that impact these knowledge areas. Scope management begins with a clear definition of the project's scope elements, which is reflected in the technical scope statement and is based on a hierarchical approach to project planning through the work breakdown structure (WBS). The project's procedures should define the WBS, and the procedures should be uniformly applied to all contracts and activities. The project scope statement is significant because it serves as the framework for resource selection, cost estimation, budgeting, and control. Projects must constantly evaluate scope changes and ensure that responsibility is properly allocated to the appropriate party based on design or construction obligations under the project's agreements. Analysis of value engineering should begin in the conception stage and continue throughout the project life cycle.

ETHICAL CONSIDERATIONS

In this chapter, you saw many examples of ways in which costs can rise because of the failure to properly control or verify scope. Scope defines the desired behavior of the project system. Much of scope management deals with planning. One of the central issues in scope planning is dealing with ambiguity. If project scope is ambiguous and doesn't identify the real needs of the customers, it is bound to result in failure.

Based on the descriptions of scope in this chapter:

1. Give three examples of how the failure to properly draft scope can have a substantial impact on the viability of a project.
2. Does the failure to properly assess the scope of a project raise possible ethical issues? If so, why?

DISCUSSION QUESTIONS

1. If you are a project manager of a megaproject like the Big Dig, what are the top ten questions you would need answered in your project scope statement?
2. Describe five ways in which the development of scope for a megaproject differs from the development of scope for a small or midsize project.
3. What is the purpose of a work breakdown structure? What are the challenges in developing a WBS for a megaproject?
4. Requirements errors continue to be a major problem in all projects. Describe the processes and procedures you would put in place to reduce and mitigate this problem to avoid extensive rework and project delays.
5. Scope creep tends to be a problem on all projects, but particularly megaprojects. Review the reasons for scope creep on the Big Dig and discuss how these problems might have been prevented with better planning and project structure.
6. Develop a work breakdown structure for constructing a new eight-room home with four bedrooms and a budget of $400,000. Be sure to include the deliverables and three levels of activities. After you finish, you learn you will be constructing that same home 2000 times more in varied climates. Would you do anything differently?
7. Why is the triple constraint a critical factor in scope management? Why is quality sometimes considered a fourth constraint? Isn't quality really a part of scope?

8. Review the three sample specifications highlighted in this chapter, and explain why project managers often fail to prevent ambiguity, which would help avoid delay and prevent disputes and costly litigation. How would you have changed the language in these three specifications to avoid ambiguity and uncertainty?

9. What did Sir Winston Churchill mean when he said that "plans are of little importance, but planning is essential?" Is this advice relevant to the planning of a megaproject?

REFERENCES

Anderson, S., K. Molenaar, and C. Schexnayder, C. 2006. *Guidance for Cost Estimation and Management for Highway Projects During Planning, Programming, and Preconstruction*. National Cooperative Highway Research Program (NCHRP) Report 574. Washington, DC: Transportation Research Board (TRB) of the National Academies. September.

Board on Infrastructure and the Constructed Environment. 2003. *Completing the "Big Dig": Managing the Final Stages of Boston's Central Artery / Tunnel Project*. National Academy of Engineering. Washington, DC: National Academies Press.

Boehm, B. W. 1981. *Software Engineering Economics*. Englewood Cliffs, NJ: Prentice Hall.

Booz-Allen & Hamilton Inc. and DRI/McGraw-Hill. 1995. *The Transit Capital Cost Index Study*. Washington, DC: U.S. Department of Transportation, Federal Transit Administration.

BRA (Boston Redevelopment Authority). 1996. "Boston's Population Doubles—Everyday." *Insight: A Briefing Report on a Topic of Current Interest, Policy Development and Research Department*. Boston, MA.

Burati, J. L., J. J. Farrington, and W. B. Ledbetter. 1992. "Causes of Quality Deviations in Design and Construction." *ASCE Journal of Construction Engineering and Management* 118(1): 34–49.

Callahan, Joel T. 1998. *Managing Transit Construction Contract Claims*. Transportation Research Board, TCRP Synthesis 28. Washington, DC: National Academies Press, 1–59.

C/AT (Central Artery [I-93]/Tunnel [I-90] Project). Specifications for Highways and Bridges: General Requirements and Covenants of Construction Contacts (Division I Specifications). Boston: Massachusetts Highway Department.

C/AT (Central Artery/Tunnel Project). Standard Bid Documents. Boston: Massachusetts Highway Department.

C/AT (Central Artery/Tunnel Project). 2004. Finance Plan. Boston: Massachusetts Turnpike Authority, 47–48.

C/AT (Central Artery/Tunnel Project). 2005. Finance Plan. Boston: Massachusetts Turnpike Authority.

CA/T (Central Artery/Tunnel Project). 2007. Cost and Schedule Update. Boston: Massachusetts Turnpike Authority.

Chang, Andrew Shing-Tao. 2002. "Reasons for Cost and Schedule Increases for Engineering Design Projects." *Journal of Management in Engineering.* ASCE. January 29–36.

CIDA (Construction Industry Development Agency). 1995. *Measuring Up or Muddling Through: Best Practice in the Australian Non-Residential Construction Industry.* Construction Industry Development Agency and Master Builders Australia. Sydney, Australia, 59–63.

FHWA (Federal Highway Administration). 2010. *Federal-Aid Policy Guide (FAPG).* Order 1321.1C, FHWA Directives Management, GO11.9. Washington, DC: U.S. Department of Transportation, Federal Highway Administration.

FHWA (Federal Highway Administraiton). 2011. *Performance Contracting Framework.* Fostered by Highways for LIFE. Washington, DC: U.S. Department of Transportation, Federal Highway Administration.

Firesmith, D. G. 2002. "Requirements Engineering." *Journal of Object Technology* 1(5):83–94.

GAO (General Accounting Office). 1999. *Mass Transit: Status of New Starts. Transit Projects with Full Funding Grant Agreements.* GAO/RCED 99-240. Washington, DC: U.S. General Accounting Office.

Harbuck, R. H. 2004. "Competitive Bidding for Highway Construction Projects." *AACE International Transactions.* Association for the Advancement of Cost Engineering. EST.09.1–EST.09.4.

Hufschmidt, Maynard M., and Jacques Gerin. 1970. "Systematic Errors in Cost Estimates for Public Investment Projects." In *The Analysis of Public Output,* edited by J. Margolis. New York: Columbia Press, 267–279.

Hunter, N. 2012. Interview with Nicole Hunter, former cost engineer in the Construction Controls Group and contracts administrator, Central Artery/Tunnel Project. June 9 and June 18.

Johnson, P., M. Leenders, and A. Flynn. 2011. *Purchasing and Supply Management.* 14th ed. New York: McGraw-Hill.

Luberoff, D., A. Altshuler, and C. Baster. 1993. *MegaProject: A Political History of Boston's Multibillion Dollar Artery / Tunnel Project.* Cambridge, MA: Taubman Center for State and Local Government, Harvard University.

Mackie, Peter, and John Preston. 1998. "Twenty-one Sources of Error and Bias in Transportation Project Appraisal." *Transport Policy* 5:1–7. Institute for Transport Studies, University of Leeds, UK.

Merrow, Edward W. 1986. *A Quantitative Assessment of R&D Requirements for Solids Processing Technology Process Plants.* Santa, Monica, CA: Rand Corporation.

Merrow, Edward W. 1988. *Understanding the Outcomes of Mega Projects: A Quantitative Analysis of Very Large Civilian Projects.* Santa Monica, CA: Rand Corporation.

Merrow, Edward W., Kenneth E. Phillips, and Christopher W. Myers. 1981. *Understanding Cost Growth and Performance Shortfalls in Pioneer Process Plants.* Santa Monica, CA: Rand Corporation.

NASA (National Aeronautics and Space Administration). 2010. *Error Cost Escalation through the Project Life Cycle*. Abstract. Houston, TX: Source of Acquisition, Johnson Space Center.

NIST (National Institute for Standards and Technology). 2002. "Software Errors Cost U.S. Economy $59.5 Billion Annually." NIST News Release. (May.) Washington, DC: U.S. Department of Commerce.

OIG (Office of the Inspector General). 2004. *A Big Dig Cost Recovery Referral: Poor Contract Oversight by Bechtel / Parsons Brinckerhoff May Have Led to Cost Increases*. Boston: Commonwealth of Massachusetts.

PMI (Project Management Institute). 2013. *A Guide to the Project Management Body of Knowledge (PMBOK® Guide)*—Fifth Edition. Newton Square, PA: Project Management Institute.

Rothman, J. "What Does It Cost to Fix a Defect?" StickyMinds.com. February 2002. Available at www.stickyminds.com/stgeletter/archive/20020220nl.asp. 2003.

Semple, C., F. T. Hartman, and G. Jergeas. 1994. "Construction Claims and Disputes: Causes and Cost/Time Overruns. *Journal of Construction Engineering and Management* 120(4):785–795.

Touran, A., and P. J. Bolster. 1994. *Risk Assessment in Fixed Guideway Transit System Construction*. Washington, DC: Federal Transit Administration.

United States v. Spearin. 1918. 248 U.S. 132.

U.S. Department of Transportation, Federal Highway Administration. 2010. *ORDER, FHWA Value Engineering Policy*. May 25.

Chapter 6

Schedule

This is no time for ease and comfort. It is time to dare and
endure.

—Sir Winston Churchill

INTRODUCTION

In his famous quote "Until we can manage time, we can manage
nothing else," Peter F. Drucker defined the significance of time in
managing projects. The triple constraint highlights the reality of all
projects—that one side of the triangle cannot be changed without
affecting the others. This chapter focuses on the impact of time on
all aspects of managing large-scale projects, from the establishment
of a timeline to the life cycle of complex projects and the problems
encountered along the way. Solutions to these problems are discussed,
along with recommendations for accelerated project delivery and the
essential tools to control and mitigate delay. Simply stated, being on
time requires an elaborate structure, an integrated system, and, most
important, careful planning at the front end.

SCHEDULE-DRIVEN PROJECTS

The Big Dig is known for cost and schedule delays, yet in the words of one
project official, *"The project was driven and controlled by meeting schedule
mandates."* (Primack 2006). An extensive analysis of the project's cost and
schedule in 2003 by an independent board of the National Academies noted
the difficulty of ascertaining the true cost of schedule because of the constant
interaction between the triple constraints of scope, schedule, and cost (Board
2003, 13).

Megaprojects are often of long duration—between 5 and 20 years, or longer
for some oil and gas concessions, which can run as long as 30 to 40 years.

The Big Dig was no different, with a 23-year time frame from development of the environmental assessment in 1983 to substantial completion in early 2006. Lengthy projects create multiple unknowns, ambiguity, uncertainty, and risk that do not exist in projects of much shorter duration. Calculating the price and availability of concrete and steel 23 years away is difficult enough, let alone determining whether the soil conditions will be sufficient to build complex structures based on environmental factors and erosion over time. It is important to note that there is less likelihood of maintaining continuity of management in long-duration projects. In a study of more than 1000 project managers researching the "greatest problem of project management," the findings revealed that organization, resource, and time issues were the three most cited problems (Hussain and Wearne 2005).

According to a 2002 GAO report, *Preliminary Information on the Timely Completion of Highway Construction Projects*, the time required to complete an average highway project varies widely. The time will depend on the size of the project, its complexity, and the public interest in the project. Some projects may take as few as 3 years, while others may take more than 13 years. Because there was no gold standard on time to complete projects set by the Federal Highway Administration (FHWA), the Big Dig's completion date evolved over time. While original projections predicted the completion date of 1998, as late as 1995 the finish date had officially crept to 2001. The 2001 date was later revised due to further changes to the schedule, and a new estimated completion date of 2004 resulted, which was later revised to the final completion date of 2006.

THE BIG DIG'S TIMELINE: A LONG AND WINDING ROAD

The long timeline of the Central Artery/Tunnel Project is shown in Table 6.1. The timeline stretched from 1975, when the funding for the I-93 tunnel was first approved by FHWA, to 1991 when the first Final Environmental Impact Statement/Report (FEIS/R) was approved (CA/T 1990), to the restoration of Boston city streets and the construction of the Greenway in 2007. Some might contend that rather than being a 23-year project from environmental assessment to completion, it was really a 30-year project that commenced upon initial approval of interstate funding by the FHWA and Congress in 1975.

Schedule Management Philosophy

On the Big Dig, schedule milestones were initially developed based on aggressive progress without contingency. The project always put a high priority on meeting its schedule milestones, though it was not always successful in reaching these goals. Achieving schedule commitments minimizes public disruption, avoids even greater delay and costs, and will deliver the benefits of the completed project to the public and businesses as soon as practicable.

Table 6.1   The Big Dig Timeline: Project Schedule Evolution from 1976–2007

Date	Event
1975	The Federal Highway Administration and the House and Senate Public Works Committee approved the inclusion of the Central Artery/Tunnel Project in the 1975 interstate cost estimate (ICE).
1983	Work begins on Final Environmental Impact Statement/Report (FEIS/R).
1985	Final Environmental Impact Statement/Report approved.
1986	Bechtel/Parson Brinckerhoff begins work as management consultant.
1987	Congress approves funding of project. Building acquisition and business relocation begins (no private homes taken).
1988	Final design process under way. Exploratory archaeology digs begin.
1989	Preliminary/final design and environmental review ongoing.
1990	Congress allocates $775 million to project.
1991	FHWA issues record of decision, the construction go-ahead. Final Supplemental Environmental Impact Statement approved. Construction contracts begin to be advertised and awarded. Construction begins on the Ted Williams Tunnel and South Boston Haul Road.
1992	More than $1 billion in design and construction contracts under way. Dredging and blasting for the Ted Williams Tunnel ongoing. Downtown utility relocation takes place. Archaeologists find seventeenth- and eighteenth-century artifacts.
1993	South Boston Haul Road opens. All 12 tube sections for the Ted Williams Tunnel are placed and connected on the harbor floor.
1994	Charles River Crossing design approved. New set of loop ramps open in Charlestown.
1995	The first major milestone, the Ted Williams Tunnel, officially opens.
1998	Peak construction years begin. Construction begins on the Charles River Crossing.
1999	Overall construction is 50 percent complete. New Broadway Bridge opens. Leverett Circle Connector Bridge opens.
2000	Nearly 5000 workers are employed on the Big Dig.
2001	Overall construction is 70 percent complete.
2002	Leonard P. Zakim Bunker Hill Bridge is completed, with phased opening of lanes from 2003–2005.
2003	Three major milestones are reached: I-90 Connector from South Boston to Rt. 1A in East Boston opens in January. I-93 Northbound opens in March. I-93 Southbound opens in December.
2004	Elevated Central Artery (I-93) is dismantled. The tunnel from Storrow Drive to Leverett Circle Connector opens, which provides access to I-93 North and Tobin Bridge.
2005	I-93 South is fully open. The completely renovated Dewey Square Tunnel is opened. Permanent ramps and roadways at the I-90/I-93 Interchange and in other areas are opened. The two cantilevered lanes on Leonard P. Zakim Bunker Hill Bridge, to handle traffic from the Sumner Tunnel and Boston surface streets to I-93 North, are opened.
2006	Substantial completion of the CA/T Project is reached in January.
2007	Boston city streets are restored. Construction of the Rose Kennedy Greenway and other parks continues.

Source: Central Artery Tunnel/ Project. 2007. Cost and Schedule Update.

Throughout the life of the project, management continued to enforce an aggressive schedule utilizing a schedule philosophy that requires establishment of schedule offsets when new issues impact the schedule (CA/T 2000). Schedule offsets include mechanisms to keep the schedule on track such as additional resources, changes in scope, or acceleration of the schedule. The early success of the philosophy was evidenced by the opening of one of the major project milestones, the Initial Leverett Circle, slightly ahead of schedule, in October 1999, and the later opening of another major milestone, the full I-93 Southbound tunnel on March 5, 2005. The project recognized this as a significant achievement because it was opened on the first day of the three-month schedule window identified in the Cost and Schedule Update (CA/T 2005).

Though the project schedule achieved milestone success early on, the Big Dig did not always run on time. In 2003, the National Academies issued a report on the project delays, with the following critical analysis and recommendations.

"[M]eeting the CA/T Project's schedule targets continues to be a problem. Despite an emphasis on reaching the milestones on time, slippage continues, thereby reducing public confidence in CA/T management" (Board 2003). The Report further emphasized that the slippage was due to the focus on short-term details of the project's activities, rather than evaluating the project risk as a whole in advance of potential occurrence (Board 2003). The problem was particularly evident due to the continuous postponement of the opening dates of I-90 and I-93. The Academies Report recommended, "that project managers should strategically evaluate future schedules by determining what critical tasks needed to be done without fail and how long these activities will likely take." Moreover, "published completion dates should be developed around realistic workflows and schedule risks, with modest allowances for unknown issues" (Board 2003).

Milestone Management   The Big Dig project managers developed a dynamic unit, the Milestone Manager Group, to help manage and overcome project delays that resulted from the unpredictable nature of several aspects of the work. To manage the schedule process, the project was subdivided into four major milestones, shown on the Map in Figure 6.1. The milestone process provided real-time project performance data and was used to forecast project delays and develop new work sequences. Before the development of this organization, the I-90 connection to Logan Airport was thought to be 12 months behind schedule. The Milestone Manager Group initiated schedule accelerations that resulted in an estimated eight months of schedule recovery, resulting in the connection finally opening on January 18, 2003 (CA/T 2003).

1. First Major Milestone: Ted Williams Tunnel (TWT) and I-90 Connector (Third HarborTunnel) Opened in 1995   Construction began on the Big Dig in September 1991 on the Bypass Road through South Boston to take truck traffic off

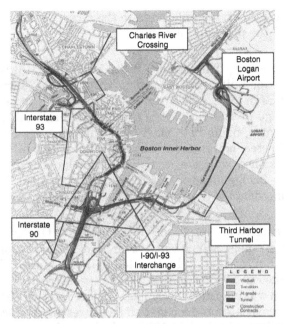

Figure 6.1   Project Milestones: (1) Third Harbor Tunnel (Ted Williams Tunnel),
(2) Interstate 93, (3) Interstate 90 and I-90/I-93 Interchange, (4) Charles River Crossing
Source: Central Artery/Tunnel Project. 2003. Finance Plan.

neighborhood streets and on the third tunnel to cross Boston Harbor. Four years later, the first major milestone, the opening of the tunnel—dedicated to and named after baseball legend Ted Williams—took place on December 15, 1995. The tunnel doubled Boston's cross-harbor tunnel capacity from four lanes to eight. The .75-mile underwater part of the 1.6-mile tunnel was built using a dozen steel tube sections, each longer than a football field, that were sunk into a trench on the Boston Harbor floor and connected together.

In 2003, despite enormous challenges, the Central/Artery Tunnel Project met three major milestones in 1993, described here, and in 2005, the majority of construction work was completed on the I-90/I-90 Interchange, and on I-93 Southbound. The project reached substantial completion on January 13, 2006.

2. The Massachusetts Turnpike Extension and I-90/I-93 Interchange   The second major milestone, the Massachusetts Turnpike (I-90) Extension, opened to traffic on January 18, 2003. The turnpike, which once abruptly ended on the edge of the downtown area, now runs from Seattle, Washington, to Logan International Airport in East Boston. The construction of the I-90 Extension involved some of the most complicated and challenging engineering on the Central Artery/Tunnel Project. It required tunnel jacking, the construction of a casting basin for immersed tube tunneling and cut-and-cover tunnel construction. This direct, 3.5-mile route to the airport saves drivers as much as 45 minutes off the previous journey.

3. Charles River Crossing The Leonard P. Zakim Bunker Hill Bridge, the only one of its kind ever built, was opened in three stages, several lanes at a time, between March 2003 and early 2005. In addition to being the widest cable-stayed bridge in the world, it is the first "hybrid" cable-stayed bridge in the United States, using both steel and concrete in its frame. The main span consists of a steel box girder and steel floor beams, while the back spans contain post-tensioned concrete. A parallel four-lane bridge, the Leverett Circle Connector Bridge, opened to traffic in October 1999. Together, these bridges more than doubled the cross-river capacity, to 14 lanes.

4. The Thomas P. O'Neill, Jr., Tunnel (I-93 tunnels) One and a half miles of underground tunnels, which went over and under major transit lines along Boston's main corridor and connected to the Leonard P. Zakim Bunker Hill Bridge, opened in 2003 (Figure 6.2). The reconstruction of I-93 through downtown Boston was enormously complex. Before heavy construction began, utilities had to be relocated and mitigation measures put in place. Then, slurry wall construction began in the mid-1990s, which required underpinning of the existing elevated Central Artery before excavation. Once I-93 North opened under the footprint of the elevated Central Artery, Big Dig crews began demolishing the aging elevated highway. That work was finished in 2004, after southbound traffic was also shifted underground and the artery was devoid of vehicles for the first time in half a century.

Figure 6.2   I-93 Southbound: The Big Dig's Last Major Milestone
Source: Central Artery/Tunnel Project.

MAJOR PHASES OF PROJECT DELIVERY

PMI's *A Guide to the Project Management Body of Knowledge (PMBOK® Guide)*—Fifth Edition (PMI 2013) describes the various phases that most projects move through as the project life cycle. These phases typically include initiation, planning, execution, and closing. Complex projects are much more difficult to define in terms of the traditional project life cycle, as the processes are repetitive and recurring throughout the life cycle of the project, and it is difficult to define where one phase ends and the next begins. Initiation of some parts of the project may occur very late in the life of the project, while closure has already been achieved on other parts of the project.

The delivery of large-scale projects requires a focus not only on the long up-front planning phase but also on the long-term operations and finance, "particularly since initial design and initial choice of technology commit the owner of the facility (public or private) to the resultant cost of maintenance and operations for three to five decades" (Miller 1997).

Several major portions of the Big Dig project were completed early on, including the Ted Williams Tunnel in 1995, while the significant demolition, excavation, and construction had not yet begun on the I-93 underground tunnel through Boston. Table 6.2 defines the various distinct, but interrelated,

Table 6.2 Major Phases of Infrastructure Project Development and Delivery on the Big Dig

Process Phases	Activities
1. Planning	Purpose, stakeholder participation, cost-benefit analysis, Environmental Feasibility Study, interagency coordination, finance commitments
2. Conceptual design	Public hearings, financing authorization, environmental approvals, right-of-way (ROW) plan
3. Preliminary design	Right-of-way development, route layout, design criteria, utility locations, surveys, geometric alignments
4. Final design	Required over 40 separate design contracts ranging from less than $1 million to over $50 million; activities included ROW acquisitions, traffic control plans, utility drawings, permits and licensing, final cost estimates, and contractor bid solicitation
5. Public bidding	Contract documents, bid advertising, prebid conferences, review bids in accordance with criteria
6. award	Select lowest qualified bidder and draft contract
7. Construction	Required over 110 separate general contractors to be awarded contracts ranging from $5 million to $400 million to initiate start-up, perform scope, systems commissioning, contract administration, traffic control, inspection, and materials testing
8. Testing, operations, and maintenance	Required coordination of multiple state and federal agencies including the MBTA, Massport Authority, and police departments throughout the city

stages and activities of the project. Important highway project research emphasizes that schedule risk analysis must consider the effects of programmatic schedule decisions, the inherent errors in the schedule estimation technique used, and external physical constraints (NCHRP 2006, 7).

The Planning Stage

Miller and Hobbs, in their research on the study of best managerial practices in complex large-scale construction and engineering projects, learned that the long, complex, and critical front end of projects was essential to ensuring project success. The basic premise of the research is that competencies developed to deal with crises, uncertainty, unexpected events, and emerging complexity should result in higher payoffs than relying solely on formal planning structures and processes. Their research reflected that the front ends of projects were very long—seven years on average—and often very expensive (up to 33 percent of the total budget) (Miller and Hobbs 2006). The management of the front end, or conceptual phase, as it is commonly called, was critical and showed significantly more impact on project performance than the management of the engineering, procurement, and construction phase. Project research as far back as the 1970s shows that the ability to influence the outcome of a project is the greatest and costs are the lowest in the earliest stages (Paulson 1976).

The planning stages of a project are often unpredictable and go through many phases before project funding is secure. The various phases of planning a large public project include:

1. The formation and structure of the owner/sponsors coalition
2. The acceptance of the project by the stakeholders and local community
3. The public dialogue and review of the alternative concepts of the project
4. The development of the regulatory, environmental, and governance framework
5. Unanticipated changes in the political environment, and governmental approvals, licensing, and funding commitments

From a project management perspective, PMI's the *PMBOK® Guide* briefly describes the planning effort required in the schedule management plan, which is used to illustrate the scheduling methodology and establish criteria for developing and controlling the project schedule. In general, a project schedule can be an effective communication tool to help stakeholders understand how proper time management of project activities could support the deliverables stated in the project management plan.

Careful up-front schedule planning would help the project manager and the project team to properly allocate, adjust, and monitor cost and resources associated with project activities. The schedule management plan thus provides a structured approach to project planning that provides visibility to project progress on both critical and noncritical work and a greater understanding of the corresponding time contingencies. As part of risk management, a robust schedule management plan also helps identify threats and opportunities that often arise due to unanticipated changes to the project baseline (Carson 2010). From a supply management perspective, the schedule management plan can help the project management team develop necessary documents for a claims dispute resolution system, penalty and incentive plan for supplier performance, and supplier resource identification and allocation plan that most likely would be required to address changes that are part of a megaproject.

PERCEPTIONS OF STAKEHOLDERS ON APPROACHES TO REDUCE HIGHWAY PROJECT COMPLETION TIME

In 2003, the GAO reported the findings of a study based on the perception of state and federal agency officials on the most promising approaches to reduce project completion time for federally funded highway projects. Respondents from 33 organizations rated 13 approaches to reduction of completion time that fell into three key areas: (1) improving project management, (2) delegating environmental review and permitting authority, and (3) improving agency staffing and skills. Specific recommendations on the 13 approaches included the following, all of which are relevant to the Big Dig (GAO 2003):

- Involve stakeholders early so that technical, environmental, policy, and other issues can be resolved in a timely manner and hold public information meetings early and often to provide information on projects that are planned or under way.
- Establish project milestones and performance monitoring systems. Specify key dates, such as when final design must be completed, and manage the project to meet the dates.
- Employ context-sensitive design. Design projects that consider the community's environmental and social context so that projects are consistent with the values of the community.
- Provide training. Determine the skills available at state transportation departments in relation to federal and state requirements to complete each phase of highway projects and establish training for shortfalls.

Fast-Tracking

Fast-track construction is a methodology of project delivery in which the sequencing of construction activities enables some portions of the project to begin before the design is completed on other portions of the project. The Big Dig utilized fast-track design and construction delivery methods to reduce costs and overall project time. This process works best when the design of each work package is complete and the impact of requirements of the later segments can be anticipated. The downside is changes and overruns if work packages have to be started before the design work is done.

Initially, the Big Dig's fast-track schedule projected the Supplemental Environmental Impact Statement (SEIS) approval by 1988, construction started by 1990, the tunnel completed by 1994, and the project completed by 1998. As the project was not substantially completed until 2006, in hindsight this was a very ambitious schedule.

In 1993, the project had 56 final design sections or packages, with a prime contractor for each. At the same time, the project had 132 construction packages for which contracts would be issued. Some design packages had several construction packages, while others had only one construction package (Hughes 2000). Research shows that complex projects like the Big Dig are best managed by breaking down the project into phases that include conceptual design, preliminary design, final design, and construction. Though normally these phases would occur consecutively, due to the use of fast-tracking on the Big Dig, some contracts would start construction while others had not yet started design.

For instance, on the Big Dig, work packages had completed the civil design phase, but they frequently required modifications to accommodate projectwide systems that were designed in later packages. The project's position that it had realized a 3:1 cost-benefit ratio by utilizing fast-track methods (i.e., the accelerated schedule saved $3 for each $1 of additional costs, attributed to using fast track) has been criticized based on a review of the Big Dig's fast-track process. As noted in the National Academies Report, one downside of fast-tracking was the high rate of claims and changes on the project (Board 2003, 16).

One positive example of the minimization of schedule impacts through fast-tracking was the construction of the civil/structural tunnel components at the same time that the mechanical, electrical, and Integrated Project Control System design was being completed (CA/T 2003).

IMPACT OF DESIGN DEVELOPMENT ON SCHEDULE

An important example of the impact of design development on schedule involved the design of one of the project's major engineering challenges, the Fort Point Channel Crossing, as shown in Figure 6.3. The Fort Point Channel project involved the construction of tunnels under the South Station railroad tracks, over Boston's major transit system, the MBTA's Red Line, and between two major buildings, the U.S. Postal Annex and the Gillette Company World Headquarters, eventually connecting Interstates 90 and 93 with the Ted Williams Tunnel.

As reported by the Massachusetts State Auditor's Office in February 2000, "At least two factors contributed to the cost increases and schedule delays for designing and constructing the Fort Point Channel Crossing: MassHighway's

**Big Dig
Casting Basin
in Boston's
Fort Point
Channel**

Figure 6.3   Fort Point Channel Crossing
Source: Central Artery/Tunnel Project.

inability to resolve in a timely manner the debate about the adequacy of B/PB's circular cofferdam preliminary design and the delay in resolving Ramp 'L' design problems" (OSA 2000).

The debate over whether to consider alternative design changes for the Fort Point Channel recommended by design and geotechnical contactors concerning the excavation support system lasted 18 months. The report also revealed that the other major delay involved design of the ramp leading from the interstate to the Ted Williams Tunnel. Federal highway officials maintained that the design of the ramp jeopardized the safety of traffic farther down I-90. This design dispute dragged on for almost three years before the realignment was satisfactorily settled. The State Auditor's Office reported that the design delays increased construction costs by approximately $13 million and the project incurred resdesign costs of $6.4 million. The problems that result from delays became more apparent in late 2000 when $300 million was required for schedule maintenance requiring the infusion of additional funds.

Thus, design development can be a critical factor in the delay of a project, if all parties cannot agree on the resolution to design alternatives within a reasonable time period. Interestingly, State Auditor Joseph

DeNucci noted that his concern was not with the eventual solution to the problem but, rather, with the lengthy amount of time it took for a resolution (OSA 2000).

SCHEDULE AND COST INTEGRATION

The key to directing and managing the project schedule was project schedule integration. Maintaining a master schedule for 132 major contracts was essential in ensuring that the project baseline and budget were realistic and that costs were controlled through maintenance of the project schedule. The management, coordination, and scheduling of this massive project emanated from the Central Artery/Tunnel Project's Control Center. The project's Control Center, like Churchill's war room, contained numerous diagrams and maps and dealt with the daily confusion of coordinating the activities of the joint-venture engineers and the extensive network of contractors and consultants (Hughes 2000). The project controls organization was responsible for preparing the diagrams and schedules from the work packages. Daily communication with the contractors was essential to ensure that milestones were reached, and when there were delays on the critical path, contractors were responsible for developing needed changes and resolving critical problems.

In addition to maintaining the project schedule, the project's Control Center was also responsible for tracking costs so that potential problems were identified in advance, before budget shortfalls became insurmountable. Because construction was taking place in an inner city, the Control Center was also faced with issues concerning traffic congestion, emergency response, fire, safety and health, and the monitoring of events and accidents. The project ultimately established one of the most sophisticated control monitoring systems, whereby 400 cameras monitored all activities on the project sites as well as within the parameters of the city and beyond.

Schedule Controls Plan

Due to the sheer size of the Big Dig project, all schedule-related information was controlled through a hierarchical process managed by the Planning and Scheduling Department of the project's Controls Center (illustrated in Figure 6.4).

The project controls plan, shown in Table 6.3, lists the five levels of the time control program at the Big Dig, starting at the bottom with the detailed summary schedules prepared by the construction contractors, and then elevated to the section design consultants (SDCs) who were responsible for preparing performance and progress reports for each major deliverable. The management consultant was responsible for developing the interface schedule reflecting the owner's milestones and summarizing the activities for each major project area, broken down by phase. The complexity of this

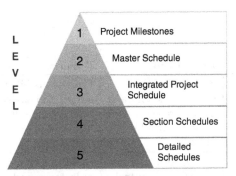

Figure 6.4 Hierarchy of Schedules Used on the Central Artery/Tunnel Project (CA/T)
Source: CA/T Project Procedure No. 207.

detailed process was compounded by the broad level of involvement from many participants, including federal, state, and city agencies, utility companies, private businesses, community groups, consultants, and suppliers.

Critical Path Method (CPM)

> The Critical Path was delayed while awaiting the approval of the Environment Impact Statement as you could not do eminent domain or other things until the environmental study was complete.
>
> —*Fred Salvucci, former Massachusetts*
> *secretary of transportation*

Managing schedule was a mammoth undertaking at the Big Dig and involved a large staff of engineers who managed the coordination of schedules among numerous projects. The project schedule was updated frequently for each and every design and construction package. Milestones and construction progress were updated monthly and shared with stakeholders in the project management monthly reports and the project's semiannual finance plans.

To keep track of schedule, the Critical Path Method (CPM) was used. CPM is a technique used to predict project duration by analyzing which sequence of activities has the least amount of scheduling flexibility. The method uses a mathematical algorithm to derive a logical and efficient order of activities and events. CPM has common attributes with the Project Evaluation Review Technique (PERT); however, CPM adopts a more controlling approach to schedule estimation, whereas PERT allows for probabilities and variances. For purposes of progress monitoring and reporting, the project's annual reports typically utilized simple bar charts with associated activity information.

Table 6.3   Central Artery Tunnel Project, Project Controls Plan

Level	Time Control Program	Description	Purpose	Responsible Party
1	Milestones	Summarize the activities(s) for each major project area, broken down by phase	Provide visibility at a high and easily understandable level of the project	Management consultant (consultant)
2	Master schedule	Major intermediate milestones, control points, and interfaces committed via planned and executed contracts	Reflects owner's milestones and establishes time criteria for all contract packages	Consultant
3	Integrated project schedule	Project interface schedule, which reflects a comprehensive summary of the scope of work from levels 4 and 5	Shows schedule integration requirement for each design and construction package	Consultant
4	Section schedules	Critical Path Method (CPM) network schedules, which represent all milestones, control points, activities, and scope for individual phases of the project on a section-by-section basis.	Reflects schedule requirement by package and actual progress by major deliverable	Preliminary design (consultant) After contract award section design consultant (SDC)/ contractor
5	Detailed schedules	Working level, CPM schedules integrated and interfaced by phase, area and/or organizational responsibility	Reflects detailed schedule requirements by package, phase, organizational responsibility, and actual progress by major deliverable	Preliminary design (consultant) After contract award (SDC)/ contractor

Source: (Schedule) Control Programs.

Under the CPM, the critical path is the sequence of activities that must be completed on time for the entire project to be completed on schedule. It is the longest-duration path through the project and represents the shortest amount of time in which a project can be completed. If an activity on the critical path is delayed by one day, the entire project will be delayed by one day unless another activity on the critical path can be finished a day earlier than planned.

Noncritical paths have float or slack associated with them. Total slack is the amount of time an activity can be delayed without delaying the finish date of the project. Free slack is the amount of time an activity can be delayed without delaying its successor activities. Ownership of float is typically a subject of controversy. The contractor wants to use float as a management tool to manage resources and keep the project on schedule. The owner usually desires to retain ownership of the float to reduce the impact of owner-initiated delays. Thus, ownership of float needs to be addressed in the contract documents to avoid costly disputes when delays occur.

In the Big Dig, with more than 9000 activities, multiple critical and non-critical paths existed within each contract and impacted several of the major milestones. Each of the multiple paths had to be evaluated independently, and each had risk exposures that required unique mitigation and control strategies. In addition to multiple critical paths, numerous paths were near critical and required close monitoring for exposures and schedule slippage. During the course of the project, constant planning was required to address potential new critical paths that arose due to resequencing or unanticipated events in the project schedule. Figure 6.5 demonstrates the complexity of multiple critical paths.

Critical Risk Exposures (CREs)

On the Big Dig, in addition to measuring the critical path, each contract involved an analysis of critical risk exposures. These varied from contract to

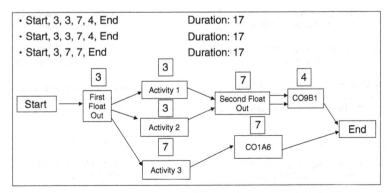

Figure 6.5   Network Diagram: Three Critical Paths
Source: Central Artery Tunnel Project Milestone Report.

contract, and as these exposures changed on a contract, so did the critical path. For example, major risk exposures that impacted schedule included design development, hazardous material removal, complexity of interfaces between contracts, unanticipated site conditions such as unchartered utilities, obstructions from old piles and seawalls, unexpected ground conditions, and archeological sites. Critical risk exposures were identified in the project's finance reports and in the project management monthly reports, as these exposures could have serious impacts on project schedule whether or not these impacts occurred on a critical path. Noncritical paths had to be carefully monitored for serious exposures that could change the status of that path to a critical path.

Time Control Processes

The critical processes in time control and the packaging of the project's numerous activities are highlighted in Figure 6.6. Starting with the owner's requirements and working from the bottom up, work packages were developed for all project contracts. The packages included extensive environmental and regulatory requirements based on the fact that the project was built through an inner city, with residents, businesses, government agencies, visitors, and

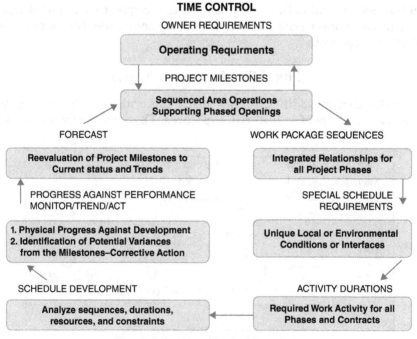

Figure 6.6   Time Control Processes
Source: Central Artery/Tunnel Project Control Procedures.

tourists impacted by the daily traffic disruption, and the dust, noise, and air quality generated by heavy equipment and excavation activity. Estimating activity durations and relationships on megaprojects is complicated by the sheer number of work packages and schedule requirements that require complex quantitative analysis. Schedule development included the analysis of resources, sequences, durations, and the constraints such as regulatory requirements and interfaces between contracts and external stakeholders.

Various tools and techniques were utilized to assess the status of project milestones, substantial completion, schedule variance, delay analysis, and the cost of schedule recovery versus schedule acceleration.

Tracking Schedule Progress

The program manager of large-scale complex projects must manage to the schedule by tracking actual progress against the schedule and comparing it to planned progress. The project managers should manage the schedule details within their projects, and the program manager should manage the cross-project schedule at the summary level. When a variance between planned versus actual schedule performance is identified, the program must institute techniques to avoid the impact of schedule delay.

Standard schedule control techniques utilized in projects include adding resources, managing slack time, outsourcing, and reducing scope to get the schedule back on track (Milosevic et al. 2007). To increase the probability of success, buffers are often introduced, depending on the size and complexity of the program.

One of the critical components in tracking schedule progress is the application of the earned value methodology (EVM). EVM integrates project scope, cost, and schedule measures to measure project performance and progress. The calculation of earned value must be consistently based on the physical progress of the work. The consistency by which work is measured ensures earned value accuracy. Earned value is used to determine current status of the project as well as long-term performance trends. On the Big Dig, earned value was used to forecast future performance, determine variances from budget, and project completion date and costs. PMI's the *PMBOK® Guide* provides an excellent overview of the principles of EVM and its application to any industry. A few of the earned value terms and formulas used on the Big Dig to measure schedule performance are listed as follows.

- Earned value (EV): Percent of the planned budget that has been completed multiplied by the planned budget—for example, if the total budget is $100 million and 20 percent of the work is completed, the earned value is $20 million.
- Planned value (PV): Estimated value of work planned at any point in time.
- Actual cost (AC): The sum of the cost of the work completed.

- Schedule variance (SV): The difference between the earned value and the planned value for the work completed to date. $SV = EV - PV$.
- Schedule performance index (SPI): The ratio of earned value to planned value. $SPI = EV/PV$.

Time Control Programs and Reports

In addition to the hierarchy of schedules and the time control processes and procedures, the project had numerous programs and reporting requirements that allowed input into the schedule process on a daily basis. For example, as shown in Table 6.4, there was an early identification and trend program and frequent meetings were held between the various project managers and senior project management to assess the project schedule and potential exposures and to identify actual versus scheduled progress.

PROJECT DELAYS

Ben Franklin, one of America's most influential Founding Fathers, described the value of time this way: *"Lost time is never found again."*

If this is true, what do you do when a project is late? When delayed, all projects face this difficult analysis as to how to recover lost time. The main question is whether it is more cost effective to recover schedule or to extend the schedule. Both schedule recovery (sometimes called *schedule acceleration*) and the extension of schedule are commonly used on projects to address delay, but each has its pros and cons.

Lost time is very expensive, as reflected in the large liquidated-damage provisions found in many construction contracts—sometimes as large as $1 million a day. Settlements for lost time are likewise huge, in the millions of dollars. In one case, a five-month delay cost the contractor $30 million, or $1.5 million for each week the project was delayed. To understand the impact of delay on the Big Dig, an analysis of the cost of recovering lost time versus the cost of delaying the project is presented here.

Schedule Recovery

Schedule recovery is when a project implements initiatives to overcome serious obstacles to the critical or near-critical paths. As an example, on the Big Dig, if a critical path activity fell behind planned progress by more than five percent, and the cause of the delay was within the contractor's control, the resident engineer, after consulting with the area construction manager, requested a recovery plan from the contractor that explained the proposed actions to regain lost time (CA/T Procedure 601). Some examples of schedule recovery mechanisms used on the Big Dig are described in Table 6.5.

Table 6.4   Time Control Programs and Reports

Time Control Programs and Reports	What	Why	How	When
Early identification and trend programs	Identify potential schedule variances for milestone	Provide client with early notice of potential schedule variances and establish subsequent action	Continuous evaluation of schedule	Continuous
Quarterly assessments	Review of management consultant work program schedule status	Provide owner with quarterly work program schedule status	Identify status of actual versus scheduled progress for management consultant	Quarterly
Progress meetings	Meetings between contractors and resident engineers	To identify potential exposures	Compare actual versus scheduled progress	Weekly
Project management monthly (PMM)	Comparison of actuals versus planned for consultants/contractors	Assess on a monthly basis the performance of each contract	Comparison of actual progress versus planned progress	Monthly
Finance plan/cost schedule updates	Milestone baseline report	Identifies recovery plans and exposures	An all-years' schedule summary	Semiannually
Change order control program	Changes to consultant/contractor contract schedule	Identifies, authorizes, and tracks changes to contract time	Negotiated with consultant/contractor	Continuous
Deliverables report	List of major contract deliverables for management consultant	Provide actual versus contracted status	Letter providing current status of major contract deliverables	Annually

Source: Central Artery/Tunnel Project. 1996. Controls Plan, Procedure 6.4 Time Controls Program.

Table 6.5   Schedule Recovery Mechanisms

Schedule Recovery Mechanism	Methodology
1. Acceleration (adding more resources)	Schedule is accelerated through overtime, weekend shifts, or adding resources and equipment to speed up completion time.
2. Reducing scope	Scope is modified through design changes to simplify or remove scope and allow contractors earlier access to a work site.
3. Fast-track construction	The sequencing of construction activities enables some portions of the project to begin before the design is completed on other portions of the project. The Big Dig utilized fast-track design and construction delivery methods to reduce costs and overall project time. This process works best when the design of each work package is complete and the impact of requirements of the later segments can be anticipated.
4. Resequencing and staged access	This allows contractors to work in all available areas.

Source: Central Artery/Tunnel Project. March 15, 2000. Finance Plan Update.

Extension of Schedule

At the Big Dig, schedule recovery was always the first approach, rather than extending the schedule, as it is usually the less costly option. This was due to the fast-track nature of the project, as a delay for one contractor always affects several other interfacing or successor contractors. For instance, if contractors were scheduled to build a tunnel box in the casting basin on January 1, 2000, and the casting basin would not be completed until June 1, 2000, there would be a six-month delay that had to be recovered through one of the four mechanisms listed in Table 6.5.

Based on quantitative assessments, as a general proposition, it is more economical to pay acceleration costs to maintain schedule than to extend the schedule and pay the added contractor overhead and construction management costs. When a project is late, these significant cost exposures include the following:

1. Delay costs to contractors (extended time for overheads—labor/equipment)
2. Escalation costs for existing and unawarded contracts
3. Additional project management costs for maintaining a presence longer

The estimated additional cash needed if the project had been delayed would have been $330 million. The project completed a "Road User Benefit" study to demonstrate that the benefits of project acceleration could be worth as much as approximately $1 million per day to achieve the I-90 and I-93 milestones. Based on the projected delays, accelerating the project was worth about $200 million for I-90 and $146 million for I-93 (CA/T 2000).

THE BIG DIG LESSONS FROM PRACTICE: CALCULATING DELAY COSTS—BOTTOM UP

Delay costs on the Big Dig were calculated by preparing two separate scenarios: (1) a six-month design delay and (2) a twelve-month construction delay. The worst-case situation for both design and construction delay combined was evaluated. For simplicity, delays were applied at the peak workloads and for a sustained duration. The bottom-up estimate more accurately reflected the impact of delays, as it took into consideration the resource type and the work being performed. A relatively lower delay cost during design was indicative of the ability to quickly mobilize and demobilize consultant design staff. Higher delay costs during the construction phase reflected the fact that mobilization and demobilization of staff are not viable options for short-term sporadic delays in a construction environment. The bottom-up delay costs captured the higher end of delay costs by applying a sustained level at the peak staffing level. Delay costs may actually be lower if the delays occur earlier in the project, when staffing levels are much lower. The bottom-up method segregated the specific costs and clarified the relationship between the functional components and the contingency components of the estimate.

Comparison of Delay versus Recovery Costs

In 2000, the Central Artery/Tunnel Project staff calculated the total delay cost of not proceeding with recommended acceleration initiatives on I-90 and I-93 to be $416 million, and total costs of acceleration of the I-90 and I-93 contracts to be $357 million, as shown in Table 6.6.

Table 6.6   Estimating Delay and Recovery Costs

Delay Costs	Recovery Costs
Access by interfacing contractors	Earlier access to site
Extended contractor overhead	Additional labor but less overtime
Bid escalation for unawarded contracts for one year	Avoidance of bid escalation
Additional cost for construction management and project administrative staff	Reduction in staff

Source: O'Brien Kreitzberg Cost Validation Study, 3-10–3-11.

Solution: In addition to the costs in column 1 of Table 6.6, further delay would prevent realization of significant transportation and land use benefits by approximately one year. User benefits were approximately $600,000 per day (more than $12 million per month) for the I-90 segment and $400,000 per day (more than $8 million per month) for I-93. Adding these factors into the calculation further weighs toward the schedule recovery options selected by the project. Based on a comparison of the costs of delay versus the cost of acceleration and contrasting the additional cost of delay of $59 million, the project decided to proceed with the schedule recovery options highlighted in column 2 of Table 6.6 to realize the full savings.

INCENTIVES AS TACTICS FOR KEEPING ON SCHEDULE

> Incentives are not strategy, they are tactics. Defensive measures.
>
> *—Carlos Ghosn*

We cannot conclude this chapter without discussing the impact of incentives on early completion of a contract or milestone. Incentives are tools used by an owner or project manager in an effort to align the goals of other project participants with those of the owner. Contract incentives typically reward or penalize a project contractor or team for failure to meet agreed-upon performance requirements. Positive incentives typically have some type of financial benefit, whereas negative incentives generally result in a financial loss, such as a penalty or reduction in fees. Project incentives must be aligned with key business success opportunities. Incentives should be made measurable and objective, using relevant benchmarks, and those benchmarks should be monitored, controlled and enforced throughout the life of the project.

Is it true that incentives get people to work harder? Are they likely to produce a better product? Are they likely to produce it faster? Are they likely to get work done in a safer way? It is remarkable that surprisingly little research has been done on this subject, yet for some time the practice of using incentives has been acceptable practice to the Federal Highway Administration (FHWA).

The contract provision of incentives/disincentives (I/D) for early completion compensates the contractor a certain amount of money for each day identified critical work is completed ahead of schedule and assesses a deduction for each day the contractor overruns the I/D time. Its use is intended primarily for those critical projects where traffic inconvenience and delays are to be held to a minimum. The amounts are based upon estimates of such items as traffic safety, traffic maintenance, and road user delay costs.

FHWA Policy on Incentives

The FHWA policy that prohibited participation in bonus payments for early completion was rescinded effective July 13, 1984, based on studies showing that I/D provisions are a valuable, cost-effective construction tool (FHWA 1989). Present FHWA policy allows for approval of I/D provisions that are in compliance with the intent of the FHWA program. This may include but is not limited to: (1) provisions for early completion of critical improvements that result in significant savings and/or positive benefits to the traveling public and (2) provisions that allow for product acceptance with pay adjustments.

When using I/D for early completion to minimize public inconvenience, maximize public safety, and reduce total costs to the traveling public, important provisions recommended by FHWA include the following:

1. The pay schedule should relate money and time.
2. Incentive payments should have a specified maximum time.
3. Disincentive payments should be charged continuously until the critical elements of the project have been completed.

In 2000, the Big Dig's project management consultant was awarded a new contract that included extra profits if the project's final $14 billion price tag was reduced by $250 million. It is significant, however, that there was no penalty in the contract if the Big Dig was not completed on time, and the five-year contract could be extended a year if work was delayed (Palmer 2000). Public policy experts have criticized project structures that provide for incentives when things go right but no penalties when things go wrong (Primack 2006).

Incentive Models for Megaprojects

Incentives play an important role in construction contracts, but they, alone, do not assure project success. Structuring an effective incentive program can be a complex undertaking. The basic principle of incentive contracting is simply to take advantage of a contractor's general objective to maximize his profits by giving him the opportunity to earn a greater profit if he performs the contract efficiently. A major benefit of incentives is the potential for creating a more cooperative relationship between the contracting parties and to strengthen the cultural shift away from the traditional, adversarial approach to contracting. Some models of successful incentive structures and programs include the following:

1. An excellent example of incentives that went right was the Big Dig's Safety and Health Awards for Recognized Excellence (SHARE) program. As described in Chapter 9, this program managed to dramatically reduce anticipated worker and third-party injuries and resulted in record-breaking lost time and occupational safety and health recordables well below national averages.

2. The United Kingdom's Terminal 5 Project at Heathrow Airport provides another model for incentivizing contractors. Unlike typical contracts where the risks are shared, the project owner, the British Airports Authority (BAA), developed a unique type of cost-plus incentive contract in which the owner pays the constructor the actual cost plus a profit margin. BAA assumed full responsibility for most of the risk, insured the total program, and worked collaboratively in integrated teams to develop innovative solutions to complex problems (Doherty 2008).

3. Incentives based on competitive factors such as contract provisions that require frequent reviews, termination for failure to meet milestones, and renegotiation of major contract terms including compensation and performance requirements will allow project owners and sponsors greater leverage in negotiating more favorable terms in the future. If a public owner has agreed to a long term contract without measurable performance requirements the government's ability to renegotiate or terminate these contracts is severely limited.

4. Whatever structure is used, incentives will not work without specific measurable performance goals in the contract. These incentive fees may be based on long-term goals related to achieving overall project cost and schedule performance goals during a given year, or they may be based on fiscal management, value engineering, quality management, risk and safety management, or other specific activities. However, the performance time must be sufficient to assess whether or not the goals have truly been achieved or whether in meeting schedule and cost goals, quality and safety have been sacrificed. Meeting schedule and cost goals should never be traded for safety and quality, thus sometimes requiring the deferment of incentive payments until all aspects of project performance can be verified.

Further research is critically needed on the impact of incentives and disincentives on project performance so that governments can implement more effective public policy for future projects.

Liquidated Damages

In discussing incentives/disincentive provisions, a clear distinction needs to be made between the intent of I/D provisions and liquidated damages. Although they have similar mechanisms, the purpose or function of each is different. The liquidated damages policy has as a prime function the recovery of construction, engineering, and/or additional costs associated with the contractor's failure to complete the project on time. The I/D provision is intended to motivate the contractor so that work will be completed on or ahead of schedule and under budget in compliance with all requirements. Liquidated damages provisions apply to all projects; however, I/D provisions apply only to special projects.

LESSONS LEARNED

1. Understand the impact of a schedule-driven project on quality, cost, and risk, and document all assumptions.
2. Delay in approval of Environmental Feasibility Studies can impact the critical path and the overall project budget.
3. Disputes over design development can have a serious impact on schedule and the critical path. The potential exposure from delay caused by design development issues needs to be included in the project budget and finance plans.
4. Fast-tracking has both benefits and limitations. Fast-tracking works best when the design of each work package is complete and the impact of requirements of the later segments can be anticipated. The downside is changes and overruns if work packages have to be started before the design work is done.
5. Contingencies should be built in for both schedule and cost and updated on a regular basis, but not less than annually, to determine the true cost of the project.
6. Plan for uncertainty by funding a contingency for construction delays and delays caused by third-party exposures such as regulatory changes and utility relocations.
7. Consider from the inception of the project the kind of incentive that will optimize positive behavior and produce a better product, and the type of penalty that will reduce negative behavior, and then enforce these provisions.
8. Distinguish between schedule recovery and schedule delay, and assess the impact of delayed realization of transportation and land use benefits; add these factors into the cost of schedule recovery options.
9. Ownership of schedule float must be detailed in the contract documents to avoid costly disputes.

BEST PRACTICES

1. Cost recovery is always difficult, but it's harder when you complicate it with a system driven by schedule. Clear specifications on responsibility for fault should be built into every contract, and those provisions should be rigidly enforced.
2. As a basis for progress monitoring and progress payment, the owner should receive from the contractor a weekly progress report that indicates actual start and finish dates for all activities in progress, percentages of completion, and activities that the contractor plans to start the following week.
3. The full impact of fast-tracking should be considered from the inception of the project, and potential exposures should be incorporated into the project budget.

4. Build in contingencies not just for cost but also for time.
5. The local community may not like delays, but if you communicate directly with the traveling public they will be more supportive.
6. Addressing schedule problems early on will minimize the negative impact on scope and budget. Patterns of delay on a megaproject must be analyzed for root causes, as falling behind on megaprojects results in substantial additional cost and can impact scope or quality decisions.
7. Maintain short reporting periods so that corrective actions may be taken earlier in the project.
8. Engineers should be given more responsibility in developing schedules so that more realistic schedules can be produced, and they will be more committed to keeping those schedules.

SUMMARY

The most effective way to manage schedule in a complex organization like the Big Dig is to focus on the following strategies: (1) development of a schedule hierarchy that includes a bottom-up analysis; (2) establishment of an integrated change control process; (3) creation of a milestone management system that monitors and controls the problems of multiple critical and near-critical paths and critical risk exposures; and (4) development of an incentive structure that motivates workers to not only keep on schedule but also meet all performance requirements including risk, quality, and budget. Keeping the project on time on a complex megaproject requires an elaborate structure, an integrated system, and, most important, careful planning on the front end.

ETHICAL CONSIDERATIONS

As you learned in this chapter, recovering costs from the designer for errors and omissions and recovering back charges from contractors for failure to follow specifications and contractual obligations are critical factors in controlling costs. Cost recovery is always difficult, but it's harder when you complicate it with a system driven by schedule. Clear specifications on responsibility for fault should be built into every contract, and those provisions should be rigidly enforced. When something goes wrong:

1. Is it the owner's fault for advertising bids before design was complete?
2. Is it the contractor's fault for going ahead and building the structure with insufficient drawings?
3. What are the ethical questions that are raised here? What are the implications for schedule-driven projects?

DISCUSSION QUESTIONS

Project, program, and portfolio managers all face the same key questions when addressing the project schedule. On a megaproject, these questions are compounded. Respond to each of the following questions, drawing examples from your assigned readings as well as the project management literature.

1. How will you manage the interdependencies among the project management areas?
2. Why must projects have both incentives and disincentives to ensure early contract completion? What is the difference between these two strategies? Do you think incentives or disincentives would be more effective, and why?
3. How will you track, review, and regulate progress to meet performance objectives?
4. What processes and procedures will you need to perform integrated change control?
5. To maintain project schedule, what types of data should be collected during reporting periods?
6. If the project needs to be accelerated, what kinds of activities would be the primary focus? Why? If the project needs to be delayed, what are the major financial risks and impacts that the project faces? Why?
7. What are the major issues a megaproject must address concerning the critical path? What options are available if activities on this path are delayed?
8. Provide three examples of performance measurements you would recommend for a megaproject like the Big Dig and how would you monitor, control and enforce those measurements.
9. Carlos Ghosn, famous for running two companies on the Fortune Global 500 simultaneously, describes incentives as follows: Incentives are not strategy, they are tactics. Defensive measures. Do you agree with this opinion? Why or why not?

REFERENCES

Board on Infrastructure and the Construction Environment. 2003. *Completing the Big Dig: Managing the Final Stages of Boston's Central Artery/Tunnel Project, Committee for Review of the Project Management Practices Employed on the Boston Central Artery/Tunnel ("Big Dig")*. National Academy of Engineering, National Research Council, Transportation Research Board of the National Academies (National Academy). Washington, DC: National Academies Press.

Carson, C. W. 2010. "Design and Development of a Schedule Management Plan." PMI Global Congress Proceedings, Dublin, Ireland.

CA/T (Central Artery [I-93]/Tunnel [I-90] Project). 1990. *Final Environmental Impact Statement Report (FEIS / R)*. Boston: Massachusetts Department of Public Works.

CA/T (Central Artery/Tunnel Project). 1996. Controls Plan. Time Controls Program. Boston: Massachusetts Highway Department.

CA/T (Central Artery/Tunnel Project). 1996. Finance Plan. (February.) Boston: Massachusetts Highway Department.

CA/T (Central Artery/Tunnel Project). 2000. Finance Plan. Boston: Massachusetts Turnpike Authority.

CA/T (Central Artery/Tunnel Project). 2001. Finance Plan. Boston: Massachusetts Turnpike Authority.

CA/T (Central Artery/Tunnel Project). 2003. Finance Plan. (October.) Boston: Massachusetts Turnpike Authority, 21–25.

CA/T (Central Artery/Tunnel Project). 2005. Finance Plan. Boston: Massachusetts Turnpike Authority, 6.

CA/T (Central Artery/Tunnel Project). 2007. Project Schedule Evolution from 1976–2007 Cost and Schedule Update. Boston: Massachusetts Turnpike Authority.

CA/T (Central Artery/Tunnel Project). Project Procedure, Section 601, Schedule and Progress, Schedule Review and Acceptance, Resident Engineer Follow-up Actions.

CA/T (Central Artery/Tunnel Project). Procedure No. 207, Hierarchy of Project Schedules.

Doherty, S. 2008. *Heathrow's Terminal Five: History in the Making*. Chichester, West Sussex, England: John Wiley & Sons, Ltd.

FHWA (Federal Highway Administration). 1989. *Technical Advisory*, Incentive/Disincentive (I/D) for Early Completion. T 5080.10. February 8.

GAO (U. S. General Accounting Office). 2002. *Highway Infrastructure: Preliminary Information on the Timely Completion of Highway Construction Projects*. Katherine Siggerud, acting director, Physical Infrastructure Issues. Testimony before the Committee on Environment and Public Works, U.S. Senate. Washington, DC: U.S. General Accounting Office.

GAO (U.S. General Accounting Office). 2003. *Highway Infrastructure: Perceptions of Stakeholders on Approaches to Reduce Highway Project Completion Time*. Report to the Ranking Minority Member, Committee on Environment and Public Works. U.S. Senate (GAO-03-398). Washington, DC: U.S. General Accounting Office.

Hughes, T. P. 2000. *Rescuing Prometheus*. New York: Vintage Books, 239–240.

Hussain, R., and S. Wearne. 2005. "Problems and Needs of Project Management in the Process and Other Industries." *Transactions of the Institution of Chemical Engineers* Part A (April).

Miller, J. B. 1997. *America's Emerging Public / Private Infrastructures Strategy: The End of Privatization*. Cambridge, MA: Massachusetts Institute of Technology.

Miller, R., and B. Hobbs. 2006. "Managing Risks and Uncertainty in Major Projects in the New Global Environment." In *Global Project Management Handbook*, 9–2 and 9–11.

Milosevic, D., R. J. Marinelli, and J. M. Waddell. 2007. *Program Management for Improved Results*. Hoboken, NJ: John Wiley & Sons, Inc., 213.

NCHRP (National Council Highway Research Program). 2006. *Washington*, DC: Transportation Research Board of the National Academies.

OBK (O'Brien Krietzberg). 2000. *Cost Validation Study of the Central / Artery Tunnel Project*. Boston: Massachusetts Turnpike Authority.

OSA (Massachusetts Office of the State Auditor). 2000. *A Review of the Central Artery / Tunnel Project Cost Recovery Program*. Report No. 98-4061-3. February.

Palmer, T. 2000. "Cost Incentives Drive Boston's Latest 'Big Dig' Highway-Tunnel Contract." *Boston Globe*.

Paulson, B. 1976. "Designing to Reduce Construction Costs." *ASCE Journal of the Construction Division, Journal of Construction Engineering and Management*. From a paper presented at ASCE Conference, San Diego, CA. April 1976, 587–592.

PMI (Project Management Institute). 2013. *A Guide to the Project Management Body of Knowledge (PMBOK® Guide)*—Fifth Edition. Newtown Square, PA: Project Management Institute.

Primack, P. 2006. "Learning from the Big Dig." *Commonwealth: Politics, Ideas and Civic Life in Massachusetts*. Boston: Massachusetts Institute for a New Commonwealth (MassINC), 61.

Salvucci, F. 2012. Interview with Fred Salvucci, former Massachusetts secretary of state. June 22.

Chapter 7

Cost History

Murphy's Law, enhanced: "Anything that can go wrong will go wrong...at the most inopportune time...and with the most damaging results." And from Murphy's more realistic relative comes O'Toole's Law: "Murphy was an optimist."

INTRODUCTION

The characteristics of megaprojects are unique, involving complex technology and numerous uncertainties, diverse stakeholder management, abundant claims and changes, political realities, and significant public concerns. Therefore, megaprojects require specialized knowledge of cost estimation and cost estimation management, which are critical to the project's success. Training in such specialties often comes after major problems have arisen, when it is far too late to be effective.

The Big Dig, as with most megaprojects, is well known for its numerous cost escalations and its rapidly increasing budget, with a final cost of approximately $14.8 billion. This chapter breaks down the project's cost elements and explains the reality behind them.

MEGAPROJECT COST ESTIMATION RESEARCH

On admitting program management failure I would say that what we've gotten for a half billion dollars is an unpronounceable acronym [DIMHRS].

—*Robert Gates, 22nd U.S. secretary of defense*

The preceding quote from former U.S. defense secretary Robert Gates highlights the impact of the massive failure of a major government program. The Defense Integrated Military Human Resources System (DIMHRS) was

214

an enterprise program within the U.S. Department of Defense (DoD). As the largest enterprise resource planning program ever implemented for human resources, DIMHRS was to subsume or replace more than 90 legacy systems and bring all payroll and personnel functions for the U.S. Army, and eventually the entire military, into one integrated Web-based system. In February 2010, after 10 years and $850 million, as well as numerous delays, technical problems, and other issues, the DoD cancelled the program. Though this is an extreme example of a government program gone wrong, cost increases and failures on megaprojects are common, as evidenced by the growing research on project cost estimation. For example, the U.S. Government Accountability Office (GAO), in a 2008 study of 72 major defense acquisition projects, found cost overruns of 26 percent, totaling $295 billion over the life of the projects. It is significant that, of the 72 programs assessed that year, no program had proceeded through system development meeting the defense acquisition program's best practices standards for mature technologies, stable design, and mature production processes—all prerequisites for achieving planned cost, schedule, and performance outcomes (GAO 2008).

Infrastructure projects known for high costs are numerous and include the English Channel Tunnel (the "Chunnel"), the Great Belt Rail Tunnel, the Denver International Airport, and Wembley Stadium for the 2012 Olympics in London, which holds the record as the most costly stadium ever built at $1.98 billion. In their review of large public works projects over the last century, Flyvbjerg et al. (2002) concluded that megaprojects are consistently underestimated, a phenomenon often attributed to the desire of the project advocates to have their projects approved. This conclusion is shared by others (Miller and Lessard 2000; Merrow 1988).

Additional reasons for cost increases include inaccurate scope, unreasonably aggressive schedules, and political pressure to stay within budget (Chang 2002). Large projects also have long lives and idiosyncratic features that contribute to their complexity (Esty 2004). Merrow's widely cited 1988 report explores costs, problems, and operations of megaprojects by examining 52 civilian projects ranging in cost from $500 million to over $10 billion (in 1984 dollars). He observes that most of the projects in his database met their performance goals, many met their schedule goals, but few met their cost goals (Merrow 1988). He concludes that the most important correlate of cost growth and schedule slippage is the relationship between a megaproject and the governments within whose jurisdiction it is built. Among the factors he cites are problems with environmental regulations, health and safety rules, and government restrictions on labor and procurement practices that conflict with the desires of the project managers (Merrow 1988).

In a major study of megaprojects, Altschuler and Luberoff, two Harvard scholars, noted that dramatic cost escalation of the kind seen on the Big Dig, though a shock locally, "was not out of the ordinary for a major highway project," citing the examples of the Century Freeway and the Woodrow Wilson Bridge near Washington, D.C. An important conclusion they gleaned from the study: "While private rent-seekers and public entrepreneurs are invaluable sources of energy and ingenuity in the evolution of urban mega-projects, local champions of environmental protection, of neighborhood preservation, and of fiscal sobriety have no less valuable roles to play. Further, in seeking the wisest balance among these multiple perspectives, there are no good substitutes for representative democracy, empowered and required to approve all major projects, and a vibrant local pluralism" (Altschuler and Luberoff 2003).

COST GROWTH HISTORY ON THE BIG DIG

> Beware of the little expenses; a small leak will sink a great ship.
>
> —*Benjamin Franklin*

As shown in Figure 7.1, the initial estimated cost of the Big Dig in 1985 was $2.56 billion, but in 2007 the project reached a final budget of approximately $14.8 billion, almost six times the original estimate. Explanations for this massive project cost increase abound and range from excessive spending on improvements for nearby neighborhoods and private businesses to unanticipated subsurface conditions, to accounting assumptions, to the long length of the project. Project management costs also increased. This was due to extended staffing resulting from schedule extensions and the challenges of managing unique and varied construction problems with complex interfaces

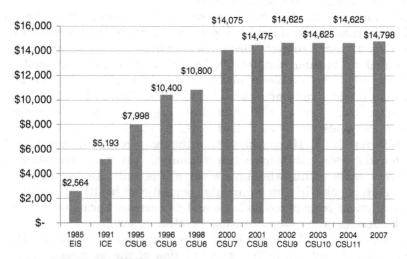

EIS = Environmental Impact Statement
ICE = Interstate Cost Estimate
CSU = Cost and Schedule Update

Figure 7.1 Cost History, Central Artery/Tunnel Budget (1985–2007)
Source: Central Artery/Tunnel Project (CA/T). 2007. (May.) Cost/Schedule Update.

and numerous diverse and often conflicting stakeholder interests. In 2007, the project prepared a history of the project scope and cost since inception (CA/T 2007), which is summarized in Table 8.1 in Chapter 8. Though it provides a year-by-year description of the major increases in scope and the cost escalations, it fails to break down the specific reasons for and the details behind these cost increases. The large increases for costs, contingency, design development, and to maintain the project schedule raise systemic problems in the project's cost growth history.

Extensive research, audits, and financial reporting provide evidence of the major causes for this cost growth, though these numbers are far from exact. Our focus here is on these six key Big Dig cost growth areas: (1) changes in preliminary concept and design development, (2) subsurface conditions, (3) schedule delays, (4) inflation, (5) potential change allowances, and (6) political realities.

1. Changes in Preliminary Concept and Design Development

In 1985, the initial cost estimate of $2.56 billion for the Big Dig was based on preliminary concepts before detailed technical studies had been completed (Table 7.1). In the years that followed, the project design was changed in response to environmental concerns and community demands. As noted by the Big Dig's management consultant, the process of developing cost estimates for the Big Dig was therefore evolutionary, as it was not possible at the beginning to anticipate with precision all final design and program decisions that would be made by the state and the other interested parties, as well as the extent and nature of unanticipated conditions that impact cost and schedule (B/PB 2003).

One major change made in the early years was shifting the proposed location of the tunnels under the Fort Point Channel in response to historic preservation rules and the concerns of the Gillette Corporation, whose world headquarters were in the proposed path of the project's tunnels. Other major changes were the redesign of the airport interchange based on the concerns of the residents of East Boston and the redesign of the Charles River Crossing that connected the Central Artery with four local roadways. Environmental compliance alone increased project cost by an estimated $3 billion. The major environmental change was disposal of excavated material on Spectacle Island, to create a harbor island park, instead of in the waters outside of Boston Harbor.

To address concerns from a host of groups, including the City of Boston and the City of Cambridge, the final design concept was not approved until 1994, almost 11 years after the issuance of the first Environmental Impact Report (EIS), and at an additional cost of a billion dollars. According to the Central Artery/Tunnel Project's finance reports, the Big Dig entered into more than 1500 separate mitigation agreements, accounting for at least one-third of the project's total costs. Mitigation agreements were entered

Table 7.1   1985 Project Cost Estimate

1985 CA/T Project Cost Estimate	($, millions)						
Construction Items	North Area	Central Area	South Bay	South Boston	Boston Harbor	East Boston	Project Total
Tunnel Structures	43	204	153	128	155	96	779
Ventilation Building and Equipment	7	17	11	18	0	11	64
Total Facilities and Equipment	0	0	0	4	0	0	4
Grade-Separated Structures	87	18	85	44	0	18	252
Lateral Support and Underpinning	36	271	126	38	0	87	558
Earthwork	13	89	50	52	39	37	280
Dredging	0	0	0	0	6	0	6
Roadways at Grade	2	7	6	3	0	5	23
Utility Relocations	4	40	28	6	0	8	86
Miscellaneous	14	33	80	7	3	15	152
Construction Total	206	679	539	300	204	276	2,204
Engineering and Contingencies (10%)	21	68	54	30	20	27	220
Right-of-Way	43	7	24	44	0	22	140
Total Project Cost	270	754	617	374	224	325	2,564

Source: Massachusetts Department of Public Works. August 1985.

into with the project's numerous stakeholders concerned about such matters as improvement of park areas; traffic congestion; alternative forms of transportation; materials disposal; dust, rat, and noise control; bridge design; wetlands; waterways; and air and water quality. The project's Mitigation Program Office worked closely with the project Public Information Office and the Community Liaison Office to disseminate information regarding construction mitigation during both the design and construction periods.

2. Subsurface Conditions

Apart from the numerous design development challenges caused by outside influences, the most difficult problems on the Big Dig involved the subsurface conditions faced during design and construction. Subsurface conditions that materially differ from data in preconstruction documents require a change in design and construction plans and contractual requirements. The combination of high water table and filled land mandated techniques in earth support, dewatering and reinjection, ground freezing, and excavation that had never before been implemented.

As described by one Bechtel engineer, "The soil beneath the city has a little bit of everything." The Big Dig tunnels had to be dug through four distinctly different types of soil—fill at the surface, followed by organics (silt, sand, etc.); a marine soil known as Boston "blue clay"; and, finally, a layer of boulders, gravel, and clay (glacial till) sitting atop the bedrock (Einstein 2012).

A particularly large and deep deposit of the blue clay complicated proposed excavations to construct tunnels connecting the Ted Williams Tunnel, the Central Artery tunnels, and the Massachusetts Turnpike. Even small, shallow excavations would collapse without support. The solution was to combine the clay with cement, a "deep soil mixing" technique developed in Japan that makes the soil harder and thus easier to excavate, and makes it act as a buttress. Even that was not simple. To access the areas where soil needed to be improved, existing structures had to be moved. The tunnel ground freezing and jacking operations produced another level of unknown conditions and construction claims.

These differing site claims addressed groundwater, soil instability, uncharted utilities, archeological discoveries, environmental problems, safety and health issues, frequent design changes, and changes in schedules. Construction costs increased throughout the project and across all contracts as a result of these subsurface conditions. As of September 30, 2004, the project reported that differing subsurface conditions represented about 19 percent of the almost $2 billion in requested claims and changes—a big number by any count.

3. Schedule Delays

Schedule delays were another significant reason for cost increases on the Big Dig. The impact of schedule delays on project budgets is often seriously underestimated because delays can impact funding, particularly when the project involves important community interests such as transportation and environmental concerns. In a 2006 interview, the Big Dig's former assistant project director, James Rooney described the problem:

> When I was at the [Big Dig], Bechtel pushed hard that cost follows schedule, that if you stick to the schedule, the rest will sort itself out.
>
> **(Primack 2006)**

As discussed in Chapter 6, the Big Dig was a schedule-driven project with little or no contingency budget for delays. This problem became apparent in 2000, when $300 million was needed for schedule maintenance, requiring the infusion of additional funds. The term *schedule maintenance* deserves definition. It refers to money additional to the value of the contract that the owner

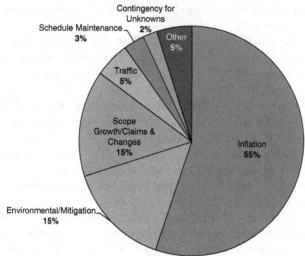

Figure 7.2   Reasons for Cost Growth on the Big Dig
Source: W. Edwards. "Project History." Presentation to the National Research Council
and the National Council of Engineering Committee for Review of the Project
Management Practices Employed on the Central Artery/Tunnel Project, October 21, 2002
(Board 2003).

pays the construction contractor to maintain the schedule required by his contract. The only reason the owner should have to pay additional monies to the construction contractor is to cover additional contractor expenses incurred as a result of an owner-caused change in the contract of the construction contractor, a change that would delay completion of the work as required by the contract. Figure 7.2 shows that schedule maintenance in 2002 cost 3 percent of the total budget.

Every Big Dig contract had a provision that required the contractor to pay what are known as *liquidated damages* (damages agreed upon ahead of time) if the schedule was delayed due to the fault of the contractor. Conversely, when the owner was the cause of the delay, the increased costs were paid by the owner—in effect, the taxpayer. This might occur, for example, if the owner required design changes that were not in the original contract. However, the owner was not responsible for paying for schedule delays on Contractor B's work caused by Contractor A, assuming the two contractors had no legal relationship.

Lessons Learned: Owner-Caused Delays   An example of an owner-caused change occurred on the Big Dig when the management consultant was forced to issue requests for proposals (RFPs) before the subject design had been completed. This was the result of a federal funding rule that required spending allotted federal money by a specific date, whether or not construction was complete, or losing it altogether. Those incomplete bid packages resulted in extra costs to the project due to changes in the contract documents from the time of bid to the time of completion of the design, which was after the bids had been received by the construction contractors.

The first lesson here is that no request for proposal should ever be released for bid until it is complete. Knowingly releasing an incomplete bid package contributed to increased costs in construction, which are always far greater than increased costs associated with completing the design. Steel and concrete are always far more expensive to change than are paper and ink! Common sense cried out for this rule to be changed to at least allow appeal and review on an individual basis. An alternate solution to this particular problem is to include the fund expiration dates in your schedule as a major milestone and track your progress toward completing all the necessary paperwork to ensure that RFPs or bid documents are released in a timely and complete manner.

The second lesson learned is that all project budgets should have contingencies built into them not only for cost but also for time. To prevent this problem, all projects within the program should (1) establish a schedule reserve with an associated contingency or (2) establish funds to cover schedule slips, or both.

4. Inflation

Extensive project research demonstrates that a key factor in the cost overruns for many projects is the effect of inflation, and the Big Dig was no different (Akinci and Fischer 1998; Arditi et al. 1985; Board 2003; Booz·Allen 1995; Hufschmidt and Gerin 1970; Merrow 1988; Pickrell 1990; Pickrell 1992; Touran and Bolster 1994).

Project schedule changes, particularly extensions, caused by budget constraints or design changes can result in unanticipated increases in inflation costs even when the rate of inflation has been accurately predicted.

It is best to think in terms of the time value of money and recognize that there are two components to the issue: (1) the inflation rate and (2) the timing of the expenditures. Many projects have a fixed annual or biannual budget, and project schedules must often be adjusted to ensure that project funding is available for all contracts as needed. Estimators frequently do not know what expenditure timing adjustments will be made (Board 2003; Booz-Allen 1995; Callahan 1998; Hufschmidt 1970; Semple et al. 1994; Touran 1994).

The time value of money can adversely affect projects when: (1) project estimates are not communicated in year-of-construction costs, (2) the project completion is delayed and therefore the cost is subject to inflation over a longer duration than anticipated, and/or (3) the rate of inflation is greater than anticipated in the estimate. The construction industry has varying views regarding how inflation should be accounted for in the project estimates and in budgets by funding sources. In the case of projects with short development and construction schedules, the effect of inflation is usually minor; however, projects having long development and construction durations can encounter unanticipated inflationary effects.

The results of these inflation effects are evident in the Big Dig. The original estimate for this project, which was developed in 1982 and based on the Federal Highway Administration (FHWA) guidelines in the *Interstate Cost Estimate (ICE) Manual*, excluded inflationary factors.

As highlighted in Figure 7.2, 55 percent of the reported increase in cost as of 2002 was estimated by the project team to be due to inflation. The project's estimate of inflation was derived from the *Engineering News-Record*'s Building Cost Index (BCI) and the Construction Cost index (CCI) combined into a single index (Board 2003). The calculated yearly average inflation rate using the BCI and CCI indexes for the 24-year span of the project from 1982 to 2006 was equal to about 3 percent "per year." Considering that in 2002 the approximate growth in the budget was $12 billion ($14.6 billion minus the original cost estimate of $2.6 billion), the shockingly high number of approximately $6.6 billion was attributed to inflation. This figure has never been explained nor justified but was accepted by the project owner, the project sponsor (the FHWA), and the National Academies Review of the Central Artery/Tunnel Project in 2003 (Board 2003).

Significantly, the McCormack Institute estimated in 1997 that about 30 to 35 percent of the cost of the project could be attributed to the required tunneling and interchange construction alone, about 25 to 30 percent to the measures needed to mitigate the impacts of the construction and meet required environmental standards, and up to 40 percent to account for inflation and cost escalation resulting from a 25-year design and construction period (McCormack 1997).

5. Potential Change Allowance (PCA)

The Big Dig project's contingency budget, known as the potential change allowance (PCA) was utilized to estimate the costs for non-schedule-related contract changes. For example, a non-schedule-related contract change might include an increase in cost to the contractor due to a change in the law that caused the contractor to have to spend more for environmental mitigation efforts. A schedule-related contract change might result from a severe snowstorm that excused the contractor from performance until the storm subsided, under the project's force majeure clause. Contractor requests for increases in cost resulting from underground site conditions, due to the inherent unknowns of underground construction, uncharted utilities, obstructions such as old piles and seawalls, groundwater conditions, weak soil strengths, and discovery of hazardous materials were all addressed in the contracts as contractor responsibility and thus were not permitted PCA requests.

The PCA is the estimated cost value that has been allowed above the fixed-price bid because all contractor-caused schedule growth was absorbed within the fixed-price contract. These changes were a result of general administrative changes such as revised regulatory or mitigation requirements, design development, and other changes. PCA exposures increased throughout the project and were not offset by cost containment or cost recovery initiatives. Each construction contract forecast included a contingency or PCA for unknown or unforeseeable change orders. When the Rev. 6 budget was developed in March 1995, it included a PCA rate of 7 percent for unawarded contracts. This equated to an all-years rate of 10.6 percent.

The project arrived at a PCA rate of 7 percent through detailed analysis of the completeness of the contracts and how the unknowns would be charged to the contractor's account and should therefore be covered in the contractor's bid. This was a number justified in detail, with the assumption that the terms of each contract would be enforced, and it included the cost of every unit of crushed stone and the removal of every shovel of dirt.

What was not anticipated at the time was that the terms and conditions of the contracts that safeguarded the owner's budget would be subject to requests for numerous claims and changes, causing project delays and rising costs. By the fall of 1999, the PCA exposures were trending beyond the rates assumed in the Rev. 6 budget; by 2000, based on a major project review and audit and the results of an analysis of 19 contracts, an additional cash requirement of $908 million was determined to be necessary (Deloitte 2000). By 2000, the project cost estimate reflected a PCA of 23 percent for completed contracts, 23 percent for currently active contracts, and 17 percent for the to-be-awarded contracts, for an overall project blended rate of 22 percent (CA/T 2000). In 2007, that blended rate grew to 27 percent (CA/T 2007).

Lessons Learned: All project participants need to carefully understand the methodologies behind potential change allowances (PCAs) for contractors, and once the rate of a PCA is determined it should be consistently enforced throughout the life of the project. Once a PCA rate methodology is established, it should not be changed. Every time the PCA rate is increased, the original contract rights are essentially waived, resulting in predictable higher project costs.

The National Academies Infrastructure Board, in its extensive report on the Big Dig, found that while individual contracts had been analyzed for exposures to changes, comprehensive risk and contingency management tools and processes did not appear to be in place (Board 2003). It is one thing to determine the contingency amount that will be allowed; it is another to enforce the agreed-upon rate.

The report recommended that "[t]he MTA should initiate contingency management procedures that include continual comprehensive risk analysis to quantify and refine contract contingencies, individual contract contingency tracking, and a contingency drawdown plan that includes contingency use forecasts" (Board 2003). The advice was well heeded, resulting in the project expanding the claims and changes function, which grew to be one of the largest operations on the project, with close to 100 employees at its peak.

Project contingencies were reported on a monthly basis in each project monthly management report (PMM). The monthly reports reflected the transfer of funds to and from the construction cost account and to the management and CEO contingencies.

6. Cost Accounting History and Political Realities

> Never base your budget requests on realistic assumptions,
> as this could lead to a decrease in your funding.
>
> —*Scott Adams, Dilbert*

In 2002, the project's management team presented an overview of the reasons behind the project's cost growth history to an independent review team of the National Academies, as shown in Figure 7.2. The reported factors behind the growth increase included inflation (55 percent), environmental/mitigation (15 percent), scope growth (8 percent), accounting changes (7 percent), traffic (5 percent), schedule maintenance (3 percent), contingency for unknowns (2 percent) and other (5 percent). Though these factors did exist, they do not fully explain the fundamental reasons behind the dramatic increase in costs over the life of the project.

The Big Dig Estimated Budget in 1994

> This Truth is incontrovertible. Panic may resent it, ignorance may deride it, malice may distort it, but there it is.
>
> —*Sir Winston Churchill (1916)*

Of monumental significance in any discussion of cost on the Big Dig must be the report from the Massachusetts Office of the Inspector General (OIG) released in March 2001 (OIG 2001). Based on an investigation of more than 100,000 pages of Central Artery/Tunnel (CA/T) Project records from 1994 to 2001, the OIG discovered that the true cost of the project was actually known in 1994.

The OIG's research determined that in the last quarter of 1994, the project's management consultant, Bechtel/Parsons Brinckerhoff (B/PB) had completed the most detailed assessment of cost-to-completion to that time. That cost assessment predicted the real baseline for costs to be approximately $14 billion, as shown in Figure 7.3. And before the end of 1994, B/PB so advised the project's owner, who was also their client, the Massachusetts Highway Department (MHD).

Importantly, the OIG's investigation also revealed that shortly after they had been provided with this up-to-date cost information, in early 1995, the

B/PB's December 1994 Forecast

Item	$M	Item	$M
Final Design	679	Prior to ICE (Interstate Cost Estimate)	255
Other Consultants	116	All Rights Credit	225
Force Accounts	356	Contract C08A1 Rt. 1A (Deferred)	135
Right-of-Way	94	Metropolitan District Commission Agreement	85
Program Management	1,712	Excluded Scope Items	261
Police Details	63	Mitigation Agreements	61
PCA (Potential Change Allowance)	831	PCA Over11%	526
Construction Contingency	651		
Ft. Point Channel	1,268	Total Exclusions	1,548
Central Artery Area (11,17,18)	1,206	To-Go Escalation 8/94 to Completion	1,215
Area North of Causeway (15,19)	1,228		
Insurance Program	635		
Other Construction	2,189	Total "Apples-to-Apples" BIG DIG Forecast:	
Subtotal:	11,028		$13,791,000,000.00

Figure 7.3   Bechtel/Parsons Brinckerhoff (B/PB) 1994 Forecast
Source: Office of the Inspector General. *A History of Central Artery/Tunnel Project Finances 1994–2001.* Commonwealth of Massachusetts.

MHD directed its management consultant (B/PB) to reduce projected costs from $13.78 billion to $7.7 billion. Obviously, this could only be done on paper, not in the reality of construction.

Ironically, the OIG concluded that "[m]easured against B/PB's $13.78 billion 1994 estimate, the Big Dig has been constructed on time and on budget. Moreover, B/PB has been paid almost $3 million in incentive fees for maintaining the Project on-time and on-budget based on the old 'official' estimate of $10.8 billion" (OIG 2001, 15).

If the true costs were known in 1994, why were those costs not reflected in the project's budget until 2000? No one really knows the answer to that question, or at least, no one who does know the answer has ever made it public. However, based upon events occurring at that time, it is thought that if the true cost of the project were made known in 1995, the federal government would abruptly end funding of the remaining and largest part of the CA/T Project. Should that happen, federal funding would continue only through completion of the Ted Williams Tunnel, scheduled for the end of 1995. But there would be no additional federal funding for the I-90 and I-93 roadways, which made up the bulk of total project cost and which were the essential parts for relieving Boston's crippling vehicular congestion. A $2 billion project that grew to $7 billion was about the limit of continued federal support. A $14 billion cost would have surely doomed the project.

In that case, the dedicated I-90 roadways and tunnels on either end of the Ted Williams Tunnel, and the I-93 tunnels and bridge in their entirety, would never have been built. Should that have occurred, the state's only option would have been to perform major structural rehabilitation to the severely debilitated elevated artery that first opened to full traffic in 1959. But it would not have increased capacity, thereby condemning the city to continually increasing traffic gridlock for the foreseeable future. That would have sounded a death knell for the City of Boston and for the economy of much of New England. In 1994, the federal government had committed to a total budget of only $7.7 billion, with the federal contribution at approximately 60 percent.

Without question, the project could not have been completed at that time without federal support. Among other initiatives, MHD's directive to B/PB required reducing to-go contract estimates by 13 percent, reducing the potential change allowance (PCA) from 26 percent to 7 percent, eliminating the 18 percent contingency allowance from every to-go contract, excluding more than $1billion in nonproject costs, and excluding to-go escalation (inflation costs) from the total cost of construction (OIG 2001, 5–6). However, in 1995 the Federal Highway Administration (FHWA) reviewed the proposed changes and directed Big Dig officials to add back in approximately $2.4 billion of the recommended exclusions, resulting in a new budget estimate of $10.4 billion (CA/T 2000).

Despite the serious reductions in cost mandated by Big Dig and FHWA government officials, the reality was that the accounting assumptions in 1995 "became part of the 'semantic' definition of the Big Dig's total cost," and "a multi-billion dollar minimizing factor for every cost estimate that followed" (OIG 2001, 9).

By 2000, however, project scope changes, contractor claims, rising construction costs, and changes in allowable accounting practices made it impossible for the MTA to maintain its zero-budget-growth mandate (B/PB 2006). In 2000, the project's budget was rebaselined, as shown in Figure 7.1, to $14.075 billion.

The June 16, 2000, Finance Plan Update was used as the base cost and schedule estimate to which all future finance plans were compared. In June 2000, the project revealed a dramatic increase in costs of $1.8 billion based on the project's knowledge about the current risk and scope. Though the costs impacted budgets across the project, it was also a sign of further increases to come. As an example, the impacted categories of work and the reasons for the increase are highlighted in Table 7.2.

Cost Estimation Research   It is appropriate to conclude this chapter with research that highlights the Big Dig cost history conundrum, which may never be fully resolved. If the true costs of the project had been actually known in 1994, as reported by the Office of the Inspector General (OIG 2001), would the budget have continued to grow if the owner had accepted the almost $14 billion cost estimation in 1994, rather than rebaselining the budget in 2000? Since the budget grew after 2000 from $14 billion to approximately

Table 7.2   Big Dig Additional Cash Requirement

Category	Reasons	Increase in $Millions
Construction Schedule Maintenance	Differing site conditions, obstructions, complex interfaces	$292
Potential Change Allowance	Differing site conditions, mitigation efforts (noise, environmental), revised construction techniques	$442
Exposures to Unawarded Contracts	Additional material disposal, traffic maintenance, staging refinements, hazardous material, scope and pricing adjustments	$529
Force Accounts—Work completed for other government agencies and private utility companies essential to modernization of the transportation systems in and around the greater Boston area	City of Boston traffic, Gillette's relocation, Amtrak service work, utility relocation, transit work (MBTA), airport settlements, and mitigation of abutters concerns	$107
Right-of-Way Settlements/Judgments	Land acquisitions and eminent domain takings	$88
Design	Construction Phase Services (CPS)—technical reviews, material samples, value engineering, and contractor claims	$88
Project Management (Including MTA staffing costs)	Extended need for consultant services through 2004	$299
Insurance		0

Source: Central Artery/Tunnel Project. 2000. (June 16.) Finance Plan Update, J 22–36.

$14.8 billion at substantial completion in 2006, the 1994 proposed cost estimation at $13.8 billion was under the final budget by approximately $1 billion. Comparing this shortfall to total project costs, it is less than 7 percent, which is not unusual for a project of this size and complexity.

The case study in Figure 7.4 and the graph in Figure 7.5 highlight the reality that cost growth was a systemic problem on the Big Dig and was not entirely related to one contract or one reason. The important lessons learned here are valuable for future projects. Political will and integrity are

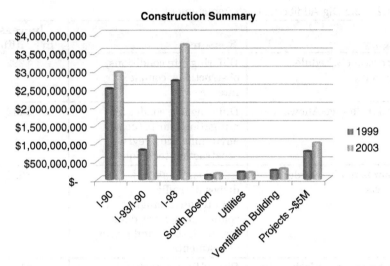

Figure 7.4   The Costs of the Three Major Construction Components of the Big Dig:
I-93, I-95, and the I-93/I-95 Interchange
Source: V. Greiman and R. Warburton. 2009. Excerpts from "Deconstructing the Big Dig:
Best Practices for Mega-Project Cost Estimating." Project Management Institute
Global Congress.

Growth of I-93 Contracts

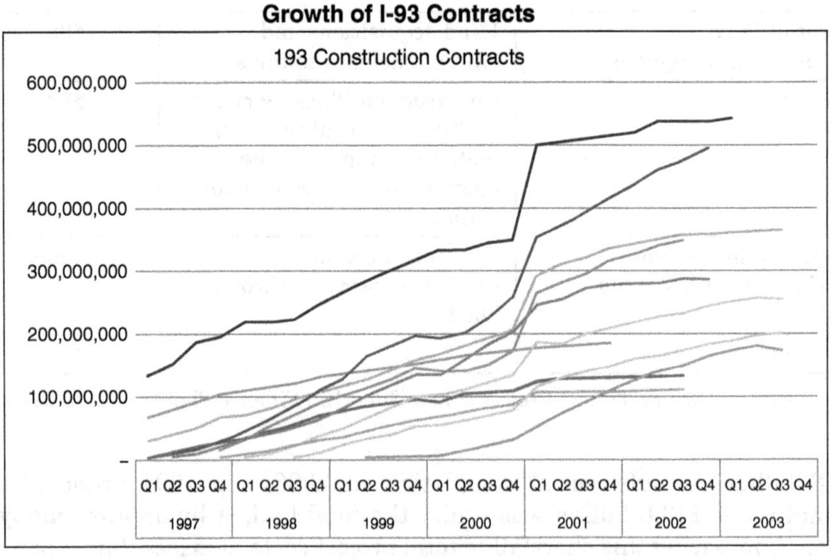

Figure 7.5   Reconstruction of I-93 Contracts
Source: V. Greiman and R. Warburton. 2009. Excerpts from "Deconstructing the Big Dig:
Best Practices for Mega-Project Cost Estimating." Project Management Institute
Global Congress.

essential leadership qualities that require project managers to insist upon and accept accurate cost estimations regardless of the reality and the risk that the project will never be fully funded by the anticipated sponsors. This is a lesson not only for project management consultants and contractors who have the option to reject the opportunity to work on a project that is not fully funded, but also for project owners who must be willing to accept the political reality that some projects may not proceed due to the unwillingness of sponsors to commit billions of dollars for public undertakings that pose substantial risk. Unfortunately, because the details of the 1994 budget were not revealed and only the general categories of cost were disclosed, as shown in Figure 7.3, it is not clear how those numbers might align with the 2006 budget by the project's cost centers and line items.

THE BIG DIG COST CONSTRUCTION SUMMARY

The three major components of construction were I-93, I-90, and the I-90/I-93 Interchange. The financial costs of these three components are shown in Figure 7.4, and amount to approximately $8 billion. The design (JV) accounts for another $2 billion of construction cost.

No single event or technological challenge seemed to have caused the cost growth on the Big Dig. This can be seen in several ways. In Figures 7.4 and 7.5, all components show similar proportional growth. Cost growth was also distributed uniformly across contracts. This is illustrated in Figure 7.5, where the cost growth of the various contracts making up I-93 is again very similar.

The primary methodology used to develop the reconstruction of the I-93 contracts shown in Figure 7.5 was to first examine the project's extensive financial data, including semiannual financial reports, monthly cost estimates, budget assumptions, inflation projections, state and federal audit reports, and historical data, and then to review and contrast the literature on cost escalation on megaprojects with the practices and strategies utilized by management on the Central Artery/Tunnel Project. Figure 7.5 shows the time period from 1997 to 2003 across the horizontal axis and the amount of the cost growth on the vertical axis. The rise in costs is consistent for all contracts for all years.

LESSONS LEARNED

1. Megaprojects require specialized knowledge of cost estimation and cost estimation management.
2. Megaprojects have extended lives, and unique features that contribute to their complexity and cost.
3. Releasing incomplete bid packages always leads to increased costs in construction.

4. Project schedule changes, caused by budget constraints or design changes can result in unanticipated increases in inflation costs even when the rate of inflation has been accurately predicted.
5. All project participants need to understand the methodologies behind potential change allowances (PCAs) for contractors, and once the rate of the PCA is determined it should be consistently enforced.
6. All project participants must have the political will to walk away from a project that is not fully funded by the anticipated sponsors even if the funding formula is legislatively mandated.
7. Identify early on in the project the systemic causes of cost growth and correct the underlying causes immediately.
8. Assess the project's governance structure to ensure that appropriate decision making and oversight authority is in place to prevent cost escalation and make changes to the structure as necessary.

BEST PRACTICES

1. Develop an interdisciplinary approach to cost estimating by including on the cost estimation team design and engineering experts, system engineers, quality assurance experts, risk management and safety experts, schedulers, test and evaluation experts, financial managers, and cost estimators and experienced construction personnel.
2. Protect estimators from internal and external pressures to provide low cost estimates.
3. Establish uniform estimating assumptions and procedures that provide guidance and minimize ambiguity to avoid conflicts and overly optimistic assumptions that can lead to cost overruns and totally inaccurate estimates and budgets.
4. Identify project risks and uncertainties early and use these explicitly identified risks to establish appropriate contingencies.
5. Determine how frequently estimates will be prepared (or updated) during the preliminary design phase. Agree upon the percent design completion when each of these estimates is prepared. Define the triggers that will require the update of an estimate (i.e., a set periodic basis, when design changes occur, or through some other triggering mechanism).
6. Develop procedures to ensure that preliminary design estimates reflect all elements of project scope (related to design, construction administration, construction, force accounts, insurance right-of-way, environmental, etc.) as defined at the time preliminary design estimates are prepared.
7. Adjust historical data used as a basis for preparing preliminary design estimates for schedule, location, and other project-specific conditions.
8. Determine what types of contingency accounts you will need, how contingency amounts are incorporated into the estimates, and what variables contingency amounts will be based on—total estimated cost,

identified project risks, approved scope modifications, or some other variables.

9. Communicate the preliminary design estimates to executive management and/or the public as a range of values with an indication of reliability.

10. Document all steps, assumptions, and significant changes in cost estimates throughout the life cycle of a project. Classify the reasons for changes under specific categories such as internal and external causes, and then classify the category of the change under scope, incorrect initial cost estimates, unforeseen events, schedule adjustments, and lack of thorough understanding of unknown (risk) factors.

11. Establish a set of formalized and institutionalized procedures for conducting estimate reviews. What staff outside of those responsible for preparing the estimate are involved in the review? How does your project team verify an estimate?

12. Decide whether project value or project complexity triggers additional reviews. If so, what are these trigger values?

13. Document estimate basis, assumptions, and backup calculations thoroughly, and continuously test these assumptions and calculations.

14. Anticipate external cost influences such as community concerns, inflation, market forces, regulatory and political changes, and unforeseen events, and incorporate them into the estimate.

15. Allocate the risk of cost escalation to the responsible designer or contractor and enforce the contract.

16. Include cost escalation in current dollars and continually review the escalation formula to ensure it is capturing true and complete cost data.

17. Hire an independent engineer to review change order requests and make sure they align with contractual provisions and are typical for the construction industry.

18. Use earned value as a methodology for holding contractors accountable, however this methodology will only work when the project's baseline is validated.

SUMMARY

This chapter has endeavored to describe the complex and often confusing cost history of the Big Dig. Extensive research on cost escalation for megaprojects in general and for the Big Dig in particular clearly indicates that controlling costs requires political will and protection of the process from internal and external pressures commencing at the inception of the project. Integrity of the cost estimation process is critical if projects are to deliver quality services to the true owners of the system, the citizens and taxpayers of the local community. Chapter 8 examines the various strategies, tools, and techniques that were used to control and manage costs on the Big Dig.

ETHICAL CONSIDERATIONS

Based on the cost overruns on the Big Dig and the extensive scholarly research on cost management, it appears that most large-scale projects are chronically underestimated. In responding to the following, think about the ethical and legal implications that may arise from serious cost overruns and how you would address these problems as a project manager.

1. Does it matter that projects are underestimated?
2. What are the implications for governments? For project sponsors? For citizens?
3. How can the risk of low cost estimates be prevented in large public projects?
4. What are some emerging areas of research that could assist in reducing the reality of consistent underestimation of large projects?

DISCUSSION QUESTIONS

1. What was the root cause of the cost overruns on the Big Dig? How could these overruns have been prevented?
2. What are the typical causes of projects that are over budget? Were the causes of cost overruns on the Big Dig typical of most projects, unique to large-scale megaprojects, or unique only to the Big Dig?
3. How would you avoid the problem discussed in this chapter of cost overruns caused by inflationary factors? What cost estimating tools and controls would you utilize to prevent overruns caused by inflation?
4. What are your options once you identify the root causes of your budget overruns if you are midway through a project?
5. Assume you are a project manager on a large-scale project and you learn that your boss has fraudulently inflated or deflated the budget. What are your responsibilities to the project? What are your responsibilities to the larger organization? How badly do you want to keep your job?
6. How would you incentivize project managers, consultants and contractors to deliver a project on schedule and budget?

REFERENCES

Akinci, Burcu, and Martin Fischer. 1998. "Factors Affecting Contractors' Risk of Cost Overburden." *Journal of Management in Engineering* 14(1):67–76.

Altschuler, A., and D. Luberoff. 2003. Megaprojects: The Changing Politics of Urban Public Investment. Washington, DC: Brookings Institution, 116–117 and 293.

Arditi, David, Gunzin Tarim Akan, and San Gurdamar. 1985. "Cost Overruns in Public Projects." *Project Management* 3(4): 218–224.

Board on Infrastructure and the Constructed Environment. 2003. *Completing the "Big Dig": Managing the Final Stages of Boston's Central Artery / Tunnel Project*. National Research Council and National Academy of Engineering of the National Academies, Committee for Review of the Project Management Practices Employed on the Boston Central Artery/Tunnel ("Big Dig") Project, Division on Engineering and Physical Sciences. Washington, DC: National Academies Press, 23–24.

Booz·Allen & Hamilton Inc. and DRI/McGraw-Hill. 1995. *The Transit Capital Cost Index Study*. Alternative Procurement Methods, Washington, DC: U.S. Department of Transportation, Federal Transit Administration. –

B/PB (Bechtel/Parsons Brinckerhoff). 2003. "The Boston Globe's Big Dig: A Disservice to the Truth." *A reply from Bechtel Parsons Brinckerhoff.* February 20.

B/PB (Bechtel/Parsons Brinckerhoff). 2006. *The Big Dig: Key Facts about Cost, Scope, Schedule, and Management.* December.

Callahan, Joel T. 1998. Managing Transit Construction Contract Claims. Transportation Research Board, TCRP Synthesis 28. Washington, DC: National Academies Press, 1–59.

CA/T (Central Artery/Tunnel Project). 2000. Finance Plan Update. (June 16.) Massachusetts Turnpike Authority, 22–36.

CA/T (Central Artery/Tunnel Project). 2007. Cost and Schedule Update. (May.)Massachusetts Turnpike Authority.

Chang, Andrew Shing-Tao. 2002. "Reasons for Cost and Schedule Increases for Engineering Design Projects." *Journal of Management in Engineering* (ASCE):29–36 (January).

Deloitte & Touche, LLP. 2000. *Cost Schedule Update Report (CSU 8)*. Prepared for the Central Artery/Tunnel Project.

Edwards W. 2002. "Project History." Presentation to the National Research Council and the National Council of Engineering Committee (NRC) for Review of the Project Management Practices Employed on the Central Artery Tunnel Project. October 21.

Einstein, D. 2012. *Laying the Groundwork: How Bechtel Geotechnical Experts Help Projects Succeed by Overcoming Everything from Boston Blue Clay to Athenian Schist*. San Francisco: Bechtel Corporation.

Esty, B. 2004. *Modern Project Finance*. Hoboken, NJ: John Wiley & Sons, Inc.

Flyvbjerg, B., M. S. Holm, and S. Buhl. 2002. "Underestimating Costs in Public Works Projects: Error or Lie?" Journal of the American Planning Association 68(3):279–295.

GAO (U.S. Government Accountability Office). 2008. Report to Congressional Committees, Defense Acquisitions: Assessments of Selected Weapon Programs. GAO-08-467SP.

Greiman, V., and R. Warburton. 2009. Excerpts from "Deconstructing the Big Dig: Best Practices for Mega-Project Cost Estimating." Project Management Institute Global Congress.

Hufschmidt, Maynard M., and Jacques Gerin. 1970. "Systematic Errors in Cost Estimates for Public Investment Projects." In *The Analysis of Public Output*, edited by J. Margolis. New York: Columbia Press, 267–795.

Interstate Cost Estimate *(ICE) Manual*. (1982). Washington, DC: Federal Highway Administration.

Massachusetts Department of Public Works. 1985. Central Artery/Tunnel Project Cost Estimate. (August.)

McCormack Report. 1997. *Managing The Central Artery / Tunnel Project: An Exploration of Potential Cost Savings*. The John W. McCormack Institute of Public Affairs. Boston: University of Massachusetts.

Merrow, Edward W. 1988. *Understanding the Outcomes of Mega Projects: A Quantitative Analysis of Very Large Civilian Projects*. Santa Monica, CA: Rand Corporation.

Miller, R., and D. Lessard. 2000. *The Strategic Management of Large Engineering Projects: Shaping Institutions, Risks and Governance*. Cambridge, MA: MIT Press.

OIG (Office of the Inspector General). 2001. *A History of Central Artery / Tunnel Project Finances 1994–2001*. Report to the Treasurer of the Commonwealth, Robert A. Cerasoli, Inspector General. Boston: Massachusetts Office of the Inspector General. (March.)

Pickrell, Don H. 1990. *Urban Rail Transit Projects: Forecast Versus Actual Ridership and Costs*. DOT-T-91-04. U.S. Department of Transportation. (October.)

Pickrell, Don H. 1992. "A Desire Named Streetcar: Fantasy and Fact in Rail Transit Promotions and Evaluation." *Journal of the American Planning Association* 58(2):158–176.

Primack, P. 2006. "Learning from the Big Dig." *Commonwealth: Politics, Ideas and Civic Life in Massachusetts*. Boston: Massachusetts Institute for a New Commonwealth (MassINC), 61.

Semple, C., F. T. Hartman, and G. Jergeas. 1994. "Construction Claims and Disputes: Causes and Cost/Time Overruns." *Journal of Construction Engineering and Management* 120(4):785–795.

Touran, Ali, and Paul J. Bolster. 1994. *Risk Assessment in Fixed Guideway Transit System Construction*. Washington, DC: Federal Transit Administration. (January).

Chapter 8

Cost Management

> Everyone is entitled to his own opinion, but not to his own facts.
>
> —*Daniel Patrick Moynihan*

INTRODUCTION

In Chapter 7, we discovered that many factors contribute to the dramatic cost increases on megaprojects and, in particular, on the Big Dig. The reasons behind these cost increases can vary from project to project, but all projects require that certain essential processes and procedures be in place to ensure the Project is completed within the approved budget. In accordance with *A Guide to the Project Management Body of Knowledge (PMBOK® Guide)*—Fifth Edition, the essential processes for effective cost management include:

1. *Planning*: Determining the resources, people, equipment, and materials necessary to perform each project activity.
2. *Cost estimating*: Developing an approximation of the costs of the resources needed to complete each project activity.
3. *Cost budgeting*: Allocating the overall cost estimate to individual work items, that is, how much money will be spent and when it will be spent.
4. *Cost control*: Controlling changes to the project budget.

Each of these processes interacts with the others and with all of the processes and procedures in the other project management knowledge areas as well. Many of the processes and procedures described in this chapter go beyond the typical approaches used by project managers to manage cost. The reason for a special approach to cost management is evident: Megaprojects involve numerous technological and design complexities, heightened risk and uncertainty, and, most important, intensive and rigorous public scrutiny. This chapter covers the framework essential to controlling and managing the ever-changing cost elements of large-scale projects, and the essential cost management processes used on the Big Dig.

1. THE PROJECT BUDGET PROCESS AND COST HISTORY

To develop a budget that is going to be used for many years, a sound methodology, assumptions, and basis of estimate must be prepared at the beginning. Whenever the actual cost deviates from the budget in the course of the project, decision makers will want to examine the methodology, assumptions, and basis of estimate to determine whether the deviation is from an estimating error, subsequent scope changes, or poor performance. An early review of the Big Dig's management of costs revealed that "the project's methodology and basis for projecting costs was unclear and somewhat confusing" (Peterson 1995).

Every project should have a baseline that is generally derived from control accounts that in turn are derived from the sum of all the work packages in that specific account plus contingency reserves. With several hundred major work packages, the process of developing an accurate, up-to-date baseline on the Big Dig was a major challenge. Ideally, if properly calculated, the baseline should remain the same throughout the life of the project. Unfortunately, as evidenced by the growing literature on cost estimation, rarely are megaproject baselines accurately forecasted from the inception of the project. As shown in Table 8.1, the cost history of the Big Dig grew dramatically from its original baseline of \$2.5 billion in 1985 to \$14.789 billion in 2007.[1]

2. COST CENTERS

During most of the project's life span, the baseline was managed through the first seven cost centers shown in Table 8.2. An eighth center (I-90 remediation) was added in 2006 to address certain costs associated with the I-90 tunnel accident, which resulted in extensive rework. The budgeted costs as of May 2007 through 2009 and beyond are highlighted in Table 8.2. By far, the largest cost center was construction, at almost \$9.6 billion. The three cost centers that were most consistent throughout the project life were the force accounts, right-of-way, and insurance premiums, due to better knowledge and certainty about the potential uses of these funds.

3. COST MANAGEMENT TEAM

Within the Big Dig Integrated Project Organization, the responsibility for coordination of cost and schedule was under Construction Controls

---

[1]In June 2009, the Massachusetts Department of Transportation (DOT), the successor to the MTA, released an unofficial Updated Cash Flow Status showing total costs at \$14.813 billion. These numbers will fluctuate slightly until all claims have been settled.

Table 8.1   Cost and Scope History

Date	Scope	Cost
August 1985	Original Environmental Impact Statement—conceptual design	$2.564 billion (1982 dollars)
1987	$657 million South Boston Haul Road, right-of-way Acquisitions, Escalation from 1982 to 1985 dollars	$3.175 billion
1989 Interstate Cost Estimate (ICE)	$799 million for high-occupancy lanes, I-90 tunnel covers, Route 1A interchange, changes in AASHTO standards	$4.43 billion (1987 dollars)
1991 ICE	$299 million Dewey Square tunnel, landscaping, railroad relocation, material disposal program, $458 escalation from 1987 to 1989 dollars	$5.780 billion
1991 Adjusted Project Forecast (APF)	$255 million for West Virginia Fire Tunnel Test, utilities, $332 million escalation	$5.780 billion
1992 APF	$354 million insurance, right-of-way, $309 million escalation	$6.443 billion
1992 APF	Charles River Crossing $324 million, $219 million insurance, $104 million escalation	$7.740 billion
March 1995 Cost and Schedule Update (CSU) 6	$258 million all project cost centers, excluded inflation	$7.998 billion
1995/1996 Finance Plan	$1.153 billion inflation for remainder of project, $255 million pre-ICE costs, $984 million exclusions/third-party contributions	$10.4 billion
1996 Finance Plan Update (FPU)	Inflation, plus insurance credit	$10.4 billion
1997 FPU	$400 million bid results, noise, dust, traffic mitigation, and deletion of future air rights	$10.8 billion
1998 FPU	Inflation, plus insurance credit	$10.8 billion
1999 FPU	Inflation, plus insurance credit	$10.8 billion
March 2000 FPU	$321 million design development, $292 million construction schedule, $60 million design, $260 million project management, $302 million construction changes, $90 million force accounts, $72 million right-of-way	$12.2 billion

(continued)

Table 8.1 (*Continued*)

Date	Scope	Cost
June 2000 FPU	$140 million awarded contracts, $203 million unawarded contracts, $17 million force accounts, $28 million design during construction, $16 million right-of-way, $39 million project management	$13.5 billion
October 2000 CSU 7	$132 million awarded construction, $71 million unawarded construction, $(23) million right-of-way, $(3) million insurance, $28 million force accounts, $270 million design, $15 million project management, $236 million contingency	$14.075 billion
October 2001 CSU 8	$118 million awarded construction, $32 million unawarded construction, $4 million right-of-way, $(50) million insurance	$14.475 billion
April 2002 Approved 2002 Finance Plan	$12 million right-of-way, $150 million insurance, $(12) million contingency	$14.625 billion
October 2002 CSU 9	$172 million awarded construction, $(99) million unawarded construction, $5 million right-of-way, $(37) million insurance, $(5) million force account, $11 million design during construction, $100 million project management, $(147) million contingency	$14.625 billion
October 2003 CSU 10	$75 million construction, $14 million right-of-way, $(20) million insurance, $(1) million force account, $8 million design, $63 million project management, $(139) million contingency	$14.625 billion
October 2004 CSU 11	$77 million construction, $(15) million right-of-way, $(21) million insurance, $(1) million force account, $3 million design, $12 million project management, $(55) million contingency	$14.625 billion
May 2007 Updated Cost Estimate	$115 million construction, $(2) million right-of-way, $19 million insurance, $54 million I-90 ceiling repair, $(12) million force account, $10 million design, $107 million project management, $(117) million contingency	$14.798 billion
2008	As of August 2008, the budget was holding at $14,798 billion	$14.798 billion

Source: Central Artery/Tunnel Project Cost and Schedule Update (CSU). May 2007.

Table 8.2   Budget by Cost Center

Uses by Cost Center	Actual through 2006 plus budgeted through 2009 and beyond ($Million)
1. Construction	9,597
2. Force accounts	588
3. Design	1,062
4. Right-of-way	590
5. Project management	2,259
6. Insurance premiums	624
7. Contingency	25
8. I-90 incident remediation (added in 2006)	54
Total	$14,798 billion

Source: Central Artery/Tunnel Project (CA/T). Updated Cost Estimate. May 2007.

(see Figure 8.1). The construction schedule manager and the construction cost manager reported directly up to the construction controls manager, who reported directly to the project's program manager. The program budget manager had a dotted-line report to the construction controls manager so that budget, cost, and schedule were linked.

The first step in ensuring costs are properly identified and controlled is to develop an integrated team of various experts to develop the cost baseline at the inception of the project. If the baseline is inaccurate, the

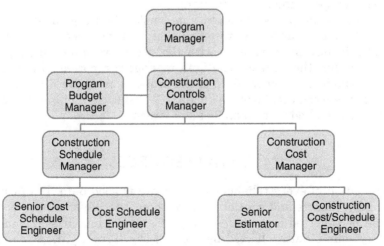

Figure 8.1   Construction Controls Organization, Central Artery/Tunnel Project, 2000
Source: Central Artery/Tunnel Project, Integrated Projection Organization.

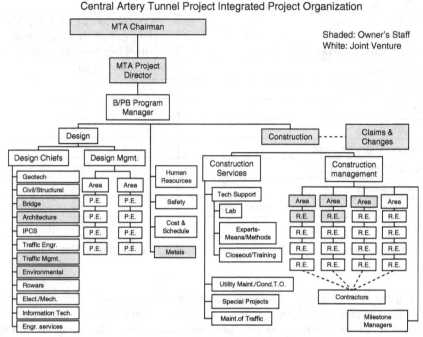

Figure 8.2   Project Organization Chart
Source: Central Artery/Tunnel Project, Integrated Project Organization.

measurements will be useless. The cost estimation team should include design and engineering experts, system engineers, quality assurance experts, risk management and safety experts, schedulers, test and evaluation experts, financial managers, and cost estimators.

As shown in the project's design and construction organization chart in Figure 8.2, area managers were given the primary responsibility for both cost and schedule management, with the necessary information gathered and used within their areas. The area managers reported to the program manager, who in turn reported up to the project's executive director. Within each area, the work breakdown structure (WBS) was organized by contract, so that each area had its own budget and forecast.

4. DATA RESOURCES

The foundation of every reliable cost estimate is good data. Data collection is a lengthy process and continues throughout the life span of the project. Data can be collected in numerous ways. Table 8.3 lists basic primary and secondary source data collected by the Big Dig. Primary data are original source documents and should always be used prior to resorting to secondary data, which are derived rather than obtained from an original source. Many of

Table 8.3   Basic Primary and Secondary Data Sources

Data Type	Primary	Secondary
Design documents and drawings	X	
Work breakdown structures	X	
Bid documents	X	
Accounting records	X	
Data surveys and forms	X	
Cost reports	X	
Historical databases	X	
Expert advice	X	
Program briefings	X	X
Technical experts	X	
Government reports	X	X
Technical databases	X	X
Contracts	X	
Contractor estimates and risk assessments		X
Cost proposals		X
Cost research and studies		X

Source: Adapted from Central Artery/Tunnel Project Procedures.

these resources are typical of data collected by other organizations, including the Department of Transportation (DOT), the Department of Defense (DoD), and the National Aeronautics and Space Administration (NASA).

5. COST CONTROL TOOLS

A. Design Evolution

The Big Dig project's methodology for controlling cost increases during design evolution was the first of its kind for a major public transportation project and has been used by the Federal Highway Administration (FHWA) as a model for nationwide implementation. To control cost increases, the focus was on cost containment and a refusal to tolerate design enhancements unless they were truly critical to the operation of the system. The project's first budget did not include any cost allowances for added design enhancement. Moreover, the project initiated a design-to-cost budget program that required each design team to agree to a not-to-exceed construction cost for its design. The specified construction cost could be adjusted only for owner-initiated scope or pricing changes (FHWA 2011).

B. Finance Plan

As with any project of the size and complexity of the Big Dig, financial planning is an ongoing activity carried out cooperatively between the state and federal governments.

A large project with an extended schedule spans several state and federal funding cycles, requiring reliance on future legislative and congressional actions. While the future reliance is justified based on a long history of transportation finance legislation, it nonetheless prevented the development of a complete Central Artery/Tunnel financial plan based on specific authorized revenue sources. Instead, certain assumptions about future conditions were made in every financial plan (MHD 1994).

Commencing in 1996, the project filed an annual finance plan with the FHWA and a semiannual finance plan with the Massachusetts legislature. The FHWA (through TEA-21) now requires finance plans for all projects over $1 billion. First instituted on the Big Dig, the finance plan allows FHWA and states to identify funding and costs and address them before they become significant issues. This is a proactive measure that has enhanced federal project oversight. The finance plan was utilized as the base cost and schedule estimate to which all future finance plans were compared.

The finance plan presents the integrated cost, schedule, and funding status for the project. It requires project cost estimates to be prepared in "year of expenditure" dollars; agency accountability must be increased for the proposed financing in the plan; significant changes to the project scope in the annual finance plan must be accurately disclosed. Also, FHWA requires annual updates to the plans and obtains independent verification of the financial data provided by the states in these plans. The key elements of the finance plan are highlighted in Table 8.4.

Project Financing and Revenues All finance reports provided an update on the overall components of funding for the project, including the percentage of federal and state aid. The base plan was compared with the funding sources, and, as shortfalls arose, additional revenue was identified. Table 8.5 illustrates how the finance plan was updated to show the change in funding sources from year to year as well as the future forecast for funding.

C. Project Management Monthly (PMM)

An aggressive monthly cost and schedule tracking process was developed in 1996, enhanced in 2000, and presented to the public through project management monthly (PMM) reports. This "early indicator" enabled items that might benefit the project to be flagged for early implementation and items that might have negative impacts to be rigorously studied and corrected

Table 8.4   Key Elements of the Big Dig's Financial Plan

Element	Description
(1) Executive Summary	Provided an overview of the current scope and financial status of the project, set out assumptions for the future, and suggested ways of managing the complex relationships between funding sources, requirements, and schedule, which were vital to project success.
(2) Project Description	Described the history of the project, the most recent milestones, the challenges of future construction, and the benefits of the project.
(3) Project Timeline	Described recent accomplishments in detail, along with detailed background on the target milestones and the percentage of completion of each contract; described future events as well as the challenges faced in reaching those events.
(4) Cost Estimate	Documented the status of the project's cost accounts by construction segment; actual expenditures were shown as contrasted with budgeted expenditures; key information included the base cost estimate, the current cost estimate, the net increase or decrease, and the cost to complete the project.
(5) Key Budget Assumptions	Some examples of budget assumptions were the impact of a competitive marketplace, the effect escalation had on the budget, and the budget assumptions for the potential change allowance (PCA), which is the estimated value above the fixed bid price. As the project progressed, and after all construction contracts were awarded, the PCA became the major factor influencing the ultimate project cost.
(6) Audits	The results of all independent assessments and audits were attached to the finance plan. Audits were conducted on a wide range of activities including the project's cost recovery, value engineering, and the claims and changes program, along with detailed audits of the project's costs and schedule.
(7) Project Cost Risks	Typical cost risks analyzed for the finance plan included: (a) assessment of claims and changes—each annual finance plan budgeted for the potential cost of change orders and contractor claims on all contracts; (b) pricing methodology-the budget was developed based on an assessment of open issues and claims that warranted merit. In addition, the budget included a contingency, based on a professional judgment taking into account two factors (a) an exposure amount if the project's analysis was understated and the issue was litigated and (b) amounts at which the project believed each contractor would ultimately settle to close all of its issues and claims. These assessments were based on input from the front-line claims managers and other senior management conversations/negotiations with the contractors (CA/T 2004).

(continued)

Table 8.4   (Continued)

Element	Description
(8) Potential Contractor Insolvency	Insolvency of a contractor was a significant risk, as it could create cash flow and credit issues that could impact the ability of the contractor to finish the project work. During the course of the project, there was a significant threat of insolvency from one of the project's main contractors with significant critical path work. Though the project required all contractors to carry surety bonds, the process of realizing funds may not be immediate or fully able to recover all costs.
(9) Implementation Plan	This section included a description of the project schedule milestones, the project schedule status, and the project schedule risk.

Source: Central Artery/Tunnel Project.

Table 8.5   Cash Flow by Funding Source ($ in millions)

Source	Cumulative as of FY03	FY 2004	FY 2005	FY 2006 and Beyond	Total Revenues
Federal	6,492	369	182	6	7,049
State bond	1,462	53	60	13	1,588
State interest on MTA funds	45	0	0	0	45
MTA	1,351	15	11	281	1,658
MassPort	302	0	0	0	302
GANs	1,500	0	0	0	1,500
Transportation Infrastructure Fund (TIF)	1,424	258	543	117	2,343
Insurance trust interest	50	6	5	79	140
TOTAL	12,626	701	801	497	14,625

Source: Central Artery/Tunnel Project. 2004. Finance Plan (October 1.) Massachusetts Turnpike Authority.

at the earliest possible time. It also ensured public disclosure of project issues. The PMM was used to keep all project stakeholders up to date on key project activities, including construction progress, forecasts, safety and health statistics, labor and minority business usage, and total federal obligations, as shown in the "Lessons from Practice" text box.

LESSONS FROM PRACTICE: KEY SECTIONS OF THE PROJECT MANAGEMENT MONTHLY (PMM)

- Planned versus Actual Cash Flow, Total Federal Obligations, and State Cash Flow Trend
- Construction progress vs. planned progress on a contract-by-contract basis
- Inclusion of both definitive and speculative cost exposures and recoveries
- Project contingency and CEO management reserve status
- Potential Change Allowance (PCA) and Future Allowance for all construction contracts
- Key indicators such as staffing levels, overtime usage, actual labor and direct expense expenditures
- Monthly Safety recordable and lost time rates
- Status of insurance expenditures and trust fund balances
- Disadvantaged Business Enterprise Utilization v. Goals
- Summary of Management Consultant's Work Program, Scope and Budget

Source: CA/T (Central Artery Tunnel Project). 2002. Project Management Monthly (PMM) (January). Massachusetts Turnpike Authority.

D. Budget, Cost Commitment, and Forecast Report

One of the basic assumptions of project budgets is that the forecast for future construction projects and other cost centers is complete and accurate. On the Big Dig, substantial project resources were devoted to forecasting, and commitments and forecasts were reported on a monthly basis in the PMM. The Budget, Cost, Commitment and Forecast Report (Figure 8.3) illustrates the extensive information that had to be compiled by each cost center for these monthly reports. Additionally, third-party scope managed by the project, but paid for by external parties, was reported and updated consistently throughout the project. This included work for other transportation agencies including Massport Authority and Boston's transit system, the MBTA. This report consolidated information by each cost center at completion values based on the last cost/schedule update (CSU). It then calculated a forecast based on anticipated cost needs. The total dollar amounts of construction placed under contract was included, along with to-go commitments and contracts that had been approved for payment.

Central Artery/Tunnel Project
Budget, Cost, Commitment, and Forecast Report

$ in Millions

BUDGET ITEMS	CSU7 BUDGET	POTENTIAL FORECAST	COMMITMENTS TO-DATE	COMMITMENTS TO-GO	AUTHORIZED INVOICES TO-DATE	AUTHORIZED INVOICES TO-GO
Construction Packages	9,059	9,050	7,362	1,687	5,889	3,161
Force Accounts-Construction	445	442	380	62	327	115
Section Design Contracts	996	996	945	50	882	114
Force Accounts-Design	151	151	130	21	92	59
Geotech Contracts	31	31	32	-1	25	6
Right-of-Way	572	574	552	22	552	22
Joint Venture	1,917	1,917	1,530	387	1,509	408
MTA Staff	45	45	5	39	5	39
Unallocated Surface Restoration	30	30	0	30	0	30
Owner-Controlled Insurance	572	572	556	16	528	44
Management Contingency	258	268	0	268	0	268
TOTAL PROJECT	14,076	14,076	11,492	2,581	9,809	4,266
MBTA and Other Betterment*	423	428	358	70	241	187

Total Costs
January 31, 2001

Provides overview statistics about Project's Budget

Info consolidated by project cost centers

At completion Values

Anticipated cost needs

The last Cost/Sched. Update (CSU) budget

To-Date Values

Approved for payment

Placed under contract

3rd Party Scope managed by the project but paid by 3rd party

Figure 8.3   Budget, Cost, Commitment, and Forecast Report
Source: Central Artery/Tunnel Project. 2001. (January 31.) Massachusetts Turnpike Authority.

E. Earned Value Methodology

One of the critical components in measuring project status on any project is the application of the earned value methodology (EVM). Earned value is used to determine the value of work completed compared to the budgeted cost of work completed and the actual cost. The basic idea behind EVM is that the current performance metrics can be used to forecast long-term performance trends and, ultimately, the final cost and delivery date. On the Big Dig, earned value was used to forecast future performance, determine variances from budget, monitor the progress of the design and construction work, and project completion date and costs. A few of the control metrics that were used to measure schedule performance were listed in Chapter 6, and a few of the metrics useful in measuring variance from budget and cost performance are listed here.

- *Earned value* (EV): Percentage of the planned budget that has been completed multiplied by the planned budget; for example, if the total budget is $100 million and 20 percent of the work is completed, the earned value is $20 million.
- *Actual cost* (AC): The sum of the cost of the work completed.
- *Budget at completion* (BAC): The amount budgeted.
- *Cost variance* (CV): The difference between the earned value and the actual costs for the work completed to date (EV − AC).
- *Cost performance index* (CPI): The ratio of earned value to actual cost (EV/AC).
- *Estimate at completion* (EAC): How much it will cost at completion? (BAC/CPI.)
- Estimate to complete: How much more will it cost? (EAC − AC.)
- Variance at completion (VAC): How much over or under budget? (BAC − EAC.)

F. Mitigation

Mitigation activities such as noise, dust, and clean air programs were incorporated in the budget primarily during the design process. These activities are the direct result of construction, and the mitigation activities were covered in each contract as being the responsibility of the construction contractor. The construction contractor was responsible for mitigating effects of the contractor's construction activities, while the management consultant was responsible for ensuring the contractor fulfilled his responsibilities in accordance with the terms and conditions of his contact to do the same. Since the Big Dig project involved numerous interfaces with other government agencies and private entities including utility companies, environmental consultants, and private contractors, it was essential that the responsible party controlled the risk. An early review of the project identified a significant number of items for which responsibility had not been established. It was recommended that a contingency pool be established to account for those items that were not clearly, but might have been, the project's responsibility (Peterson 1995). According to various financial reports and research studies, mitigation was a major factor in cost escalation caused by demands of the local communities and businesses and has been estimated to represent more than one-third of total project costs, though this number has never been fully substantiated (McCormack 1997).

G. Variance Reports

Commencing October 1, 2000, the Big Dig project submitted to the FHWA its overall "budget vs. potential forecast variance report" on a semiannual basis. This report contained explanations of any and all variances by project element, segregated into the following three categories:

1. *Firm variances requiring budget revision:* These include, but are not limited to, the value of actual contract awards (or executed change orders), approved scope changes to be incorporated during design, and expected settlement amounts for asserted construction claims.
2. *Variances subject to further adjustment:* These require future management corrective action or other alternative remedies.
3. *Speculative forecast variances:* These are difficult to quantify and price but could have a positive or adverse effect on the future cost of the CA/T Project and/or the statewide program.

H. Bottom-up Assessment of To-Go Project Costs

Starting in 2000, and once every six months thereafter, the Big Dig project conducted a bottom-up estimation of to-go project costs. Bottom-up estimating is defined in the fifth edition of the *PMBOK® Guide* as aggregating the estimates of the lower-level components of the work breakdown structure (*PMBOK® Guide* 2013). Bottom-up estimating is an extremely helpful technique in project management, as it allows for the ability to get a more refined estimate of a particular component of work. Individual estimates are developed to determine what specifically is needed to meet the requirements of each of these smaller components of the work. The estimates for the smaller individual components are then aggregated to develop a larger estimate for the entire task as a whole. In doing this, the estimate for the task as a whole is typically far more accurate, as it allows for careful consideration of each of the smaller parts of the task. It then combines these carefully considered estimates rather than merely making one large estimate, which typically will not as thoroughly consider all of the individual components of a task.

On the Big Dig, bottom-up estimating required detailed analysis of each work package. Allowances were included for potential but relatively unknown issues including cost increases, reductions, and offsets. The results were contained in the PMM and annual finance plans. Detailed cost-based bottom-up estimating requires a great deal of knowledge about construction methods, supply systems, labor markets, and method productivity specific to the area where the work is being performed. It also requires more time to prepare a detailed estimate than that needed for estimating methods that simply apply bid averages to work items. This is because the estimator must conceptualize the construction process in order to prepare an accurate estimate. The benefits include a basis for controlling project costs.

I. Contingency Funding as a Means of Control

Contingency funding is defined in various ways in project management and is sometimes referred to as *contingency reserve, contingency allowance*, or *management reserve*. PMI's the *PMBOK® Guide* guidelines provide that "the contingency reserve may be a percentage of the estimated cost, a fixed number, or may be developed by using quantitative analysis methods."

The contingency process begins with a risk analysis to develop issues that enable the quantification of a project-contingency allowance. As a project passes through its various phases, including planning, design, pre-construction, and construction, and as more is known about the project, the contingency becomes more defined. Various factors impact contingency budgets, including omissions, underestimated quantities, changes in the law or regulations, environmental requirements, and unexpected conditions.

Contingencies can be managed through the claims and changes process and can be defined in the contract. Contingency budgets commonly range from 5 percent to 10 percent, but on complex projects contingency budgets generally are much higher, in the 20 to 30 percent range. For example, on the English "Chunnel" project, the contingency budget or cushion was reported as 25 percent of estimated project costs and was still insufficient to cover all costs, resulting in increased borrowing and equity infusions throughout the life of the project (Grant 1997).

Inconsistent application of contingencies causes confusion as to exactly what is included in the line items of an estimate and what is covered by contingency amounts. Contingency funds are typically meant to cover a variety of possible events and problems that are not specifically identified, or to account for a lack of project definition during the preparation of early planning estimates. Misuse and failure to define what cost contingency amounts cover can lead to estimation problems. In many cases, it is assumed that contingency amounts can be used to cover added scope, and planners seem to forget that the purpose of the contingency amount in the estimate was lack of design definition. Projects run into problems when the contingency amounts are applied inappropriately (Anderson et al. 2006; Noor and Tichacek 2004; Ripley 2004).

Table 8.6 The Big Dig's Contingency Budget as of September 2003

Contingency Categories	Purpose	Control	Responsibility	2003 Contingency Funding
1. Construction (PCA)	Allocations for risks and exposures that were not allocated to the contractor in the contact documents, such as design development	Managed through the potential change allowance (PCA) process and claims and changes process	Management consultant/ later in the project, the owner managed the claims and changes process	$900 million
2. Management contingency	Allocations for project costs, elements other than construction	Federal oversight and external audits	Project director	$294 million
3. CEO management reserve	Growth in owner's staff, such as funding for the claims and changes program	Federal oversight and external audits	Project director	$40.9 million

Source: Central Artery/Tunnel Project Management Monthly. September 2003.

As shown in Table 8.6, contingencies were budgeted in three categories on the Big Dig: (1) construction contingency, (2) management contingency, and (3) CEO contingency.

J. Potential Change Allowance (PCA)

As described in Chapter 7, the potential change allowance (PCA) process was used to estimate the costs for non-schedule-related contract changes. For example, a non-schedule-related cost might be the cost of additional design work or the cost of construction due to expanded scope. A schedule-related cost would be, for example, extension of the schedule for three months because there was delay on a critical path caused by circumstances beyond the contractor's control, such as flooding of an adjacent work site.

The PCA is the estimated cost value that has been allowed above the fixed-price bid. On the Big Dig, these changes were a result of unanticipated site conditions, general administrative changes such as revised regulatory or mitigation requirements, design development, and other factors. This measurement of change in the PCA was essential in controlling project costs

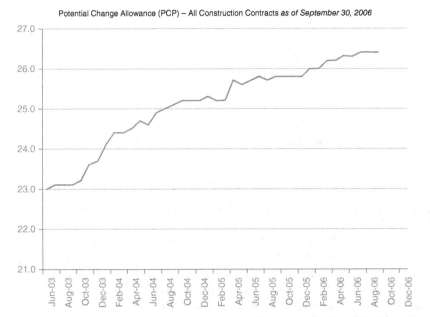

Potential Change Allowance (PCP) – All Construction Contracts *as of September 30, 2006*

"All Identified Issues" includes contract issues and contractor claims that are included in the Project's Potential
forecast ($14.625B) even though the Project has not yet determined merit.
This data point is being provided for reference only.

Figure 8.4   Potential Change Allowance as of September 2006
Source: CA/T Project Management Monthly. September 2006.

and making sure the project budget was sufficient to cover these costs. The percentage allowance encompasses contract issues and contractor claims that are included in the project's potential budget forecast even though the project had not yet determined merit. Figure 8.4 shows, on the horizontal axis, the timeline of the project for the period June 2003 to December 2006, and, on the vertical axis, the percentage changes to the contract bid price budgeted (except scope changes and transfers). The steady increase in the PCA from 2003 to 2006 indicates that the project budget had an insufficient cushion to cover potential claims, risk was not properly allocated in the contracts, the contracts were not being enforced and/or design errors or omissions resulted in a significant increase in contractor claims.

LESSONS FROM PRACTICE

The PCA shown in Figure 8.4 highlights the increase in the potential claims allowance (PCA) from 23 percent in 2003 to 26.5 percent in 2006 at project substantial completion. This increase in the PCA raises the question of why claims were increasing throughout the life of the project and whether claims should have been paid if the contractor failed to complete the requirements set forth in the detailed specifications.

All projects must examine the PCA process to ensure that costs are never increased based on obligations that have been allocated to the designer or contractor in the contract specifications or other documents or agreements.

An increase in the PCA during the life of the project raises a red flag that must be investigated immediately to prevent cost escalation from getting out of control.

Source: CA/T Project Management Monthly (PMM). 2006.

K. Management Reserves

Management reserves are typically established to address "unknown unknowns" and are reserved for unplanned changes to project scope and cost; however, on the Big Dig, management reserves were generally used for increases in project staff to address emergency response needs, legal requirements, or public information demands. This application of management reserves is inconsistent with both the EVM and the *PMBOK® Guide*. Management reserves usually can be used only after high-level project approval and are not contained in the baseline, but should be included in the total budget for the project. These reserve funds are needed to cover major unforeseen risks and are controlled by the project manager and the owner of the project. Management reserves can be based on historical data and judgments concerning the uniqueness and complexity of the project. With proper project planning, these funds will never be used.

L. Independent Outside Audits

A global accounting and consulting firm was placed on contract to validate project developed cost and schedule assessments. These periodic reports contained numerous recommendations for cost and schedule control and cost containment. In addition, audit reports were issued by independent agencies including the National Academy of Engineering, independent auditors, and state and federal audit agencies.

For instance, as claims increased dramatically during the peak years of the project from 1999 to 2003, a new protocol was established to handle these claims and changes based on the recommendations of an outside audit. An important feature of the claims and changes program was the requirement of independent audits of claims that had been conducted during the claim resolution process rather than after that process had been completed. Some examples of the findings of these reports are highlighted in Table 8.7.

Best Practices   Few would dispute that independent outside audits are a necessary control mechanism for megaprojects; however, compliance with

Table 8.7   Central Artery Tunnel/Project Audit Recommendations and Compliance

Audit	Recommendation	Implemented
Deloitte Project Assessment	Recommended increase in CSU 7 budget of $2.214 billion to complete the project and $280 million for contingency reserves.	Project revenues were increased to meet the additional increase in the project budget, and contingency reserves were increased (Deloitte 2003 Project Assessment).
Office of the Inspector General	Recommended corrective actions to increase cost recovery efforts against both designers and contractors.	Based on OIG recommendations, corrective actions were implemented, resulting in recovery of millions of dollars for defective design and workmanship (OIG 2000).
FHWA Task Force Report	The secretary of transportation requested the governor of Massachusetts to reevaluate the appropriateness of the MTA's continuing role in day-to-day management and control over the project.	The governor changed the MTA manager, but MTA continued to manage the day-to-day activities of the CA/T Project (FHWA 2000).

Sources: Central Artery/Tunnel Project. Office of Inspector General 2000 Audit; FHWA 2000 Task Force Report; and Deloitte & Touche 2003 Project Assessment.

these reports is not always certain. Projects must be held accountable and demonstrate where audit recommendations are adopted, as well as where they are rejected and the reasons why the recommendations will not be implemented.

M. Claims and Changes

As described in Chapter 11, the Claims and Changes Program on the Big Dig was one of the largest operations on the project, with more than 100 employees. During the peak years of construction, this program managed more than 13,500 claims, many of them involving nonroutine, complex contractual obligations and unforeseeable events. As a result of this growing backlog of claims, project management had to take a new look at the dispute avoidance/resolution program. This involved establishing a claims resolution plan that called for a collaborative process between the contractors and the owner and a sophisticated dispute avoidance/resolution program that elevated issues to successively higher levels of management through a dispute review board (DRB). Key to the success of this program was the requirement of reassessing and revising it as the needs and priorities of the project evolved (Dettman et al., 2010).

Hiring an independent engineer to review change order requests and making sure they align with contractual provisions and are typical for the construction industry is essential to cost control. For the CA/T Project, change order requests included items such as unidentified utilities, design changes due to the desires of third parties, interface coordination with other contracts, minor alignment changes, revisions to entrance and exit areas such as ramp location and enhancements to original design, and some incomplete bid documents due to federal funding rules.

In 2003, Deloitte and Touche (D&T), the company that conducted the Commonwealth of Massachusetts's independent assessment of the project's cost and schedule, found that the project did not adequately document the value of outstanding claims. Although D&T did not believe the project's cost estimate should be increased, it recommended that the project closely manage and monitor the settlement of claims so that project costs would not increase in the future (D&T 2003). The assessment further determined that the number of claims continued to grow despite project efforts to resolve claims. For example, from August through December 2003, an average of 418 new claims were received and an average of 406 claims were resolved. As a result, the total number of unresolved claims as of March 2004 had increased to 4,805 (CA/T 2004, Appendix E, 11).

It is significant that, in December 2002, the authority chairman directed the project's Claims and Changes Department to establish a plan to resolve the pending backlog of unresolved claims. To accomplish this task, the Claims and Changes Department developed an expedited closeout plan and increased its staff from 84 in June 2003 to 111 in November 2003 to handle its workload of outstanding claims (CA/T 2004).

N. Cost Recovery

Broadly used, the term *cost recovery* refers to the process by which "public and private owners file claims against design and construction management professionals for the costs claimed to be attributable to errors, omissions, or other 'deficient' or unsatisfactory performance" (Hatem 1996). Cost recovery is based on the recognition that all design and construction projects contain some errors and omissions, the design engineer should be expected to perform to the professional standard of care applicable to the services provided, and that the cost recovery policy applies to errors and omissions. Since 1994, the project had an FHWA-approved cost recovery program that allowed the project to approve change orders, pay the consultant contractor for the work, and seek reimbursement from the FHWA, before determining whether the change was, in fact, due to a design error (CA/T 2004).

The Office of the Inspector General criticized the oversight of the cost recovery program as not being truly independent, since the management consultant (consultant) was charged with not only reviewing the work of the contractors and section design consultants they were overseeing but also providing technical assistance to the Cost Recovery Committee that included the owner and the Federal Highway Administration. State procedures also called for the consultant "to identify issues of potential cost recovery," which meant the state relied on the consultant to point out flaws in its own designs and management (OIG 2000). It is important to note that the management consultant had been tasked with this responsibility early in the project at the request of the project owner.

In 2002, in response to the OIG's concerns, the Massachusetts Turnpike Authority legal department and the Office of the Attorney General began vigorously pursuing cost recovery against Big Dig contractors through a restructured cost recovery process, and, in 2003, a retired state court judge was appointed to lead the process. This renewed effort recouped millions of dollars for the Commonwealth of Massachusetts. Between 2003 and 2005, the OIG also redirected its oversight to focus on cost recovery issues, resulting in some important recommendations. In addition to the revamped cost recovery effort, special legislation was enacted that extended the statute of limitations for seeking cost recovery and added an additional level of scrutiny to the process.

The important lessons learned on the Big Dig about the cost recovery process from the perspective of the owner include the following:

- Cost recovery should commence at project start-up and continue beyond project closure until all potential cost recovery actions have been completed.
- Cost recovery should include actions against designers, contractors, and consultants for design and construction management issues and overpayments.
- The cost recovery processes and procedures should be clearly understood by all project stakeholders and embedded in all project contractual and legal documents.
- The establishment of a cost recovery committee of experts is an important tool in ensuring all possible efforts have been undertaken by the owner to recover costs from designers and contractors.
- The cost recovery team should be made up of independent experts to avoid conflicts or the appearance of impropriety.
- Legislation should be implemented to ensure that the state's statute of limitations extends sufficiently beyond project completion to allow for sufficient time to recoup all monies due for deficient performance.

In 2000, the Massachusetts Office of the Inspector General, after an extensive review of the project's cost recovery program, issued the recommendations shown in the following text box:

RECOMMENDATIONS OF THE MASSACHUSETTS OFFICE OF THE INSPECTOR GENERAL ON COST RECOVERY (OIG 2000):

1. Use the cost recovery program to send a clear message that all design professionals on the Project will be held accountable for their design work.
2. Avoid conflicts of interest by making sure the government and not the management consultant contracts directly for any services aimed at assessing the management consultant's liability for design deficiencies
3. Reassess the Cost Recovery Program's goals and criteria for judging program success or failure.
4. Provide training and guidelines to increase the likelihood that those closest to the issues in the field, including resident engineers, identify cost increases caused by deficient design.
5. Explore and vigorously pursue cost recovery opportunities that go beyond the current program boundaries to include recovery actions for construction management issues and indirect cost overpayments to consultants.

Source: Office of the Inspector General (OIG) (December 2000). A review of the Central Artery/Tunnel Project Cost Recovery Program, Robert a Cerasoli Inspector General, Commonwealth of Massachusetts.

O. Cost and Schedule Containment Initiatives

The cost and schedule containment programs were a major focus of project management and included (1) cost and schedule reduction initiatives, (2) early identification and trend analysis, (3) a claims avoidance program, and (4) partnering and alternative dispute resolution, among other initiatives. Significant cost savings totaling $750 million were realized from cost containment actions, including $60 million for disposing of 17 million cubic yards of excavated material (Bechtel 2006). A summary of each of these initiatives is found in Chapter 5.

P. Value Engineering and Value Engineering Change Proposal Programs

The value engineering (VE) and value engineering change proposal (VECP) programs reduce project costs through design and constructability reviews by engineers, consultants, and contractors. These reviews typically identify new or different ways of designing and constructing scope items that lead to cost and, often, schedule savings. The VECP program solicits value engineering proposals from contractors, and, if implemented, the contractor and the project share the cost savings evenly. The section design consultant VE program solicited value engineering proposals from design consultants for inclusion in the final design. These programs, among others, are discussed in more detail in Chapter 5 but are mentioned here in recognition of the contribution of these programs to cost control.

Q. Owner-Controlled Insurance Program

The owner-controlled insurance program (OCIP) (see Chapter 9) provided a centralized cost-controlled process for managing construction and third-party claims. The superb safety record kept insurance claims lower than expected for a project of this magnitude. Moreover, the program eliminated the need for each contractor or consultant to purchase commercial insurance, thus eliminating overlapping coverage and allowing the project to realize the economies of scale.

An owner-controlled insurance program should be evaluated through a detailed cost-benefit analysis. There are some disadvantages to OCIPs, including increased administrative costs and a disincentive for the contractors to work safely if the contractor's own insurance record will not be impacted by poor performance. However, on the Big Dig, the benefits clearly outweighed the disadvantages through the project's incentivized safety program, resulting in superior safety records, reduced costs through a centrally managed program, elimination of delay in paying claims, and better loss control because of collaboration with insurers, risk management, and safety.

6. STRATEGIES TO ADDRESS COST ESCALATION

In 2006, the Transportation Research Board's Final Report for Cost Estimation and Management for Highway Projects identified eight strategies to address cost escalation and linked these strategies to 18 different causes of cost escalation on highway projects in the United States. Notably, the research concluded that most efforts in cost estimation have focused on creating tools to improve cost estimates, when in reality tools were needed to manage the costs after the estimates were completed. The National Cooperative Highway Research Program (NCHRP) team arrived at this state-of-the-practice review through an exhaustive literature review and in-depth interviews with federal, state, and local transportation agencies, transportation consultants, and nontransportation owners (Anderson et al. 2006).

Of the 18 factors, the following 5 factors, highlighted by the NCHRP in its report, had a particularly significant impact on project cost growth at the Big Dig (Anderson et al. 2006, 124).

1. *Project bias:* The intentional underestimation of costs in order to ensure a project is funded (see OIG 2001 report).
2. *Schedule-driven projects:* Extensions caused by budget constraints or design challenges can cause unanticipated increases in inflation cost effects even when the rate of inflation has been accurately predicted. (Conversely, federal funding requirements caused some early bid packages to be released before they had been completed). This alone increased costs. Importantly, the impact of the project's chosen delivery method (design-bid-build) unfortunately has never been evaluated in terms of the additional costs it may have imposed on the project.
3. *Engineering and construction complexities:* Project technological complexities caused by the project's location or purpose can make early design work very challenging and lead to internal coordination errors between project components. Internal coordination errors can include conflicts or problems between the various disciplines involved in the planning and design of a project. Constructability problems that need to be addressed may also be encountered as the project develops. If these issues are not addressed, cost increases are likely to occur.
4. *Faulty execution:* Faulty execution by the department of transportation (DOT/FHWA) in managing a project is one factor that can lead to project cost overruns. This factor can include the inability of the DOT representatives to make timely decisions or actions, failure to provide information relative to the project, and failure to appreciate construction difficulties caused by coordination of connecting work or work responsibilities (Board 2003; Callahan 1998; Chang 2002; Merrow et al. 1981; Merrow 1986; Merrow 1988; Touran and Bolster 1994). In 2000, the Federal Highway Task Force on the Big Dig issued a report summarizing 34 recommendations for oversight of highway projects (FHWA 2000).
5. *Inconsistent application of contingency:* Inconsistent contingency application can be both an internal factor contributing to underestimation during the planning stage and a contributor to cost overruns during the execution of the project. During the project execution, contingency funds, instead of being applied to their dedicated purpose, are inappropriately applied to construction overruns and then are not available for their intended purpose (Noor and Tichacek 2004; Ripley 2004).

LESSONS LEARNED

1. Engineering and construction complexity can cause early cost estimates to be inaccurate and unrealistic; therefore, megaprojects require specialized knowledge of cost management. Federal funding rules must change so that projects are not required to spend money or lose it if the project procurement process is delayed.
2. If the project is schedule driven, understand the impact of this approach on cost, quality, risk, and design and budget, accordingly.

3. Market competition is a critical factor in costing contracts, and baselines on long-duration projects must be adjusted as the market changes.
4. The earned value methodology should be utilized from the inception of the project and must be consistently based on the physical progress of the work and a realistic baseline.
5. Develop cost management tools and measurements from project inception, and consistently enforce procedures based on these measurements.
6. Make sure your cost control tools highlight vital signs to indicate warnings of potential problems, then act immediately upon those warnings.
7. Large-scale projects are beset by an overly optimistic bias at their inception, which must be reconciled by statutory budget requirements, rigorous oversight, and independent reviews that are mandated by public laws and regulatory standards.
8. The purpose of construction contingency and other contingency accounts and management reserves should be clearly defined and procedures should be followed regarding the rules for drawing down these accounts so they are used for the intended purposes.
9. Budget sufficient management reserves to reflect potential staff increases.
10. The potential for schedule delays should be built into the project's construction contingency and inflation cost estimates.
11. Cost and schedule risks must be clearly allocated in the contractual documents, and contracts must be enforced based on those allocations.
12. Project reports should lend themselves to ready analysis—particularly with regard to such concerns as the uncertainty of forecasts and the trade-off possibilities between time reductions and cost increases.

BEST PRACTICES

1. Develop policies and procedures to define the project's method of cost management.
2. Establish a baseline against which measurement of costs can be made and against which a properly evolved budget can be formed from uniformly developed cost estimates.
3. Challenge the status quo and look for innovative ways to eliminate, reduce, and recover costs.
4. Document estimate basis, assumptions, and backup calculations thoroughly and frequently test these assumptions and calculations.
5. Separate construction contingencies from the project's management reserve, apply contingencies consistently, and never utilize contingencies to add or modify scope.
6. Anticipate external cost influences such as community concerns, inflation, market forces, regulatory and political changes, and unforeseen events, and incorporate them into the estimate.

7. Allocate the risk of cost escalation to the responsible designer or contractor, and enforce the contract.

8. Measure the physical progress of the work in parallel with the cost of that work set off against the budget by determining what level of value has been earned by the completion of the work against the budget under the earned value methodology.

9. Develop fully integrated cost and resource project schedules to provide greater understanding to managers and/or the public in tracking and managing the whole project.

10. Include cost escalation in current dollars and continually review the escalation formula to ensure it is capturing true and complete cost data.

11. Hire an independent engineer or appoint a committee of independent experts to review change order requests and make sure they align with contractual provisions and are typical for the construction industry.

12. Create estimate transparency with disciplined communication of the uncertainty and importance of an estimate.

13. Create cost containment mechanisms for timely decision making that indicate when projects deviate from the baseline.

14. Apply rigorous project reporting and controls that include earned value systems, forecast time, and cost to complete, and maintain historical data with which to benchmark project performance.

15. Remember that earned value has no value unless your budget is realistic and contracts are enforced in accordance with contractual obligations and project standards.

SUMMARY

This chapter has described the critical issues in cost estimation management and control for large-scale projects. Strategies, tools, and techniques for managing cost have been analyzed. Extensive research on cost escalation for megaprojects in general and for the Big Dig in particular clearly indicates that controlling costs requires political will and protection of the process from internal and external pressures, commencing at the inception of the project. Integrity of the cost estimation process is critical if projects are to deliver quality services to the true owners of the system, the citizens and taxpayers of the local community.

ETHICAL CONSIDERATIONS

In an important case reported by the FHWA in the United States, an inspector for the state agency overseeing the project noted that a concrete supplier had delivered precast concrete catch basins only a day after the state Department of Transportation had approved the custom design, including a framework of reinforcing steel. Precast concrete structures normally must cure for at least a week before shipment.

The inspector reported the discrepancy to the resident engineer, who noted handwritten markings on one of the catch basins indicating that it was standard stock, not a custom product. The engineer directed destructive testing on one of the catch basins and found no reinforcing steel. After twice blaming the matter on truckers who "mistakenly" loaded the wrong stock, the concrete supplier finally admitted his company had falsely certified that it provided materials meeting contract specifications. The supplier was suspended from the state's prequalification program, had to identify and replace deficient structures at a substantial cost, and paid $500,000 in criminal and civil penalties. This case also illustrates concerns that can arise about safety of the traveling public and the service life of transportation facilities when taxpayers do not get what they pay for as a result of unethical behavior. Experts agree that prevention and deterrence of ethical lapses in any organization depend on the effectiveness of the internal controls and oversight.

1. Do you feel the punishment was severe enough in this case, considering the potential safety issues for the traveling public? Why or why not? If it was not severe enough, what further penalties would you suggest?
2. What are some of the vital controls that can be implemented on projects to assist managers in uncovering unethical conduct as reported in this case?

DISCUSSION QUESTIONS

1. Of the 17 cost control tools described in this chapter which do you think are the three most important tools and why?
2. What is the impact on a project when a project's funding sources are insufficient to meet the project's cost commitments?
3. How would you structure your cost management team to ensure the proper estimation and management of cost?
4. What are some cost monitoring tools that you could utilize to provide further advance indications as to the accuracy of cost projections through Project completion that are not discussed in this chapter?
5. When can earned value be a useful tool in tracking project performance, and when will it be of no use in tracking cost and schedule?
6. Describe three vital signs that would indicate that your cost control process is out of control.
7. Research has shown that large scale projects are beset by an overly optimistic bias at their inception. How can projects prevent this systemic underestimation of cost so that the public is aware of the true cost of the project before commitment of any funding?

8. Why is market competition a critical factor in costing contracts and baselines on long duration projects and how would you mitigate the risk of under estimating the project cost based on competitive factors?

REFERENCES

Anderson, S., K. Molenaar, and C. Schexnayder. 2006. *Final Report for NCHRP Report 574: Guidance for Cost Estimation and Management for Highway Projects During Planning, Programming and Preconstruction.* Web-Only Document 98. September 2006.

Bechtel/Parsons Brinckerhoff. 2006. *The Big Dig: Key Facts about Cost, Scope, Schedule, and Management.*

Board on Infrastructure and the Constructed Environment. 2003. *Completing the "Big Dig": Managing the Final Stages of Boston's Central Artery / Tunnel Project.* National Research Council and National Academy of Engineering of the National Academies, Committee for Review of the Project Management Practices Employed on the Boston Central Artery/Tunnel Project, Division on Engineering and Physical Sciences. Washington, DC: National Academies Press.

Callahan, J. T. 1998. *Managing Transit Construction Contract Claims. Transportation Research Board.* TCRP Synthesis 28. Washington, DC: National Academies Press, 1–59.

CA/T (Central Artery/Tunnel Project). 2000. Finance Plan Update. (June 16.) Massachusetts Turnpike Authority, 22–36.

CA/T (Central Artery Tunnel Project). 2002. Project Management Monthly (PMM) (January). Massachusetts Turnpike Authority.

CA/T (Central Artery/Tunnel Project). 2004. Finance Plan. (October 1.) Massachusetts Turnpike Authority.

Chang, Andrew Shing-Tao. 2002. "Reasons for Cost and Schedule Increases for Engineering Design Projects." *Journal of Management in Engineering* (ASCE): 29–36 (January).

D&T (Deloitte & Touche). 2003. Central Artery/Tunnel Project, CSU10, Project Assessment. Prepared for Massachusetts Executive Office for Administration and Finance. October 17.

Dettman, K., M. J. Harty, and J. Lewin. 2010. "Resolving Megaproject Claims: Lessons from Boston's 'Big Dig.'" *The Construction Lawyer* 30(2) Washington, DC: American Bar Association.

FHWA (Federal Highway Administration). 2011. *Lessons Learned: Summary of Lessons Learned from Recent Major Projects.* Office of Innovative Program Delivery (IPD), U.S. Department of Transportation.

FHWA (Federal Highway Administration). 2000. *Task Force Report on Boston's Central Artery / Tunnel Project.* U.S. Department of Transportation. April 11.

Grant, M. 1997. "Eurotunnel Financing." *Japan Railway and Transport Review, April.*

Hatem, D. J. 1996. "Errors/Omissions Cost Recovery Claims against Design and Construction Management Professionals." *The CA/T Professional Liability Reporter* 1.4 (1996):1.

McCormack Report. 1997. *Managing The Central Artery/Tunnel Project: An Exploration of Potential Cost Savings*. The John W. McCormack Institute of Public Affairs. Boston: University of Massachusetts.

Merrow, Edward W. 1986. *A Quantitative Assessment of R&D Requirements for Solids Processing Technology Process Plants*. Santa Monica, CA: Rand Corporation. July.

Merrow, Edward W. 1988. *Understanding the Outcomes of Mega Projects: A Quantitative Analysis of Very Large Civilian Projects*. Santa Monica, CA: Rand Corporation.

Merrow, Edward W., Kenneth E. Phillips, and Christopher W. Myers. 1981. *Understanding Cost Growth and Performance Shortfalls in Pioneer Process Plants*. Santa Monica, CA: Rand Corporation. September.

MHD (Massachusetts Highway Department). 1994. Central Artery/Tunnel Project Finance Plan. (December 30.) Massachusetts Highway Department.

Noor, I., and R. L. Tichacek. 2004. "Contingency Misuse and Other Risk Management Pitfalls." *AAACE International Transactions*: Risk.04.1–Risk 04.7.

OIG (Office of the Inspector General). 2000. *A Review of the Central Artery/Tunnel Project Cost Recovery Program*. Robert A. Cerasoli, Inspector General. Commonwealth of Massachusetts. December.

OIG (Office of the Inspector General). 2001. *A History of Central Artery/Tunnel Project Finances 1994–2001*. Report to the Treasurer of the Commonwealth. Robert A. Cerasoli, Inspector General. Commonwealth of Massachusetts. March.

Peterson Consulting Limited Partnership. 1995. Central Artery/Tunnel Project Management Review, Phase II. Boston.

PMI (Project Management Institute). 2013. *A Guide to the Project Management Body of Knowledge (PMBOK® Guide)*—Fifth Edition. Newtown Square, PA: Project Management Institute.

Ripley, P. W. 2004. "Contingency! Who owns and manages it?" *AACE International Transactions*: CSC.08.1–CSC.08.4. SAIC 2002.

Touran, A., and P. J. Bolster. 1994. *Risk Assessment in Fixed Guideway Transit System Construction*. Washington, DC: Federal Transit Administration.

Chapter 9

Megaprojects and Megarisk

There are risks and costs to a program of action, but they are far less than the long-range risks and costs of comfortable inaction.

—*John F. Kennedy*

THE ROLE OF RISK MANAGEMENT ON MEGAPROJECTS

Natural and man-made disasters around the globe, including earthquakes, cyclones, oil spills, tsunamis, devastating floods, and political unrest, remind us that catastrophic risk is all around us and, as project managers, we must be vigilant and constantly prepare for the unexpected. However, it is not just the catastrophic risk that is of concern on megaprojects, but the everyday routine performance of tasks potentially resulting in serious harm and damage claims that can exceed potential catastrophic loss. For instance, U.S. Department of Labor statistics indicate that on an annual basis slip and fall cases constitute the biggest single cause of loss on construction projects.

The Big Dig was one of the largest and most complex inner-city engineering projects ever designed, entailing many technological challenges that required a world-class risk management program (Tobin 2001). With more than 5000 workers, thousands of businesses, and more than 600,000 residents, it was critical that a framework be developed that could manage the unique and complex risk issues the project would face during its long life. Figure 9.1 depicts the risk framework that was deployed to seek mutual cooperation and agreement among multifunctional project stakeholders. The serious potential for catastrophic loss included airport disruption, immersed tube tunnel leakage and collapse, construction over subway lines and under railways, and excavation within feet of high-rise buildings. Previous high-risk projects with large owner-controlled insurance programs (OCIPs) included the Great Belt Link in Denmark, the English Chunnel, and the Sydney Harbor. However, none required tunneling through an inner city within feet of massive structures such as Gillette World Headquarters, the Federal Reserve Bank, the U.S. Postal Service, and the facilities that house many multinational corporations, area hospitals, and financial institutions. Due to the scale of

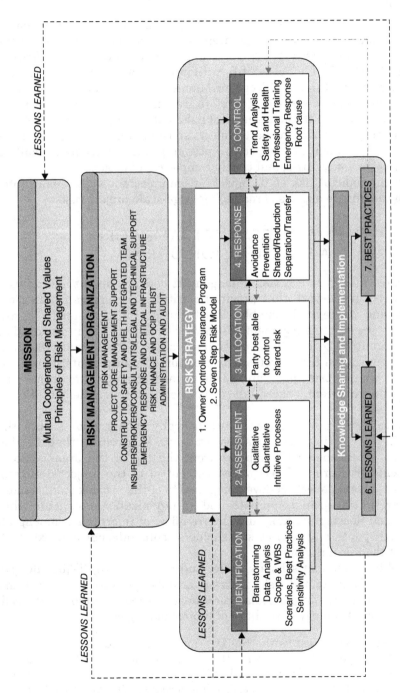

Figure 9.1   Risk Management Framework: A Shared Vision

the project, any project failure would have had a significant and long-lasting impact on the city.

Risk management is an integral part of project management, as evidenced by the risk management knowledge area included in recent versions of the Project Management Institute's *A Guide to the Project Management Body of Knowledge (PMBOK® Guide)*—Fifth Edition (PMI 2013) and the Program Risk Management Standard (Program Management Standard 2013). Successful management of projects, therefore, requires a well-strategized risk management approach through the establishment of clear project-developed risk plans and principles. The best projects show an ability to manage risks more effectively, which, in turn, contributes to positive outcomes, resulting in safer projects, lower costs, and timely completion of projects.

Though the topic of risk as it impacts megaprojects is vast, this chapter focuses on the unique aspects of managing large-scale project risk.

RISK MANAGEMENT FRAMEWORK: A SHARED VISION OF RISK

As illustrated in Figure 9.1, risk management depends upon the establishment of a risk framework that provides clarity to the program's mission, principles, and strategy. To enable robust and proactive oversight of risk at all levels, the risk management framework comprises (1) a mission that is based on mutual cooperation and shared values, (2) a formal risk management organization that involves the creation of multiple interdependent teams with shared principles, and (3) a defined strategy that focuses on continuous improvement, shared lessons learned, and the implementation of best practices.

The overall risk profile must be strategically managed to ensure the project achieves its vision and business strategy. It is critical that the risk program be established with support from the top of the organization's management structure and recognized as central to the project's success. The most important aspects of developing a state-of-the-art risk management program are an integrated approach and an organizational structure that ensures sound decision making and the free flow of information among all project participants and project stakeholders, both internal and external, throughout the life of the project.

As noted by prominent scholars Miller and Hobbs (2006), "[T]he effective management of anticipated risks in large, complex projects in general and in relational venturing in particular goes much beyond the steps in the risk management methodology of traditional project management."

In complex projects such as the Big Dig, involving public/private collaboration, it is important to recognize that "risks are manageable and that public officials can mitigate these risks if they take prudent and reasonable steps to ensure that they are... performing necessary due diligence before committing to projects..."

(USDOT 2008)

Rigid oversight must be applied not only in the conceptual stage but throughout the project development and execution stages. Effective risk management requires that the project organization have a clear overarching vision of risk, including the right team of participants, and that it structure the organization to ensure that risk is the first and most important priority.

THE DEVELOPMENT OF A RISK MODEL

Figure 9.2 shows a risk management model describing the shared risk concept based on approaches used by various organizations including the Project Management Institute, the National Institute of Science and Technology, and the U.S. Department of Energy. Risk Management is an iterative progression that involves a sequence of analysis utilizing various methodologies, tools and techniques, and processes and procedures. Thus, each time a new risk is identified, the sequence of analysis starts again and continues throughout the life cycle of the project and beyond, until all responsibilities of the risk manager are transitioned to operations.

Step 1: Risk Identification

Effective risk management relies on the identification of risks, particularly in the early phases, before the project concept has been finalized. In the early phases, it is more important to identify all the potential types and sources of risk than to actually identify individual risk events. Having a rich coalition of project participants and a large network external to the project that the owner can draw on in the search for information and solutions is essential. Risk identification involves continuous analysis and evaluation of risks based on the nature, severity, and potential impact on the project. "It

Figure 9.2   Seven-Step Risk Model
Source: Central Artery/Tunnel Project Risk Management Model.

is, for example, impossible to predict for the individual project exactly which geological, environmental, or safety problems will appear and make costs soar . . . [b]ut . . . it is possible to predict the risk, based on experience from other projects, that some such problems will haunt a project and how this will affect costs" (Flyvbjerg et al. 2002).

Step 2: Risk Assessment

Once risks are identified, the second step in the process is the assessment or analysis of the risks. Risk analysis can be a lengthy process, usually resulting in a formal report known as a *risk assessment*. A simple explanation of the process is that risk assessment deals with answering three questions: What can go wrong? How frequently does it occur? What are the consequences?

The risk manager today is, in reality, a change manager who must continuously update the assumptions and underlying principles that govern risk throughout the life cycle of the project. Original assessments must be updated frequently when a project's scope, duration, and budget changes. Assessments also change as risks are realized from identified exposures. Best practices recommend that risk assessments be updated no less than annually and, in projects subject to dramatic swings in market forces and environmental factors, more frequently in order to ensure that the project meets to-go risk exposures in the most cost-effective manner. Risk includes not only the exposures that evolve from the design and construction activities but also the risks inherent in the overall financial structure of the project and the market forces that bear on that risk.

Risk Perception   An important focus of risk assessment is to recognize the existence of differing risk perceptions. Risk perception is the subjective judgment that people make about the characteristics and severity of a risk.

Despite the fact that people generally fear flying more than driving their automobiles, the risk of being injured or of dying in a car crash far exceeds the risk of flying in an airplane. The obvious reason for their fear is the false impression that what you can control is a lower risk than one you cannot control. For example, most people feel safer behind the wheel of a car than as a passenger because they are controlling the direction and movement of the vehicle and they know their own skills in accident prevention. Yet statistics bear out the fact that risks you can control, such as remembering to utilize fall protection on a work site, result in a far greater incidence of injuries and fatalities than risks you cannot control such as personal injury and property damage from a hurricane. Examples of uncontrollable risks include train and airplane travel, terrorism, earthquakes, and pesticides in food.

Understanding risk perception is critical so that a project risk manager can avoid spending time and funding on mitigation and prevention for a risk that is unlikely to happen at the expense of failing to spend enough time on a risk that is more likely to occur and can harm a greater number of people.

Countering Risk Perception   To counter risk perception, projectwide training and educational programs are essential. Perception of risk plays a prominent role in decision making. Both individual and group differences in preference for risky decision alternatives and situational differences in risk preference have been shown to be associated with differences in perception of the relative risk of choice options. This is opposed to differences in attitude toward perceived risk (Slovic and Weber 2002). "It is important to understand that risk assessments are constructed from theoretical models which are based on assumptions and subjective judgments. If these assumptions and subjective judgments are deficient, the resulting assessments may be quite inaccurate" (Slovic 1987).

Important Factors in Assessing Risk Perception

- Assumptions must mirror reality—if a risk is overstated, resources may be devoted to an exposure that will never be realized, while other, more important exposures are ignored.
- Assumptions must be tested through historical data, current research, and expert opinion.
- Brainstorming, surveys, and checklists must be employed, and false impressions must quickly be addressed.
- Educate all stakeholders, including the public, about the reality of risk perceptions so that risks are not misunderstood.

Step 3: Develop Risk Response Strategies

Risk response is the process by which projects reduce the likelihood that risks and resulting damages will occur from known events. It is critical that risk response begin in the early stages of project planning. Risk response strategies are the approaches that risk management takes to deal with the risks that have been assessed and quantified. In the section on risk quantification, we discuss evaluating the risk in terms of its impact and probability so that identified risks can be prioritized in their order of importance. This is called *severity*, the combination of impact and probability.

Risk response strategy is really based on risk tolerance. Risk tolerance in terms of severity is the point above which a risk is not acceptable and below which the risk is acceptable. Risk tolerance also plays a major role in what risks will be accepted and what risks will be transferred or even avoided. On public projects, risk tolerance tends to be lower because of the duty to protect the public interest. Because risk is about probability, response must be determined using processes such as root-cause analysis to determine source, and a combination of likelihood and consequence estimation to assess options such as risk avoidance, mitigation, and transfer.

Step 4: Allocate Risk

Traditionally, virtually all risk associated with the design, construction, financing, operation, and maintenance of a transportation project is borne by the public sector. However, in recent years public projects have increasingly used public-private partnerships (PPPs) to transfer financial, technological, and operational risks. Proper allocation of project risk to the parties (public or private) best able to manage the risks has lowered overall risk, reduced project costs, and accelerated project delivery.

Proper risk allocation can also increase the public sector's ability to manage a large number of projects simultaneously. Public private partnerships have been used to encourage the private sector to come forward with creative ideas for improving the quality of public transportation infrastructure. When risks are understood and their consequences are evaluated, decisions can be made to allocate risks in a manner that minimizes costs and delays, promotes project goals, and aligns the construction team with the interests of the local citizens.

Step 5: Monitor and Control Risk

Risk monitoring and control is defined in PMI's *PMBOK® Guide* as the process of identifying, analyzing, and planning for newly arising risks; keeping track of the identified risks and those on the watch list; reanalyzing existing risks; monitoring trigger conditions for contingency plans; monitoring residual risks; and reviewing the execution of risk responses while evaluating their effectiveness. As risk exposures are identified and quantified, appropriate means for managing each exposure must be selected in order to minimize the cost of risk. Effective control requires technical knowledge of the exposure and processes and procedures that are regularly reviewed and enforced.

Based on the risk appetite of the project's stakeholders and the prevalent regulatory requirements, risk control measures need to be monitored and reviewed throughout the project life cycle. To this end, the U.K. Office of Government Commerce suggests the "four Ts" approach to risk management: (1) Transfer, (2) Tolerate, (3) Treat, and (4) Terminate (Vines 2007).

When analysis indicates that a risk cannot be adequately retained or controlled, it should be transferred to another party who can bear the risk at a lower cost. This includes not only transfer through insurance but also direct transfer to a contractor through hold-harmless and indemnification agreements (transferring risk). In instances where the probability of the risk event is minimal or the economic cost in mitigating such risk is astronomical compared to the project catastrophic potential or lack of proven technological advancements in megaprojects in addressing uncertainty fully, the risk should be retained and no immediate action to mitigate the risk should be taken until such time such risk is no longer considered tolerable and appropriate risk control measures need to be performed (tolerating risk). In cases where a risk cannot be eliminated entirely, control measures may be used to reduce the frequency and/or severity of some losses (treating risk). Some risks may be avoided entirely through decisions not to engage in certain activities, thus giving up the potential benefits of the risky activity in order to avoid the potential loss (terminating risk).

The risk monitoring and control process applies techniques, such as variance and trend analysis, that require the use of performance data generated during project execution. Important strategies and tools for risk control on the project are as follows:

1. Establishment of a world-class health and safety program
2. Use of root-cause analysis and evaluation to prevent reccurrence of similar events
3. Protection of critical infrastructure through security and emergency preparedness programs

Step 6: Document Lessons Learned

Lessons learned are among the most important process assets generated by projects and are recognized by the Project Management Institute as an essential influence on a project's success (PMI 2013). Unfortunately, these valuable assets are often collected either too late in the project's life to be of value or are forgotten before the organization's next project begins. All projects should have a comprehensive, coordinated, systemized, integrated lessons-learned program that cuts across all project areas and links with the umbrella organization. For instance, early in the project, the Big Dig established a representative group of core managers who met weekly to discuss and document all lessons learned from the previous week and was supported with a best practices implementation plan.

Step 7: Identify Opportunities and Implement Best Practices

Every project strives to identify best practices by comparing actual or planned project practices to those of comparable projects (PMI 2013). To avoid dooming a project to failure, you must consistently look at the best practices available (Kendrick 2009). Most effectively used as a benchmark, a "best" practice can evolve to become better as improvements are discovered on the project. Best practices are used to maintain quality in addition to mandatory legislated standards. Implementation of these practices can occur in various forms including policy memorandums, codes of conduct, or directives from senior project management. Just as important as identifying and implementing best practices is the process of changing "worst practices." Ceasing to do things wrong can be more beneficial than doing more things right. The Big

Dig project continuously identified both best- and worst-case practices. As an example, if the project experienced losses from failure to identify the location of an underground sewer pipe, practices were assessed and processes implemented that included better training, better data, and better oversight to reduce the number of these incidents in the future.

Projects succeed generally because their leaders do two things well. First, leaders recognized that much of the work on any project—even a high-tech project—is not new. Lessons learned on earlier projects can be a road map for identifying and avoiding potential problems. Second, they plan project work thoroughly, especially the portions that require innovation to understand the challenges ahead and to anticipate many of the risks (Kendrick 2009).

Business Continuity Management   Similar to the need to view risk management along the value chain (internal and external customers and suppliers) in an integrated way to ensure mutual collaboration from multiple interdependent teams and their understanding and execution of common goals, the treatment of enterprise risk management would not be complete without discussing business continuity management (BCM) in the event that disasters or complex and unique risks materialize.

Business continuity management seeks to identify potential risks or threats to an organization and allows it to plan and develop ways to react and recover from major risk events. Today's business continuity management is tied closely to crisis management that systematically deals with a disaster or a risk event as it arises. PMI's the *PMBOK® Guide* project management methodology for post disaster reconstruction, the Disaster Recovery Institute International (DRII) and the Business Continuity Institute (BCI) formulate the common body of knowledge that provides a structured and systematic approach to business continuity management. There is close similarity between project management and business continuity management, as evident in the many steps of the DRII professional practices used to develop a business continuity management program to help an organization recover from a crisis (DRII 2008).

From a project management perspective of establishing a continuity planning project to recover from a major disaster or risk event, Howe (2007) suggests grouping the components or *subject areas* of the business continuity plan described in Table 9.1 into three distinct phases:

1. *Information gathering:* This first phase consists of risk evaluation and control and the establishment of an appropriate recovery support structure, with appropriate team members assigned. A detailed business impact analysis would allow the stakeholders to gain valuable information about the impact of the risk event on the ongoing operations and help the project manager and team members develop proper continuity strategies that ensure the continuation of critical functions within the specified recovery objectives and timelines.

Table 9.1   Considerations for Implementing a Business Continuity
Management Program

Subject Area	Plan Details
Program Initiation and Management	Justify the need to establish a Business Continuity Management (BCM) framework that includes, for example, the risk mission to safeguard the safety of the general public and the project's workers, and the development of operational risk management and crisis management plans.
	Obtain management support and approval of the BCM program.
Risk Evaluation and Control	Assess the risk events and their environment that would severely impact the organizations and their resources in the event of a major disruption.
	Establish appropriate control measures to mitigate risks.
	Define a cost-benefit analysis to justify and seek approval for instituting necessary controls to mitigate crises as they unfold.
Business Impact Analysis	Define the scope of the business impact analysis (BIA) applicable to the entire enterprise with timelines for business resumption (due to disruption of airport operations, etc.) and resource requirements, and obtain the crisis management team's agreement.
	Assess the effects of loss exposure (loss control and claims management for the Big Dig, for example), disruption of delivery service, and public perception of management actions to mitigate the crisis.
	Finalize the appropriate data collection method (questionnaires, interviews, workshops/roundtable discussions).
	Establish benchmark criteria to define the criticality of functions (health and safety, operations, etc.), order of recovery, and support functions.
	Examine business process interdependencies (delivery system, supply base, regulatory agencies, and financial goals).
	Present and update the BIA report. Create appropriate records management.
Business Continuity Strategies	Compare enterprise-wide business continuity needs to business unit requirements (corporate and governmental strategies versus functional department objectives).
	Identify continuity strategy options and associated risks, e.g., maintain adequate resources to mitigate loss claims at completion-and-turnover-to-owner phase.
	Prepare and update the cost-benefit analysis of continuity strategies.

(continued)

Table 9.1   (*Continued*)

Subject Area	Plan Details
Emergency Response and Operations	Identify internal and external emergency response procedures, e.g., crisis escalation to senior officials. Public relations officer to communicate with media, public agencies, and supply base.
	Categorize disasters by types and establish the roles and responsibilities of the crisis response and management team members.
	Develop emergency response procedures such as notification of stakeholders. Analyze optimal actions by all critical management team members and their roles in times of crisis.
Business Continuity Plans	Develop and implement a business continuity and crisis management plan that includes action plans/checklists, and define the scope that identifies severity criteria that impact key business objectives.
	Establish a procedure to transition from crisis response to crisis management and business continuity.
	Develop a document to identify continuity functions (media center, transportation, etc.) and implement the plan (invoke contractual terms with suppliers).
Awareness and Training Programs	Identify key crisis members who need full business continuity training (classroom, seminars, and conferences), and suggest educational opportunities for formal certification.
	Conduct business continuity awareness sessions for management and crisis support personnel; institute electronic training modules for new employees and yearly mandatory recurring awareness training for current employees.
Business Continuity Plan Exercise, Audit, and Maintenance	Develop internal processes that fully evaluate the plan exercise steps and document the results—e.g., would the collapse of bridges under construction put the public and workers at risk and delay project completion due to the subsequent political backlash?
	Create an exercise schedule: full exercise of plan yearly with monthly incremental exercise of key functional areas.
	Prepare exercise objectives with realistic scenarios (assumptions and limitations), identify and brief exercise participants, and assign adjudicators with clear roles and responsibilities.
	Execute and audit the exercises and report results and recommendations to senior management. Coordinate ongoing maintenance of exercise plans and change control procedures (quarterly schedule).

Table 9.1   (*Continued*)

Subject Area	Plan Details
Crisis Communications	Identify and develop a crisis communications program that fosters open communications with internal stakeholders (business units and corporate, crisis and support teams) and external stakeholders (customers, suppliers, the public, media, and regulatory agencies).
	Establish primary and secondary media briefing centers and advertise the role of the public relations officer.
	Identify sources of media outlets to communicate to in the event of a crisis.
	Establish exercise objectives (test validity of corporate Web portal information and media, radio and television contacts) annually.
Coordination with External Agencies	Review the ongoing relationship with suppliers, insurance providers, and regulatory bodies to identify and coordinate emergency management procedures focusing on (1) regulatory compliance such as health and safety standards and (2) financial and resource needs in the event of a crisis.
	Coordinate and exercise emergency planning with external agencies annually. Report exercise results to senior management and government regulators with the corrective action plan and owners.

Source: Disaster Recovery Institute International (DRII).

2. *Plan development:* This second phase includes the actual development of the business continuity plan that provides details about the appropriate emergency response and escalation procedures. This detailed planning phase takes into account the health and safety of all project stakeholders, especially the public and workers on megaprojects like the Big Dig.
3. *Business continuity transformation:* Howe describes this phase as "a true transformation when a business continuity planning project becomes an ongoing corporate-wide process" (Howe 2007, 122). To this end, DRII (2008) advocates the need to establish appropriate crisis communications with stakeholders including the coordination with external agencies that encompass all levels of the government and emergency responders. The communication process needs to follow applicable laws and regulations that govern emergency response management. In this phase, it is important that awareness and training programs be developed that would allow project stakeholders to acquire the necessary knowledge and awareness to handle a crisis as it develops. Last, emergency response and recovery exercises in the business continuity plan

need to be evaluated and validated on an ongoing basis with the exercise results documented, and lessons learned captured and used to update the management plan.

When these three business continuity management phases are properly integrated with the risk management framework described in this chapter, and commitment is available at the highest level of the organization, the impact on the enterprise of a crisis or major risk event that is likely to occur during a megaproject could be lessened. This holistic approach to risk management could minimize the potential disruption to critical functions of the organization and reduce costs and schedule delay, at the same time ensuring public and worker health and safety.

THE BROAD CONTEXT OF RISK FOR THE BIG DIG

> You must put your head into the lion's mouth if the performance is to be a success.
>
> —*Sir Winston Churchill*

Each of the risk categories in Table 9.2 presents a tremendous risk challenge on large, complex projects requiring the establishment of an integrated project team in the early start-up phases of the project. Other chapters in this book have elaborated on various strategies to manage cost, schedule, and financial, political, and operational risk. This chapter, however, focuses primarily on risk category number 10 in Table 9.2, the management of catastrophic, uncertain, and accidental risks. This major category of risk was the primary responsibility of the Central Artery/Tunnel Project's Risk Management Program.

Mission

The overarching risk mission at the Big Dig was clear: to instill a project culture where safety was considered the most important value. It was a well-understood mandate that pervaded every aspect of project decision making from the early planning stages through project completion. Initial research from the U.S. Department of Labor reflected that in 1992, when project construction began, the fatality rate for a construction project of this size was 52 fatalities based on anticipated labor hours worked (DOL 1992). As the project grew in duration and complexity, so did that anticipated number. This alarming statistic caused the project to develop a mission based on a zero-accident philosophy, which required a framework of mutual cooperation, shared values, and strong governance. Considerable efforts were required to maintain a first-class loss prevention, risk mitigation, loss control, and safety and health team. The program was based on principles that were regularly

Table 9.2 General Risk Categories

Risk Category	Description	Responsible Party	Reference
1. Completion	Scope, schedule and budget, testing and commissioning	Management consultant (consultant)/ contractor/designer	Chapters 5–8
2. Construction	Adequacy of design, defects in equipment or materials, means and methods, technology threats, unforeseen events, availability of labor and materials	Consultant/ contractor/ designer	Chapters 5–9
3. Operational	Market demand and technical capacity, maintenance	Operator	Chapters 2, 10, and 11
4. Integrated project organization	Conflicts, mutual trust, partnership disputes	Shared (owner/ consultant/contractor/ designer)	All chapters
5. Technical	Design, latent defect, technology failure	Consultant/contractor/ designer	Chapters 2, 5, 9–11
6. Environmental	Meeting environmental requirements, health and safety, quality, construction, maintenance, and operational risk	Shared	Chapters 2, 5, 9–11
7. Political and regulatory	Delays, permitting, change in law, technical requirements, expropriation	Owner	Chapters 2, 4, 6, 9, and 11
8. Sociocultural	Transparency, moral hazard, and environmental justice	Shared	Chapters 2–4
9. Financial	Funding sources, revenue, and cash flow	Owner	Chapter 2
10. Force majeure/ catastrophic, accidents, and uncertainty	Natural perils, human error, economic perils, and technological hazards	Insurer/owner/ consultant/contractor/ designer/operator	Chapter 9

Table 9.3   Principles of Risk Management

Risk Management Principles
1. Develop a shared vision of risk that aligns with the strategic management goals of the organization.
2. Instill a project culture where safety is considered the most important value.
3. Require coherent policies that set forth clear objectives, goals, and standards that serve as a road map for implementation.
4. Address the inevitability of change in every aspect of risk management.
5. Involve the public and the stakeholders at every step of the risk management process.
6. Determine the degree of risk the owner is willing to accept and the risks the owner is not prepared to accept, and those risks that can be shared based on a consistent risk methodology.
7. Focus on opportunities to advance project goals, and not just negative risk and threats.
8. Manage risk from the conception stage of the project through the transition to operations.

reviewed and enforced. The principles in Table 9.3 were reviewed at various phases of the project to ensure that they were aligned with the overall goals of the organization.

RISK MANAGEMENT ORGANIZATION

As shown in Figure 9.3, an integrated risk management structure was developed at the Big Dig to provide oversight of the risks the project faced by assembling a team of worldwide risk experts, brokers, and insurers to identify, assess, mitigate, and control risk. Risk management is at the core of every project regardless of size, industry, or complexity, and risk was a central focus of the Big Dig from every perspective. The CA/T's risk mission was the operation of a world-class risk management program for engineering and construction, loss control, and safety and health that focused on both opportunities and threats. Regular meetings were held with brokers, insurers, and contractors to discuss current and future risks in order to make sure appropriate resources and processes were in place to respond to and control these risks. For every contract on the Big Dig, contractor meetings were held before construction commenced in order to discuss risk identification, assessment, response, and control with the contractor's risk manager and health and safety managers as well as with the contract resident engineer and area manager. Detailed plans were developed for dealing with identified risks, and expert advice was sought concerning the people, processes, and tools and techniques for controlling these risks. Risk Management also worked closely with the project's chief financial and budget officer, the OCIP

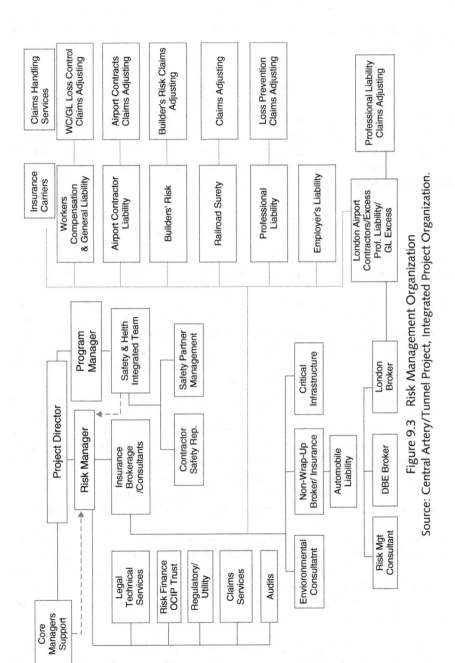

Figure 9.3 Risk Management Organization

Source: Central Artery/Tunnel Project, Integrated Project Organization.

trust investment adviser, regulatory counsel, environmental consultants, utility managers, quality assurance, legal and technical services, emergency response, and the claims adjusters and loss control representatives for each of the insurers.

RISK STRATEGY

As a consequence of the complexity of the Big Dig, the project's risk strategy was developed to address the enormous uncertainty and propensity for change that the project faced throughout its long life. This involved recognition and adherence to the concept of managing risk using the seven-step risk model outlined as follows.

Step 1: Big Dig Risk Identification

Though many sources of information can be used to identify and assess risk on complex projects, the following were the most critical for the Big Dig:

- *Brainstorming:* Expert advice and technical judgment. The process for risk identification on the Big Dig began with assembling a team of experts, including the risk management organization, project management and labor, the core project management team members, technical experts, internal and external stakeholders, and insurers and brokers, as well as construction safety representatives.
- *Project data and documentation from comparable projects and industry practice:* This included the review of historic resource data sheets, environmental impact reports, documentation from prior projects with similar concerns, and geotechnical, structural, and supportive engineering reports. In order to assess workers' compensation loss, data was reviewed from the workers' compensation rating and inspection bureau of Massachusetts, labor and industries minimum prevailing wages, and analysis of the project's procurement, cost estimates, and schedule.

The Boston Harbor Clean-Up Project, the largest court-ordered compliance actions in the history of the Clean Water Act, took place at the doorstep of the Big Dig. Though a very different project technologically, since it involved tunneling through water and not digging through an inner city, the Boston Harbor Project provided important lessons for risk management in project organization, integration, and governance.

- *Analysis of project scope and work breakdown structure:* Understanding the work breakdown structure (WBS) is crucial to evaluating risk, and the data and documentation provided must be thoroughly reviewed and analyzed by experts in the field. Use of the WBS reduces the chance that a risk event will be missed. On the Big Dig, contractors' risk and safety representatives were responsible for submitting their risk reports to their respective managers, and, in turn, these reports were analyzed by risk management and safety and health representatives.

- *Loss scenario analysis:* Scenario analysis is one of the most common techniques used for analyzing risk. The disciplines of management science and scenario building form the backbone of risk management (Miller and Lessard 2000). To prepare for scenarios on the Big Dig, discussions were held with numerous entities and extensive documentation was analyzed. As a starting point, seven major areas of the project were identified, and activities associated with the area, as well as loss scenarios that might be expected, were analyzed. For example, the immersed tube tunnels were to be constructed in dry dock and installed in the Fort Point Channel crossing over the MBTA Red line tunnel with a minimum of 2 feet of clearance (see Figure 9.4).

Loss Scenarios   Loss scenarios included:

- Train collision due to derailment, bridge collapse, or signaling error or malfunction
- Major gas explosion in a heavily traveled public area
- Collapse of a bridge while under demolition or construction
- Aircraft damage or airport disruption due to construction activities
- A derailment or collision and shutdown of a major manufacturing operation due to malfunction of the water intake system

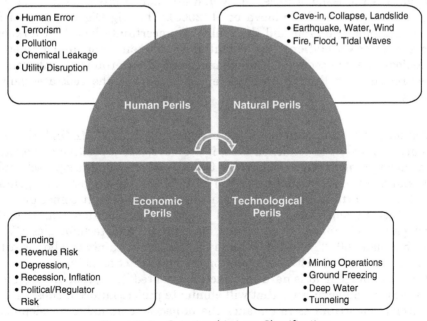

Figure 9.4   Catastrophic Loss Classification

Once the scenarios were identified, the probability and impact of the event was analyzed through both qualitative and quantitative processes. Risk analysis on the Big Dig included worst-case scenarios in order to estimate maximum possible loss. The experience with flooding and fire in the Denmark Great Belt rail tunnel illustrates the pertinence of these scenarios, as do the cost overruns and fire in the case of the Channel Tunnel (Flyvbjerg et al. 2003). In both of these cases, a failure to include such scenarios caused the cost of each of these projects to rise without sufficient mitigation or allocation of risk to reduce the impact. On the Big Dig, these types of scenarios were incorporated into the risk analysis and the insurance program.

Management of Uncertainty and Catastrophic Potential   In megaprojects, the understanding of catastrophic potential and uncertainty become critical for effective decision making and ultimately ensure project success or failure. Although the probability of a catastrophic event can be determined, the real unknown is the extent of damage that may be realized. For example, the probability of a seasonal hurricane might be high, but the damage of the resulting storm may be totally unpredictable. On the other hand, uncertainty as contrasted with catastrophic potential can have many meanings and is not easily subject to traditional risk methodologies and analysis.

Keynes defined uncertainty as a state in which individual actors find it impossible to attribute a reasonably definite probability to the expected outcome of their choice (Keynes 1937).

The recent literature and trends in project management stress the need to readdress the issue of uncertainty and attempt to integrate it as part of project management (Perminova et al. 2008). The Big Dig was known for its catastrophic potential and the reality of uncertainty based on unknowable subsurface conditions, the potential for human error, and numerous technological advancements. The management of uncertainty is inherent in megaprojects, and thus must be accepted as part of the risk assessment process.

Uncertainty as an Opportunity   Risk as defined by PMI's *PMBOK*® *Guide* is an uncertain event or condition that, if it occurs, has a positive or negative effect on one or more project objectives. Objectives can include scope, schedule, cost, and quality. As further described by PMI and the project management literature, uncertainty is not always a threat to projects. It sometimes can be used as an opportunity to exceed goals and expectations through the development of innovative processes, procedures, and technologies (Ward and Chapman 2003). As noted by some scholars, uncertainty can be regarded as one of the characteristics of evolution (Perminova et al. 2008).

Project management is naturally success oriented; thus, risk management must focus on opportunities that will eliminate project failure modes, as well as develop opportunities to enhance the project's sustainable development. This means a continuous, proactive process of identifying and assessing program risk strategies and plans, monitoring processes that are deficient, and developing opportunities for success.

A few examples of risk strategies used to create opportunities on the Big Dig included the following:

- Use of partnering approaches to improve understanding of stakeholder needs and concerns
- Initiation of scenario planning to stimulate innovation and test current processes
- Implementation of an owner-controlled insurance program to better control risk
- Development of an emergency response and critical infrastructure protection program to monitor risk
- Integration of the project risk, safety, health, and loss control teams to build understanding and relationships
- Mandatory reporting of near misses, unsafe conditions and at risk behavior
- Training of project safety staff on the benefits of incentive programs in motivating workers
- Employment of root-cause analysis to prevent the same and similar accidents from occurring in the future

Major Catastrophic Losses   Since the early 1990s, total economic losses from natural catastrophes in the United States alone have averaged tens of billions of dollars per year. These disasters cause death and injury, damage property and the natural environment, interrupt business activities, and disrupt society generally. Damages from natural catastrophes in the United States are rising and are expected to continue to increase in the future (Lloyds 2011).

To understand the impact of catastrophic loss worldwide, the major impact of catastrophes over the last two decades is highlighted in Table 9.4, based on estimates from world's largest underwriters and insurers.

Classification of Catastrophic Loss   Catastrophic loss generally has a low probability but high damages if the events do occur. Infrastructure development is often at risk, as it was during the 2004 tsunami in the Indian Ocean, which set back development in parts of Southeast Asia for more than 20 years (UNDP 2009). Catastrophic loss can be classified into four categories: human perils, natural perils, technological perils, and economic perils, as illustrated in Figure 9.5. Serious loss potential existed in all four categories during the Big Dig, however, because of the technological challenges, human and technological perils were a major focus of the project's risk strategy.

Catastrophic Potential at the Big Dig   Figure 9.5 highlights the potential for catastrophic loss on a major contract on the Big Dig as described in the Big Dig's Lessons from Practice.

Table 9.4   Major Catastrophic Loss

Event	Estimated Loss
Hurricane Katrina (2005)	$43 billion–$60 billion
World Trade Center (2001)	$30 billion–$40 billiion
BP Deepwater Horizon (2010)	$25 billion–$40 billion
Hurricane Andrew (1992)	$18 billion
California earthquake (1994)	$12.5 billion
Hurricane Hugo (1989)	$ 4.2 billion
Japan Typhoon Murielle (1991)	$ 6.4 billion
Hurricane Georges (1998)	$ 2.9 billion
Hurricane Floyd (1999)	$ 2.0 billion
Oakland, CA, fire (1991)	$ 1.7 billion
IRA bombing, London (1993)	$ 1.0 billion

Source: Lloyds of London, Munich Re, Swiss Re.

Fort Point Channel

Figure 9.5   Photo of Fort Point Channel
Source: Central Artery/Tunnel Project.

The Big Dig's Lessons from Practice   The most significant risk exposure on the Big Dig was the construction and installation of the six concrete immersed tube tunnel sections under Boston's Fort Point Channel, given the close proximity of the works to the Gillette Company's World Headquarters, the Red Line Tunnel (the fourth-oldest subway in the world), and the U.S. Post Office. The shaded area in Figure 9.5 shows the six immersed tunnel tubes that were fabricated in the casting basin area. These tubes were floated out, during two construction phases, into the channel via land-secured winches and cranes. They were then guided to their permanent location using a global positioning satellite system. Once in position, they were lowered below the surface of the Fort Point Channel and supported by 110 steel reinforced caissons or drilled shafts. These tunnel tubes and caissons fit together like Legos and match up within 1/16 inch of perfection. Two of the tunnel tubes rest permanently exactly 4 feet above Boston's subway system, the Red Line. The largest tunnel box weighs about 50,000 tons. The potential exposure would have been enormous if the tunnel had collapsed on the subway beneath it, causing bodily injury and property damage.

Mitigation measures were substantial, including construction over the Red Line during nonpeak hours, the installation of gates to isolate the subway from the main train station, the availability of a nearby barge with clay to fill the leak quickly in the event a caisson were to penetrate a tunnel wall, duplicate water cooling lines for Gillette World Headquarters, the use of satellite positioning systems to guide the tunnels into place, supporting the tunnel boxes above the Red Line tunnel by drilling 110 steel reinforced caissons or drilled shafts below the surface of the channel, the building of a dam around the casting basin, and the doubling of insurance coverage.

Outcome: In May 2004, this contract was substantially complete without touching its catastrophic potential. However, significantly on September 22, 2001 a massive leak erupted beneath the tunnel tubes, gushing 70,000 gallons a minute into the site, submerging heavy machinery, and bringing key Big Dig contracts to a halt for several weeks. It was one of the largest construction setbacks on the Big Dig resulting in substantial delays in the opening of the Massachusetts Turnpike connector to Logan Airport. The cost of the flood was estimated by the project to be at least $41 million (Lewis and Murphy 2003). The losses were ultimately paid by the contractor. Lessons learned from this event include the importance of preconstruction risk planning, extensive mitigation, independent design review and safety critical failure analysis and design verification by the owner, and constant risk monitoring and control activity.

Step 2: Big Dig Risk Assessment

The focus in the Big Dig Risk Assessment was on three elements: hazards, exposures, and risk, as defined here:

- *Hazards* are the real or potential conditions (natural, accidental, or human) that cause injury to people, that cause loss or damage to property, or that interfere with the operations of the project or the government owner.
- *Exposures* are the affected loss elements, such as third-party injury, worker injury, or damage to property and equipment or the work itself, natural environment, or agencies or governments representing the public.

- *Risk* as a measure of uncertainty, is two-dimensional, capturing both the expected number (frequency) and the magnitude (severity) of an undesired occurrence or loss.

Relationship between Known, Unknown, and Realized Risk   Figure 9.6 shows the relationship between known, unknown, and realized risk. *Known risks* are generally defined as those that have been identified and analyzed, making it possible to plan responses for those risks. They can be based on expert opinion, experience, and quantitative and qualitative analysis. Known risks are assessed, mitigated, and controlled, but they may or may not occur.

Unknown risk is the risk that events will occur on projects even though they cannot be estimated or even identified in advance. These risks must be managed proactively, through contingency plans and project controls. Unknown risk can surface at any point in the project, resulting in surprise and, sometimes, dramatic losses. On the Big Dig, unknown risk was proactively managed through excess insurance coverage, contingency plans, and control mechanisms such as a centralized safety program, root-cause analysis, and emergency response.

Realized risks are the expenses that have already been incurred in a project and must be paid regardless of whether there is proper insurance. Realized events are those events that occur from both known and unknown risks and can impact the scope, cost, and schedule of a project. On the Big Dig, these realized, but previously unanticipated, risks included:

- Utility disruptions caused by a failure to properly identify sewer pipes that had been placed many decades or even centuries earlier
- Flooding caused by adjacent airport floodgates that were not operable

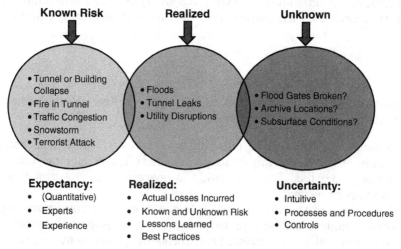

Figure 9.6   Risk Reality and Impact of Unknowns

- Subsurface obstructions including archives that had to be preserved during recovery
- Groundwater or soil conditions that were not detected despite extensive testing

Realized risks should be carefully analyzed for possible trends or patterns that would provide lessons for the future, such as additional risks or practices that should be modified going forward. Uncertainties can be managed through intuitive processes based on experience rather than quantitative or qualitative analysis and contingencies and controls (Agor 1990; Lindkvist 2011). An intuitive approach involves using data to support decisions and justifications that have already been made, given the experience of the project professionals. This approach is difficult to use in public projects because it is the most immature approach, and it involves perception of truth and facts, independent of the reasoning process.

Key Factors in Risk Assessment at the Big Dig

The Big Dig, like most complex infrastructure projects, involved many levels of decision making, each of which included an assessment of risk and some plan of managing that risk. Periodically issuing a risk assessment creates an opportunity to inform project managers of the priorities of risk management and the essential strategies that must be implemented to counter potential harmful events. An assessment uncovers and evaluates historical information and past risk assessments, analyzes current risk potential, and provides guidance for future decisions. Not to be confused with value engineering, the focus of the risk assessment is not on increasing the safety in design or construction operations, or saving money through changes in these operations, but instead the focus is on risk control techniques to reduce the frequency and severity of loss. The primary purpose of risk assessment is to identify and evaluate risks in a way that supports informed decision making. Risk assessment analysis should use the best approaches that properly capture the probability and severity of adverse consequences, as well as identify positive effects for opportunities.

Qualitative Risk Analysis   The primary purpose of qualitative risk assessment is to prioritize identified risks. The process of qualitative risk analysis is to assess the likelihood that a specific risk will occur and the impact on cost, quality, or performance, including both negative effects for threats and positive effects for opportunities, if it does occur. Sponsors and owners should organize risk management brainstorming sessions. Outside experts, independent consultants, future stakeholders, and project sponsors must evaluate all potential loss exposures in terms of their expected frequency and severity of occurrence. A risk matrix, as shown in Figure 9.7, can be used to show how risks can be classified as high, medium, or low based on

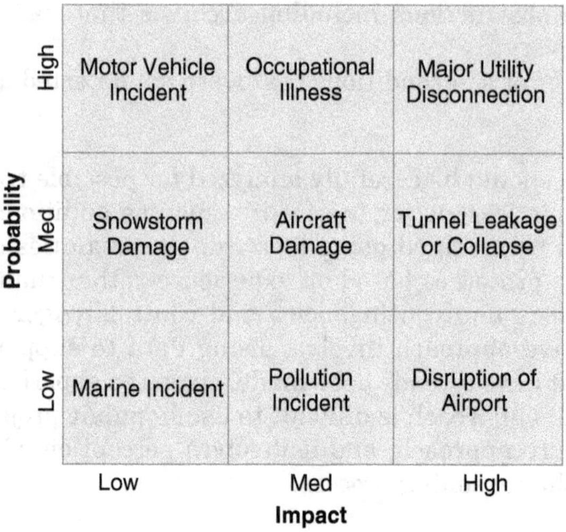

	Low	Med	High
High	Motor Vehicle Incident	Occupational Illness	Major Utility Disconnection
Med	Snowstorm Damage	Aircraft Damage	Tunnel Leakage or Collapse
Low	Marine Incident	Pollution Incident	Disruption of Airport

Probability (vertical axis: High, Med, Low)

Low   Med   High
Impact

Figure 9.7   Qualitative Risk Analysis

probability and impact. Close attention should be paid first to those risks that fall in the probability and impact ranges of high/high, high/medium, and medium/medium. A more detailed matrix can be used to identify the specific type of liability that may occur, such as damage to property, bodily injury, general liability, builders' risk, and environmental and professional liability.

Quantitative Risk Assessment   Quantitative risk assessment is about estimating specifics for risks—focused primarily on the highest-priority exposures. Quantification of risk consists of evaluating risks and interactions to assess the range of possible project outcomes. The measurement and evaluation phase involves the application of probability theory, statistical analysis, and loss forecasting methodologies and predictions. A single risk factor can result in many outcomes. For example, collapse of a major portion of project work may result in flooding, explosion, property damage, personal injury cleanup, and replacement costs. Common tools for quantitative risk assessment include decision trees, influence diagrams, and Monte Carlo simulation and sensitivity methods (Han and Dikmann 2004; Meredith and Mantel 2012). A decision tree is a diagram that depicts key interactions among decisions and related chance events as they are understood by the decision maker (*PMBOK*® *Guide*). Like decision trees, simulations can also handle both threats and opportunities, as well as sequential events.

A variety of methodologies were used to quantify risk on the Big Dig, including trend analysis based on loss histories for similar projects within the same area, insurance industry informal indications for expected losses for workers' compensation insurance, expert judgment, and Monte Carlo simulations and sensitivity analysis. The benefits of quantitative risk analysis for both public and private projects include (1) evaluating the uncertainty in the requirements and the overall risk that this places on stakeholders, (2) establishing contingency levels, (3) improving the accuracy of project cost estimates, (4) determining the impact of retained and transferable risks, and (5) choosing between alternative technologies or approaches with different risk profiles (Cooper et al. 2005).

Step 3: Big Dig Risk Response

On the Big Dig, risk response involved every aspect of the project and included an extensive environmental impact study that took years to complete and was finally released in November 1990, almost six years after the concept of the project had begun (Massachusetts Executive Office of Environmental Affairs, 1990). The magnitude of construction impacts and the implementation of appropriate mitigation measures was a concern for many, especially those who felt their homes and businesses would be directly affected. Regular responsive communication with the public is essential for an effective mitigation program. Extensive meetings were held with the local community and businesses during the early design phase of the project to identify these concerns and to develop a comprehensive mitigation program. These efforts resulted in the establishment of the Mitigation Program Office (MPO) along with the Public Information Office (PIO), which remained until the project was substantially complete.

Mitigation officers were assigned to contracts for design and construction within a project geographic area. The officers worked closely with all project staff to coordinate mitigation activities 24/7 and were in constant contact with the resident engineer on the assigned site. The PIO's priority was to create a high level of public understanding about the project. This included regular public meetings on the project status, weekly news columns, signs, highway advisory relations campaigns, an information hotline, emergency response, and project displays and maps. Table 9.6 highlights some of the more significant response measures. Typical risk response methodologies that were used on the project are highlighted as follows:

Avoidance: Risk may be prevented by eliminating scope or through procedural changes. For instance, on the project, unsafe construction practices were replaced with procedures that had less inherent risk. In the conception stage, a bridge design was altered to prevent congestion and environmental hazards.

Loss Prevention: The safety and health program and the loss control program, the mitigation program office, emergency response, and root-cause analysis were used as mechanisms for controlling losses and ultimately preventing many potential losses included in the project's risk assessment. To prevent losses, project engineers and area construction managers were authorized to order a shutdown of a construction site with known hazards.

Loss Reduction: Mitigating the effects of losses that do occur through rapid response and claims handling. The project employed both an integrated claims and changes process and a 24/7 emergency response center to mitigate losses. Loss runs prepared by the project's insurer were reviewed on a monthly basis to identify patterns of unsafe behavior, loss trends, and necessary changes in procedures.

Separation: Physically or legally separating aspects of the project that present risks and thereby lessening interactive exposures. To prevent the impact of potential flooding due to construction near water, building gates were installed and a dam was erected to separate the impact of losses from one work site seeping into another work site.

Duplication: Having additional records, equipment, or people to ensure that losses will be mitigated. On the Big Dig, backup systems were commonly used when there was concern that an essential electrical system or water cooling line might be displaced or damaged during construction.

Transfer of Risk: Allocating risk to another party. This commonly occurs through contractually obligating another party such as the contractor, to accept liability for loss or damage. On the Big Dig, the potential for catastrophic loss was transferred through the project's owner-controlled insurance program (OCIP), and liability for construction risks was transferred to the designers and contractors through contractual indemnification and a hold harmless agreement.

Owner-Controlled Insurance Program (OCIP)   Various options were considered to manage the complexity of the Big Dig and address safety, health, and catastrophic loss concerns. One option was a controlled insurance program (CIP), which is used in federal highway projects and private undertakings and is considered a highly efficient control mechanism. (Schexnayder and Weber 2002). Under a CIP, the interest of the owner, designer, construction manager, contractors, and consultants are covered by one centralized insurance arrangement. In a conventional program, contractors provide their own insurance; those contractors with a good loss experience history receive better insurance rates and, therefore, have a bidding advantage as long as the contractors have invested in safety. With an OCIP, commonly known as a wrap-up program, the rate reduction, achieved through the contractor's diligence goes to the owner. There are many additional advantages to an OCIP, the most important of which include economies of scale, centralized loss control, and enhanced workplace safety. The Big Dig's OCIP was established to address this reality. A complete review of the benefits and challenges of OCIPs can be found in a publication entitled "National Cooperative Highway Research Program (NCHRP) Synthesis 308, Transportation Research Board of the National Academies 2002."

Considerations in Selecting an Owner-Controlled Insurance Program   The Central Artery/Tunnel owner-controlled insurance program (OCIP) was the largest wrap-up program ever developed, according to one of the project's major insurers, Lloyds of London. This program provided coverage for contractors, subcontractors, and designers in place of individual insurance coverage. The program included six major types of insurance coverage, as described in Table 9.5.

Many of the risks on the Big Dig were significant and potentially catastrophic, including the collapse of bridges under construction, major building damage, construction over and under major transportation lines, the shutdown of the multi-billion-dollar Gillette Operations, and disruption of airport operations. Among the myriad mitigation controversies was the regional concern about air quality (Altshuler and Luberoff 2003). The Big Dig created an archive of lessons learned applicable to subsurface conditions in inner cities and required significant analysis of liability that was not foreseen at the time risk was identified and allocated contractually.

This OCIP was not new in the construction industry and had been used in numerous projects around the globe including the Channel Tunnel, the Sydney Harbor Tunnel, the Great Belt Link in Denmark, the New York City Transportation system, the Chicago Transit Authority Green Line Rehabilitation Project, Utah Interstate 15, the New Jersey Transit Corporation Hudson-Bergen Rail Line, and the construction of many U.S. nuclear power plants. According to the NCHRP, OCIPs have been a popular way to finance wrap-up programs (Schexnayder and Weber 2002).

Due to the enormous catastrophic potential on the Big Dig, the project could never have been started without significant coverage on all lines of insurance. To implement the program, approvals had to be obtained from the Commissioner of Insurance of the Commonwealth of Massachusetts and the federal and state agencies funding the project. In 1992, 33 insurance companies and 28 brokers bid to take part in the program. A local insurance broker was selected to help implement the program's structure and assist in the program's oversight.

Structuring an Owner-Controlled Insurance Program   To determine the structure of an OCIP, the following questions must be asked (Schexnayder and Weber 2002):

- *How much of the risk should simply be assumed?*
  When financially prudent, it is usually best to retain predictable risk. Even when insurance is used, an owner retains some risk based on selected deductible levels. This is an important component of the risk acceptance decision. Large deductible programs may have many cost advantages based on economies of scale, but they also provide advantages through loss-sensitive insurance plans including:
  1. Retrospective rating plan (actual loss experience)
  2. Dividend plan (loss-sensitive guaranteed cost policy)
  3. Retention plan (higher amount of underwriting assumed by the insurer)

Table 9.5 The Big Dig's Owner-Controlled Insurance Program Coverage and Cost

Coverage	Description	Limits	Deductible	Total Cost
Workers' Compensation	Covers injury to contractors and management consultant employees while working on the project	Statutory	$1million per person; $3 million aggregate maximum payout per occurrence	$262 million
General Liability and Excess Liability	Third-party coverage for injury and property damage	$400 million	$2 million per occurrence/$6 million loss limit per occurrence	$215 million
Builders' Risk	Covers physical damage to construction work in progress	$400 million	$25,000 (exception: $100,000 TWT tubes/Charles River Crossing)	$48 million
Railroad Protective	Coverage for bodily injury and property damage claims for work proximate to railroad property	$2 million per occurrence/$6 million aggregate per contract	No deductible	$5 million
Airport Contractors	Third-party liability for injury and property damage	$500 million	$25,000 each loss, property damage only	$8 million
Professional Liability	Covers design contractors for errors and omissions	$50 million	$500,000 per claim	$11 million
Administrative Cost	Risk management, safety, health, audit, broker, and consultants			$60 million
2008 and 2009 MADOT Updates				$15 million
Total Cost:				$624 million

Source: The Central Artery/Tunnel Project Finance Plan, 2009 Cost and Schedule Update.

The Big Dig chose a retrospective rating plan along with the large deductible in order to maximize potential savings from a centrally managed program. The insurance premium for a retrospective rating plan is based on incurred loss at the expiration of a rating period. The final premium is based on the actual losses incurred. When the purchaser of such a plan controls losses, there can be a substantially lower premium as compared with guaranteed cost insurance and the benefits of loss control accrue to the insured immediately. With retrospective policies, there is a maximum premium that places an upper limit on the effect of poor loss experience and a minimum premium that places a limitation on the potential savings resulting from a good loss experience.

- *What coverage should be included in the OCIP?*

Most of the insurance premiums that an owner compensates a contractor for in a traditional project bid situation are those related to workers' compensation and liability insurance, which are almost always included in the OCIP. However, since the project work itself was at great risk due to the potential for tunnel collapse, structural concerns, and the introduction of new technologies, it was essential that builders' risk, airport contractor's liability, professional liability, and railroad protective insurance be purchased in order to address these concerns.

- *What limits should be purchased? Is excess coverage desired?*

Catastrophic risks should be insured when coverage is available at a reasonable price. Limits should be based on qualitative and quantitative analysis of risk and excess coverage is desirable when the projected impact of the loss is high. The project had large limits of $400 million for general liability and builders' risk and $500 million for airport contractor's liability due to a number of scenarios with potential damages in excess of $100 million.

- *How do you manage the insurance budget?*

A trust was established in 1996, retroactive to program inception in 1992, in order to collateralize the project's obligations to share losses but also to share the income of the trust. The trust was chosen to segregate the funds from other insurer funds and to restrict use of the funds for insurance purposes only.

Evaluation and Benefits of the Project's OCIP As shown in Table 9.5, the cost of the Big Dig's OCIP as of substantial completion in 2006 was $609 million, which was approximately 4 percent of the total project's $14.87 billion budget. Finance updates in 2008 and 2009 increased the total cost to $624 million. In 2007, the project reported total worker compensation claims of 13,855 with 148 claims pending, and general liability claims totaling 5,532 with 92 claims pending. Though these numbers may fluctuate slightly, the enormous size of the project's loss control program is reflected in these statistics. Several reviews of the project's OCIP highlighted here indicate that there are considerable savings through reduced litigation, large-scale purchasing, enhanced safety and loss control, and reduced premiums.

In its extensive 2003 report on the Central Artery/Tunnel Project, the National Academies found that "the Project's Owner Controlled Insurance Program (OCIP) was an effective and cost-reducing response to the challenge of obtaining adequate insurance coverage for the large numbers of engineering and contracting firms involved in the project" (Board 2003). Earlier, an independent review commission had similar findings and recommended: (1) that future premiums be paid from current Trust funds, (2) that the OCIP be continued and not reverted to a contractor furnished program, (3) that $50 million should be withdrawn from the trust funds based on excess reserves to finance the CA/T Project, and (4) that a yearly analysis of the status of OCIP funding should be performed (MTA OCIP Review 2000; MTA Finance Plan 2000).

According to a GAO study on OCIPs, owners can save up to 50 percent on the cost of traditional insurance, or from 1 to 3 percent of a project's construction costs. In this study of six transportation projects, insurance savings were estimated to be between $2.9 million and $265 million through the use of OCIP insurance. Saving results from bulk buying power, the avoidance of duplicate coverage, centralized claims handling, and the reduction of litigation (GAO 1999).

Step 4: Big Dig Risk Allocation

An important theme underlying allocation of risk on the Big Dig was ensuring that the risk was allocated to the party best able to control the risk, but also, in some instances, that the risk was also shared based on considerations of efficiency and fairness. For example, catastrophic loss was shared among all project participants through the project's OCIP. In addition to allocation of risk through insurance, contractual transfer of risk was used in all construction contracts. Contractors were responsible for most construction risks including means and methods, inadequate labor force, equipment failure, quality assurance, site safety and health, and additional costs. Difficult allocations involve those where conditions are unknown, such as subsurface conditions. Often those allocations are resolved through contingencies in the budget or an equitable adjustment, or sometimes the owner has assumed these risks either by agreement or by failure to transfer this risk in the contract (*U.S. v. Spearin* 1918). Table 9.6 illustrates how major categories of risk were allocated and mitigated on the Big Dig.

Step 5: Monitoring and Controlling Risk at the Big Dig

To try to be safe everywhere is to be strong nowhere.
—*Winston Churchill*

From the inception of the project, the focus was on preemptive actions for quality and safety. The project's approach to safety and accident prevention

Table 9.6   Risk Response and Allocation

Risk	Responsible Party	Risk Response
Construction	Management consultant (consultant)/contractors/ designers	Catastrophic analysis and prevention, quality assurance, risk control training, soil tests, projectwide labor agreement, and environmental tracking system
Extension of scope and construction schedules	Consultant/contractors/ designers	When project scope and schedule changes, so must the project risk assessment. In these cases, insurance policies need to be extended and pricing and coverage need to be adjusted in order to reflect the new risks and new duration of the project.
Differing site conditions (substantial or material)	Contractors were required to give notice and to mitigate risk for an equitable adjustment to apply.	Soil sampling, structural support, as-built drawings, geotechnical investigation, and contract clause
Technology risk	Management consultant/ contractors/designers	Quality assurance and quality control, testing and audit procedures and enforcement
Operations	Owner operator Consultant/contractors/ designers for professional liability or contractor's defects liability	Contractor's defects liability, extended warranties and insurance coverage, and hiring experienced operators
Community concerns, residences and business operations	Shared among owner/ consultant/contractor/ designer)	Preconstruction videos, building monitors, business artery committee, mitigation program office, public information office, and community task force
Environmental risk	Shared in accordance with project contracts	Environmental assessment; monitoring of air, noise, and water quality; dirt transport mitigation; traffic controls; and materials testing
Financial	Project owner	State and federal participation agreement, sufficient reserves, certainty of revenue flow

(continued)

Table 9.6   (Continued)

Risk	Responsible Party	Risk Response
Political	Project owner	Centralized permitting process and labor agreements permitting all union shops in exchange for a no-strike policy
Transition to operations	Shared	Throughout the life cycle of a project, certain segments of the project become operational and are turned over to the owner. This creates increased public exposure to the infrastructure, including traffic risks and pedestrian risks that do not exist in projects under construction. The interconnectedness of the project contracts also creates risk in which damage in operations could seep into work sites and cause severe damage to work under construction. To avoid potential large losses through project completion and turnover, the resources and efforts to mitigate claims must remain at a high level to prevent increase in project losses.

Source: Project Contracts and Central Artery/Tunnel Project Finance Reports.

was founded on the zero accidents philosophy used by Bechtel Corporation in projects worldwide. This approach is based on the belief that workplace accidents are:

- Predictable
- Preventable
- Intolerable

The Big Dig project's culture was shaped by this philosophy and resulted in the development of innovative safety solutions and proactive approaches to accident prevention. It proved to not only enhance employee safety but also increase morale and productivity on the project. Figure 9.8 highlights the project's safety goals, organization, and performance measurements.

Safety Organization: Centralized and Integrated   The Risk Management Organization reflected a collaborative effort among the project's Health and Safety

Goals	Zero Accidents Safety Philosophy

- Instill a Project Culture where Safety is Considered the most important Value!
- Promote Accident prevention as a Contractor Business Imperative!
- Strive for Zero Accidents and Enforce Contracts!

Organization	Centralized and Integrated

- Establish an Integrated, Seamless, and Multi disciplined Risk Management Team!
- Develop a Dedicated Project Safety Team!
- Institute an Insurance Carrier Loss Control Program!

Performance	Measured and Accountable

- Measure by the highest standards set forth in project policy and design and construction contracts, the U.S. Occupational Safety and Health Agency Regulations (OSHA), and other applicable state and federal laws
- Publish Contractor Loss Record, Worker Lost Time Days and OSHA Recordables on a Montly Basis
- Establish a Safety and Health Awards Program for Recognized Excellence (SHARE Program)

Figure 9.8   Safety Goals, Organization, and Performance
Source: Central Artery/Tunnel Project Safety Procedures and Financial Reports.

Team, the contractor's safety representative, and the project's insurance carrier, with assigned responsibilities as designated in Figure 9.9.

Loss Control and Claims Management   The project's Loss Control Program was one of the largest programs in the country, with 13,885 workers' compensation and 5,532 general liability claims processed as of August 2007 (MTA PMM 2007). Risk Management oversaw the entire claims process through the project's audit and claims procedures. Monthly loss reports were prepared for project management and oversight and included review of the safety team accident/incident reports. Responsibilities for loss control included determination of coverage, investigation and evaluation of claims, and assessment and allocation of liability and damage. Services provided by the project's main insurer, American International Group (AIG), included medical management, loss control, vocational rehabilitation, policy administration, and premium audit.

Establishing Safety and Health Objectives, Programs, and Practices   The cornerstone of the project's safety mission was the development of an environment in which safety was always the first priority. Proactive safety goals and requirements were embedded in project contracts, policy, directives, processes, and procedures. In order to evaluate the attainment of safety goals, the project established a sophisticated metrics program. The program measured losses, accidents, safe behaviors, OSHA recordables and lost time, and increased costs, among other factors.

The project's safety and health practices were used to control the potential for anticipated risk as well as surprise events. It was essential that discipline

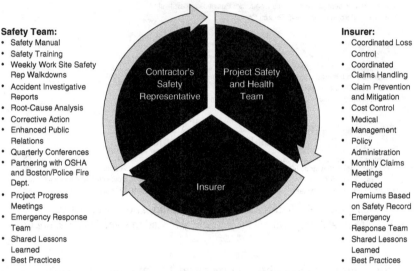

Risk Management Safety and Health Integrated Team Effort

Safety Team:
- Safety Manual
- Safety Training
- Weekly Work Site Safety Rep Walkdowns
- Accident Investigative Reports
- Root-Cause Analysis
- Corrective Action
- Enhanced Public Relations
- Quarterly Conferences
- Partnering with OSHA and Boston/Police Fire Dept.
- Project Progress Meetings
- Emergency Response Team
- Shared Lessons Learned
- Best Practices

Contractor's Safety Representative

Project Safety and Health Team

Insurer

Insurer:
- Coordinated Loss Control
- Coordinated Claims Handling
- Claim Prevention and Mitigation
- Cost Control
- Medical Management
- Policy Administration
- Monthly Claims Meetings
- Reduced Premiums Based on Safety Record
- Emergency Response Team
- Shared Lessons Learned
- Best Practices

Figure 9.9   Integrated Safety and Health Team
Source: Project Risk Management and Safety and Health Procedures.

and best practices were implemented to prevent and mitigate the possibility of catastrophic potential through occupational illness, tunnel collapse, flooding, explosions, utility disruption, or building collapse. Table 9.7 describes several of the programs and best practices.

The SHARE Program and Safety Metrics   One of the most significant impacts on worker safety was the Safety and Health Awards for Recognized Excellence (SHARE) Program. Integration of this program with Safety and Risk Management was a key element in ensuring correct oversight, input, and accountability. The program was an integral part of ensuring a safe workplace that not only prevented and reduced accidents but improved productivity, schedule, morale, and individual job satisfaction, and ultimately provided substantial cost savings to the owner and all project participants. The program was established in 1997 on a pilot basis and was extended indefinitely in June 2000. It continued to have positive impacts on construction safety, including behavioral safety changes, improved communications and education on safety issues, and continuous improvements in field support and contractor safety awareness (Board 2003).

Clear evidence of the impact the program had on worker motivation is illustrated in Figures 9.10 and 9.11. The figures show OSHA lost time and OSHA recordables consistently below national averages in every year of peak construction from 1998 through 2006. A lost time case includes any

Table 9.7 Safety and Health Programs at the Big Dig

Programs	Practices
Safety and Health Awards for Recognized Excellence (SHARE)—incentive program to prevent and reduce accidents	Continually reviewed to incorporate changes recommended by labor, management, and safety and risk management.
Substance Abuse Prevention—drug testing program	Continuous evaluation as technology and new procedures were developed.
Emergency response—prepare for and respond 24/7 to construction-phase project incidents	Consists of procedures, training, drills and exercises, and program maintenance.
Weekly health and safety inspections and report cards	Project contracts allow for safety inspection and pay item withholdings based on failure to comply with project safety requirements.
1344 Environmental commitments	Project response includes air and water quality control, rat patrol, and noise and vibration control.
Electronic identification	Provides for notification to contract management upon entry or exit on the work site.
Community and Business Artery Public Awareness Program and Utility Disruption Plan	Held weekly meetings, where new issues were addressed, including construction plans and mitigation and response efforts.

Source: Central Artery/Tunnel Project Risk Management Procedures.

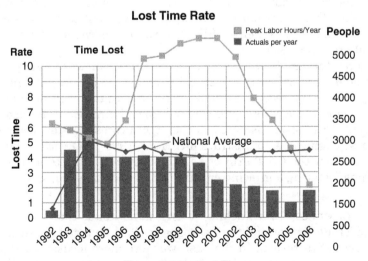

Figure 9.10   Lost Time
Source: Central Artery/Tunnel Project, Project Management Monthly (PMM).
September 2006.

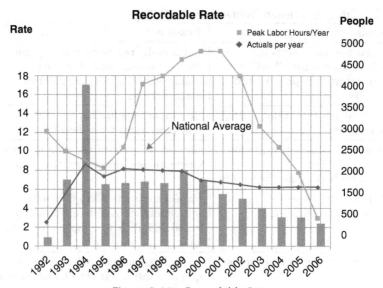

Figure 9.11   Recordable Rate
Source: Central Artery/Tunnel Project, Project Management Monthly (PMM).
September 2006.

occupational injury or illness that results in the employee being unable to work a full assigned work shift. The OSHA lost time rate represents the number of lost work days per 100 full-time employees in any given time frame. The OSHA recordable rate shows the number of employees per 100 full-time employees that have been involved in an injury or illness due to the violation of an OSHA regulation. Tracking these statistics provides a tool for identifying problems and helps OSHA determine where industries may need additional program assistance.

The successful results of the project's safety program were widely reported. The National Academies in its extensive report on the Big Dig noted that "the project's safety record for 2002 at 5.5 recordable worker injuries per 100 full-time employees is significantly below the national average of 8.2" (Board 2003). Moreover, as noted in the 1999 Process Review conducted by the Federal Highway Administration (FHWA 1999), "[O]verall, the Review Team found that the CA/T Project and the Project Contractors appear to be establishing/fostering a growing culture of Safety on the Project."

Protection of Critical Infrastructure   There is no doubt that the attacks on the World Trade Center and the Pentagon in 2001 changed minds about the consequences of terrorism. In the past, we were more focused on significant damage in a localized area such as the bombing of embassies or the USS *Cole*. Today, we confront the possibility of much wider attacks including cyber, nuclear, biological, and chemical weapons.

Prior to September 11, 2001, emergency preparedness was not widely recognized as a necessary function within organizations. Such programs typically consisted of informal policies and procedures that did not readily integrate during a response to a significant event. Since the terrorist attacks on the United States, federal, state, and local agencies have realized the need for an integrated, comprehensive emergency preparedness program that includes the following (USDHS 2009):

Security and Emergency Preparedness Project Requirements
1. Vulnerability assessment
2. Emergency management plan
3. Standard operating procedures
4. Training program
5. Drills and exercise program

As described in the 2008 Critical Infrastructure Report issued by the Organization for Economic Co-operation and Development (OECD), in most countries the word *critical* refers to infrastructure that provides an essential support for economic and social well-being for public safety and for the functioning of key government responsibility. For example, the general definition of critical infrastructure in the overall U.S. National Infrastructure Protection Plan (NIPP) is:

Systems and assets, whether physical or virtual, so vital that the incapacity or destruction of such may have a debilitating impact on the security, economy, public health or safety, environment, or any combination of these matters, across any Federal, State, regional, territorial, or local jurisdiction.

For investment policy purposes, this definition is narrower:

Systems and assets, whether physical or virtual, so vital to the United States that the incapacity or destruction of such systems and assets would have a debilitating impact on national security.

Hurricane Katrina Response Plan   One of the most sophisticated response plans ever developed resulted from the lessons learned from Hurricane Katrina, the most destructive hurricane to ever strike the United States (NOAA 2007). This monumental event prompted an extraordinary national response that included all levels of government—federal, state, and local—the private sector, faith-based and charitable organizations, foreign countries, and individual citizens. People and resources were amassed to the Gulf Coast region to aid in the emergency response and to meet the needs of countless victims. Their actions saved lives and provided critical assistance to Hurricane Katrina survivors. However, despite these efforts, the response to Hurricane Katrina fell far short of the seamless, coordinated effort that had been envisioned under the National Response Plan created in 2003

(White House 2006). Hurricane Katrina obligated the federal government to reexamine how it is organized and resourced to address the full range of catastrophic events—both natural and man-made. The storm and its aftermath provided the government with the mandate to design and build such a system, as described in the Federal Response to Hurricane Katrina.

The Federal Response to Hurricane Katrina: Lessons Learned (2006) After reviewing and analyzing the response to Hurricane Katrina, the federal government documented 17 lessons learned. Several of the more important lessons, as they relate to megaproject management, are listed here (White House 2006).

1. *National Preparedness:* The Federal Government should work with its homeland security partners in revising existing plans ensuring a functional operations structure and a clear accountable process for all national preparedness efforts.
2. *Citizen and Community Preparedness:* DHS should develop a single national campaign to promote and strengthen citizen and community preparedness.
3. *Public Safety and Security:* DOJ [Department of Justice] in coordination with HLS [Homeland Security] should build operational plans, procedures, and policies to ensure an effective Federal law enforcement response.
4. *Public Health and Medical Support:* The Department of Health and Human Services (DHHS) in coordination with DHS [Department of Homeland Security] should strengthen the Federal government's capability to provide public health and medical support during a crisis.
5. *Public Communications:* DHS should develop an integrated public communications plan to better inform, guide, and reassure the American public before, during, and after a catastrophe.
6. *Critical Infrastructure and Impact Assessment:* DHS working collaboratively with the private sector should revise and finalize the National Response Plan to be able to rapidly assess the impact of a disaster on critical infrastructure.
7. *Environmental Hazards and Debris Removal:* DHS in coordination with EPA should oversee efforts to gather environmental data and provide the public and emergency responders with information, to determine whether it is safe to operate in a disaster environment.
8. *Training, Exercises, and Lessons Learned:* DHS should establish specific requirements for training, exercise, and lessons-learned programs linked through a comprehensive system and common supporting methodology across all government agencies.

Critical Infrastructure Controls at the Big Dig The public perception of a terrorist threat creates another type of risk for large infrastructure projects. Readiness and response are critical, whether there is an attack or not.

Project Security and Emergency Response

Figure 9.12   The CA/T Project Security and Emergency Response Program Elements
Source: Adapted from the Central Artery/Tunnel Project Emergency Response Programs.

Therefore, resources and efforts must be committed to assessing the Big Dig project's vulnerabilities to attack, to preparing appropriate emergency responses, and to addressing continuity/contingency plans to recover from a potential attack. Security and response efforts are the critical element in addressing this risk. Security was an obvious challenge, given the open, multiple access points and sprawling nature of the project and related elements of the Metropolitan Highway System. The project's response, shown in Figure 9.12, included a project security and disaster plan, appointment of full-time security staff, safety and security efforts among the contractor community, a terrorism risk assessment based on Total Security Services International, Inc. (TSSI) studies of potential terrorism vulnerabilities and responses, and the most advanced traffic management and incident response system in the world. This system included more than 400 video cameras, 130 electronic message signs, 30 infrared height detectors, and 6 emergency response stations in operation 24 hours a day.

Workplace Accidents

> The harsh reality of labor statistics reminds us that "every day in America, 12 people go to work and never come home. Every year in America, 3.3 million people suffer a workplace injury from which they may never recover. These are preventable tragedies that disable our workers, devastate our families, and damage our economy."
>
> —*Secretary of Labor Hilda Solis, April 28, 2011 blog*

Out of 4070 worker fatalities in private industry in calendar year 2010, one-fifth (751, or 18.5 percent) were in construction (USDOL 2011a). This number is alarming, considering the catastrophic potential on the Big Dig. The zero accidents philosophy on the project was extremely effective in reducing the possibility of workplace fatalities but could not eliminate it entirely. During the heaviest construction phases of the Big Dig, the project was exceptionally safe. There had been 4 workplace fatalities, one of which occurred off the project site. The projection, using Bureau of Labor statistics, had been 52 at the inception of the project but increased as the labor force grew (USDOL/IIF). The largest liability cases were all "third-party over" claims, in which injured workers sue another contractor (not their employer) for work-related injuries, including pain and suffering within their claim.

Efforts to reduce construction failures by studying their causes has led to a meaningful reduction in incidents. A large majority of construction failures has been attributed to human error. The Occupational Health and Safety Administration continually studies the reasons for project failures and, each year, identifies the most frequently cited OSHA standards violations, as listed in Table 9.8. The focus of risk management at the Big Dig centered on the determination of the root cause for each and every incident.

Root-Cause Analysis

> All human actions have one or more of these seven causes:
> chance, nature, compulsion, habit, reason, passion, desire.
>
> —*Aristotle (384 BC–322 BC)*

Table 9.8   Top 10 Most Frequently cited OSHA Standards Violations in 2011

1. Fall protection, construction (29 CFR 1926.501)
2. Scaffolding, general requirements, construction (29 CFR 1926.451)
3. Hazard communication standard, general industry (29 CFR 1910.1200)
4. Respiratory protection, general industry (29 CFR 1910.134)
5. Control of hazardous energy (lockout/tagout), general industry (29 CFR 1910.147)
6. Electrical, wiring methods, components and equipment, general industry (29 CFR 1910.305)
7. Powered industrial trucks, general industry (29 CFR 1910.178)
8. Ladders, construction (29 CFR 1926.1053)
9. Electrical systems design, general requirements, general industry (29 CFR 1910.303)
10. Machines, general requirements, general industry (29 CFR 1910.212)

Source: U.S. Occupational Safety and Health Administration, FY 2011 (USDOL 2011b).

Root-cause analysis (RCA) has been defined by the U.S. Department of Energy as:

> any analysis that identifies underlying deficiencies in a safety management system that, if corrected, would prevent the same and similar accidents from occurring, and to identify the lessons to be learned to promote the achievement of better consequences.

(USDOE 1992)

RCA has been used in the defense, energy, construction, and nuclear power industries as a primary mechanism for risk assessment and the development of best practices to avoid reccurrence of harmful events in the future. The practice of RCA is predicated on the belief that problems are best solved by attempting to address, correct, or eliminate root causes, as opposed to merely addressing the immediately obvious symptoms. RCA is often considered to be an iterative process and is frequently viewed as a tool of continuous improvement.

Root-cause analysis is not a single, sharply defined methodology; there are many different methodologies, tools, processes, and philosophies for performing RCA. However, several very broadly defined approaches can be identified by their basic approach. These include safety-based, production-based, process-based, failure-based, and systems-based approaches. Root-cause analysis was performed on all major incidents or repetitive events at the Big Dig and was an essential tool in loss mitigation and control. Figure 9.13 illustrates how root-cause analysis has been used by the U.S. Department of Energy in safety management.

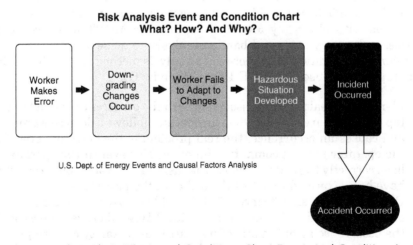

Figure 9.13   Risk Analysis Events and Conditions Chart Events and Condition Analysis
Source: DOE Guideline: Root Cause Analysis Guidance Document.
DOE-NE-STD-1004-92. February 1992-.

Table 9.9　Root-Cause Analysis Process

Error: Worker miscalculates location of an underground sewer pipe.
Downgrading change occurs: Follow-on worker fails to take into account all elements concerning the placement of steel beams near location of sewer pipe.
Worker fails to adapt to changes: Beam is drilled into sewer pipe.
Hazardous situation: Sewer pipe breaks.
Incident occurred: Work site and adjacent building are flooded.
Accident occurred: Three workers and five pedestrians are seriously injured, building is damaged, and the project works are damaged due to flooding.
Root-cause investigation is conducted.
Insurance claims triggered: General liability (injury to pedestrians and damage to building), workers' compensation (injury to workers), builders' risk (damage to work itself), professional liability (design error or omission).

To illustrate the process set forth in Figure 9.13, Table 9.9 provides an example of the various steps applied in a root-cause analysis.

Root-Cause Evaluation: Management Oversight and Risk Tree (MORT) Risk Factor Analysis　The MORT system was developed by Bill Johnson in the 1970s for the U.S. Atomic Energy Commission, now the U.S. Department of Energy (DOE), to improve safety in the nuclear industry. The system contains approximately 1500 items arranged into a large/complex fault tree used primarily for accident investigation, but also for inspection, audit, or appraisal purposes.

Events and causal factors analysis (ECFA) is an integral and important part of the MORT-based accident investigation process. It is often used in conjunction with other key MORT tools, such as MORT analysis, change analysis, and energy trace and barrier analysis, to achieve optimum results in accident investigation. Any root-cause analysis method that includes these basic steps may be used (USDOE 1992, Appendix G).

1. Identify the real problem associated with the occurrence and list it as the top event. As an example, when an operator follows a defective procedure and causes an occurrence, the real problem is the defective procedure; the operator has not committed an error. However, if the operator had been correctly trained to perform the task, the operator could reasonably have been expected to detect the defect in the procedure.
2. Determine the significance of the problem. Were the consequences severe? Could they be severe next time? How likely is recurrence? Is the occurrence symptomatic of poor attitude, a safety culture problem, or another widespread program deficiency? Base the level of effort of subsequent steps of your assessment upon the estimation of the level of significance.

3. Identify the causes (conditions or actions) immediately preceding and surrounding the problem (the reason the problem occurred).
4. Identify the reasons why the causes in the preceding identification step existed, working your way back to the root cause (the fundamental reason that, if corrected, will prevent recurrence of this and similar occurrences throughout the facility and other facilities under your control). This root cause is the stopping point in the assessment of causal factors. It is the place where, with appropriate corrective action, the problem will be eliminated and will not recur.

Creating a Culture of Fact Finding and Behavior-Based Safety   Closely connected with the root cause analysis was the mandatory reporting of near misses, unsafe conditions and at risk behavior. Daily briefings and tool box talks are a minimum requirement for communicating health and safety issues across projects and worksites. On the Big Dig a culture of fact finding rather than fault finding was essential to encourage reporting and was seen as an opportunity to foster learning and continuous improvement. To build this culture mandatory training was required in partnering, dispute resolution, fact finding, behavior-based safety and behavioral change. After several near misses early on in the project the importance of reporting unsafe conditions and near misses, fact finding and behavioral training was recognized across the project as essential to the prevention of future incidents and conditions that would create unsafe working environments and serious risk for all project participants.

Step 6: Document Lessons Learned

On megaprojects, the regular communication of previous actions taken and lessons learned is essential to improving decision making, operational procedures, and project performance. At the Big Dig, the project core management team met weekly to identify and develop corrective actions based on lessons learned. These lessons were communicated projectwide through directives, policy memorandums, and updates to the project's *Lessons Learned Manual*. Learning from past experience is critical to future performance on all projects. Since you can't manage what you don't measure, metrics were integral to the lessons learned process. Highlighted here are a few important lessons learned from the Big Dig about Risk Management.

Step 7: Identify Opportunities and Implement Best Practices

At the Big Dig, best practices were continually implemented based on the identification of opportunities. This required the continual use and analysis of metrics, reports, evaluations, standards, regulations, audits, brainstorming sessions, expert opinion, root cause analysis, reporting of unsafe conditions, fact finding, behavioral analysis, stakeholder input, and lessons learned. Best practices were adopted and continuously updated and implemented through the project's directives, policies, processes, and procedures. Table 9.7 highlights some of these programs. Selected examples of these practices for risk management are summarized in Table 9.10.

LESSONS LEARNED

1. A risk management framework with a shared vision, an integrated organization structure, and a strategic risk model must be developed from the conceptual phase of the project to ensure effective risk preparedness. Converting from a traditional contractor-controlled program to an owner-controlled program will be costly and will delay the implementation of projectwide practices.
2. Owner-controlled insurance programs have proven to be effective mechanisms for large-scale projects with multiple contractors and complex governance systems if they are properly structured and integrated into the project mission and procedures.
3. Risk sharing is essential to mitigate losses, reduce cost, and maintain relationships both internal and external to the project.
4. A mission of safety and health must take priority and rebel against cost, schedule, and scope constraints, but never against quality.
5. To change behavior, workers must be incentivized through recognition and awards based on clearly understood criteria and expectations, as well as penalized for wrongful behaviors.
6. Political leaders, the public, the business sector, and local communities must be educated on the benefits of risk mitigation options and the impact if these options are not accepted.
7. Stakeholder participation is critical to understanding risk perception, and all project participants as well as the public must be educated to prevent faulty decision making.
8. Risk management strategies used in large-scale complex projects like the Big Dig must expand upon traditional project management methodologies and tools and techniques and introduce innovative practices not readily available in the project management literature.
9. Project organizational, governance, and contractual structure are key factors in mitigating risk.
10. Project culture is a by-product of organizational, governance, and contractual structure and must be continually assessed to ensure a safe and healthy project environment.
11. Creating a culture of fact finding rather than fault finding and rewarding behavioral change are important factors in risk mitigation and control.
12. Reporting of all incidents, unsafe conditions, and at risk behavior is essential to foster learning and continuous improvement.

BEST PRACTICES

Table 9.10   Best Practices in Risk Management

Practice	Approach
1. Promote a shared vision.	Effective risk management requires that the project organization have a clear, overarching understanding of risk and that it structure the organization to ensure that risk management is the first and most important priority of the organization.
2. Establish shared values.	Project managers must create a collaborative environment and instill a culture and focus on safety and health.
3. Develop a collaborative communication structure.	Establish a trusting and transparent process among all project participants through regular reporting of incidents and sharing of lessons learned.
4. Integrate the risk management organization throughout the project.	The responsibility for risk management must be shared, systemic, and assimilated across all project disciplines.
5. Prepare for the inevitability of change.	Control risks by continually scrutinizing hazards, exposures, regulations, standards, processes, procedures, technology, claims, and updates to cost, scope, and schedule.
6. Develop innovative processes and procedures.	Megaproject managers cannot rely only on traditional mechanisms to manage risks but must focus on innovative ways of identifying, assessing, mitigating, and controlling risk.
7. Address the cause, not the symptom, of an outcome or behavior.	Processes such as root-cause analysis and root-cause evaluation should be used for all project risk events to prevent reccurrence.
8. Measure what you monitor, and hold all actors accountable.	Risk metrics and monitoring techniques must be put in place at the inception of the project and used throughout the life of the project, and performance requirements must be consistently enforced.
9. Establish a program with reward and penalty features based on specific performance goals to incentivize workers.	Programs such as Safety and Health Awards for Recognized Excellence (SHARE) should be used to mitigate contractor recordables and lost time and ultimately ensure a safer project.
10. Focus on opportunity as well as risk.	Opportunity management should focus on innovation, fact finding, behavior based safety and seeking out the potential for change in a given situation.

SUMMARY

Megaprojects require a nontraditional approach for managing risk that must be conceived and developed before project commitments are finalized in the conceptual phase. Risk management requires a shared vision and mutual cooperation among all project stakeholders. The project's organization must be structured to respond quickly to events and to establish open communication and a collaborative environment. All participants must be educated and updated on the underlying assumptions and dynamics of the ever-evolving processes of risk identification, assessment, allocation, response, and control. Finally, lessons learned and root-cause determinations must be communicated to all project participants, and best practices must be developed and integrated into all aspects of the project's organization.

CASE ANALYSIS: AUSTARIA POWER PLANT CASE STUDY

Assume you have been asked to serve as project manager to the Austaria Power Plant (APP) Project to build an electrical power plant in the developing country of Austaria that will be 45 percent financed by the government of Austaria and 55 percent financed by an international consortium of investors including 35 percent by a United States company. When it is complete, the plant will be 100 percent owned by the government of Austaria. The plant will be responsible for the generation, transmission, and distribution of electrical power and will be operated by the main state-owned electrical authority in Austaria (Austaria-Elec). The power plant is to be built within several miles of a poor residential area of the main city in Austaria. This is a unique project and is the first of its kind in this country. The country is a postconflict country now living in peace, and it has no experience with industrial projects of this magnitude. The country also has an unskilled labor force and language barriers. The project will take seven years to complete and is estimated to cost around $2 billion. The people of the area are concerned about environmental and health and safety issues, as well as risk to the residents and businesses in the area. Fortunately, a similar power plant was built in a neighboring country, and the same technology and contractors will be utilized on the project in Austaria.

Based on the Austaria Power Plant Case Study respond to the following questions:

1. Prepare a risk matrix showing: (a) the risks involved, (b) how you would mitigate those risks, and (c) to whom those risks should be allocated? The sponsors? The government? The contractors? The designers? Other stakeholders?

2. What mechanisms would you utilize to control the risks you have identified in question 1?
3. Describe your three major concerns for moving forward with this project.

ETHICAL CONSIDERATIONS

The contractor of the ABIG Construction Company is reviewing plans for the megaproject on which he is working and discovers that the specification was underestimated for the amount of support needed for the project's cable-stayed bridge. In this type of bridge, the roadway is supported by cables attached directly to the supporting tower (or towers) of the bridge. He estimates that he will have to spend more money and time to shore up additional support for the bridge since it is a fixed-price contract. The contractor estimates that the additional cost could be in the $500,000 range for a $3 million contract. If he builds the bridge in accordance with the specifications, he will have satisfied the requirements of the contract and will be paid in full.

1. What, if any, are the risks, insurance issues, and the legal and ethical factors that the contractor faces?
2. What would you advise the contractor to do, and why? Assume you are the risk manager on the project and you learn about the contractor's dilemma from one of your project managers. Your boss tells you this is a construction matter and it is not a problem that risk management should resolve.
3. What would you do, as the risk manager, to address this problem?
4. What are your ethical responsibilities?

DISCUSSION QUESTIONS

1. How do you avoid complacency when your project has repeatedly been successful at inherently hazardous or difficult tasks?
2. What should the risk manager have done in advance planning for potential hurricanes in New Orleans described in the Federal Response to lessons learned in this chapter?. How can you mitigate the losses in advance if it is probable that an act of God will occur in the location of your project (i.e., earthquake damage or flooding)?
3. How would you conduct a quantitative and qualitative analysis of the consequences of a disaster, such as a fire in your plant? What type of data would you require? What would your standard form of measurement be?

4. What should the role of a risk manager be in a project versus in a program? Are the roles identical? What are the differences?

5. Should the risk manager in a megaproject be responsible for construction risks? Cost and schedule risks? Political risks? Environmental risks? Does it depend on the size of the project? The location of the project? The type of project (infrastructure versus research and development)? What factors would you consider in structuring your risk management services?

6. The *PMBOK® Guide* states: Project Risk has its origins in the uncertainty present in all projects. It defines known risks as those that have been identified and analyzed, making it possible to plan responses for those risks. Specific unknown risks cannot be managed proactively, which suggests that the project team should create a contingency plan. Describe three recommendations you would make to manage unknown risks.

7. Risk managers often face ethical decisions concerning conflicts of interest, transparency, environmental obligations, and political risk. Provide an example of an ethical dilemma a risk manager might encounter and explain how you would resolve this dilemma.

8. How would you prioritize actions in a risk assessment? Would you look at: Impact of the risk? Probability of the risk? Public concerns? Perceptions of risk? Stakeholder expectations? Other concerns?

9. Distinguish between a hazard and a risk. As a risk manager, would you manage a hazard differently than a risk? Explain why or why not. Should certain risk issues have a higher priority than others?

10. How would you identify risk opportunities on a project?

11. Are the risk responses for threats more important than the risk responses for opportunities? Why or why not?

12. How would you create a culture of fact-finding rather than fault finding on a project with serious safety concerns and near misses?

13. What are the most important factors to consider in changing behaviors?

14. Assume you were hired as director of risk management to develop a risk program for a new tunnel project in the United States. The project director has given you full authority to develop the high-level framework and structure for this project. Describe the top ten questions you would ask the project director before beginning your responsibilities as director of risk management.

15. Assume you are the risk manager for an inner-city project similar to the Big Dig. Develop a checklist of 10 items for the project team to assist them in identifying, assessing, responding to, and controlling risk on their construction site. For example, a few items on your checklist might be the following:

- Are scope changes reported to Risk Management before finalizing commitments?
- Is Safety and Health consulted on ways to reduce workplace accidents?
- Are the root causes of accidents investigated and is appropriate action taken to prevent future occurrences?

REFERENCES

Agor, W. H. 1990. "The Logic of Intuitive Decision Making: An Agenda for Future Research." In *Intuition in Organizations*, edited by W. H. Ago, 263–264. Newbury Park, CA: Sage Publications.

Altschuler, A., and D. Luberoff. 2003. *Megaprojects: The Changing Politics of Urban Public Investment*. Washington, DC: Brookings Institution, 107–108.

Board on Infrastructure and the Constructed Environment. 2003. *Completing the "Big Dig": Managing the Final Stages of Boston's Central Artery / Tunnel Project*. National Research Council and National Academy of Engineering of the National Academies, Committee for Review of the Project Management Practices Employed on the Boston Central Artery/Tunnel ("Big Dig") Project, Division on Engineering and Physical Sciences. Washington, DC: National Academies Press, 1.

Cooper, D., S. Grey, G. Raymond, and P. Walker. (Broadleaf Capital International.) 2005. *Project Risk Management Guidelines: Managing Risk in Large Projects and Complex Procurements*. West Sussex, England: John Wiley & Sons, Ltd, 187–188.

DRII (Disaster Recovery Institute International). 2008. *Professional Practices for Business Continuity Practitioners*. Falls Church, VA: Disaster Recovrey Institute International.

FHWA (Federal Highway Administration). 1999. *Central Artery / Tunnel Project Comprehensive Audit of the Project Safety and Health Team*.

Flyvbjerg, B., N. Bruzelius, and W. Rothengatter. 2003. *Megaprojects and Risk: An Anatomy of Ambition*. Port Chester, NY: Cambridge University Press, 85.

Flyvjberg, B., M. K. Holm, and S. L. Buhl. 2002. "Understanding Costs in Public Work Projects: Error or Lie." *Journal of the American Planning Association* 68(3):287.

GAO (General Accounting Office). 1999. (June.) *Transportation Infrastructure: Advantages and Disadvantages of Wrap-Up Insurance for Large Construction Projects*. Report to the Chairman, Subcommittee on Transportation, Committee on Appropriations, U.S. Senate. GAO/RCED-99-155, 3.

Han, S. H., and J. E. Diekmann. 2004. "Judgment Based Cross-Impact Method for Predicting Cost Variance for Highly Uncertain Projects." *Journal of Construction Research* 5(2):171–192.

Howe, J. 2007. "Project Initiation and Management." In *The Definitive Handbook of Business Continuity Management*, edited by A. Hiles. 2nd ed. West Sussex, England: John Wiley & Sons Ltd.

Kendrick, T. 2009. *Identifying and Managing Project Risk: Essential Tools for Failure-Proofing Your Project*. 2nd ed. New York: AMACOM.

Keynes, J. M. 1937. *The General Theory of Employment*, Quarterly Journal of Economics, 51, February, 209–23, reprinted in J. M. Keynes (1971–1989), Volume XIV.

Lewis, R., S. P. Murphy, and T. C. Palmer 2003 (February). The Boston Globe. Boston: Globe Newspaper Company.

Lindkvist, L. 2011. "Knowledge Integration in Product Development Projects: A Contingency Framework." In *The Oxford Handbook of Project Management*, edited by P. W. G. Morris, J. K. Pinto, and J. Soderlund, Chapter 19, 472.

Lloyds of London. 2011. *Managing the Escalating Risks of Natural Catastrophes in the United States*. London, England, 3.

Massachusetts Executive Office of Environmental Affairs. 1990. Central Artery (I-93) Tunnel (I-90) Project, Environmental Impact Study (EIS), Part IV, Book 1 of 2. EOEA #4325. November.

Meredith, J. R., and S. J. Mantel. 2012. *Project Management: A Managerial Approach*. 8th ed. Hoboken, NJ: John Wiley & Sons, Inc., 254–258.

Miller, R., and B. Hobbs. 2006. "Managing Risks and Uncertainty in Major Projects in the New Global Environment." *Global Project Management Handbook*. New York: McGraw-Hill, 9-11–9-12.

Miller, R., and D. Lessard. 2000. *The Strategic Management of Large Engineering Projects: Shaping Institutions, Risks and Governance*. Cambridge, MA: MIT Press.

MTA (Massachusetts Turnpike Authority). 2000. Central Artery/Tunnel Project Finance Plan. October 1, 10–11.

MTA (Massachusetts Turnpike Authority). 2000. Review of Owner-Controlled Insurance Program (OCIP Review). *October* 3.

MTA (Massachusetts Turnpike Authority). 2006. Project Management Monthly (PMM). June 30, 9.

MTA (Massachusetts Turnpike Authority). 2007. Project Management Monthly (PMM). August 31, 8.

NOAA (National Oceanic and Atmospheric Administration, U.S. Department of Commerce). 2007. *Hurricane Katrina—Most Destructive Hurricane Ever to Strike the U.S*. February 12. www.katrina.noaa.gov.

OECD (Office of Economic Co-operation and Development). 2008. *Critical Infrastructure Report*. Paris, France: Office of Economic Cooperation and Development, 3.

Perminova, O., M. Gustafsson, K. Wikstrom. 2008. "Defining Uncertainty in Projects—A New Perspective." *International Journal of Project Management* 26(1) (January) 73–79.

PMI (Project Management Institute). 2013. *A Guide to the Project Management Body of Knowledge (PMBOK® Guide)*—Fifth Edition. Newton Square, PA.

PMI (Project Management Institute). 2013. *The Standard for Program Management*. 3rd ed. Newtown Square, PA.

Schexnayder, C. L., and S. L. Weber. 2002. *Owner Controlled Insurance Programs: Synthesis 308*. National Cooperative Highway Research Program (NCHRP), American Association of State Highway and Transportation Officials, Transportation Research Board of the National Academies.

Slovic, P. 1987. "Perception of Risk." *Science* 236(479):280–285.

Slovic, P., and E. Weber. 2002. "Perception of Risk Posed by Extreme Events." Presentation at Risk Management Strategies in an Uncertain World, Palisades, NY. April 2002, 12–13.

Tobin, J. 2001. *Great Projects: The Epic Story of the Building of America, from the Taming of the Mississippi to the Invention of the Internet.* New York: Free Press, 253.

UNDP (United Nations Development Program). 2009. *The Tsunami Legacy: Innovation, Breakthroughs and Change Report.* Coordinated by Kuntoro Mangkusubroto, Chair of the Tsunami Global lessons Learned Steering Committee. April 24.

United States v. Spearin. 1918. 248 U.S. 132.

USDHS (U.S. Department of Homeland Security). 2009. National Infrastructure Protection Plan: Partnering to Enhance Protection and Resiliency, 3.

USDOE (U.S. Department of Energy). 1992. *DOE Guideline: Root Cause Analysis Guidance Document.* DOE-NE-STD-1004-92. Washington, DC: Office of Nuclear Energy, Office of Nuclear Safety Policy and Standards. February.

USDOL (U.S. Department of Labor). 2011a. Top 10 Most Frequently Cited Standards for FY 2011. U.S. Occupational Safety and Health Administration (OSHA). www.osha.gov/Top_Ten_Standards.html.

USDOL (U.S. Department of Labor). 2011b. National Census of Fatal Occupational Injuries in 2010 (preliminary results). August 25. www.bls.gov/news.release/pdf/cfoi.pdf.

USDOL/IFF (U.S. Department of Labor). 1992. *Injuries, Illnesses and Fatalities (IIF).* Bureau of Labor Statistics. www.bls.gov/iif/.

USDOT (U.S. Department of Transportation). 2008. (July 18.) *Innovation Wave: An Update on the Burgeoning Private Sector Role in U.S. Highway and Transit Infrastructure.* Section VI: Managing Risk in PPPs, 1. Federal Highway Administration.

Vines, P. 2007. "Operational Risk Management." In *The Definitive Handbook of Business Continuity Management,* edited by A. Hiles. 2nd ed. West Sussex, England: John Wiley & Sons Ltd.

Ward, S., and C. Chapman. 2003. "Transforming Project Risk Management into Project Uncertainty Management." *International Journal of Project Management* 21(2) (February):97–105.

White House. 2006. *The Federal Response to Hurricane Katrina: Lessons Learned.* Response led by Frances Frago Townsend, Assistant to the President for Homeland Security and Counterterrorism. February.

Chapter 10

Quality Management

> Quality is never an accident; it is always the result of high intention, sincere effort, intelligent direction and skillful execution; it represents the wise choice of many alternatives.
>
> —*William A. Foster*

INTRODUCTION

Writing a book on project management would not be complete without a serious focus on *quality*. As Aristotle (384 BC–322 BC) vividly described it, "Quality is not an act, it is a habit." To take this one step further, in projects we should not focus just on controlling quality but, rather, on ensuring that quality is embedded in everything we do. Quality is not just processes and procedures but a vision that should be at the forefront of every project manager's mission.

This chapter focuses on the vision, strategy, organizational structure, and processes and procedures that encompass a superior quality management program. Most important are the ethical obligations of the project participants in assuring delivery of a quality product. The lessons from the Big Dig, both successes and failures, are described to assist future project managers in understanding not only what can go wrong, but what can go right. Quality management begins at the conceptual stage and continues through closure and the transition to operations. Quality must be carefully planned as part of the project's governance structure and must be continuously improved. Quality never ends because it forms the basis for the ultimate product that is delivered and must last as long as the projected lifetime of that product or infrastructure.

Finally, in this chapter, two successful case studies and two tragic case studies—including the I-35 Mississippi River Bridge collapse and the Big Dig's tunnel roof failure—demonstrate the application and impact of quality management, not only during the life of the project but long after the project has ended.

WHAT IS QUALITY?

Before analyzing how we measure and manage quality, the question must be asked, "What is quality?" The term *quality* is one that is often used in daily conversation but frequently without much thought as to its meaning.

Pioneers of quality control, including Shewhart, Deming, Juran, and Crosby, defined quality in various ways. Deming (1986), influenced by Shewhart (1939), defined *quality* as a predictable degree of uniformity and dependability, at low cost and suited to the market. Crosby (1986) defines quality as conformance to requirements. Juran (1995) saw quality as fitness for purpose and, in his quality handbook, recognized that quality means "freedom from deficiencies" (Juran, 1999).

According to the American National Standards Institute (ANSI) and the American Society for Quality (ASQ), *quality* is defined as "the totality of features and characteristics of a product or service that bears on its ability to satisfy given needs" (Evans and Lindsay 2011). Similarly, the Project Management Institute (PMI) defines *quality* as "the degree to which a set of inherent characteristics fulfill requirements." This definition is taken directly from ISO 9000:2000 (p. 7), published by the International Organization for Standardization, and it basically means that the owner defines the requirements and the project fulfills these requirements.

These definitions of *quality* focus heavily on the "fitness for intended use, or how well the product [or service] performs its intended function" (Evans and Lindsay 2011, 16). In addition, this notion of quality emphasizes the need for a project to successfully meet specific and measurable product or service characteristics or attributes. Following that line of reasoning, does this mean that if the requirements are poor, the project contractor must fulfill these requirements regardless of the quality? Who in the organization is responsible for quality? The project director? The designers? The contractors? The owner/customer?

Knowing how to ensure quality is one of the most difficult aspects of project management and is made more so by the demands of complex technology, innovative practices, numerous stakeholders with diverse interests, and the pressures of meeting schedule and budget. As noted by one Big Dig engineer:

> Quality is not just the product of procedural implementation, but is directly a result of integrated organizational governance and design.
>
> *—Keith Diggans, facilities engineer,*
> *Central Artery / Tunnel Project*

We are reminded that the project "triple constraint" includes time, cost, and scope. Sometimes quality is mentioned as a fourth constraint. However, that concept has been critiqued for the right reasons. "A project manager should never, never, ever trade off quality during project implementation" (Rose 2005).

Project goals and project managers are often incentivized for their ability to stay on schedule and within budget. In some projects, managers are rewarded for a project that comes in ahead of schedule and under budget, and those rewards can be substantial. However, rarely do we incentivize project managers for quality, because it is a major assumption of project management that quality must be controlled and ensured. The problem with incentivizing quality is that after many decades of research, differing views about how to measure quality persist. Is quality measured by utilizing the best materials? Following plans? No rework? Durability? Satisfying stakeholders beyond expectations? Design process and testing? Or meeting construction codes and standards? When there are conflicting views and requirements, which take priority?

The answers to these questions may lie in the meaning of quality in today's global business environment, where companies and their top management need to demonstrate their commitment to continuous improvement to create a competitive advantage and enhance their financial return. To this end, quality management has evolved largely from focusing on product quality, with its strict adherence to conformance to design specifications and reduction in manufacturing defects, to the more integrated view of quality called Total Quality Management (TQM) or, simply, Total Quality (TQ).

This system approach to quality, accepted by many large U.S. companies and major universities (Evans and Lindsay 2011), requires that all stakeholders along the value chain be fully engaged "in improving processes, products, services and the culture in which they work" (Johnson et al. 2011). You may have heard about the failure of many quality initiatives at various companies in different industries over the years. Lessons learned from these failures often point to a lack of commitment or a loss of focus from top management, coupled with insufficient involvement of the key internal and external customers to relentlessly pursue continuous improvement at all phases of the product life cycle.

Kaizen, the Japanese name for continuous improvement that is incremental and systematic, depends on the engagement of all stakeholders in the organization. In an increasingly global economy, this kaizen philosophy also involves the corporation's suppliers and customers to ensure that customer's needs and expectations are ultimately met. Indeed, it is critical that everyone in the organization gain a good understanding of what the customers expect from the products and/or the services that the company provides. In addition to planning for quality, it is essential to involve the key suppliers early in the process to ensure quality excellence. This is especially important on megaprojects, where multiple interdependent stakeholders are involved throughout the project life cycle.

In addition to the quality control tools mentioned here, companies often use *dashboards* that visually depict the health or performance of a few key quality metrics. This visual representation of the quality data helps project stakeholders make appropriate decisions that could link and align the process quality control measures to the strategic goals and objectives of the project and the organization. On the subject of appropriate decision making in today's environment, rampant ethical issues and dilemmas in the business world have forced corporate executives to devise strategies that would allow their companies to compete effectively in a world of increased regulatory controls.

To ensure sustainable corporate growth, successful business leaders proactively promote the idea that good organizational decision making should not only center strictly around short-term financial results but should also focus on environmental and social concerns that are the basis of the triple-bottom-line corporate framework (Ball et al. 2010). This should be a key consideration on megaprojects where the environment and the health and safety of all stakeholders along the value chain are essential parts of the project's mission.

ELEMENTS OF QUALITY MANAGEMENT

A Guide to the Project Management Body of Knowledge (PMBOK® Guide)— Fifth Edition (PMI 2013) states that there are three elements essential to quality management, defined here. These three elements permeate every industry and have great significance to megaprojects. Without implementing the processes of quality planning, assurance, and control, the project will surely fail.

Quality planning: The process of identifying quality requirements and/or standards for the project and product, and documenting how the project will demonstrate compliance.

Quality assurance: The process of auditing the quality requirements and the results from quality control measurements to ensure appropriate quality standards and operational definitions are used.

Quality control: The process of monitoring and recording results of executing the quality activities to assess performance and recommend necessary changes.

Planning for Quality: Philosophy

> For you to sleep well at night, the aesthetic, the quality,
> has to be carried all the way through.
>
> *—Steve Jobs*

Success in the delivery of projects requires a commitment to the highest standards of quality. Quality can never be compromised or negotiated. Understanding a project's philosophy on quality is key to preventing and reducing requirements errors and must be understood from conception. Quality requires time, up-front expenditures, resources, support from project management, independent oversight, and an integrated project structure.

Key questions that must be answered in designing a quality program include the following:

1. What is the project's commitment to quality?

    Is it a top priority? A constraint on cost and schedule? Does it provide for enforceable penalties for noncompliance? Will the project commit to quality for the entire life cycle?

2. How will quality assurance be structured?

    What is the scope of the quality management system, organizational structure, governance structure, and quality management resources?

3. Is quality assurance integrated into the project?

    Does quality assurance have a relationship to design, construction, risk management, geotechnical, safety and health, legal, claims and changes, and procurement?

4. Are the quality standards and requirements broad or limited?

    Are there contractual provisions? Laws and regulations? Project policy and directives?

5. What are the quality control tools?

    Is a full range of tools going to be employed, including deficiency reporting, inspections, training, control checks, review of project changes, cause-and-effect analysis, corrective action plans, and insurance?

Quality Planning: Emphasis on Requirements   Quality is often thought of as expensive and time consuming, thus causing quality to be treated as less important or a lower priority. This opinion is, in reality, a myth. Studies have shown that the cost of rework can be significantly greater than doing it right the first time. Moreover, failure can generate liability costs that are far more expensive. If it is a schedule- or cost-driven project, as many projects are, there must be a structure in place to ensure that quality is never sacrificed for cost or schedule despite the political forces, the financial hurdles, or the economic realities. Quality begins with process. A project's processes and procedures are the first step in ensuring quality. One could argue that quality is free, if you contrast it with the alternative of a failure of quality.

In his famous study of software requirements in 1981, Boehm estimated that the late correction of requirements errors could cost up to 200 times as much as correcting such requirements during engineering (Boehm 1981). Later studies have confirmed the requirements problem on a much larger scale. The often quoted 1994 Standish CHAOS Report, involving a survey of more than 8000 information technology projects undertaken by 350 U.S. companies determined that one-third of the projects never completed and one-half succeeded only partially. When asked about the causes of such failure, executive managers identified poor requirements as the major source of problems. Recent studies by the Standish Group indicate that project failures continue to rise. Improving the quality of requirements has thus been a matter of much concern across industries (Standish 1994 and 2010).

Donald Firesmith, of the Software Engineering Institute, has written extensively about the criticality of quality requirements. In one article, he summarizes the essential characteristics of quality requirements (see "Merit of Quality Requirements" textbox).

MERIT OF QUALITY REQUIREMENTS

A. Is each quality requirement:
1. Mandatory:
   Not just an unintended architecture, design, or implementation constraint?
2. Feasible:
   Based on endeavor, technology, and physical limitations? Simple statements of goals such as "The system shall be 'secure'" or "The system shall be 'reliable'" are not good requirements because they are infeasible, as no system is totally secure or reliable, or they are ambiguous because they do not say how secure or reliable they need to be.
3. Scalable:
   Clear as to just how much quality is required?
4. Unambiguous:
   So that all stakeholders and developers will interpret it the same way?
5. Verifiable:
   Tested, demonstrated, inspected?
6. Correct:
   In that it meets some real need of the stakeholders?
7. Prioritized:
   So that it can be allocated to an appropriate build or release?
8. Traced:
   To its source?
B. Does each quality requirement have an associated:
1. Rationale?
2. Verification method?

Source: Donald Firestone, "Quality Requirements Checklist," Journal of Object Technology 4(9) (November-December 2005).

Quality Assurance: System Overview to Confirm Product Is Working

Quality assurance (QA), simply stated, is the process of evaluating overall project performance to ensure that the project will satisfy the relevant quality standards. It is a process-centered approach to ensuring that a company or organization is providing the best possible products or services. Quality assurance also supports continuous improvement. The key input for quality assurance is the quality improvement plan, and a key output is quality improvement of the project. The key tools for determining quality assurance are the audit and process analysis. When an organization has a viable QA system, clients are more confident that the final product or service will be developed and delivered with quality (Abdulaziz and Tawfiq 1999).

Quality Control: Measures Product to Determine It Meets Standards

Quality control is a process that is used to ensure a certain level of quality in a product or service deemed necessary to the organization. The basic goal of this process is to ensure that the products or services that are provided meet specific requirements, standards, and characteristics, such as being dependable, satisfactory, safe, and fiscally sound.

Organizations that engage in quality control typically have a team of workers who monitor specific project results to determine whether they comply with relevant quality standards. The goal of the quality control team is to identify products or services that do not meet a company's specified standards of quality to find ways to eliminate causes of unsatisfactory results. The job of a quality control team might involve stopping production or service until the problem has been corrected. The main outputs of quality control are status reports, performance data, process improvements, rework, approvals, and completed surveys and checklists.

Quality Control Tools   Quality control involves developing the tools to identify the causes of quality problems and to measure performance based on data. Quality control tools consist of inspections, reviews, performance data, and walk-throughs. The total system within which quality control and quality assurance activities are carried out is known as the *quality control program*.

Statistical methods are very important for quality control and include histograms, cause-and-effect diagrams, checklists, and control charts. Figure 10.1 shows a fishbone diagram, also known as an Ishikawa diagram. This tool helps to analyze a process to identify the possible causes of errors. As illustrated, the head of the fish represents the defect, and the inputs to the process are the bones of the fish. Another control process commonly used for quality control is the control chart (Figure 10.2). Control charts are used to show how a process behaves over time. Control limits are the lines that are two or three standard deviations on either side of the centerline or the mean of a normal distribution.

When a measurement is outside the control limits, it should be investigated to determine the probable cause of the condition. Six Sigma is another common tool used to improve processes by eliminating defects. It is widely used in the

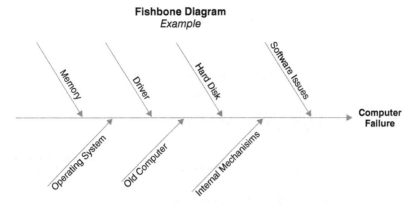

Figure 10.1   Ishikawa Fishbone Diagram

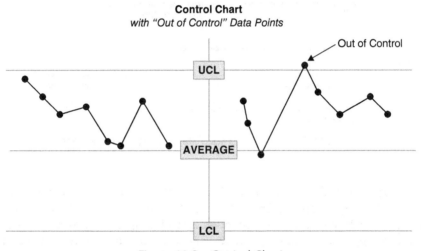

Figure 10.2   Control Chart

health care, engineering, and manufacturing industries and was developed by Motorola in 1986. Companies that use Six Sigma can expect to generate less than 3.4 defects out of 1 million opportunities. Another important tool for quality control is the root-cause analysis described in Chapter 9.

Quality Control Standards   ISO 9000 and the 9001 standards published in 2008 are models of quality standards that set minimum requirements for activities to achieve a quality product acceptable to the customer. The standards are published by ISO, the International Organization for Standardization, based in Geneva, Switzerland, and they are available through national standards bodies. ISO 9000 deals with the fundamentals of quality management systems, including the eight management principles on which

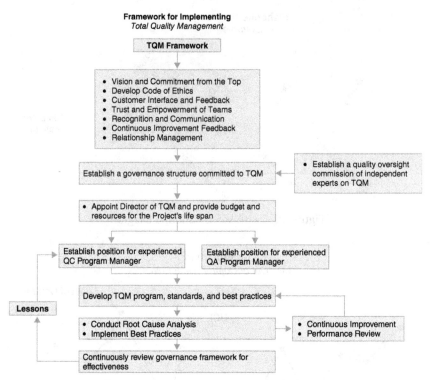

Figure 10.3   Framework for Total Quality Management

the family of standards is based. Figure 10.3 provides a framework and processes for implementing TQM. The eight principles are as follows: (1) customer focus, (2) leadership, (3) involvement of people, (4) process approach, (5) system approach to management, (6) continual improvement, (7) factual approach to decision making, and (8) mutually beneficial supplier relationships. ISO 9001 deals with the requirements that organizations wishing to meet the standard have to fulfill.

CONTINUOUS IMPROVEMENT

> Success is a lousy teacher. It seduces smart people into
> thinking they can't lose.
>
> —*Bill Gates*

One of the major goals of quality management is the focus on continuous improvement. *Continuous improvement* is defined as an ongoing effort to improve products, services, or processes. Improvement can be "incremental" or "breakthrough," all at once. Dr. W. Edwards Deming, who is considered by

Figure 10.4   Elements of TQM in the Construction Process

many to be the father of modern quality control, made popular the four-step quality model used on most projects today:

Plan: Identify an opportunity and plan for change.
Do: Implement the change.
Check: Use data to analyze the results of the change and determine whether it made a difference.
Act: If the change was successful, implement it on a wider scale and continuously assess your result. If the change did not work, begin the cycle again.

All of the Big Dig project's tools, techniques, processes, and procedures required continuous improvement assessment—for example, the change order process, inspection reports, audits, deficiency reports, and the field engineer's daily reports. Elements of TQM in construction are shown in Figure 10.4.

QUALITY PROGRAMS AT THE BIG DIG

Due to the innovative technology used on the Big Dig and the enormous level of uncertainty involved, quality assurance and quality control were integrated into the project at all levels through an integrated quality assurance program. The joint-venture management consultant controlled most of the Big Dig's quality assurance work, and each construction firm holding a major contract also was required to hire a quality assurance manager. The sheer size and complexity of the Big Dig necessitated a quality program that favors a more controlled environment with extensive oversight, similar to those used in government defense programs, at nuclear power plants, and in energy-related industries.

Total Quality Management-or TQM, as it is commonly known—is an integrative philosophy of management for continuously improving the quality of products and processes. The concept of TQM was used on the Big Dig, as quality was not just a concern of the project engineers but was integrated throughout the project, with a strong commitment from the project owner. The project established numerous quality assurance (QA) and quality control (QC) processes and procedures both on the design side and the construction side of the project. Primary responsibility for quality control of the project belonged to the contractor, in accordance with the project's contracts, policies, and procedures (CA/T 2000c). However, quality assurance was the responsibility of the section design consultants (SDCs) on each contract, who worked in collaboration with the field engineers (FEs) to conduct oversight, perform audits, and resolve disputes between and among the project owner, contractors, and designers (CA/T 2000a). Table 10.1 highlights the essential quality considerations, used on the Big Dig, for developing a framework and vision for a quality program in a megaproject.

1. Quality Program Considerations

Table 10.1   Quality Program Considerations

Quality Program Considerations	Implementation
Philosophy	Senior management commitment to provide the vision, strategy, and sponsorship
Governance	Quality head reports directly to project director to ensure transparency and expert knowledge and oversees the quality engineering field team
Integrated Organization	Shifting focus from traditional modes of quality control and conformance to total quality implementation at every level of an organization
Criticality of Requirements	Specifications that have uniform characteristics that mandate quality compliance
Quality Control	Sophisticated data and quality analysis tools including root-cause analysis and structured and unstructured approaches
Continuous Improvement	Focus on high-level involvement of the project teams and management in sustained incremental problem solving
Quality Assurance	Uniform, consistent inspection and audit process in every contract

2. Governance and Organizational Integration

On quality—you can only elevate individual performance
by elevating that of the entire system.

—W. Edwards Deming

Quality must be integrated into every aspect of the organization and especially into the project teams. As shown in Figure 10.5, projects need to be
organized so that quality control and quality assurance are central to the
organization's goals. In 2002, a director of quality management (DQM) was
hired by the project owner to scrutinize the contractors' quality assurance
programs as well as the Big Dig's as a whole. Though this was a positive step,
criticism was expressed by the cochairman of the Massachusetts legislature's
Transportation Committee that the owner should have hired the DQM in the
early stages of the project rather than during the peak years of construction
(Lewis 2002). A major lesson learned here is that quality assurance must
be overseen from the inception of the project by the project owner so that
uniformity in practice and procedure is enforced across large-scale projects.
Significantly, neither the federal nor the state government required a centralized quality assurance and quality control program at the owner's level
at the inception of this megaproject. The DQM plays an important role in
ensuring that all core functions of the project work cooperatively. It is critical

Figure 10.5   Quality Organization

that the DQM be supported through expert knowledge, additional resources, sufficient budget, schedule allowances, insurance, and risk management.

The organizational chart in Figure 10.5 shows a model structure for a centralized quality management program where the DQM reports directly to the project director and oversees the project's engineering team responsible for quality assurance and oversight of each contractor's quality control program. If the owner is to maintain control of the quality process, it is essential that the DQM report directly to the owner's project director and have the support of the core management team. Total Quality Management requires a framework that not only integrates quality into the core functions of the project but also allocates responsibility for quality management from the bottom up, with clear requirements and a commitment to quality that emanates from the top levels of the organization down, so that quality permeates each layer of management (Figure 10.5).

3. Independent Quality Assurance Oversight and Continuous Improvement

Quality management requires independent oversight. To provide the necessary independence and expertise to the project owner, an independent quality assurance task force (oversight committee) should be established. The committee should be composed of quality experts to assist in identification and resolution of problem quality issues. The National Aeronautics and Space Administration (NASA) has done this through formal mandated governance policy known as NASA Procedural Requirements (NPR7120.5D). This is a good model for all large-scale projects. Similar to the Big Dig, it requires both program and project oversight and approval before moving through the various phases of the project.

Quality management also mandates continuous improvement. Since contractors are usually more concerned with profit maximization, it is critical that the quality management program focus on continuous improvement and prevention of defects and requirements errors. Responsibility should be allocated based on a team structure that reinforces the goals and requirements of the quality program. In construction and infrastructure projects, the responsibility for quality control is normally with the contractor. However, on large projects, it is critical that the consultant, designers, contractors, and owner work together to ensure a collaborative environment and shared mission of quality excellence.

Important questions that must be asked when allocating responsibility for quality assurance and quality control are the following:

1. Does the party managing quality have sufficient resources, access to senior management, and control through an integrated quality management program?

2. Does the party have an understanding of the core attributes of and standards of quality including the know-how and technological expertise?
3. Can the responsible party bear the consequences of the risk?
4. Is their sufficient collaboration and support from other project disciplines including procurement, risk, finance, communications, and safety management?

4. Quality Planning for the Big Dig

On the Big Dig, the construction contracts required Quality Control to be performed by the contractor and all contractors to submit a quality plan that had to meet certain conditions before construction work began. Quality was one of the most highly regulated areas of the project, and all quality standards were set forth in the project's detailed contracts and the Quality Procedures (CA/T 2000a, 2000b, 2000c). All contractors submitted the quality plan before the project's preconstruction workshop that included the quality personnel, the quality activities, and the resources to be employed to ensure that the work met the project's quality requirements.

The project's quality specifications were rigid and subject to federal and state regulation (MHD 2000). Fabricators of project materials were required to be on the owner's approved list prior to the bid opening date, and only approved fabricators were allowed to perform the work. A key element of the quality process was testing. Before construction began, the contractor was obligated to develop a testing plan based on the contract specifications. Testing that was subcontracted to one of the project's approved testing labs required the contractor to confirm that testing laboratories maintained quality requirements.

As an illustration of deficiencies in quality planning by the federal government, the U.S. Department of Transportation's Office of the Inspector General conducted a quality audit of the Big Dig in December 1996 (OIG 1996). The objective of the audit was to evaluate the FHWA's oversight of the project's testing procedures. The audit concluded that the FHWA provided limited oversight of the project's testing procedures, and the OIG found weaknesses in the project's quality of workmanship, disposition of failed materials, and implementation of the Materials Manual. As a result, the Big Dig incurred $1,784,000 in additional expenses for repairs. In response to the audit and the OIG's recommendations, oversight of the project's testing procedures was strengthened to ensure that construction and materials used in the project were in accordance with applicable specifications. It is significant that the OIG stated, "Although the monetary effect cited in this report for three contracts is relatively small, the issues raised illustrate weaknesses which have the potential to escalate into larger problems as construction proceeds to completion over the next 8 years" (OIG 1996).

The important lesson here is that despite best efforts and rigid procedures, early oversight can enhance and strengthen quality programs in a positive way for future planning, whether through an independent oversight committee or an external governmental audit process.

5. Allocation of Responsibility

Quality means doing it right when no one is looking.

—Henry Ford

The responsibility for quality control is normally with the contractor. However, on large projects, it is critical that the consultant, designers, contractors, and owner work together to ensure a collaborative environment and shared mission of quality excellence. On the Big Dig, quality performance was controlled primarily by the resident engineers and the field engineers at the contract level.

Mandatory training programs for resident engineers, field engineers, and other construction personnel was conducted to assist in the performance of quality assurance and quality control responsibilities. Training was a requirement on the project for both safety and health and quality control and was built into the project's policy, procedures, plans, and specifications. In the United States, the Occupational and Health Administration (OSHA) is responsible for the enforcement of safety on construction sites. Since quality and safety are in many respects intertwined, each can have an impact on the other. Training in the OSHA requirements can include training in team building and problem solving. Important questions, concerning leadership for quality assurance and quality control, are:

1. Does the party managing quality have the leadership skills necessary to implement change?
2. Has the party built a trusting relationship with the project teams?
3. Can the party motivate the project teams to implement a change of culture as necessary?
4. Are the lessons learned about quality being communicated project-wide?

6. Quality Assurance for the Big Dig

The Big Dig had extensive and complex quality assurance and control procedures that were enforced by the project's management consultant. For example, the Big Dig's Project Procedure 301, in some sense, was a reiteration of the goal of project quality assurance under the PMI standards. The procedure stated in pertinent part, "[T]his Quality Assurance Program provides a systematic approach for meeting the quality policy and provides focus on quality in balance with cost and schedule." In essence, the quality policy was designed to satisfy needs and expectations of the project owner in accordance with contract requirements and to perform the work in accordance with the drawings, specifications, and project procedures.

The quality assurance procedures and directives were contained in the Resident Engineer's Manual, Section 500, "Construction Monitoring and Quality Control," Project Procedure 1239. These procedures provided for "Quality Control Walkdowns" by technical experts, customized inspection checklists and a technical manual, and "Contractor Quality Control Program Enforcement." The quality assurance manager (QAM) and the quality control manager (QCM) worked closely with their staff to promote a team approach to quality assurance and control, to audits and inspections, and to the development of innovative solutions to complex problems.

The Quality Assurance Audit, System Review, and Surveillance Program describe the QAM's responsibility for performing system reviews and auditing to evaluate the effectiveness of the quality program and follow-up to verify implementation of recommendations and corrective actions (CA/T 2000b). The procedure described in Table 10.2 also establishes the core and department manager's responsibilities for supporting the program and responding to issues raised during these activities.

7. Quality Control Requirements

The quality control requirements at the Big Dig were extensive and permeated every phase of the project from preliminary design through closure. The most important project procedures in terms of true integration of quality process into the project contracts were the General Requirements and Covenants of Construction Contracts, which required contactors to submit their quality control plan (QCP) and quality control manager (QCM) for approval and describes the contents of the QCP in general terms. The structure of the project's quality program required the Technical Services Group to review the QCP and the qualification of the QCM as requested by the resident engineer.

Quality requirements were contained in each contract and included the items listed here. These requirements were amended from time to time as the project evolved. For example, in 1996, when the project's Safety and Health Program was first implemented, this required additional information to be collected on lost time and OSHA recordables as well as the preparation and submittal of a Safety and Health Program by each contractor.

- Plans, specifications, technical provisions
- Codes and standards reflecting federal, state, and industry practices
- Contractor quality program
- Full-time quality control manager of large contracts
- Standardized inspection cards and special process details
- Field inspections/audits
- Quarterly and biweekly contractor meetings on quality control issues

Table 10.2   Central Artery/Tunnel Project Quality Surveillance Program Procedure

Type of Audit	Purpose of Audit	Tools and Techniques	Responsible Party
1. Prime Contract and Compliance Audits	Verification by examination and objective evidence that the organization is producing the required deliverables in accordance with owner's guidelines	Evaluation of compliance to the contract, established requirements, procedures, and practices, including the review of contents and effectiveness of the work product. Deliverables: (1) postaudit conference, (2) quality assurance audit report	Quality assurance manager or lead auditor (reports directly to the project manager)
2. System Review and System Review Report	Evaluates previously identified processes or systems for their implementation and effectiveness and identifies deficient areas and opportunities for improvement	Flowcharts are compared to project procedures to identify differences, interviews, and other problem identification and data-gathering techniques. Deliverables: (1) system improvement recommendations (SIR), (2) system review team conclusions, (3) system review report	System review team leader appointed by the quality assurance manager
3. Compliance audit	Verifies that elements have been effectively implemented in accordance with requirements	An audit checklist is used for each audit, which considers information from previous audits, and deficiencies requiring correction are documented on the Corrective Action Request (CAR) form.	System review team leader
4. System Improvement Recommendation	Formal recommendations by the system review team	Construction quality control procedures are used to measure conformance with quality standards and required actions.	System review team

		Contractor
5. Remedial Action	Steps taken to correct the individual items identified as being deficient	Corrective action to preclude recurrence is recommended for serious deficiencies or generic problems. If sufficient time or information is not available to determine the magnitude or cause of a problem, action is further investigated.
6. Surveillance	Unscheduled activity performed to verify a particular requirement or activity	Corrective Action Request (CAR) used to identify issues Deliverable: General Surveillance Report — Lead auditor
7. Root-Cause Analysis	Looking beyond identified deficiencies to determine how extensive the problem is and what is the cause of the problem	Various tools and techniques — Lead auditor
8. Corrective Action System	Instances other than during the course of a formal audit or surveillance when it is necessary to document a condition adverse to quality and the corrective action taken	CAR procedure — Lead auditor

Source: Central Artery/Tunnel Project Quality Surveillance Program Procedure No. 302, Rev. 4 (April 11, 2000).

- Deficiencies documented, discussed, and corrected
- Nonconformance documentation
- Payment withholdings applied for unresolved items
- Contract closeout and review of quality control deficiencies

8. The Deficiency Report

The Deficiency Report (DR) process (Resident Engineer Manual Section 504), was used primarily for significant problems. An example of a Deficiency Report is shown in Table 10.3. Deficiency reports were critical in accounting for contractor's compliance with specifications and also as a warning that failure to comply with contractual requirements may result in temporary suspension from the project or, for high-risk situations, termination from the project permanently.

Table 10.3   Deficiency Report, Central Artery/Tunnel Project

Deficiency Report Information	Description	Responsible Party/Provision
Contractor, Date of Deficiency, Date Issued, Pay Item No.	Contract C11A1, 2/2001, 3/2001, 95277	Field engineer
Requirement	Concrete shall be cured for a minimum of five days for standard contract and areas cured shall be inspected once a day.	Contract specification
Deficiency	Contractor is not complying with contract curing requirements.	Resident engineer
Recommended Action	Contractor's QC manager shall review requirements with field engineer. Contractor's field staff shall perform checks, inspections, or surveillances.	Resident engineer
Compliance	Contractor will complete a concrete postplacement report daily for duration of the curing period.	Resident engineer
Corrective Action Taken	Curing requirements are reviewed and approved.	Contractor quality control manager
Design Change	Not required.	Project engineer
Corrective Action Verified	All actions taken—no further concrete on this contract.	Resident engineer

Source: Resident Engineer Manual Section 504.

9. Materials Controls

Construction materials engineering and testing is a critical component in the process of quality assurance and quality control, but this component was magnified on the Big Dig due to the large volume of activities and the complex geotechnical evaluations required for a project within an inner city. The project maintained multifaceted materials testing laboratories, both on and off site, equipped with soils testing equipment to provide moisture content, bearing ratios, density data, boring data for soils and rock, and asphalt testing. A few examples of the internal and external testing processes are highlighted in Table 10.4.

10. Value Engineering Change Proposal (VECP) Program

This chapter cannot be concluded without mentioning the importance of the application of value engineering in relation to quality. Value engineering can be defined as a systematic method to improve the "value" of goods and services by using an examination of function. *Value*, as defined, is the ratio of function to cost. Value can therefore be increased by either improving the function or reducing the cost. It is a basic principle of value engineering that quality not be reduced as a consequence of pursuing value improvements. In the United States, value engineering in the federal government is specifically provided for in Public Law 104-106, which states: "Each executive agency shall

Table 10.4   Materials Controls, Central Artery/Tunnel Project

Job-Site Testing	Off-Site Testing
Review welder's certification to the statewide certification program.	Review and approve structural steel fabricators at plants.
Verify contractor's process for metals/coating against their QC program.	Verify fabricator's process for metals/coating against their QC program.
Review/witness structural steel erection activities.	Conduct plant inspections for structural steel, precast concrete elements, ready-mix concrete, asphalt plants, soils and aggregate source, and segmental bridge fabrication.
Conduct testing for high-strength bolting.	Perform QA inspection at fabrication plants.
Advise the contractors for surface preparation and coating for corrosion protection.	Witness nondestructive testing.

Source: Central Artery/Tunnel Project Materials Testing Process.

establish and maintain cost-effective procedures and processes for analyzing the functions of a program, project, system, product,...." As described in earlier chapters, the application of value engineering in major projects like the Big Dig is critical to effective quality management.

11. Case Studies on Quality Assurance and Control

Quality as a Success or Failure Factor

> We have forty million reasons for failure, but not a single excuse.
>
> —*Rudyard Kipling*

Project management views of success have evolved over the years, but, traditionally, success has been defined as the sponsor's return on investment. In their research of project success frameworks, Morris and Hough (1987) found that success varies across the project and product life cycle and that success is both subjective and objective. Factors they identified as contributing to success include project functionality (financial and technical), project management (budget, schedule, and scope), business performance, and project termination (reasonable and efficient).

More recent studies have concluded that success factors encompass the contribution that the project made to the strategic mission of the firm (Cleland and Ireland 2002), and the success of not just the project but the entire organization (Turner and Muller 2004). Significantly, there is little mention in the project management literature of quality management as a success factor, but, rather, lack of quality management is often mentioned as a reason for failure. Since quality is defined as meeting a customer's requirements, it is often assumed that quality is built into the project documents and, thus, is a part of scope rather than a separate factor in project success. The following four cases illustrate the impact of quality on a project's success or failure, and the difficulties projects face once a failure occurs. The first two cases had successful outcomes in terms of quality assurance and quality control of the specific aspects of the project they were overseeing. The last two case studies highlight the tremendous risk in megaprojects, the reasons for quality failure, and lessons learned for the future.

- Case Study 1: Boston Harbor Waste Water Treatment Project
- Case Study 2: Quality as a Success Factor: U.S. Environmental Protection Agency (EPA) Case Study
- Case Study 3: The Collapse of the I-35 Mississippi Highway Bridge in Minneapolis
- Case Study 4: The Big Dig: 2006 Ted Williams Tunnel Ceiling Failure

Case Study 1: Quality as a Success Factor: Boston Harbor Waste Water Treatment Project

> Success is not final, failure is not fatal: it is the courage to continue that counts.
>
> —*Sir Winston Churchill*

The $3.8 billion Massachusetts Water Resource Authority (MWRA) Boston Harbor Cleanup Project, mandated by a 1984 federal court ruling by Judge Paul G. Garrity, is often cited for its exceptional quality assurance/quality control programs. Considering that Boston Harbor in the 1980s had a reputation for the most polluted waters in the United States, quality assurance and control were a critical component of providing an effective wastewater treatment facility on Boston's Deer Island. One of the most important aspects of the success of this massive cleanup facility, completed in 1995, was the extensive preconstruction planning as documented in the project's hundreds of reports, audits, and inspections (NPS 2002, MWRA 1993, MWRA 1997). Moreover, more than 300 technical reports and more than 1000 scientific papers on the subjects of Boston Harbor and Massachusetts Bay document the successful environmental conditions and changes since the new treatment facilities were brought on line. Notably, according to the MWRA, no adverse effects attributable to the discharge have ever been found, and the beaches and ecosystem of Boston Harbor have rebounded (MWRA 2009). Despite the enormous environmental success of the project, it was not without disasters, including the loss of two commercial divers in a high-risk underwater tunnel tragedy, attributed to a failure to consider less risky but more costly options (Swidey 2009).

Case Study 2: The Big Dig: U.S. Environmental Protection Agency Clean Construction Program   The Big Dig had extensive environmental regulations that had to be met throughout the project life cycle. One of these requirements is highlighted in the following Central Artery/Tunnel Project Contract Requirement: All pieces of construction equipment must have a diesel oxidation catalyst (DOC) and cannot idle in excess of five minutes.

To fulfill this requirement, the project began exploring the option of retrofitting equipment in September 1998 because of the close proximity to sensitive receptors. The program initially looked to retrofit a total of approximately 50 pieces of construction equipment. However, due to the number of vehicles used in the tunnel construction, there were more than 100 pieces of construction equipment participating in the program. Equipment targeted for retrofitting was located near sensitive receptors such as residential communities and hospitals, used in tunnel work for health and safety consideration of the workers, and included any equipment that was slated to remain on the project work site for the longest duration of the contract life.

Diesel oxidation catalysts were selected for the Big Dig because of the reduction in hydrocarbons (HCs), carbon monoxide (CO), and particulate

Figure 10.6   Tunnel Project Wall Demolition as of November 2003
Source: Central Artery/Tunnel Project.

matter (PM), the ease of installation, and the relatively inexpensive cost. The reduction of HCs helped to alleviate the odors and impacts to air quality. Another factor considered when selecting DOCs was the inclusion on EPA's Verified Technology list and the fact that the technology was well proven. According to contractor experience, the equipment retrofitted did not experience any adverse operational problems. Figure 10.6 shows in the background the heavy equipment used for demolition that was subject to the U.S. EPA construction equipment regulations.

Along with DOCs, the project explored the use of lower emission diesel fuel, specifically LUBRIZOL's PuriNOx product. Switching to the new fuel resulted in lower nitrogen oxide (Nox) emissions and reduced smoke. The only performance problems reported by operators were that the vehicle required slightly more power in deep mud and that slightly more fuel was consumed. A reduced idling policy was established and enforced, requiring all operators to turn off equipment that was not in active use. Prior to the project, there were two major concerns expressed by contractors. The first was the potential effect on the equipment warranty as well as the potential effect on equipment performance. The second was whether the emission control equipment would affect the performance of the construction equipment. However, after using the retrofitted equipment, contractors did not experience any adverse operational problems and did not have to perform any additional maintenance. Overall, the program was a huge success and contributed significant benefits to the entire project community (USEPA 2012).

Case Study 3: The Collapse of the I-35 Highway Bridge, Minneapolis, Minnesota
Failure of Quality Assurance: Lessons from Practice Facts: On August 1, 2007, the unimaginable happened: The I-35W highway bridge over the Mississippi River in Minneapolis experienced a catastrophic failure in the main span of the deck truss. As a result, 1000 feet of the deck truss collapsed, with about 108 feet plunging into the 15-foot-deep river, taking a school bus filled with children and 111 vehicles with it (see Figure 10.7). As a result of the bridge collapse, 13 people died, and 145 people were injured.

Proximate cause: The National Transportation Safety Board (NTSB) determined that the probable cause of the collapse was the inadequate load capacity, due to a design error, of the gusset plates at the U10 nodes, which failed under a combination of (1) substantial increases in the weight of the bridge, which resulted from previous bridge modifications, and (2) the traffic and concentrated construction loads on the bridge on the day of the collapse. Contributing to the accident was the generally accepted practice among federal and state transportation officials of giving inadequate attention to gusset plates during inspections for conditions of distortion, such as bowing, and of excluding gusset plates in load rating analyses.

Outcome: As a result of its investigation, the Safety Board issued a series of recommendations, including the development and implementation of a bridge design quality assurance/quality control program, to be used by the states and other bridge owners, that includes procedures to detect and correct

I-35 Highway Bridge Collapse, August 1, 2007
Minneapolis, MN

Figure 10.7   NTSB PHOTO: Collapsed Bridge Center Section (Looking Southeast)
Source: National Transportation Safety Board (NTSB). 2007. Accident Report.
NTSB/HAR-08/03, PB2008-916203. Collapse of I-35W Highway Bridge, Minneapolis,
Minnesota, August 1. p. 19.

bridge design errors before the design plans are made final, and modify the approved bridge inspector training to address inspection techniques and conditions specific to gusset plates. Remarkably, the investigation determined that, even though the bridge design firm knew how to correctly calculate the effects of stress in gusset plates, it failed to perform all necessary calculations for the main truss gusset plates on the bridge. Moreover, neither federal nor state authorities evaluated the design of the gusset plates for the I-35W bridge in sufficient detail during the design and acceptance process to detect the design errors in the plates, nor was it standard practice for them to do so. Though the I-35W bridge had been rated under the National Bridge Inspection Standards as Structurally Deficient for 16 years before the accident, the conditions responsible for that rating did not cause or contribute to the collapse of the bridge.

Case Study 4: The Big Dig: 2006 Ted William Tunnel Ceiling Failure

Failure of Quality Assurance Lessons from Practice   Though the Project had implemented numerous successful safety, health, risk and quality control programs throughout the life of the Project, in 2006 the Project faced its most serious violation of the public trust since Construction began in 1992. In July 2006, massive suspended ceiling panels fell in the Ted Williams Tunnel and crushed a passing car below. The passenger was fatally injured and the driver had minor physical injuries. The safety accident investigations and analysis was conducted by the National Transportation Safety Board (NTSB). An extensive NTSB Report determined that the proximate cause of the accident was "the use of an epoxy anchor adhesive with poor creep resistance, that is, an epoxy formulation that was not capable of sustaining long-term loads."

The Report identified six major causes:

1. The failure of the designer and management consultant to identify potential creep in the anchor adhesive as a critical long-term failure mode and to account for possible anchor creep in the design, specifications, and approval process for the epoxy anchors used in the tunnel.
2. A general lack of understanding and knowledge in the construction community about creep in adhesive anchoring systems.
3. Failure of the Contractor to provide the Central Artery/Tunnel project with sufficiently complete, accurate, and detailed information about the suitability of the company's Fast Set epoxy for sustaining long-term tensile loads.
4. Failure of the Sub-Contractor, to determine that the anchor displacement that was found in the high-occupancy vehicle tunnel in 1999 was a result of anchor creep.
5. Failure of Contractor and Management Consultant, subsequent to the 1999 anchor displacement, to continue to monitor anchor performance in light of the uncertainty as to the cause of the failures.

6. Failure of the owner to implement a timely tunnel inspection program that would likely have revealed the ongoing anchor creep.

As a result of its investigation, the Safety Board made Safety Recommendations to the Federal Highway Administration, American Association of State Highway and Transportation Officials, Departments of Transportation of the 50 States and the District of Columbia, International Code Council, ICC Evaluation Service, Inc., Powers Fasteners, Inc., Sika Chemical Corporation, American Concrete Institute, American Society of Civil Engineers, and Associated General Contractors of America (NTSB 2006).

NASA System Failure Case Studies   In June 2008, the National Aeronautics Space Administration issued a case study on the 2006 NTSB Highway Accident Report and raised the following questions for consideration by the NASA community:

1. Are cost and schedule pressures detracting from safety-critical design and/or design verification? Is there an effective pathway to express your concerns?
2. Are safety-critical maintenance activities being identified and conveyed to others by the proper authorities? Are inspections implemented in a timely manner?
3. Have all stakeholders worked to understand root causes associated with any unexpected results or off-nominal behaviors in development, testing, or integration?
4. Are you fully knowledgeable concerning the performance characteristics of all the materials you are working with (including polymers, composites)? Are you assuming engineering accountability or are you delegating?

LESSONS LEARNED

1. Foster a quality management philosophy that demonstrates a commitment to quality management that is integrated into project cost, schedule, and scope decision making at all levels of the organization.
2. Establish a quality governance structure that is integrated into a centralized quality management system led by a director of quality management (DQM).
3. Develop an organizational reporting structure that ensures the DQM has a direct reporting line to the owner organization's CEO.
4. Establish an independent quality assurance oversight committee composed of quality experts to assist in identification and resolution of problem quality issues.
5. Develop high-level criteria for the selection of a director of quality management, quality control personnel (QCP), and quality control managers (QCMs) for each contract and provide ongoing training that

focuses on continuous improvement of quality control and quality assurance processes.

6. Provide the DQM with the authority to approve all QCP and QCMs with direct and indirect reporting lines to the DQM.

7. Provide the DQM with the authority to issue a stop work order based on various criteria established in the project construction contracts and agreements including high-risk activities or previously identified problem areas.

8. Implement problem prevention programs into the project correction processes.

9. Provide a transparent and open process for all project participants to express their concerns

10. Require a uniform, consistent inspection process in each and every contract that requires approval and corrective action and then follow through with enforcement of these requirements.

11. In a design-bid-build (separately bid) or design-build project (single point of responsibility), make sure inspections continue upon turnover to the government or private owner.

12. Utilize sophisticated data and quality analysis tools such as formal root-cause analysis, quality, and metrics and trending that enable fact-based analysis and decisions.

13. Make sure all quality managers, project team members and high level project management understand root causes associated with any unexpected results or off-nominal behaviors in development, testing, or integration.

14. Make sure inspections are being conducted in a timely manner and that safety-critical maintenance activities and long term critical failure modes are being identified and conveyed to others by the proper authorities.

15. Conduct training based on theory and practice, and train all members of the project management teams, including high-level project managers, on quality assurance, quality control, and continuous improvement.

16. Conduct regular quality assurance meetings with all personnel involved in quality assurance activities, including internal project managers and external contractor managers.

17. Conduct quality audits in a uniform, comprehensive manner by a sophisticated independent quality engineer.

18. Vigorously enforce contract provisions for quality control, quality assurance, and continuous improvement programs.

19. Ensure that cost and schedule pressures are not detracting from quality assurance and quality control.

20. Quality managers should be responsible for performing system reviews and auditing to evaluate the effectiveness of the quality program and follow-up to verify implementation of recommendations and corrective actions.

BEST PRACTICES

1. An owner's director of quality management (DQM) should be appointed from the inception of the project with a direct reporting line to the organization's CEO and oversight responsibility for the project's quality assurance engineers.
2. Quality plans should incorporate a clear delineation of oversight and decision-making responsibilities of the owner, the management consultant, and the contractors for quality assurance and quality control.
3. An extensive quality assurance and quality control assessment should be conducted and approved before construction commences.
4. Quality training should be a requirement for all project employees involved in any aspect of construction oversight, and training should commence prior to the construction phase and continue through all stages of the project.
5. Emphasize the need for strict compliance with project testing procedures and pertinent regulations, and recover project costs resulting from the contractor's failure to abide by contract provisions.
6. Require that, prior to certification, the state ensure that material closeout reports include necessary documentation for all materials that have been tested and incorporated into the project and review such documentation for compliance with contract specifications.
7. Flexibility should be built into the project structure, giving the project manager the ability to deal with challenging circumstances that require innovative solutions.
8. Quality analysis methodology, standards, and tools should be utilized that focus on problem prevention and identification of safety critical design and long-term critical failure modes.
9. Oversight of quality control training and competence by the project contractors should be conducted by an independent authority on a regular basis.
10. Deficiency reports, construction change orders, and inspection reports must be reviewed on a regular basis by an independent quality assurance/control auditor to assist in the identification of trends, patterns of abuse and potential risks on the project.
11. Data on quality control for all project activities should be available and not limited only to select groups.
12. A quality assessment should be prepared at the inception of the project and should be updated on a regular basis to identify new risks and troublesome patterns, with recommendations for correction.
13. Enforcement and prevention mechanisms should be included in the project contracts that have serious consequences, including penalties for noncompliance and termination of contracts for more serious violations.
14. Inspections should occur on a regular basis to identify high risks, patterns of abuse, perilous trends, and lack of enforcement.

15. Testing laboratories should be independent of the consultant that oversees the project so that effective testing of project construction materials can be performed by independent experts.
16. The project's quality program should be integrated with risk management so that a shared vision of risk, safety and quality is central to the project's mission and goals.

SUMMARY

Quality management requires a commitment, vision, and strategy and a focus on continuous improvement and expert knowledge. Quality can never be ignored, compromised, or negotiated. Process and procedures that govern quality must be integrated into the project and managed consistently and uniformly throughout the project. Root causes of quality failure and safety critical design and long-term critical failure modes must be identified and understood and shared through the implementation of lessons learned and best practices.

ETHICAL CONSIDERATIONS

1. In the introduction to this chapter, William A. Foster is quoted as follows: "Quality is never an accident; it is always the result of high intention, sincere effort, intelligent direction and skillful execution; it represents the wise choice of many alternatives."

   In the field of project management there is much confusion as to what quality "is" and what it "isn't." Do you agree with William A. Foster's definition of quality? Why or why not? Can you think of a better definition? What are the ethical implications for project managers when quality fails?
2. When megaprojects fail because of a quality error, no matter how large or small, who should be held accountable? The designer? The project owner? The management consultant? The contractor? Subcontractors? All of the foregoing parties? Is the failure of quality an ethical violation? Should any of the parties be penalized? If so, how? Is a failure of quality always the result of design error or omission, or can quality failures occur in other ways? Explain.
3. Develop a definition of a failed project. Is a failed project one with cost overruns? Delayed performance? Quality failures? Risk failure? Or is a failed project one that never finishes because the project runs out of funding sources?

DISCUSSION QUESTIONS

1. Assume you were hired as director of quality management to develop a quality program for a new tunnel project in the United States. The

project director has given you full authority to develop the high-level framework and structure for this project. Describe the top ten questions you would ask the project director before beginning your responsibilities as director of quality management.

2. Do you agree with the statement that quality should drive a project rather than cost and schedule? How would you convince your project director that quality must always supersede the triple constraint of cost, time, and scope? What evidence would you provide to the project director who firmly believes that all projects must be schedule driven to contain costs and keep on budget?

3. Based on the Big Dig tunnel collapse case study, explain the root causes of the failure of quality in this case. Describe the quality assurance and quality control strategy, processes, and procedures you would put in place to prevent future tragedies on highway and tunnel projects?

4. Explain the root cause of the failure of quality in the Mississippi Bridge Failure case study. Why did the National Transportation Safety Board conclude that, though the bridge had been rated as structurally deficient for 16 years, that rating did not cause or contribute to the accident?

5. The following statement in italics was contained in the final NTSB Report on the I-35W Bridge Collapse in Minneapolis. What is alarming about this statement, and what should project managers do to address the problems inherent in this statement in their own projects?

   Moreover, neither Federal nor State authorities evaluated the design of the gusset plates for the I-35W bridge in sufficient detail during the design and acceptance process to detect the design errors in the plates, nor was it standard practice for them to do so. (NTSB Report I-35W Bridge Collapse 2007)

6. Why are failures of quality control often attributed to project failure, and yet quality success stories like the Big Dig's Clean Air initiatives, in balance, are not given sufficient consideration?

7. Contrast quality management with risk management. How are they alike? How are they different?

8. How would you identify safety critical design and long-term critical failure modes on your project, and what type of procedures would you implement to ensure that these concerns were properly monitored and controlled?

9. Describe in your own words the meaning of the following quote by one of America's best-known entrepreneurs as it might apply to managing quality on a large scale project like the Big Dig.

   Success is a lousy teacher. It seduces smart people into thinking they can't lose.

   —Bill Gates

REFERENCES

Abdulaziz, A. B., and H. A. Tawfiq. 1999. "ISO 9000 Quality Standards in Construction." *Journal of Management in Engineering* (November-December): 41–45.

Ball, D., J. Geringer, M. Minor, and J. McNett. 2010. *International Business: The Challenges of Global Competition.* 12th ed. New York: McGraw-Hill/Irwin.

Boehm, B. 1981. *Software Engineering Economics.* Englewood Cliffs, NJ: Prentice-Hall.

CA/T (Central Artery/Tunnel Project). 2000a. Project Procedure 301, Revision 3. Project Quality Assurance Program.

CA/T (Central Artery/Tunnel Project). 2000b. Project Procedure 302, Revision 4, April 11. Construction Quality Surveillance Program.

CA/T (Central Artery/Tunnel Project). 2000c. Project Procedure 1234. Construction Field Personnel Orientation and Training (required technical and other instructions).

Cleland, D., and L. Ireland. 2002. *Project Management: Strategic Design and Implementation. Vol.* 1. 4th ed. New York: McGraw-Hill.

Crosby, P. B. 1986. *Quality without Tears.* New York: McGraw-Hill.

Deming, W. E. 1986. *Out of the Crisis: Quality, Productivity and Competitive Position.* Cambridge, MA: MIT Press.

Diggans, Keith. 2012. Interview with Keith Diggans, Facilities Engineer, Central Artery/Tunnel Project. June 21 and 22.

Evans, J., and W. Lindsay. 2011. *Managing for Quality and Performance Excellence.* 8th ed. Mason, OH: South-Western Cengage.

ISO 9000. 2000. International Organization for Standardization. Geneva.

Johnson, P., M. Leenders, and A. Flynn. 2011. *Purchasing and Supply Management.* 14th ed. New York: McGraw-Hill, 171.

Juran, J. M. 1995. *The History of Managing for Quality in the United States.* Milwaukee, WI: ASQ Quality Press.

Juran, J. M., and A. B. Godfrey. 1999. *Juran's Quality Handbook.* 5th ed. New York: McGraw-Hill, 2.1–2.2.

Lewis, Raphael. 2002. "Big Dig Hires Quality Manager Official: Had Left Job Unfulfilled for Three Years." Boston Globe, April 27, B.1.

MHD (Massachusetts Highway Department). 2000. (August 15 Revisions.) MHD Division I Standard Specifications and Supplemental Specifications and CA/T Supplemental Specifications to Construction Details of the Standard Specifications for Highway and Bridges (Division II) for Central Artery (I-93)/Tunnel (I-90) Project in the City of Boston. Vol. I and Vol. II of Contract Package.

Morris, P. W. G., and G. H. Hough. 1987. *The Anatomy of Major Projects: A Study of the Reality of Project Management. Vol.* 1. Chichester, UK: John Wiley & Sons, Ltd.

MWRA (Massachusetts Water Resources Authority). 1993. *The Boston Harbor Sludge Abatement Monitoring Program: Soft Bottom Benthic Biology and Sedimentology, 1991–1992 Monitoring and Surveys*. Charlestown, MA: MWRA, Commonwealth of Massachusetts.

MWRA (Massachusetts Water Resources Authority). 1997. *Final CSO Facilities Plan and Environmental Impact Report*. Charlestown, MA: MWRA, Commonwealth of Massachusetts.

MWRA (Massachusetts Water Resources Authority). 2009. *The Boston Harbor Project: An Environmental Success Story*. Charlestown, MA: MWRA, Commonwealth of Massachusetts.

NASA (National Aeronautics and Space Administration). 2009. Space Flight Program and Project Management Requirements, NASA Interim Directive (NID) for NASA Procedural Requirements (NPR) 7120.5D, and the Standing Review Board Handbook. Washington, DC: National Aeronautics and Space Administration.

NASA (National Aeronautics and Space Administration). 2008. *System Failure Case Studies, Tunnel of Terror*. Volume 2, Issue 5 (June).

National Defense Authorization Act. 1996. 110 stat. 186 Public Law 104–106, 14 USC 1711. February 10.

NPS (National Park Service). 2002. *Boston Harbor Island—A National Park Area*. Massachusetts Water Resources Scoping Report, prepared by Mark D. Flora. Technical Report NPS/NRWRD/NRTR-2002/300. Washington, DC: National Park Service, Water Resources Division.

NTSB (National Transportation Safety Board). 2006. Ceiling Collapse in the Interstate 90 Connector Tunnel Boston, MA, July 10, 2006. Accident Report, NTSB/HAR-07/02, PB2007-91620.3.

NTSB (National Transportation Safety Board). 2007. Collapse of I-35W Highway Bridge, Minneapolis, Minnesota, August 1, 2007. Accident Report, NTSB/HAR-08/03, PB2008-916203.

OIG (Office of the Inspector General). 1996. *Audit Report: Quality of Construction, Central Artery / Third Harbor Tunnel*. Federal Highway Administration Region I, Report Number: R2-FH-7-007. December 19. Washington, DC: U.S. Department of Transportation, 1.

PMI (Project Management Institute). 2013. *A Guide to the Project Management Body of Knowledge (PMBOK® Guide)*—Fifth Edition. Newtown Square, PA: Project Management Institute.

Rose, K. 2005. *Project Quality Management: Why, What and How*. Boca Raton, FL: J. Ross Publishing, Inc., 6.

Shewhart, W. A. 1939. *Statistical Method from the Viewpoint of Quality Control*. Foreword by W. Edwards Deming, 1986.) Washington, DC: The Graduate School, the Department of Agriculture. Republished by Dover Publications.

Standish Group. (1994 and 2010). *The CHAOS Chronicles, 1994 and 2010*. Boston: Standish Group International, Inc.

Swidey, N. 2009. "Trapped." *Boston Globe Sunday Magazine, August* 9, 2009.

Turner, J. R., and R. Müller. 2004. "Communication and Co-operation on Projects between the Project Owner as Principal and the Project Manager as Agent." *European Management Journal* 22(3):327–336.

USEPA (U.S. Environmental Protection Agency). 2012. Case Studies, Clean Construction USA Program. www.epa.gov/diesel/construction/casestudies .htm (last visited March 28, 2012).

Chapter 11

Building a Sustainable Project through Integration and Change

> There is nothing more difficult to take in hand, more perilous to conduct, or more uncertain in its success, than to take the lead in the introduction of a new order of things.
>
> —*Niccolo Machiavelli*
> *The Prince (1532)*

INTRODUCTION

> If you do not change direction, you may end up where you are heading.
>
> —*Lao Tzu*

This chapter introduces the important concept of project integration management and its impact on managing change and sustainability. The importance of integrated processes, especially on long-term projects, has become a key requirement of all project management methodologies. Integrated project management is commonly defined as the combining of all of the major dimensions of project management under one umbrella and involves applying a set of knowledge, skills, tools, and techniques to a collection of projects.

Integration management introduces the important need for collaboration in building a sustainable project. How megaprojects use integrative tools to enhance the likelihood of project success is an important theme of this chapter. The question of how projects are integrated to foster collaboration and sustainability is a developing field in project management and an area for much-needed research. To build a sustainable project that lasts long beyond project completion requires meeting the following goals: (1) building awareness,

(2) ensuring community involvement, (3) developing a diverse base of support, and (4) promoting systems change. Integration and change management are critical to accomplishing these goals.

PROJECT INTEGRATION VERSUS COLLABORATION

PMI defines program integration management to include:

> The processes and activities needed to identify, define, combine, unify, and coordinate multiple components within the program. It coordinates the various program management activities across the program life cycle.
> **(*The Standard for Program Management* 2013)**

Often defined as a criterion for project success, project integration essentially means achieving coordination and collaboration among project teams, internal and external stakeholders, project controls and responsibility centers, and the entire organization.

The terms *integration* and *collaboration* are often used interchangeably, when, in practice, they have distinct meetings. *Integration* is a tool that is often used on projects to achieve collaboration. In contrast, *collaboration* is generally defined as a model of professionals working together to accomplish a goal. Thus, integration requires collaboration as a precondition to be effective; however, collaboration does not necessarily require integration. For instance, a project may have separate groups or individuals who work together collaboratively, yet this collaboration is not necessarily embedded in the project's organizational framework.

The coordination needs of a megaproject may create unique interdependencies between the larger organization, and the numerous separate projects and programs that comprise the organization. Project related coordination requirements are often quite complex. Project managers should consider the following questions before embarking on an integrated project framework:

- What types of functions or activities require coordination in the project—risk management, cost and schedule control, quality assurance, change control, conflict management, dispute resolution?
- What is the best way to achieve this integration—organizational and governance change, policy changes, contractual obligations, relationship building, education and training, development of new processes and procedures?
- How may these needs change over time? Integration may be implemented at various phases of the project, depending on project goals and objectives during each phase. For example, an integrated construction change control process may be needed during project construction but not during the earlier conceptual and design phases.

THE RELATIONSHIP BETWEEN PROJECT INTEGRATION AND CHANGE MANAGEMENT

> We see the world the way we do not because that is the way
> it is, but because we have these ways of seeing.
>
> —*Ludwig Wittgenstein,*
> *Philosophical Investigations 1953*

Project management was developed over many centuries as a means for organizations to manage change. Change management has been written about extensively in the literature as a result of technological advances and the focus on project sustainability and complexity over the last several decades. How and when we see the need for change is a critical component of project success. Change impacts all aspects of a project's organization including procurement, design, construction, cost, schedule, risk, quality, sustainability, human resources, and technology.

Megaprojects, by their very nature, are creatures of change. The environment of megaprojects—the pace, the pressure, the tension and uncertainty, the widespread fears and skepticism—combined with the sheer volume of difficult decisions create a herculean task that can quickly overwhelm even the most capable project managers and the most sophisticated organization. As if the challenges of the long up-front formation and planning phase are not difficult enough, projects are then faced with the difficult work of the execution phase. Either phase, if poorly led and managed, can prevent the progression of an otherwise successful project.

As a result, project integration is, without a doubt, the ultimate change management challenge. For a project organization to successfully integrate multiple polices, processes, and procedures, leadership in change management is a key requirement. On megaprojects, the need for change is driven by internal factors such as technological challenges, uncertainty, and risk complexity, and external challenges such as the regulatory environment, stakeholder expectations, and unpredictable markets. Integration management is concerned with facilitating the process of change through strategies, structures, and processes and can serve as a road map for understanding and managing change.

Managing Change in Projects

Change is inevitable in projects because that is why we create projects—to innovate, advance a new idea, and explore new ground. The challenges of managing change are well described in the following words of the man who came to be regarded as the symbol of independent India:

> A "No" uttered from the deepest conviction is better than a
> "Yes" merely uttered to please, or worse, to avoid trouble.
>
> —*Mahatma Ghandi*

The words of Ghandi are so relevant to projects today. As noted by historians, Ghandi's philosophy was not theoretical but one of pragmatism. Managing a megaproject is not about popularity or unifying opinion, but rather about leading change. Change management has been defined as "a structured and systemic approach to achieving a sustainable change in human behavior within an organization" (Todd 1999). It can be reactive, coming from outside the organization, or proactive, coming from within the organization. Resistance to change is a common reaction in most organizations, and projects are no exception (Paton and McCalman 2008; Pendlebury et al. 1998). Political change is particularly prevalent in large projects, as are ethical and legal change. Because change comes in different forms, and from different sources, a variety of systems, structures, and programs are needed to manage it. *A Guide to the Project Management Body of Knowledge (PMBOK® Guide)*— Fifth Edition (PMI 2013) links organizational strategies and priorities to portfolios and programs, and between programs and individual projects. PMI defines the responsibility for managing change differently for projects, programs, and portfolios, as summarized in Table 11.1.

Change and Integration at the Big Dig: The Complex Network of Internal and External Controls   The Big Dig project was managed both from within the organization and through an extensive external network of auditors, stakeholders, community advocates, regulators, congressional oversight committees, and participants from the federal and state transportation systems. The management of the coordination and scheduling of this colossal project emanated from the Central Artery/Tunnel Project's Control Center.

Internal controls included such processes as the prequalification of contractors, contract packaging, detailed bidding requirements, the cost containment program, cost recovery, value engineering, the project labor agreement, quality assurance and quality control, and the owner-controlled insurance program. External controls included the community advisory board, rating agencies and bond underwriters, regulatory authorities, internal and

Table 11.1   Comparative Overview of Project, Program, and Portfolio Management

Discipline	Projects	Programs	Portfolios
Change Management	Project managers expect change and implement processes to keep change managed and controlled.	The program manager must expect change from both inside and outside the program and be prepared to manage it.	Portfolio managers continually monitor changes in the broad environment.

Source: Adapted from *A Guide to the Project Management Body of Knowledge (PMBOK® Guide)*—Fifth Edition, p. 8 (PMI 2013).

external contract audits, peer reviews, and special oversight by the Central Artery Executive Oversight and Coordination Commission.

Because the adaptability to change was central to the project's success, substantial time and resources were devoted to developing, improving, and implementing change policies and procedures and to measuring the impact of change on project goals and deliverables. There was a constant tension among project managers trying to balance the right kinds and number of procedures with the reality that if a procedure existed it must be enforced.

In deciding how to integrate processes and procedures, project, program, and portfolio managers all face the same key questions:

1. What processes and integrative actions are crucial to project completion on my project?
2. How will I manage the interdependencies among the project management areas?
3. How will I track, review, and regulate progress to meet performance objectives?

Dimensions of Integration and Change Management

As the nature of activities change, so did the roles of the owner, the consultant, the designers, and the contractors. In the previous chapters of this book, the integration of scope, schedule, cost, risk, and quality were described, as well as the various tools and techniques utilized to manage these integrated programs.

As shown in Table 11.2, complex megaprojects require not only the integration of numerous processes and people but also the integration of communities

Table 11.2   Dimensions of Project Integration Management

People Dimension	Integration of the people dimension requires an understanding of the relationship between the resources dedicated to the change and the people impacted by the change. Managing the change relationship is key to the success of project integration.
Process and Procedures Dimension	Integrating processes and procedures involves aligning the strategic goals of the technical activities with the people who will perform these activities. Key questions involve when and how the processes will be implemented.
Knowledge Dimension	Different types of knowledge require different ways, methods, and actions of knowledge creation and sharing across projects and across the organization. The sharing of knowledge through training, shared databases, financial reporting, implementation of best practices, and lessons learned is an essential factor in project integration management.

of knowledge, including business process innovation, strategic management, socioeconomic impact, public policy, and quantitative and qualitative analysis across disciplines. Partnership alliances are critical to successful megaproject management, and engagement between the public and private sectors is essential. Due to the many risks and potential catastrophic loss that the project faced, process became all the more important. Throughout each phase of the project, processes were reviewed and sometimes amended based on lessons learned or changes in owner and stakeholder requirements. Critical to the implementation of a process was the importance of integration and collaboration among the participants to ensure that these innovative processes were properly delivered.

Project integration and change management occur across several dimensions. Three significant dimensions to project integration management are as shown in Table 11.2.

The ability to develop, implement, and manage change starts at the top. Since the Big Dig was structured as a program rather than a project, the roles of both the project director and the program manager in implementing change were significant. Project managers were retained based on their experience working on complex projects and their proven ability to develop and implement change processes and procedures. The program manager had responsibilities not only for overseeing the work of the project's resident engineers but also for managing the constant influx of internal and external stakeholder demands through numerous processes and procedures. In the absence of a formal designation, the project's portfolio management responsibilities were assumed by the project director, who reported directly to the chairman of the board.

INTEGRATION OF PROJECT DELIVERY

Integrated Project Delivery (IPD), as defined by the American Institute of Architects (AIA), is a project delivery approach that integrates people, systems, business structures, and practices into a process that collaboratively harnesses the talents and insights of all participants to optimize project results, increase value to the owner, reduce waste, and maximize efficiency through all phases of design, fabrication, and construction (AIA 2007). Integrated projects are distinguished by highly effective collaboration among the owner, the prime designer, and the prime contractor or management consultant, commencing at the early design phase and continuing through to project turnover.

Though almost all of the project's processes were integrated because of the many challenges faced by the project's core management team, as a general rule not every project uses every process all the time. Each of the major contracts on the Big Dig involved intensely complicated technical, legal, and financial issues and numerous processes and procedures as well as a complex regulatory scheme. In addition to design and construction integration processes, operational integration processes are essential to conduct testing, training, and transfer of infrastructure and facilities. In every contract on the project, prior to transfer to operations, a detailed plan was prepared that incorporated a skills training program and operational requirements well in advance of project opening.

Configuration Management: Project Delivery Systems

Configuration management (CM) as a formal management approach was developed by the U.S. Air Force (USAF) in the 1950s as a technical management discipline. Today, the CM process is widely used by military engineering organizations to manage complex systems, such as weapon systems, vehicles, and information systems. Outside of the military, the CM process is used in engineering projects, including civil engineering to build roads, bridges, canals, dams, and buildings. It is a process for establishing and maintaining consistency of a project's performance, both functional and physical attributes, with its design and operational requirements throughout the project's life cycle.

Configuration management can be likened to what is known as the "project delivery method" in construction projects.

The Associated General Contractors of America (AGC) defines the project delivery method as "the comprehensive process of assigning the contractual responsibilities for designing and constructing a project..." (AGC 2004). Though different types of delivery methods for design and construction are employed in the United States, the three most common methods are design-bid-build (DBB), design-build (DB), and a newer, more integrated approach, construction manager at risk (FHWA 2012.). (See Table 11.3). The earliest empirical research comparing these delivery systems concluded that design-build delivery speed was at least 23 percent faster than construction management at risk, and 33 percent faster than design-bid-build (Konchar 1997).

The Big Dig's Delivery Approach

On the Big Dig, integration problems were more challenging because the project's delivery approach separated design from construction through its traditional design-bid-build model. This delivery mode meant that construction could not be bid until after design was completed, thus separating the design responsibilities from the construction responsibilities on each of the project's 132 major contracts. The emerging project management research contends that true integration requires a design-build or construction manager at risk model from the inception of the project.

Because contracts on the Big Dig were negotiated separately with designers and contractors, collaboration was more difficult when conflicts developed

Table 11.3   Project Delivery Methods

Delivery Method	Characteristics	Comments
Design-bid build (DBB; the Big Dig's delivery method)	The traditional delivery system whereby the owner either completes the design using its own professionals or retains a designer, and after design is complete the owner and/or the owner's consultant solicits fixed price bids from contractors.	Owner owns the details of design during construction and can be held liable for errors and omissions. There is limited contractor input into the design, and low bid can encourage claims and changes.
Design-build (DB)	The owner contracts with a single entity to perform both design and construction under a single design-build contract. On megaprojects, portions or all of the design and construction may be subcontracted.	Chain of responsibility is simplified, and as in CMR the contractor has input into the design process. As the design-builder controls the delivery process, research has shown this has the greatest prospect of reducing delivery time.
Construction manager at risk (CMR)	Integrated team approach. The owner contracts separately with a designer and an at-risk construction manager. The contractor usually has significant input into the design process.	Aim is to engage construction expertise early in the design process to enhance constructability and manage risk, without the owner relinquishing control over the design.

among the project's most important stakeholders. Under a design-build model, both the designer and constructor are retained at the same time, thus developing a strong working relationship from the start through shared goals and methodology. Combining the design, construction, and operations under a single point of responsibility enhances the likelihood that the project will be more united in its goals and will eliminate the tensions that too frequently arise when design and construction are segmented such that the designers blame the contractors for errors in construction and the contractors blame the designers for errors and omissions. The enormous claims and changes that were filed in this project highlight the conflicts and tensions between the designers and the contractors and emphasize the need for a more uniform and centralized approach to construction management.

In hindsight, some have argued that structuring a competition for a single contract for the management services may have resulted in a better understanding of roles and responsibilities within the project team. In general, the party who is accountable for the project scope and cost must have proper incentives to perform. However, when the Big Dig was conceived, the federal funding rules required the separation of design and construction, resulting in project objectives that focused on the federal regulations. Although no federal project has ever been left unfinished, there is often uncertainty as to the scope or the total cost of the project. The criticism of the design-bid-build model is well taken to the extent that a project is allowed to receive federal funding before the project is designed and before it is has received environmental approval. Some early research on the Big Dig concluded that the design-bid-build process limits the effectiveness of value engineering and the potential to obtain the "best value" for public money (Mahoney 1998).

The FHWA has, in recent years, encouraged the use of a design-build model, as designer and contractors are retained at the same time, developing a strong working relationship from the start of the project through shared goals and methodology. Recent research by the U.S. National Cooperative Highway Research Program has also revealed the benefits of the CMR model based on its integrated team approach (NCHRP 2010).

INTEGRATED PROJECT ORGANIZATION

During the peak construction years, one approach used to cope with the changing integration needs was to change the project structure from a traditional program management model into an integrated project organization (IPO). An IPO is an organization where both the owner's employees and the management consultant's employees work under one organization structure. This change was made because management decided that an integrated organization would enhance collaboration and reduce conflict at a time when it was desperately needed. This transition to an IPO was made in 1999, just as construction activity was peaking.

Although adopted for the stated purpose of streamlining the management structure and trimming costs, it also had the effect of blurring accountability and responsibilities and discouraging proactive project management.

This transition to the IPO was met with mixed reviews. In its Report on the Big Dig, the National Academies stated (Board 2003):

> The implementation of the IPO has complicated the control of expenses for the B/PB management-consultant team.

One of the criticisms of the Big Dig during the process of integration was the loss of independence and the "cozy" relationship developed between the public- and private-sector managers of the project. Mary Richards testified in 2003 on behalf of the Massachusetts Organization of State Engineers and Scientists (MOSES) that the reduction in the ranks of the public government professionals has been so reduced and "the ranks of private contractors has increased so dramatically that the lack of oversight on public construction projects has spawned a greater potential for the waste, fraud and abuse of tax dollars"—a problem not limited to the Big Dig. (Richards 2003). In a

November 2001 report, the FHWA warned that "current overall construction and materials staffing levels are below the minimum needed."

Though organizational integration, as distinct from integration of project management processes and procedures, is widely supported in the project management literature and was recognized as a credible solution at the Big Dig, it was not without its critics. Particularly, those who felt integration of the project management organization may have impacted the integrity of the government watchdog because of the dual role of the government as regulator and owner. Public projects must maintain independent oversight of the projects they regulate, and, to the extent that independence is compromised, the use of an IPO should be carefully scrutinized to ensure that the public trust is maintained.

INNOVATIVE PROCESS AND PROGRAM INTEGRATION AND SUSTAINABILITY AT THE BIG DIG

Developing strategies for maintaining complex projects like the Big Dig over a long period of time requires a shift from implementing a plan of action to establishing processes and programs that create an ongoing transformational and sustainable structure that will address different stakeholder interests. Long after the project is complete, the community must live with the outcomes. In establishing integrated programs and processes, the goal of the project was to maintain its operability and benefits during its lifetime. Several of the more important integrated processes utilized on the Big Dig are highlighted in Figure 11.1. These important models of integration include: (1) partnering, (2) stakeholder management, (3) claims and changes, (4) centralized audit program, (5) dispute resolution, (6) team integration, (7) utilities management, (8) contract integration, (9) risk management, and (10) budget and financing. Integration meant that each of the ten programs had centralized processes and procedures that were followed by all project participants. The benefits of integration included increased efficiency, reduced costs, reduction in redundancy, improved data integration, better procedures, one-stop service, continuous relationship building, and the development of a sustainable project.

1. Integration through Partnering

> I cannot monetize how much we saved as a result of partnering, but after awarding over $2 billion in construction, we have no lawsuits and no major disputes.
>
> —*Peter Zuk, former Central Artery / Tunnel project director (ENR 1996)*

Partnering is a form of collaboration, and projects are, by their very nature, collaborating organizations. However, project research on empirical evidence

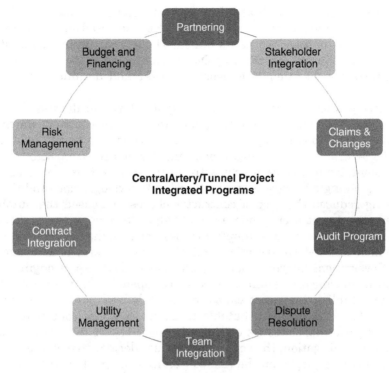

Figure 11.1   Models of Integration at the Big Dig
Source: Integrated Project Programs, Policies, Guidelines and Processes and Procedures.

concerning collaboration in projects is limited. The concept of *partnering* was first utilized by DuPont Engineering on a large-scale construction project in the mid-1980s, and the U.S. Army Corps of Engineers was the first public agency to use partnering in its construction projects. Partnering is now widely used by numerous government and construction entities around the world. It involves an agreement in principle to share project risks and to establish and promote partnership relationships to achieve business objectives. Partnering has been utilized to achieve the aspirations of early advocates of greater project integration, and it has become a widespread feature of global construction management practice (Chan et al. 2003; Wood and Ellis 2005). However, across different national and cultural contexts, researchers caution that, despite its presumed benefits, "partnering is by no means as pervasive or taken for granted as its early advocates would have liked" (Morris et al. 2011).

Partnering as described in the Big Dig's *Partnering Manual* (CA/T 1998) was initially implemented in 1992, primarily on construction contracts, but its success in construction later led to its use in design contracts, community groups, and the development of internal and interagency partnerships. Partnerships were used to improve schedule adherence, quality, safety, and

project performance, as well as to reduce costs, claims, disputes, and litigation. Almost 100 partnerships existed on the Big Dig based on contract values
ranging from $4 million to a half a billion. Though partnering is not always
contractually required, on the Big Dig it was included in all construction
contracts with a duration of at least one year and a value of $1 million
or more.

Partnering sessions were held on a regular basis to discuss the needs
of the project, to resolve problems, and to improve controls. Partnering
included leadership training, seminars, executive meetings, and other activities. The federal and state government officials and the contractor's project
management team met regularly with an independent expert to assist in
developing a single integrated team. Sharing knowledge, risk, and liability,
partnering reduced the cost of contractor claims, increased the number of
value-engineering savings proposals, and helped keep projects on schedule.

Partnering was used, for example, to assess leaks in the Fort Point Channel
area, which delayed construction and often had several causes and flow
paths. Government lawyers, aided by an independent expert engineer with
substantial marine geotechnical experience, spent more than 2000 hours
trying to establish the exact cause of the leak but could not do so with
certainty. The leak was attributable to unexpected site conditions and to
contractor performance issues compounded by pressure to meet milestones.
To avoid costly litigation, the government owner decided to mediate the issue
before two sitting judges on the Armed Services Contract Board of Appeals.
The mediation process took three months and succeeded in convincing the
parties that liability for the leak should be shared between the owner and the
contractor (B/PB 2003).

The Big Dig has used partnering to an unprecedented extent. Experts
have concluded that, because of its scope and complexity, the project would
have been simply unmanageable without partnering. Though the benefits
of partnering on the Big Dig have not been quantified, there is sufficient
data to support the conclusion that partnering contributed significantly to
the reduction of claims and the avoidance of expensive and time-consuming
litigation.

The partnering process is an alternative team problem-solving approach,
with the help of a neutral facilitator that is intended to eliminate the adversarial relationship problems between the owner and contractor by developing
a single integrated team. More simply stated, it is a way of conducting business in which two or more organizations make long-term commitments to
achieve mutual goals focused on interests, not position. Though often used in
construction, it is valuable for almost any type of business relation. Partnering promotes open communication among participants, trust, understanding,
and teamwork.

Types of Partnerships on the Big Dig   Various types of partnerships were
used on the Big Dig project; several of them are described in Table 11.4.

Table 11.4   The Central Artery/Tunnel Project Partnering Relationships

Type	Partners
Construction contacts	Primarily between the prime contractors: the owner, the sponsor, and the management consultant. Subcontractors, critical agencies, community groups, and private companies that were impacted by nearby construction were also included.
Design contracts	Usually between the design consultant and the prime contractors. Critical agencies were also involved.
Internal partnerships	Primarily between partnering teams that were developed among the prime contractors.
Interagency partnerships	Typically, the owner, the City of Boston, and the local airport (Massport) or transit authority (MBTA).
Intercontract partnerships	Interface relationships between two or more contractors.

Source: *The Central Artery / Tunnel Project Partnering Manual*. 1998.

Though the benefits of partnering have not been quantified for the Big Dig, there is sufficient data to support the conclusion that partnering contributed significantly to the reduction of claims and the avoidance of expensive and time-consuming litigation. The most important lessons about partnering learned from the Big Dig experience are as follows (CA/T 1998):

- A multiday intensive initial partnering workshop should be held at a neutral site with a neutral facilitator to teach team problem-solving approaches, with the intention of eliminating the adversarial relationship problems between the owner and the contractor by focusing on interest, not position.
- Formation of a partnering steering committee for each contract should be mandatory and should consist of individuals from all key organizations.
- The competency and neutrality of the facilitator is critical in building mutual trust and ensuring successful resolution of controversies.
- Ground rules help establish the tone of a partnering workshop. Personal attacks are not permitted. Partnering is hard on the problem but easy on the people and requires focus on the determination of the root cause of problems and not on assessment of blame.
- Subcontractors should be included in the partnering sessions. They can be crucial to the success of the project and help balance the teams.
- Risk should be shared jointly among the partners, if not otherwise allocated contractually or by agreement, to encourage innovation and continuous improvement.
- Administrative systems should be integrated, and access should be made available to each partner's resources.

- Leadership training is an important component to prepare managers for partnering. In-house training is less expensive, especially when a large number of employees are attending.
- Partnering should never replace independent and rigorous oversight of the project.

Partnering Contract Language   The following contractual language was used in all design and construction contracts on the Big Dig, creating an expectation from the inception of the project that partnering was a respected process that had the full commitment of the project owner and the project's management consultant. Though partnering was completely voluntary at the Big Dig, all construction contractors and most design consultants who were asked to consider partnering agreed to participate in accordance with the following contract language:

THE BIG DIG'S PARTNERING CONTRACTUAL PROVISION

The Owner and the Management Consultant intend to encourage the foundation of a cohesive partnership with the Design Consultant. This partnership will be structured to draw on the strengths of each organization to identify and achieve reciprocal goals. The objectives include; effective and efficient performance; completion within budget, on schedule, and in accordance with the contract documents.

The partnership will be totally voluntary. Any cost associated with effectuating this partnership will be agreed to by both parties and will be shared equally with no change in Contract price. To implement this partnership it is anticipated that the Consultant's assigned Project Manager and the Owner's authorized representative will attend a leadership development seminar at the earliest opportunity after award followed by a team building workshop to be attended by the Consultant Team and the CA/T Project Design Management Team.

An integral aspect of partnering is the resolution of issues in a timely, professional and non-adversarial manner. Alternative dispute resolution (ADR) methodologies will be encouraged in preference to the more formal mechanisms including arbitration and litigation. ADR will assist in promoting and maintaining an amicable working relationship.

After the contract award key members of the Consultant team may be invited to attend Construction Phase Partnering Workshops with the General Construction Contractor. During construction, the partnering relationship is with the Contractor, and the Consultant team is in a support role with the Owner and the Management Consultant.

Source: Central Artery/Tunnel Project, Division I Specifications.

Partnering Survey   Prior to partnership meetings, a survey was completed with all partners to better prepare for the partnering session. The following questions were among several included in the survey (CA/T 1998):

1. What major objectives do you have for the project?
2. Are there good aspects you have experienced on past projects that this team might want to include on this project?
3. Are there bad aspects you have experienced on past projects that this team may want to avoid on this project?
4. What aspects of teamwork or the construction process seem impossible to do but, if done, would fundamentally change this job for the better?
5. What are the three (3) items of greatest concern to you that should be discussed at this partnering workshop?

Characteristics of Successful Partnering   While the roles and responsibilities of the participants in the partnering relationship may vary from project to project, the overall role and responsibilities of government do not change. The benefits of partnering are extensive and include: (1) better value for the owner and recognition and protection of profit margin for contractors; (2) creation of an environment that encourages innovation and technical development; (3) elimination of duplication, better predictability of time and cost, and stability in the project environment, which leads to a more productive project with better outcomes. Partnering requires considerable effort to set up and hard work to maintain, and the rewards can be substantial; however, it also depends on the acceptance of some of the critical factors highlighted as follows:

a. *Upper management support*: Partnering must be accepted from the top of the organization, and the commitment must be demonstrated through the selection of competent management and the allocation of resources for partnering at all levels of the project hierarchy.
b. *Early involvement*: Participants should be brought to the process at the earliest possible date even before a dispute has arisen. Partnering should be used not just for problem solving but also for prevention and dispute avoidance.
c. *Positive leadership style*: Project leaders must demonstrate the attributes that promote partnering. It is critical that project leadership display a positive attitude about partnering and support decisions reached through partnering that satisfy the project criteria.
d. *Trust and respect for subordinates*: Partnering requires trust and respect for those carrying out the partnering process. Trust can be engendered through an open and transparent process, by providing access to documentation and people that will be helpful in resolving the dispute, and an independent process that is free of concerns about bias and control.
e. *Open communication*: The intention of the partnering arrangement and the necessary change in attitude must be conveyed to all people directly

and indirectly involved in the participating organizations. More than just cooperating, it is important to provide an environment where the needs and expectations of the other party are understood.

f. *Win-win approach*: All parties must constantly seek ways to improve partnering as well as project performance. People can misinterpret best intentions, and parties can become preoccupied with division and animosity that can make problem solving more difficult or impossible. Management should be prepared to continually evaluate the partnering process and make changes as necessary.

g. *Time-based issue resolution model*: Issue resolution should be achieved through a time-based structure, making sure that each step of the process has a definite time frame. For example, you may want ten days of negotiation with lower-level management before moving up the ladder. This prevents issues from getting lost until too late in the contract to do anything to resolve them. If the team cannot come to closure on an issue within a reasonable period of time, the process must be escalated.

2. Stakeholder Integration

Since an entire chapter is devoted to stakeholder management on the Big Dig, this section is included just to highlight the relationship between project integration and stakeholder management. Problems in integration on the Big Dig were a result of the sheer number of internal and external stakeholders, their interaction, and the ever-changing dynamics of managing these relationships. For example, in the early phases of the project there was an impressive outreach to the local community, particularly the residents living within close proximity of several of the project's major work sites. Community and social costs related to stakeholder expectations were vastly underestimated on the Big Dig. No one ever envisioned the costs of dealing with the media, community interests, businesses, conservationists, auditors, and neighborhood stakeholders. However, as the project progressed, stakeholder interest groups emerged and more formal processes and procedures for addressing the concerns of these groups were developed and integrated into the project framework. This is where linkages with the project integration, goal setting, and performance measurements of the Project Management Institute (PMI) must be developed, including the emphasis on life cycle and sustainability. The unexpected discovery of archaeological sites—150-year-old Revolutionary era sites and Native American artifacts—was an example of a surprise complication on the Big Dig. Delays lasted from five days to years and required substantial sums just to investigate the impacts. Approvals were required from yet another diverse set of stakeholders: historical and preservation organizations, Native American groups, environmental organizations, and utility companies.

Stakeholder integration was demonstrated throughout the project life through various stakeholder groups, including those from Chinatown, Cambridge, South Boston, and the North End. The project laborers, integrated procedures through the Project Labor Agreement, and the oversight agencies coordinated oversight and auditing of the Big Dig through the Oversight Coordination Commission (OCC). The Artery Business Committee (ABC) assisted through all phases of the project, including gaining support from the business community during the early phases and addressing concerns of the community during construction.

Project integration is critical to success; however, it must exist not only in form but also in practice. Every day, a project manager must ask this question: How can I incentivize my managers, labor, customers, suppliers, and other stakeholders to deliver their best? Processes and procedures should be developed to manage stakeholder expectations. These expectations will change throughout the life of the project, as some stakeholders, such as environmentalists and local residents, may have interests early on, at the conceptual stage, and other stakeholder interests will develop later in the project, after design is completed and construction has commenced.

3. Integrated Change Control

One of the largest integrated programs on the Big Dig was the project's Claims and Changes Program. In both the public and the private sectors, construction change orders are a normal and essential part of the construction management process. Change orders are necessary for making adjustments to the work scope, schedule, and costs that could not be anticipated during the planning and design process. Limiting change or growth in project scope through change orders is a fundamental tool of cost control.

The Big Dig's Claims and Changes Department was the project's internal organization comprising technical claims specialists, such as claims estimators and analysts, schedulers, and auditors. The Claims and Changes Department provided technical support staff to resident engineer field offices and reviewed and administered all claims of more than $250,000 in value. It maintained an up-to-date claims and changes database integrated into the project cost controls and financial management programs. Claims ranging from $50,000 to $250,000 were reviewed by the area construction managers, and claims ranging from $0 to $50,000 were reviewed by the resident engineers. Change orders at the project were administered by approximately 65 full-time positions, in addition to construction inspectors, field engineering, and areawide and central management staff (CA/T OCC 2003).

A *claim* was defined very broadly in the project's specifications to include "any written demand that seeks relief in any form arising out of or relating to the contract, the contract documents, or the work, including without limitation, all contract claims, statutory claims, equitable claims, and claims for extension of time...." In accordance with the Massachusetts Highway

Construction laws (Bluebook 2008), the contractor was required to bring claims within defined time periods and in prescribed ways, depending on the type of claim.

All claims were evaluated under the following criteria:

- Terms of the contract
- The deliverable
- Construction plans and specifications
- Design standards, warranty, and indemnification provisions
- The professional standard of care under the contract
- Mitigating factors affecting the consultant's or contractor's performance
- Estimate of costs or damages incurred by the owner
- Premium costs for omitted work
- Cost-benefit analysis to ensure that the cost of pursuing a matter does not exceed the amount that can reasonably be expected to be recovered
- Documented evaluation to ensure an auditable record of issue determination

Changes were granted for claims only if the specific change was authorized by law, regulation, contract, drawings, or prior approval. Typical requests for changes from contractors that were generally accepted changes included the following:

- Materially different site conditions that were not contemplated in the original specifications, and only after compliance with notification and mitigation requirements
- Changes to contractor's means and methods due to design development or other changes in the project's plans
- Scope changes that were approved by the project owner
- Revised site access restraints or work restrictions
- Delays, suspension, or schedule adjustments not due to the fault or negligence of the contractor
- Unusually severe weather as defined in the project specifications
- Variations in quantities
- Third-party conduct beyond the control of the contractor
- Regulatory changes
- Value engineering change proposals
- Defective design/design changes

Errors and Omissions Review Program Goals   In addition to responsibility for contractor claims, the Claims and Changes Department was also responsible for reviewing errors and omissions in design and construction. Typical claims generally fell into one of the following three categories:

1. *Design error*: Change in work attributed to a mistake in judgment or work incorrectly done during design.

2. *Design omission*: An oversight in the design that results in additional work that should have been included in the original contract document.
3. *Contractor backcharge*: A backcharge is, simply, the right of the project owner to bill a contractor for work that was not performed in accordance with the contract requirements. Examples of backcharges include charges for cleanup work, or to repair something damaged by another subcontractor, or for deficient construction work that resulted in increased project cost.

Claims and Changes Statistics   Over the life of the Big Dig project, the Claims and Changes Program managed more than 25,000 disputes, claims, and issues, many of them involving nonroutine, complex contractual obligations and unforeseeable events (CA/T 2007). Important aspects of change control on the Big Dig included the significance of independent fair cost estimates to evaluate contractors' claims and the important role of the project's Change Order Review Board.

In May 2000, responsibility for claims and changes of more than $250,000 was assigned to the government owner's legal staff. By 2003, based on the project's financial reports, payments for claims and changes totaled more than $1.6 billion, which included approximately 9163 modifications, with an average value of $175,000 (Board 2003). By September 2004, the total costs had jumped to more than $2 billion. The breakdown of the percentage of change by category is shown in Figure 11.2, with the largest identified categories of changes falling under different site conditions (19 percent), design development (19 percent) and other changes (32 percent).

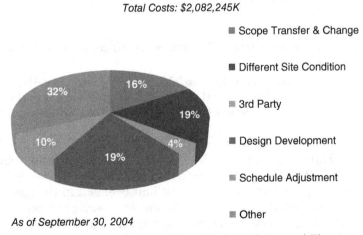

Total Costs: $2,082,245K

- ■ Scope Transfer & Change
- ■ Different Site Condition
- ■ 3rd Party
- ■ Design Development
- ■ Schedule Adjustment
- ■ Other

As of September 30, 2004

Figure 11.2   Central Artery/Tunnel Project Claims and Changes Modification Cause by Percent
Source: Central Artery/Tunnel Project. Total Cost of Contract Modifications as of September 30, 2004. Project Finance Report.

4. Integrated Audit and Oversight

More than 33 local, state, and federal audit agencies oversaw the Big Dig, including the CA/T Project Oversight Coordination Commission (OCC). The Offices of the Attorney General, State Auditor, and Inspector General constituted the Oversight Coordination Commission. These independent agencies were critical to the project's success and helped reduce costs over the long run by identifying critical project problems and serving as an advocate in the public interest. Independent state agencies, including auditors, identified existing and potential cost overruns and delays, conflicts of interest, shoddy workmanship, and patterns of contractor abuse, among other significant problems. Although costly and a diversion of the project manager's time, the role of the independent auditor on megaprojects cannot be overestimated.

A strong project-independent audit program creates transparency, provides for accountability, and identifies areas for contract review and enforcement. Some lessons learned from the Big Dig concerning the use of independent state agencies include the following: (1) assurance that the outside resources are truly independent and have the requisite expertise to know the questions to ask and the documentation necessary for an effective audit; (2) linking the auditors with insiders that are cooperative and willing to devote the time and resources necessary to provide all critical information so that the auditor's report does not provide a false sense of security; (3) recognizing that audits are not a substitute for good design, decision making, and project management; and (4) providing incentives for project personnel to support audits, recognizing that they may be the best security against a massive project failure.

The Central Artery/Third Harbor Tunnel Oversight Coordination Commission (OCC)

> Focused and proactive oversight of a project is critical for safeguarding the public interest.
>
> **(Richard Schoenfeld, former executive director of the Central Artery/Third Harbor Tunnel (CA/T) Project Oversight Coordination Commission)**

In July 1996, the Massachusetts legislature established the Central Artery/Third Harbor Tunnel (CA/T) Project Oversight Coordination Commission (CA/T OCC 1996), to coordinate the scrutiny of potential cost savings and recommend opportunities for systemic improvement in the operations of the Big Dig. This unified, integrated, independent oversight commission was the first of its kind to oversee a megaproject in the United States.

Through the efforts of the OCC, member agencies were able to consult with one another, have a better understanding of each other's responsibilities and function, and work together, sharing expertise and resources without duplicating efforts or impeding each office's constitutional or statutory mission.

The OCC was headed by an executive director, who played a vital role in assisting the commission to achieve its legislatively mandated mission, including arranging monthly commission meetings, integrating periodic plans from its members, alerting commission members to opportunities for inter-agency case development and areas of apparent duplication of effort, and developing sound working relationships with federal oversight agencies that had an interest in the project, to ensure that state oversight supplemented rather than supplanted the work of federal watchdogs (CA/T OCC 1996).

Each of the three offices represented in the OCC—the state auditor, the state attorney general, and the state inspector general—had, in one way or another, already examined aspects of the CA/T Project. Each office differed substantially in its statutory mission and powers, the analytical methods it customarily used, and the aspects of the CA/T Project it found most interesting and troubling. The goals of the OCC were to combine the expertise and statutory authority of the three offices to target management practices that invited waste, fraud, and abuse, to identify cost savings, and to pursue enforcement and recoupment actions against those who might have been engaged in fraudulent or otherwise unlawful activity (CA/T OCC 1998). Some of the differences and similarities of the three primary investigative offices are described in Figure 11.3.

Activities of the Oversight Commission   The Oversight Commission issued an annual report that summarized the activities of the commission for that year. Each year, an impressive number of reports and investigations were issued by each of the Oversight Commission offices, resulting in significant changes in the process, procedures, and operations of the Central Artery/Tunnel Project. Some examples of each agency's activities are described in the following list (CA/T OCC 2003). Following this list is an important lesson learned about project oversight on the Big Dig that has now been enacted into law in Massachusetts.

- Office of the Attorney General (OAG) activities included civil and criminal oversight, prosecution and enforcement efforts, financial recoveries, providing legal advice to the CA/T Project, defending the Commonwealth of Massachusetts in civil matters, and developing proposals for legislative action, such as passage of the civil False Claims Act.
- Office of the State Auditor (OSA) activities involved identifying system weaknesses and opportunities for savings, cost avoidance, and adhering to scheduling and performance requirements, resulting in 22 interim reports that identified hundreds of millions of dollars in excessive and avoidable CA/T Project costs as well as savings opportunities.
- Office of the Inspector General (OIG) activities resulted in 26 reports and over 150 letters that questioned more than $1 billion in CA/T Project costs overall.

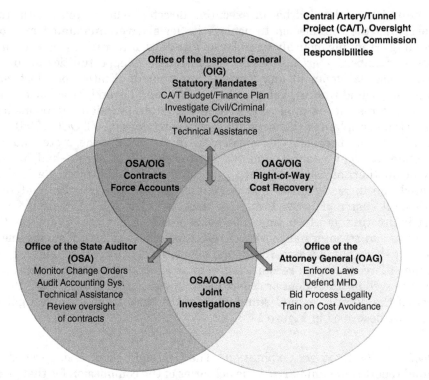

Figure 11.3   Central Artery/Third Harbor Tunnel (CA/T) Project Oversight
Coordination Commission
Source: Commonwealth of Massachusetts. Central Artery/Third Harbor Tunnel Project
Oversight Coordination Commission. Summary Report (July 1998).

Lessons Learned: Project Oversight   Drawing upon lessons learned from the CA/T Project and addressing several inadequacies and loopholes in Massachusetts's horizontal construction (i.e., roads) laws legislation was enacted that requires *independent engineers* on all public construction projects costing over $50 million (M.G.L. c. 30).

The issue of independent project reviews was raised in several contexts on the project, including independent engineers to investigate cost overruns and schedule delays, and to assist the project's board of directors with analysis of financial plans and budget requests.

Initiatives and Reviews by the External Audit Agencies and Outside Organizations   In addition to the Oversight Coordination Commission, the project used both in-house government audit staff and several outside consultant firms and organizations, most of which represent specialists in construction contract financial reviews. Postaudits conducted by both internal and external auditors focused on, among other areas, any instance of excessive, unreasonable or undocumented damages assertions made by a contractor or subcontractor related to changes or claims, technical assistance, cost recovery assistance, cost overrun assistance and review of schedules and contingency budgets among numerous other matters. Tables 11.5 and 11.6 highlight several of these initiatives and the outcomes.

Cost Containment Program   The goal of the Big Dig's cost containment program was to reduce and contain total project cost by identifying areas, ideas, and new concepts and evaluating the feasibility of such suggestions to limit or reduce costs. Under this program, a joint team of the project and the Federal Highway Administration (FHWA) senior managers reviewed in detail specific cost containment options and alternatives put on the table. By December 31, 2001, the initiative had resulted in implementing actions in excess of $500 million (CA/T OCC 2003).

Nevertheless, in testimony before Congress, a high-ranking U.S. General Accounting Office (GAO) official pushed for more aggressive goals in his comments about the CA/T Project, one of four projects nationwide the GAO had been asked to examine (USGAO 1998).

The Central Artery/Tunnel project is one of the most expensive, and in many ways, the most complex federally assisted highway project[s] ever undertaken. As we have reported in a series of reports and testimonies, state managers have worked to control the costs of the project and are taking steps to reduce them. However, the state is not meeting its aggressive cost containment goals and, unless further savings can be found, construction cost increases seem likely to push the project's total net cost higher than the current $10.8 billion estimated.

(USGAO 1998, 57)

Lessons Learned about Oversight   The most important advice is to start early. Oversight funding and coordination should be in place before megaproject design and construction begin, for at least two reasons:

1. The greatest opportunities for cost containment occur in the planning and design phase, well before construction begins. By the time construction contracts are bid, fundamental decisions about the shape and cost of the project have been made already. Changes late in the game can be costly, as CA/T Project officials demonstrated on the Big Dig's Charles River Crossing ("Scheme Z") and the Fort Point Channel Crossing (Haynes 1996).
2. The further a major project has advanced, the more firmly entrenched are its stakeholders and the more powerful the resistance to change, even when those changes may reduce the high price the public will eventually pay. Whether the legislature possesses the will to fund the oversight initiative in subsequent years will be influenced profoundly by which constituencies capture the debate and define the value—or threat—presented by additional, proactive, coordinated oversight efforts (Haynes 1996).

Table 11.5 Examples of Initiatives and Reviews by External Oversight Agencies

Review/ Initiative	Agency	Comments
22 technical assistance reviews at project's request	Office of State Auditor	Assistance included policy analysis, management reviews, recommendations on legislative initiatives related to civil and criminal penalties, changes related to consultant accountability, review of contractor and force account payment process and insurer reimbursements.
Eminent domain case	State Office of Attorney General	In March 1998, the AG won a significant decision against Spaulding Rehabilitation Hospital, which claimed the Big Dig was obligated under the eminent domain laws to pay for its relocation. The Spaulding decision saved the taxpayers as much as $124 million.
Procurement fraud	State Office of Attorney General	The AG in 1997 indicted a bidding contractor for forged signatures on a contract worth $7 million.
Contractor fraud under False Claims Act	State Office of Attorney General	In a case initiated by a relocation contractor against MHD for outstanding payments, the AG counterclaimed under the False Claims Act, resulting in savings of $600,000 and the debarment of the contractor and certain of its principals.
Review of claims and changes process	USDOT Inspector General/State Inspector General	Two extensive reviews were conducted of the claims and changes process, resulting in recommendations for improvement that were implemented by the project, including an increase in focus and resources.
Cost recovery assistance	State Office of Inspector General	Based on OIG recommendations, corrective actions were implemented to improve cost recovery efforts (MA OIG 2000).
Cost overruns	State Office of Inspector General	OIG examined the history of cost overruns and found they resulted primarily from incorrect budget assumptions made in 1994 that were accepted by federal officials (MA OIG 2001).
Review of contingency budget	Office of the State Auditor	Recommended that proceeds from air rights or land development be used to pay down bond debt to avoid $88 million in borrowing costs (MA OSA 2002)

Sources: Central Artery/Third Harbor Tunnel Project Oversight Coordination Commission. Summary Reports (September 2001 and September 2002). Massachusetts Office of the State Auditor, Massachusetts Office of the Inspector General, Massachusetts Office of the Attorney General.

Table 11.6   Independent Audits by Outside Organizations

Review/ Initiative	Organization	Year	Comments
Review of project's management and organizational structure	Peterson/ Lemley and Lorsch	1995	Resulted in the implementation of an integrated project management organization (IPO) in 1998 (Peterson 1995).
Review of potential cost savings	U-Mass McCormack Institute of Public Affairs	1997	Recommended cost savings through fast-tracking, mitigation, and scope reduction (McCormack 1997).
Analysis of schedule delays	Deloitte Touche	2000	Schedule delays in 2000 cost the project more than $300 million based on analysis of the project's critical paths and timeline (Deloitte Touche 2000).
Managing the final stages of Boston's Central Artery/Tunnel Project	National Academy of Engineering	2003	The report issued 15 findings on the adequacy of procedures for cost and schedule control, oversight of the management consultant, and transition from construction to operations (Board 2003).

Independent Oversight Programs to Prevent Abuse   In 2003, the Central Artery/Tunnel Project Oversight Coordination Commission conducted a survey of 28 potential megaprojects asking respondents to explain and assess various management models, as well as the internal and external controls used to contain and recover costs, prevent fraud, and improve controls (CA/T OCC 2003). The megaprojects identified seven key areas that deserve special oversight attention:

1. *Management model*: Maintain a technically capable, senior-level in-house management team to oversee the project, and use an independent construction manager, not involved in the design process, to provide resident engineering services, including administration of the change order process.
2. *Change order controls and administration*: Create a change order board to review every change order, and aim to keep cost increases within 10 percent of the original budget. Heighten monitoring of the design and construction claims process, to avoid delays and unanticipated scope changes that could significantly impact the critical path and associated costs of construction packages.
3. *Quality control/quality assurance*: Review design for errors, omissions, and potential cost recovery and perform multiple independent reviews.

Provide oversight via the owner's special consultant. Establish a monitoring program for ensuring the highest quality of work by contractors and suppliers.

4. *Construction bid and award process*: Prepare a well-written request for proposal, and establish and enforce design standards. Utilize incentive/disincentive programs as part of the contract. Require all bidders, contractors, and subcontractors to be prequalified and perform an integrity check of each.

5. *Mitigation impacts*: Provide oversight and monitoring of the scope and costs associated with the final environmental impact statement and subsequent mitigation agreements developed and executed during the design and construction process.

6. *Safety*: Strive for the highest levels of accident prevention, worker safety, and public protection during construction.

7. *Community relations:—public awareness*: Involve the community and encourage citizen participation in terms of oversight of the planning process and the coordination. Draw upon those people most adversely impacted by the project. Use the press as a public information program, and assign a dedicated team for community relations and mitigation.

5. Integration through a Centralized Dispute Resolution Process

Dispute Review Boards   One way to resolve disagreements between designers and contractors without getting entangled in time-consuming, expensive litigation is by providing for a dispute review board (DRB) in the project contract. The review board, a panel of experienced, respected, and impartial reviewers, takes in all the facts of a dispute and makes recommendations on the basis of those facts and the board's own expertise. This trend in "preventive law" has been taking hold all over the world, saving time, project costs, and legal fees. Research has shown that 97 percent of construction disputes using DRBs were settled without proceeding to litigation (DRBF 2007).

The Big Dig had one of the largest and most sophisticated dispute resolution processes ever implemented in the United States. Disputes were managed through the project's partnering process, the claims and changes program, and the project's dispute review board. Of the 123 major contracts at the Big Dig, 47 contracts representing nearly $7 billion in construction funds were using the DRBs. As of 2001, only 15 issues on the project needed DRB recommendations, and none of these went on to litigation (FHWA 2001).

The Big Dig was known for its efficient handling of disputes through the DRB, which handled disputes at the very lowest levels of the organizational hierarchy before proceeding to resolve the disputes at the higher levels of project management or through a formal mediation process (see Figure 11.4). The DRB and its procedures are organized before construction begins. A typical review board consists of a panel of three experienced, respected, and impartial reviewers who take in all the facts of a dispute and make recommendations on the basis of those facts and the board's own expertise. The costs of the review board are often shared by the owner and contractor, and the board's procedures are spelled out beforehand in the contract. For large, complex projects, DRBs can save enormous amounts of money and time. Disagreements are settled contemporaneous with the construction project, which allows the parties to free up time and resources and allows personnel to work on more productive things. Thus, the costs of pursuing court claims are avoided.

Dispute review boards have been successfully used in many megaprojects. The success rates of DRBs are impressive. According to the Dispute Review Board Foundation, as of 2007, 98 percent of construction disputes using DRBs were settled without proceeding to litigation. Through the end of 2006, DRBs had been planned or used in over 2000 global projects with a combined construction value of over US $100 billion. Major multilateral organizations that have recommended the DRB include the World Bank, the *Fédération Internationale Des Ingénieurs-Conseils*, (FIDIC), and the International Chamber of Commerce (ICC).

At the Big Dig, every effort was made to resolve disputes internally, which required the parties to agree to waive any claim against each other except in the case of willful conduct or default. The Big Dig's dispute resolution process required a progression from field office determination through various stages, including senior-level partnering, executive-level partnering, mediation before the dispute review board up to litigation, as shown in Figure 11.4. At any point along the way, the dispute could be resolved. As noted in the figure, the longer a dispute took to resolve, the greater the expense; thus, early resolution was always encouraged. The internal resolution of disputes allowed the integrated and collaborative process to continue throughout the life of the project. During the the project, more than 25,000 claims were generated between the contractors and the project owner.

Lessons learned from dispute resolution at the Big Dig include the following:

1. To prevent large backlogs of claims, dispute resolution programs "must have robust and experienced staffs in both the contractor and owner organizations so that claims can be addressed as they arise and do not migrate to the end of the project as part of an omnibus claim" (Dettman et al. 2010).
2. Dispute resolution methodologies should be designed to encourage conflict avoidance and dispute prevention before controversies escalate and cause serious communication breakdowns among the key stakeholders.
3. Creating proactive, innovative dispute resolution processes with independent oversight is essential in large, complex projects where schedule delays can cause serious financial losses.

Steps in Claims Dispute Resolution

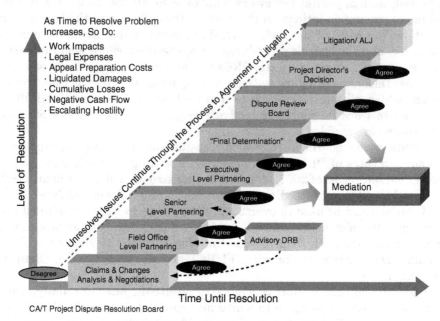

As Time to Resolve Problem
Increases, So Do:

· Work Impacts
· Legal Expenses
· Appeal Preparation Costs
· Liquidated Damages
· Cumulative Losses
· Negative Cash Flow
· Escalating Hostility

Level of Resolution

Unresolved Issues Continue Through the Process to Agreement or Litigation

Litigation/ ALJ

Project Director's Decision — Agree

Dispute Review Board — Agree

"Final Determination" — Agree

Executive Level Partnering — Agree

Senior Level Partnering — Agree

Mediation

Field Office Level Partnering — Agree   Advisory DRB

Claims & Changes Analysis & Negotiations — Agree

Disagree

Time Until Resolution

CA/T Project Dispute Resolution Board

Figure 11.4   Dispute Review Board
Source: Central Artery/Tunnel Project.

4. Constantly assess the effectiveness of the dispute review board framework and revise the processes and procedures as the requirements and priorities of the project change. As an example, if the mediation process proves cumbersome because mediators are issuing opinions through an evaluative mediation process, you may want to change the process so that the mediators merely try to facilitate a resolution between the disputing parties rather than render a formal decision. Another change might be to reduce the dispute review board from five to three members to expedite the process and save on costs.

5. The dispute review board process can be effective if the disputing parties are compelled to learn the facts and evaluate not only their position but that of the opposition and the dispute is resolved in a timely manner (Harmon 2009). This can be accomplished by requiring that each step of the process have a clear deadline so that decisions are not unduly delayed.

Alternative Dispute Resolution   Alternative dispute resolution (ADR) mechanisms like the dispute review board have been used on megaprojects around the world. ADR has been defined in many ways, but, most commonly, ADR provides procedures for settling disputes by means other than litigation and includes, in addition to dispute review boards, such mechanisms as negotiation, mediation, arbitration, and mini trials. The growing use of ADR is often attributed to the fact that the ADR processes are less costly and save time, though that is not always the case with large, complex disputes. The term *alternative dispute resolution* is, in some respects, a misnomer, as, in reality, fewer than 5 percent of all lawsuits go to trial and the other 95 percent are settled or concluded before trial. ADR methods are used in all megaprojects and can vary from one project to another. Some interesting examples of dispute resolution on megaprojects arose on the Eurotunnel project, which constructed the Channel Tunnel between England and France.

The Eurotunnel's former general counsel, Jean Naslin, in describing litigation on the Eurotunnel, stated that "disputes started the very day the first person started taking his wheelbarrow . . . [D]isputes were at the very, very heart of the whole saga." He said the project demanded ADR rather than binding procedures like arbitration and litigation due to French/English cultural differences, diversity and a multitude of contractors and banks (about 250), different securitization laws, and an "incredible" choice-of-law clause stipulating that the project's principal agreement was subject to "common principles" of English and French law, even though one country is under common law while the other has a civil law system (CPR 2005).

One of Eurotunnel's most famous disputes was the Sangatte Hostel Case (2007). This case resulted in the first major international arbitration decision against Western governments. Prior to this case, the majority of arbitral rulings against governments were rendered against non-Western countries, usually poor developing countries, which exacerbated the suspicions that arbitration systems mostly benefit large corporations in the developing world.

On January 30, 2007, the arbitral tribunal rendered a partial award to the Eurotunnel group, which brought claims against the governments of the United Kingdom and France. Claimants argued that both governments had failed to carry out their contractual duties of maintaining public order in and around the tunnel. The respondents insisted that it was Eurotunnel's responsibility to maintain order within the tunnel. Specifically, the claimants contended that between 1999 and 2002, the presence of the Sangatte Hostel for migrants, opened close to the tunnel by the French government, severely affected Eurotunnel's business because of immigrants seeking to enter the United Kingdom illegally through the tunnel. The migrants repeatedly broke into the French terminal of the tunnel. Most notably, 450 migrants broke in on Christmas Eve in 2001 and caused significant delay and disruptions because each time a migrant got into the tunnel, the company had to close the terminal and stop the traffic. The arbitral tribunal found that the claimants were entitled to damages, the exact amount of which was to be determined at a later stage in the proceedings (Sangatte 2007).

This case illustrates that alternative dispute resolution mechanisms can be used to address the rights of project stakeholders, without having to avail themselves of costly litigation in the courts, and, furthermore, that these decisions may not always be favorable to governments.

6. Integrated Project Teams

None of us is as smart as all of us.

—Ken Blanchard

One of the first efforts in structuring an integrated project organization is the establishment of integrated project teams with the common goal of designing and constructing a successful project. Critical to integrated teams is the ability of team members to adapt to new ways of delivering their services, understanding and accepting change, and developing a cooperative relationship that overrides individual concerns and behaviors.

In integrated projects, the teams are formed early in the project and are bound together by contractual relationships, common goals, and a partnering attitude. In the early years of the Big Dig, even prior to the formation of the IPO, a great effort was spent in team formation, trust building, and commitment to an integrated process. Open communication and transparency were essential to team cooperation and delegation of responsibility, and decision making to the lowest levels possible was a key aspect of developing strong team support and fostering positive attitudes. The integrated project labor agreement was an essential element in creating a unified workforce in both the development of the teams' goals and in the understanding of project expectations. An interesting feature of the labor agreement was a no-strike policy, which was granted in exchange for an all-union shop (Labor 1989).

Team building was accomplished through regular training, unified policies and procedures throughout the project, and joint workshops in which team members participated in decisions on project protocols, safety and health policies, and communication and information sharing. As contrasted with traditional delivery approaches where disputes and conflicts abound, on the Big Dig most internal disputes were avoided through the project's partnering approach, team building, and the structured dispute review board process.

7. Integration of Underground Utility Protection

One major component of the CA/T Project involved relocating and modernizing the web of existing utilities that underlie virtually the entire artery site. According to the project's utility program, all told, about 200,000 miles of copper telephone cable and 5000 miles of fiber-optic cable was installed on the Big Dig. Work began in 1993 to reroute the water, gas, electric, and telephone lines into new utility "corridors" that run alongside the underground roadway. Project planners used the relocation as an opportunity to replace Boston's aging and outdated utility infrastructure with state-of-the-art equipment, including a fiber-optic telecommunications system.

To protect against losses caused by disruption and failure of underground utilities on a massive project like the Big Dig, a state-of-the-art utility program was established. In 1996, the Big Dig initiated an integrated, comprehensive relocation program that moved 29 miles of gas, electric, telephone, sewer, water, and other utility lines maintained by 31 separate companies. After the comprehensive program was initiated in 1986, there was an 86 percent decrease in the predicted rate of infrastructure damage (Greiman 2010).

Utilities were a major risk on the project because the infrastructure was more than 150 years old and there was a complete lack of knowledge on the age, condition, and location of most of the utilities, which required submission of as-built drawings by all project contractors. The risks were substantial, and frequent claims resulted from replacement of water-damaged electrical cable, which totaled more than $1.5 million, utilities that had not been installed but were shown on as-built drawings, or damage and flooding caused by underground sewer pipes that were not identified on contract drawings. With major buildings located within feet of construction, major life safety issues existed and the risk was high that damage to the infrastructure would shut down the operations of Boston's major financial centers, including the Federal Reserve Building, International Place, and One Financial Center.

During the span of the project, 5000 miles of fiber-optic cable and 200,000 miles of copper cable were installed. This required over 80,000 hours of construction and 5000 construction workers operating 24/7. Between 1996 and 2000, the rate of utility damage decreased 86 percent and cost savings approximated $50 million. Despite many problems and risks, the utility program, overall, improved safety, quality, schedule, budget, insurance costs, and public relations.

The success of the project's massive utility program can be attributed to the early integration of more than 30 utility companies that met on a weekly basis to discuss critical incidents, potential exposures, mitigation techniques, risk allocation, contract drawings, design and construction, new technological challenges, and recommendations for resolution of those challenges. A major component of the utility oversight was the as-built process. As-builts are the latest changes in the blueprints that have been shown on new drawings to indicate the way something was built as opposed to the way it was designed. Maintaining as-builts on the Big Dig was a major undertaking, as it required keeping thousands of utility drawings up to date with all the latest changes. Figure 11.5 shows the project's 150-year-old utility system, and Figure 11.6 shows the state-of-the-art fiber-optic cable system as it looks today.

8. Integration of Project Contracts

As described in previous chapters, the project's 135 major contracts were integrated through the project control program. To be effective, contractual integration requires substantial planning, negotiation, monitoring, and enforcement. Key attributes of project contractual integration on the Big Dig included (1) development of projectwide standards and contractual provisions that required all contractors and subcontractors to adhere to standard specifications in scope of work, control of work, control of materials, public

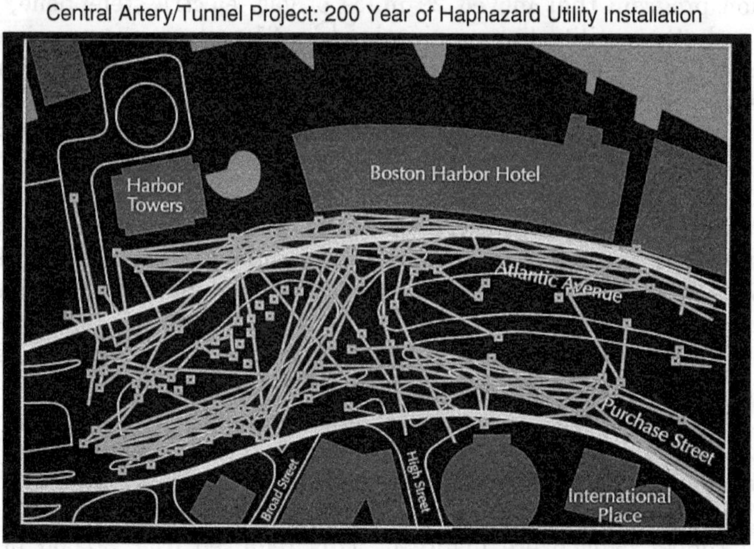

Central Artery/Tunnel Project: 200 Year of Haphazard Utility Installation

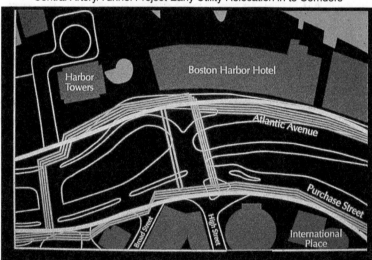

Figure 11.5   The Big Dig's 150-Year-Old Underground Utility System
Source: Central Artery/Tunnel Project Utility Relocations.

Central Artery/Tunnel Project Early Utility Relocation in to Corridors

Figure 11.6   The Big Dig's Fiber-Optic Cable System as It Looks Today
Source: Central Artery/Tunnel Project Utility Relocations.

responsibility and legal relations, risk management, quality assurance and control, and safety and health; (2) scope definition and limits and interfaces of all project work packages; (3) reporting of actual, committed, and budget costs for all project contracts and entities; (4) identification of the impacts that funding issues, schedule delays, and changes in the scope had on the project's individual work packages and on the project's milestones; (5) integrated summary schedule for all project phases by contract package; (6) integrated section schedule for each project milestone; (7) integrated task-oriented schedules by package; and (8) detailed schedule by work activity and task (CA/T OCC 1996 Control Programs).

9. Integration of Risk Management

Chapter 9 explores the integration of risk management on the Big Dig and its importance in loss control, safety, and health management. The key to success of risk management on the Big Dig was the development of an integrated safety, health, loss control, and risk management program focused on behavior-based safety from the inception of the project. Additionally, the program required an integrated team of safety representatives from both within the project company as well as within the contractor organizations. The integrated team tools included field safety reporting, baseline assessments, standardized job hazard analysis, root-cause analysis, and trend analysis.

Essential to the integration of safety and health was the project's centralized owner-controlled insurance program (OCIP), which provided coverage for contractors and other participants in place of contractors individually purchasing insurance plans. It provided greater insurance protection at the lowest possible price. A single, coordinated, integrated program on the Big Dig had advantages of economies of scale, elimination of redundant insurance services and expenses, coordinated claims adjustment, and safety/loss control services. It required all contractors in the program to create a uniform structure of risk management that included a contract risk manager, safety manager, risk control manager, and loss control manager.

10. Integrated Budget and Finance Plan

Financial information on the Big Dig was communicated to the FHWA and the public through an annual finance plan and a semiannual finance plan filed with the Massachusetts legislature starting in 1996. These plans identified the cash flow requirements of the existing budget, the cost exposures, and the available funding sources to support this cash need. In addition to the finance plans, the project used a project management monthly (PMM) that provided up-to-date information on critical budget elements such as planned versus actual progress, cash requirements, variances from the budget, claims and changes status, and project exposures and safety records.

After a bottom-to-top review of reporting procedures in 2000, the March 15, 2000, finance plan update recommended several mechanisms to improve

Table 11.7 Communication Enhancements

Reporting Requirements	Communication Format
In addition to total project cash requirements, to-go cash requirements were incorporated.	Project management monthly (PMM)
Planned versus actual progress information on a contract-by-contact basis.	PMM
Information on construction change orders, both actuals and projections.	PMM and finance plans
Status against budget at a detailed level for change orders and by major to-go cost area.	PMM
Definitive and speculative cost exposures and reductions (rough order-of-magnitude assessments).	PMM
More detailed information on project management expenses (labor and staffing levels).	PMM
Key project safety statistics.	PMM
Planned versus actual cash flow, federal obligation financial information, and progress on all revenue generation activities.	PMM
Six-month bottom-to-top assessment of to-go project costs including allowances for potential but unknown issues.	PMM and future finance plans
Updated project finance and progress information.	Available on the project's website
Quarterly review sessions with senior executive division and national FHWA officials to focus on the project's vital signs.	Quarterly review meetings
Retention of a national consulting firm to validate project cost and schedule assessments.	Available to interested federal and state agencies

Source: Central Artery/Tunnel Project Finance Plan Update. June 16, 2000.

communication with the project's many stakeholders, and these mechanisms were implemented shortly thereafter. In order to provide timely and current information, the PMM was issued within four weeks of the close of each month and reviewed at the project's monthly open meetings. These meetings were open to the public and provided an opportunity for all stakeholders to raise questions on matters of concern. Table 11.7 highlights some of the enhancements to the Annual Report and the PMM in 2000.

STRUCTURING THE CHANGE PROCESS

The openness and credibility of the process of change is very important, particularly on a megaproject where the public interest and the interests of multiple stakeholders are involved. To resolve perceived problems, a process must be in place to identify the root cause of problems, the behaviors causing the problems, the barriers to resolving the problems, and the plans to implement the change (Seidman 2001). Once the change to the policy, process, or procedure is made, then it must be monitored and enforced. Outlined here are the key steps involved in implementing changes at the Big Dig.

1. Identify the Problem

The first step in change management is to identify the problem. This is not always as easy as it appears, and the management literature abounds with research on problem identification. Simply stated, problems are often identified as evidence that objectives are not being met. One of the easiest ways of specifying problems is by reference to a set of objectives. For example, safety objectives relate to accidents and efficiency objectives relate to traffic congestion. Problems may be identified in a number of ways, including consultation, objective analysis of indicators or targets, monitoring of project conditions and trends, stakeholder feedback, and auditing the project's cost, schedule, risk, and quality programs.

2. Identify the Behaviors That Are Causing the Problem

All problems are a result of various behaviors, which may include internal or external stakeholders, processes and procedures, or ambiguity in standards or requirements. The behaviors that are causing the problem may include a failure of leadership, governance, communication, integration, or any number of factors.

It is important to note that behavior rarely has a single cause—most people behave in response to many interacting causal factors. For example, if the project management team is failing to identify exposures in time to mitigate or control the exposures, it is an indication that something is systemically wrong in the project management structure. Be sure to distinguish between causes and conditions. Causes are circumstances that you can try to change, such as policy, contractual requirements, or legal authority, and conditions are circumstances that you may not change, such as the weather on any given day.

3. Identify the Barriers to Change and the Root Causes of the Failure to Change

Barriers are those constraints that are causing the behavior, such as a law, procedure, or contractual requirement that requires the person to behave in a certain way. Assume you discover that project scope is escalating on the project due to poorly drafted contracts that do not require scope changes to be approved. Since these are matters that are within the control of the parties, a strategy must be developed that addresses the problem of poorly drafted contracts both retroactively and going forward.

4. Develop a Plan to Eliminate the Barriers and Incentivize the Responsible Parties That Can Influence Change

Possible responses to the problem of scope creep due to poorly drafted contracts may include renegotiation of the contracts or sharing of losses to the extent that the ambiguity impacts multiple parties. On the other hand, if the problem of scope creep is a failure to properly identify scope from the inception of the project, finding alternative sources of funding from the private sector, including funding from the private bond markets, generating additional revenues from tax resources, or charging additional fees to cover the costs of the infrastructure, may be an appropriate remedy.

5. Implement the Change

This could include enacting legislation that requires all projects to deliver a balanced budget, providing a disincentive for failure to reveal exposures such as reducing salaries for senior management when there are cost overruns, or determining alternative sources of funding for the project beyond the government's contribution.

6. Monitor and Control the Change That Has Been Made

Once a change is implemented, it cannot be effective unless the conduct that must change is monitored and controlled, ensuring that the change has been made. Change can be monitored in many ways, including testing, surveys, feedback mechanisms, or setting up periodic audits to make sure the change intended is actually occurring and measuring results based on those changes.

7. Enforce the Contract or Policy Change

Once a change is implemented under a new policy, the new policies must be enforced. This means holding the responsible parties accountable before patterns of abuse or neglect set in and the problem continues to escalate out of control.

LESSONS LEARNED

1. Integrative programs are valuable in developing strategies for maintaining sustainability over the long term.
2. Sustainability requires maintaining operability, services, and benefits of the project during its lifetime.

3. Integration requires the development of broad-based relationships and partnerships that foster collaboration.
4. The establishment of a government Oversight Coordination Commission that is independent of the project company can provide much-needed assistance in identifying system weaknesses, opportunities for savings, and adherence to performance requirements.
5. Frequent use of independent outside auditors promotes transparency, avoids conflicts, and provides expertise on the achievement of project goals and performance.
6. Partnering is an effective process for resolving problems before they escalate and developing innovative solutions as long as conflicts are clearly identified and addressed by project management
7. Project delivery methods need to be carefully evaluated at the inception of the project to assure the project stakeholders that projects are distinguished by highly effective collaboration among the owner, the prime designer, and the prime contractor or management consultant. To the extent that public policy or government regulations do not provide for effective delivery approaches, legislative or policy changes should be considered.

BEST PRACTICES

1. Identify sources of change, including measurements, baselines, recommendations from the project manager, the team, the owner, or other stakeholders.
2. Look at the impact of the change on cost, scope, schedule, quality, financing, and risk.
3. Once a change is made, update the status of the change on project plans, documents, estimates, baselines, insurance, and risk and monitor, control and enforce the change that has been made.
4. Manage stakeholders' expectations when changes are decided, and establish clear communication channels for all changes.
5. Develop integrated programs to manage change, such as partnering, stakeholder groups, claims and changes, audit and oversight coordination, dispute resolution, utility relocation, quality assurance and quality control, risk management, and contract integration.
6. Develop an oversight and coordination structure that is independent of the project.
7. Create alternative dispute resolution processes such as dispute review boards to reduce timely and costly litigation and to encourage cooperative relationships.
8. Investigate frequently the effectiveness of your partnering and dispute resolution processes to make sure they are delivering the benefits intended.

SUMMARY

The integration of project management with other management processes is essential to ensure a successful project and may include integrated knowledge, skills, processes, and procedures. Integration of the project processes should begin at project inception. Based on the needs of the project, integrated programs to promote collaboration should be established, including partnering, dispute resolution, coordinated oversight and audits, stakeholder integration, risk management, contract integration, and a contract claims and changes program. All projects must establish plans to develop, implement, and manage change and to preserve the project integrity and sustainability for the life of the project's assets.

ETHICAL CONSIDERATIONS

As described in this chapter, megaprojects have the potential for massive fraud, false claims, kickbacks, bribery, and public corruption. Government agencies, consultants, and contractors should pursue suspected ethics violations aggressively. Assume you have been assigned as the ethics officer for a large tunnel, bridge, and road construction project in Seattle, Washington. What processes, programs, and procedures would you put in place to reduce the likelihood of these serious crimes occurring on your project?

DISCUSSION QUESTIONS

1. Explain the relationship between project integration and change management by explaining how integration can be used to bring about change.
2. Why does your reading refer to project integration as the ultimate change management challenge?
3. Explain how integration was exacerbated by the Big Dig's organizational structure, which separated design from construction through its traditional design-bid-build model. Would it have been better to have a single point of responsibility for both design and construction? Why or why not?
4. Describe the difference between partnering and public-private partnerships by giving an example of each.
5. Review the Big Dig's Partnering Contractual Provision discussed in this chapter and describe any changes you would make to incentivize the parties to want to use the partnering process more frequently.
6. Explain why there was such a large volume of claims and changes on the Big Dig. What were the systemic problems in the project that caused the number of claims to escalate over time? If you were the project manager, what would you have done to control the large number of claims?

7. This chapter refers to the use of independent auditors that were external to the project. What are the advantages of independent audits? Describe what you believe should be the role of an independent auditor.
8. How does an audit differ from a performance control system?
9. What are the benefits of an Oversight Coordination Commission like the one used on the Big Dig? Can you recommend any improvements for structuring the Oversight Coordination Commission?
10. Assume you discover that one of the barriers to controlling costs on a project is the failure of the project managers to enforce the contract because it was ambiguously written and there is a failure to clearly allocate the responsibility for certain events. Describe the steps you would undertake to resolve this problem through a structured change process as described in this chapter.
11. This chapter begins with the following quote from the famous Chinese philosopher Lao Tsu:
    If you do not change direction, you may end up where you are heading.
    a. What did he mean by this quote, and how is it applicable to project management?
    b. How will you know when it is time to change direction in managing a project?
12. Explain the meaning of the following quote by the philosopher Ludwig Wittgenstein. How is it applicable to project change management?
    We see the world the way we do not because that is the way it is, but because we have these ways of seeing.

REFERENCES

AGC (Associated General Contractors of America). 2004. *Project Delivery Systems for Construction*. Washington, DC.

AIA (American Institute of Architects). 2007. *Integrated Project Delivery: A Guide*. Version 1. Washington, DC: AIA National Council, and Sacramento, CA: AIA California Council.

Board on Infrastructure and the Constructed Environment. 2003. *Completing the Big Dig: Managing the Final Stages of Boston's Central Artery / Tunnel Project*. National Academy of Engineering, National Research Council, Transportation Research Board of the National Academies (National Academy), Committee for Review of the Project Management Practices Employed on the Boston Central Artery/Tunnel ("Big Dig"). Washington, DC: National Academies Press.

B/PB (Bechtel Parsons Brinckerhoff). 2003. *The Boston Globe's Big Dig: A Disservice to the Truth. Reply from B / PB*. February 20.

Bluebook. 2008. *Massachusetts Bluebook of Building and Construction*. Boston: Contractors Register, Inc.

CA/T (Central Artery/Tunnel Project). 1998. *Central Artery Tunnel Project Partnering Manual*, prepared by Michelle G. Daigle and Deborah Merlino. Boston: Massachusetts Turnpike Authority.

CA/T (Central Artery/Third Harbor Tunnel Project). 1998 (July). *Oversight Coordination Commission Summary Report, Boston*: Commonwealth of Massachusetts.

CA/T (Central Artery/Tunnel Project). 2000 (March 15). *Finance Plan*. Boston: Massachusetts Turnpike Authority.

CA/T (Central Artery/Tunnel Project). 2007 (May). Cost and Schedule Update (CSU). Boston: Massachusetts Turnpike Authority.

CA/T OCC (Central Artery/Third Harbor Tunnel Project Oversight Coordination Commission). 1996. Established by Massachusetts General Laws, Section 2B of Chapter 205 of the Acts of 1996.

CA/T OCC (Central Artery/Third Harbor Tunnel Project Oversight Coordination Commission). 1998 (July). Summary.

CA/T OCC (Central Artery/Third Harbor Tunnel Project Oversight Coordination Commission). 2000. *Summary Report*. Boston: Commonwealth of Massachusetts.

CA/T OCC (Central Artery/Third Harbor Tunnel Project Oversight Coordination Commission). 2003 (May). *Summary: Megaproject Oversight Activities*. Boston: Commonwealth of Massachusetts.

Chan, A. P. C., D. W. M. Chan, and K. S. K. Ho. 2003. (July). *An Empirical Study of the Benefits of Construction Partnering in Hong Kong. Construction Management and Economics* 21(5):523–33.

CPR Institute (International Institute for Conflict Prevention and Resolution). 2005. *Resources and Data: How Mediation Is Practiced in Europe, 23 Alternatives to High Cost Litigation* 98, 99. Available at Wiley Online Library.

Deloitte & Touche 2000 (July 24). Deloitte & Touche Central Artery Tunnel Analysis of Budget and Schedule Status, Boston.

Dettman, K., M. J. Harty, and J. Lewin. 2010. "Resolving Megaproject Claims: Lessons from Boston's 'Big Dig.'" *The Construction Lawyer* 30(2).Washington, DC: American Bar Association.

DRBF (Dispute Review Board Foundation). 2007. "Estimated Use of DRBs and DBs, Success Rate of the DRB Process." *Dispute Review Board Practices and Procedures*. Seattle, WA: Dispute Review Board Foundation.

ENR (Engineering News-Record). 1996. *One Project, Many Parts, Innovative Answers* 237(8).

ENR (Engineering News-Record). 2008 (February 4). *Legal Settlements Obscure An Urban Marvel*. The McGraw-Hill Companies, Inc.

FHWA (Federal Highway Administration). 2001 (December). *Dispute Review Boards: Resolving Construction Conflicts*. Washington, DC: U.S. Department of Transportation, Federal Highway Administration, Office of Infrastructure.

FHWA (Federal Highway Administration). 2002. *Report on Construction Staffing Levels for Highway Projects*. Washington, DC: U.S. Department of Transportation, Federal Highway Administration.

FHWA (Federal Highway Administration). 2012. *Accelerating Project Delivery Methods*, Washington, DC: U.S. Department of Transportation, Federal Highway Administration.

Greiman, V. 2010. *The Big Dig: Learning from a Mega Project, Academy Sharing Knowledge*. The NASA Source of Project Management and Engineering Excellence, APPEL, 47–52.

Harmon, K. M. J. 2009. "Case Study as to the Effectiveness of Dispute Review Boards on the Central Artery/Tunnel Project." *Journal of Legal Affairs and Dispute Resolution in Engineering and Construction*. Reston, VA: American Society of Civil Engineers (ASCE).

Haynes, W. 1996. "Constructing an Oversight Plan for the Central Artery/Tunnel Project: The Long and Winding Road." Presented at the ASPA National Conference, Atlanta, GA.

Schoenfeld, Richard. 2012. Interview with former executive director of the Central Artery/Tunnel Project Oversight Coordination Commission. May 21.

Konchar, M. 1997. *A Comparison of United States Project Delivery Systems, Computer Integrated Construction Research Program*. Technical Report No. 38 (December). University Park, PA: Department of Architectural Engineering, Pennsylvania State University.

Labor Agreement. 1989. Central Artery (I-93)/Tunnel (I-90) Project Labor Agreement By and Between Bechtel/Parsons Brinckerhoff on behalf of the Massachusetts Department of Public Works and the Building & Construction Trades Council and its Affiliated Local Unions and the Building and Construction Trades Department, AFL-CIO and its Affiliated International Unions and their Affiliated Local Unions.

Mahoney, S. E. 1998. *Project Delivery and Planning Strategies for Public Owners*. Submitted to the Department of Civil and Environmental Engineering in partial fulfillment of Master's Degree. Cambridge: Massachusetts Institute of Technology.

M.G.L. (Massachusetts General Laws) Chapter 30, section 39M1/2. Project oversight; owner's representative; qualifications; procurement; powers and duties.

Mass OIG (Massachusetts Office of the Inspector General). 1998 (December). *A Review of the Central Artery / Tunnel Project's Use of Anchor Bolts on the C05B1 Tunnel Finishes Contract*. Boston.

Mass OIG (Massachusetts Office of the Inspector General). 2000. (December). *A review of the Central Artery Tunnel Project Cost Recovery Program*. Boston.

Mass OIG (Massachusetts Office of the Inspector General). 2001. (March). *A History of the Central Artery/Tunnel Project Finances 1994–2001, Report to the Treasurer of the Commonwealth*. Boston.

Mass OSA (Massachusetts Office of State Auditor). 2003 (April). *Central Artery / Tunnel Project Summary Report*. Boston.

MASS OSA (Massachusetts Office of State Auditor). 2002 (July 22). Independent State Auditor's Report on Certain Activities of the Massachusetts

Turnpike Authority's Central Artery/Third Harbor Tunnel Management Contingency October 1, 2001 through March 31, 2002, No. 2002-0510-3C, Boston.

McCormack Report. 1997. *Managing the Central Artery / Tunnel Project: An Exploration of Potential Cost Savings*. Boston: John W. McCormack Institute of Public Affairs, University of Massachusetts.

Morris, W. G., J. K. Pinto, and J. Soderlund. 2011. *The Oxford Handbook of Project Management*. New York: Oxford University Press, 161.

NCHRP Syntheses 402. 2010. *Construction Manager-At-Risk Project Delivery for Highway Programs, A Synthesis of Highway Practice*. Douglas D. Gransberg and Jennifer S. Shane, Consultants. Washington, DC: Transportation Research Board of the National Academies, National Cooperative Highway Research Program.

Paton, A. R., and J. McCalman. 2008. *Change Management: A Guide to Effective Implementation*. 3rd ed. London: Sage Publications.

Pendlebury, J., B. Grourard, and F. Meston. 1998. *The Ten Keys to Successful Change Management*. Chichester: John Wiley & Sons.

Peterson Consulting Lmtd. Partnership (Peterson Consulting), Lemley Associates, Inc., and Professor Jay Lorsch. 1995. *Central Artery / Tunnel Project, Management Review Report, Phase I and Phase II*. Boston: Massachusetts Highway Department.

PMI (Project Management Institute). 2013. *A Guide to the Project Management Body of Knowledge (PMBOK® Guide)*—Fifth Edition. Newtown Square, PA.

PMI (Project Management Institute). 2013. *The Standard for Program Management*. 3rd ed. Newtown Square, PA.

Richards, M. 2003. Massachusetts Organization of State Engineers and Scientists (MOSES). Testimony before the Massachusetts State Legislature. Boston, MA.

Sangatte Hostel. 2007. The Channel Tunnel Group Limited 2. France-Manche S.A. v. 1. the Secretary of State for Transport of the Government of the United Kingdom of Great Britain and Northern Ireland, The Permanent Court of Arbitration, The Hague.

Seidman, A., R. B. Seidman, and N. Abeysekere. 2001. *Legislative Drafting for Democratic Social Change: A Manual for Drafters*. The Netherlands: Kluwer Law International, 143–149.

Todd, A. 1999. "Managing Radical Change." *Long Range Planning* 32(2): 237–244.

USGAO (U.S. General Accounting Office). 1998. *Surface Infrastructure: Costs, Financing and Schedules for Large-Dollar Transportation Projects*. GAO/RCED-98-64.

Wood, G. D., and R. C. T. Ellis. 2005. "Main Contractor Experiences of Partnering Relationships on UK Construction Projects." *Construction Management and Economics* 23(3):317–325.

Chapter 12

Leadership

Nearly every man who develops an idea works at it up to the point where it looks impossible, and then gets discouraged. That's not the place to become discouraged.

—Thomas Alva Edison

It has been my observation that most people get ahead during the time that others waste.

—Henry Ford

INTRODUCTION

Henry Ford and Thomas Alva Edison recognized almost a century ago that successful leadership is a result of perseverance and hard work. Leadership is not about the managerial capabilities of an individual, but, instead, leadership focuses on building a vision by inspiring a team of workers to take an idea and with that idea build a better world.

> The organizational world, whether private or public sector, is shifting from formal hierarchies and management through orderly command and control processes to loosely coupled networks of different interests held in partial and fragile alignment through mutual learning and adaptation.
>
> **(Pelegrinelli et al. 2011)**

As recognized by program management scholars, traditional notions of leadership as individual tasks have been replaced by shared, collective, or distributed leadership ideas.

(Ancona et al. 2007; Pearce and Conger 2003; Hofstede 2001)

This chapter takes the lessons learned from all the preceding chapters and the leadership research and scholarship and explores the essential characteristics needed to take large-scale projects—with technical complexity, a vast amount of uncertainty, and political and environmental risk—from a concept to reality, despite the difficult burdens, threats, and obstacles faced along the way.

WHAT IS LEADERSHIP?

> They don't make plans; they don't solve problems; they don't even organize people. What leaders really do is prepare organizations for change and help them cope as they struggle through it.
>
> —*John P. Kotter (2001)*

In his scholarly work on leadership, Professor Kotter points out that management and leadership are really two distinctive and complementary systems of action, but both are necessary for success in a changing world. He explains that "management is about coping with complexity" through practices and procedures, while "[l]eadership, by contrast, is about coping with change" (Kotter 2001). On the one hand, project managers accomplish their goals by planning and budgeting, setting targets, controlling, monitoring results against the plan, and problem solving. On the other hand, leaders create a vision, develop strategies to achieve the vision, and implement the vision. Project managers use tools and techniques and processes and procedures to accomplish their goals, whereas leaders must impact human emotion, change minds, and motivate and inspire individuals to do things they have never done before or do things in a different way. Since leadership is about change management, the more that change occurs in an organization or project, the more leaders must motivate others in the project to provide leadership as well. Because projects, by their very definition, are about change, good leadership skills, as distinct from managerial skills, are critical to project success.

According to Dulewicz and Higgs (2005), leadership has been studied more than any other aspect of human behavior. Remarkably, however, there are limited references to leadership in the entire *A Guide to the Project Management Body of Knowledge (PMBOK® Guide)*—Fifth Edition:

> Successful projects require strong leadership skills. Leadership is important through all phases of the project life cycle. There are multiple leadership theories defining leadership styles that should be used as needed for each situation or team. It is especially important to communicate the vision and inspire the project team to achieve high performance.
>
> **(PMI 2013)**

In their extensive study of leadership competency profiles, Müller and Turner (2010) identified the following four factors of successful project managers in all types of projects: (1) critical thinking, (2) influence, (3) motivation, and (4) conscientiousness. The important implication from the study is the need for practitioners to be trained in the soft factors of leadership, in particular, for their types of projects. The study reflected the difference between the need for more transactional leadership and concern for process on relatively simple projects and the need for more transformational leadership and concern for people in complex projects (Müller and Turner 2010, 446). Transformational leaders are able to inspire followers to change expectations, perceptions and motivations to work toward common goals through the strength of their vision and personality.

When one considers that complex projects require the ability to achieve project integration across disciplines, influence multiple governance structures, energize numerous stakeholders, empower project teams, and create the vision for innovative technology and processes, the need for transformative leadership skills becomes more apparent. Crawford (2007) concluded that project success and competence of project management personnel are closely interrelated, and the competence of the project manager is in itself a factor in the successful delivery of projects. Significantly, however, Crawford observed that leadership is consistently ranked highest among project manager competency factors, yet by comparison it does not rank in the highest category for success factors.

In one study of 52 project managers and project sponsors from a financial services company in the United Kingdom, eight separate leadership dimensions were found to be statistically significantly related to performance based on the results of a leadership dimension questionnaire (LDQ) and a project success questionnaire (PSQ) (Geoghegan and Dulewicz 2008). (See Table 12.1.)

Another important international study conducted by two leading experts on leadership over a 20-year period with public and private organizations emphasizes that the fundamentals of leadership are the same today as they were in 1987. The study reveals the following four leadership traits coming up again and again in all countries: (1) honesty, (2) forward-looking, (3) competent, and (4) inspiring (Kouzes and Posner 2012).

Table 12.1   Statistically Significant Leadership Dimensions

Highly Significant Leadership Dimensions	Significant Leadership Dimensions
Managing resources	Critical analysis
Empowering	Influencing
Developing	Self-awareness
Motivation	Sensitivity

Source: L. Georghegan and V. Dulewicz. 2008. "Do Project Managers' Leadership Competencies Contribute to Project Success?" *Project Management Journal* 39(4):58–67.

CHARACTERISTICS OF EFFECTIVE LEADERSHIP

When everything seems to be going against you, remember that the airplane takes off against the wind, not with it.

—*Henry Ford*

What is effective leadership? This question has been answered in multiple ways across institutions and cultures. Leadership has been described as both an art and a science, depending on personal, global, and cultural contexts (Nahavandi 2012). Project leadership has been a subject extensively researched by project management scholars, and many thoughtful articles and books have been published on the topic. Emerging literature includes analysis of leadership styles, including improvisation, social development, emotional intelligence, strategic leadership, and change management. Managers are more likely to perform better or to stay longer in their positions if their personal characteristics meet the requirements of the position (Mumford 2000). A basic premise of project leadership is that project managers must manage levels of formalization and discretion in any and all projects that involve creativity among groups of knowledge workers (Naveh 2007).

Leading Diverse Cultural Environments

Leadership depends heavily on global and cultural contexts and is described differently for functional organizations versus project structures. Different organizations have different cultures that impact how the projects will be managed. For example, the fast-paced software design culture in the developing world is very different from the slow, hardware culture deeply rooted in complex engineering in the developed world, as evidenced by Siemens' experiences in India (Thomke and Nimgade 2001).

Culture has deep meanings in society and encompasses the behaviors and beliefs of a particular social, ethnic, or age group. Culture consists of the socially transmitted behavior patterns, attitudes, norms, and values of a given community (Salacuse 2003). Not only does culture arise from deep-seated beliefs, but organizations also develop cultures that impact how projects will be managed. For example, corporate culture tends to be more ingrained in longstanding traditions and top-down management, whereas project cultures tend to be more transient and are driven more from the needs of the project than the long-term views of the parent organization. Once a project is completed, the culture is gone, whereas corporate cultures can last for decades.

Project cultures are heavily influenced by the context and environment—the country—in which they are initiated and by the leaders of the projects; hence, it's important early on to establish the desired project culture, rather than just take the default.

Projects tend to be culturally diverse, as they are made up of individuals who come from many different environments; thus, they require leadership that recognizes these differences, and managers across these cultures to set common goals and a harmonized environment. On the Big Dig, this meant blending the fast-paced, profit-oriented, team-based, private-sector culture with the more deliberate, public interest, regulatory-focused, public-sector culture. One was more inward focused, to the project teams, while the other was more outward focused, to the project's external stakeholders.

Scholars have divided societies into high and low context (Hall 1976). Anthropologist Edward T. Hall's theory of high- and low-context culture helps us better understand the powerful effect culture has on communication. A key factor in his theory is context. Context relates to the framework, background, and surrounding circumstances in which communication or an event takes place. As defined by Hall, high-context cultures (including much of the Middle East, Asia, Africa, and South America) are relational, collectivist, intuitive, and contemplative (Hall 1976). This means that people in these cultures emphasize interpersonal relationships. Developing trust is an important first step in any business transaction.

According to Hall, these cultures are collectivist, preferring group harmony and consensus to individual achievement. And people in these cultures are less governed by reason than by intuition or feelings. For example, an attribute of the Asian culture is the reluctance to say "no." When a government official in China says, "That is challenging," it might mean "no" to the Chinese but "maybe" to the American.

On the other hand, low-context cultures (including North America and much of Western Europe), according to Hall, are logical, linear, individualistic, and action oriented. People from low-context cultures value logic, facts, and directness. Solving a problem means lining up the facts and evaluating one after another. Decisions are based on fact rather than intuition. Discussions end with actions. And communicators are expected to be straightforward, concise, and efficient in telling what action is expected.

A leader understands how to negotiate across cultures and break down the barriers, whether the cultural differences are the result of longstanding, deeply held beliefs or have been brought into the project environment by the merger of different philosophical and experience-based organizational cultures.

LEADERSHIP STYLES

It is better to lead from behind and to put others in front, especially when you celebrate victory when nice things occur. You take the front line when there is danger. Then people will appreciate your leadership.

—*Nelson Mandela*

There are multiple styles of leadership used by corporate managers and project managers. These leadership styles vary from one situation to the next, and styles may change throughout the course of the project. There is a general consensus in the leadership research that more inspirational leadership is needed at the beginning of a project, while during the implementation stage the project manager tends to lead by energizing, facilitating, and empowering. Listed in Table 12.2 are some of the more important leadership styles used in a project- or program-based environment.

The leadership styles described in Table 12.2 can be used at different times throughout the life cycle of the project, depending on the particular situation and overarching needs of the project. Generally, good leaders will use a combination of styles, particularly when their projects are undergoing constant change. The need to adapt a leadership styles depends on the following factors and the stage of the project:

Complexity of the project: The more challenging the project, the more the need for a transformational managerial style and empowerment of the teams so that authority is delegated to the level of expertise where decisions can be made more expeditiously. The first five leadership styles in Table 12.2 are critical for effective management of large-scale projects.

Technological change: Projects with constant change require considerable reliance on the transformative, inspirational, influencing, and empowering leadership styles. These styles are important because change requires that leaders think innovatively and openly and take uncommon risk. The resistance that is often present in projects with dramatic change can best be countered not through a directive or commanding approach, but through an inspirational and transformative approach to encourage innovative response and new ideas. Critical thinking is required to identify barriers, generate alternatives, and analyze the value of each prospective opportunity.

Duration of the project: Long-term, infrastructure projects require greater team building, inclusiveness, and empowerment, whereas a shorter project with a more tightly defined approach and more immediate demands may require more direction and support than a longer project.

Maturity level of the organization: If this is a one-of-a-kind project in an organization with less experience in project management, initially a more controlled, bureaucratic approach may be required to convince the CEO that the project structure has direction and controls. Over time, the initial structure may be revisited once upper management is convinced of the benefits and value and the alignment of the project with the organization's goals.

Experience of the team: As previously discussed, megaprojects have different teams for different purposes across the project. Partnering has been an effective tool for managing executive teams as well as construction teams across projects. Teams that have not previously worked together may require greater oversight, while long-established, well-motivated teams may be managed better with a laissez-faire or less restrictive approach. A newly established team, even if it is made up of experienced team members, may

Table 12.2   Leadership Styles

Leadership Style	Description
1. Transformational/ visionary	Defines the need for change, creates new visions, organizes commitment to these visions, and transforms individuals, teams, and organizations (Keegan and Den Hartog 2004).
2. Inspirational	Shows a high level of concern for ensuring organizational cohesiveness and encourages others to follow the vision.
3. Influencing	Emphasizes team building and decision making.
4. Empowering	Provides autonomy to team members to make decisions, select procedures, and determine how activities are completed. Places great faith and trust in the capabilities of the project team.
5. Inclusive/ participative	Encourages team participation in the decision-making process and shared involvement in developing project objectives and goals. On public projects, focuses on involvement of all stakeholders, particularly public citizens.
6. Coaching/ supportive	Assists the individuals and teams in skill enhancement, professional development, and performance.
7. Laissez-faire	From the French word meaning "to permit or leave alone." Generally used with a highly expert team that does not require assistance or advice.
8. Strategic/ tactical	Adroit in planning ahead each step and gains cooperation from the team due to expertise and knowledge.
9. Energizing	Motivates others to carry out the mission and goals of the project because of the desire to work hard and create buy-in.
10. Achieving	Results oriented and determined to complete the project regardless of burdens along the way—not a quitter, even when the hurdles are high.
11. Directive/ commanding	Top-down approach whereby teams generally follow orders, with little room for creativity. Least favorable approach in megaprojects because of difficulty of tight control over numerous projects, managers, and stakeholders.
12. Organizational	Based on project manager's position in the organization and generally evolves to greater responsibility based on support from above and flexibility of the organization.
13. Interventionist	Actively intervenes or influences something not under the project manager's control. Used when delegated responsibility has failed or a conflict has arisen.
14. Collaborator	Recognizes potential for and builds alliances, collaborations, and partnerships.

need more of a consensus/transformational emphasis. Teams with a mixture of maturity levels and expertise may need more flexible direction, such as mentoring or coaching. Teams that are colocated and meet face-to-face frequently may benefit from a more casual approach. Virtual or dispersed teams may need a more directive leadership style because they have less direct communication. Since teams are constantly evolving, the type of leadership will need to change to meet the purpose and goals of the team's mission and the stage of the project.

Organizational culture: It has often been said that culture is hard to define, but you will know it when you see it. Edgar Schein, credited with inventing the term *organizational culture*, defines it this way:

> The pattern of basic assumptions that a given group has invented, discovered, or developed in learning to cope with its problems of external adaption and internal integration, and that have worked well enough to be considered valid, and, therefore to be taught to new members as the correct way to perceive, think, and feel in relation to those problems.
>
> **(Schein 1984)**

In a functional organization with numerous reporting requirements and an inflexible structure, the project manager may have to follow the rules of the organization, thus making team building more difficult but not impossible. The challenge of the project manager is to encourage, support, and facilitate team members to create a good environment between project and functional employees. In a megaproject, there are always multiple organizational cultures to work with, as the contractor for one project may have a different culture than the contractor for another project (even within the same project—the civil engineering team may have a different culture than the electrical engineering team).

On the Big Dig, project culture was a significant challenge for the project director, the program manager, and all core managers in the project. It was particularly important to have a harmonized, integrated culture on critical issues such as risk, quality, health, safety, emergency response, and management of critical infrastructure. Culture could not be negotiated on serious matters of life, death, and project viability.

LEADERSHIP FOR THE FIVE STAGES OF PROGRAM MANAGEMENT

> I never had a policy; I have just tried to do my very best each and every day.
>
> —*Abraham Lincoln*

Leadership styles can change throughout the project life cycle depending upon the project goals, requirements, interest and influence of stakeholders

Table 12.3   Leadership for the Five Stages of Project Management

Stage	Focus	Style	Gains Knowledge By
Conceptual	Innovative ideas Realistic options Strategies Limitations/ constraints Relationship/ partnership building	Visionary Inspirational Inclusive	Research Historical data Expert advice Public participation
Start-up	Program structure Governance Alliances Goals Plan Contracts	Strategic Organizational Enabling Negotiating Democratic	Stakeholder feedback Public involvement Brainstorming Consensus building
Implementation	Team building Managing change Getting results	Empowering Facilitating Coaching Energizing Mediating Achieving	Listening Questioning Problem solving
Monitoring and Control	Assessing progress Enforcing contracts Resolving disputes	Directive Bureaucratic Interventionist	Investigating Root-cause analysis Lessons learned Resolutions
Closing	Deliverables Product verification Lessons learned Administrative closeout	Transformative Critical analysis	Team evaluations Owner/sponsor input Assessment of achievements

at various stages, and the structure, organization, and governance of the project (Table 12.3).

TEN IMPORTANT LESSONS ON LEADERSHIP FROM THE BIG DIG

1. Make Ethics and Transparency the Number One Priority

> On Lessons Learned and Organizational Culture in NASA, we never punish error. We only punish the concealment of error.
>
> —*Al Siepert, former Kennedy Space Center*
> *deputy director for administration*

The root of destruction on a public project is not that a project is behind schedule, or dramatically over budget, or even that there is a failure in project design, but rather the lack of transparency. Though the evidence supports extensive transparency on the Big Dig, with numerous public forums, a record-breaking number of independent audits, and extensive oversight from various public agencies, you can never have too much transparency, as reflected in lessons learned from the Big Dig and other megaprojects around the world. Whether it is a bolt that costs $20 or a bridge that costs $100 million, every detail and every public risk and expenditure must be disclosed and justified.

Human history tells us that ethical problems generally result not from making the wrong decision but from failing to disclose when a wrong decision is made. To maintain credibility with all stakeholders, it is important to "tell the public the truth." Whether the matter involves life or death, or simply that a project has serious budget concerns, the earlier the information is disclosed, the more likely the problem will be resolved. When a patient is sick, the sooner a diagnosis is made, the easier it is to treat the patient. If an illness or disease is permitted to linger, the likelihood is great that the patient may never fully recover.

A leader not only conveys the importance internally of openness but instills a culture of transparency that permeates the entire organization. The importance of trust and honesty has been highlighted throughout this book, particularly as it pertains to governance, stakeholder communications, and project financing. Unfortunately, the fear of losing public funding as grounds for nondisclosure of costs happens too often on public projects (Flyvbjerg et al. 2003). Project leaders of the future must confront these deficient practices of the past and establish more effective ways to manage the political realities of public endeavors. All project leaders face ethical dilemmas. A failure to properly address these dilemmas as they arise will only result in greater damage to the project, the people who benefit from the project, and the larger society.

2. Focus on the Project Vision

> There are no constraints on the human mind, no walls around the human spirit, no barriers to our progress except those we ourselves erect.
>
> —*Ronald Reagan*

As described in the earlier chapters of this book, the Big Dig had a long history, both politically and economically. However, a great idea means nothing without a visionary behind it who, with persistence and perseverance, can bring that vision to reality. The hurdles, political obstacles, and community activism were legendary on the Big Dig. Perhaps no project in history faced greater obstacles led by a few visionaries that kept it moving forward. The project ultimately resulted in a dramatic change to a city once famous for its ugly green highway in the sky.

There are many stories of the Big Dig's long up-front planning, the cobbling together of local coalitions from Boston's neighborhoods, and working with Congress and legendary Speaker of the House Tip O'Neill, who convinced President Ronald Reagan and his resistant secretary of transportation that it was the right thing to do. This was no easy task, and the mastermind behind this effort, Fred Salvucci, former secretary of transportation and an MIT engineer, credits another MIT engineer, Bill Reynolds, as the inspiration for his thinking about the Big Dig (Salvucci 2012). Remarkably, after 10 years of planning and perseverance, the funding was obtained. It would be another 15 years before the project was completed. During this time, the project leadership needed to inspire and motivate thousands of workers and project teams to do what they had never done before, so that the vision would finally become a reality. The desperate belief in the benefits of and need for this transformation, and the beautification of a city that had been divided for decades, kept this vision moving forward. However, without Fred Salvucci's and Bill Reynolds's persistence and strategic ingenuity, the project would have remained only a dream for future generations, while the environment and the old elevated highway system continued to deteriorate.

3. Encourage Transformation through Innovation and Advancement

> At Microsoft there are lots of brilliant ideas but the image
> is that they all come from the top - I'm afraid that's not
> quite right.
>
> —*Bill Gates*

Since projects are about change, the best leaders understand that transformations occur when innovation and creativity are encouraged and rewarded. Projects should not be about assessing blame but about moving forward and making progress toward an ultimate goal. Large, complex projects often have long start-up times (Miller and Hobbs 2005). An analysis of these cases reveals that the long front end is a result of careful planning and vision. Throughout this book, examples of innovation in technology as well as in process and procedures have been discussed. A true leader has the ability to inspire others to develop ideas that will advance the goals of the project and, ultimately, the organization. The project delivered many technological marvels, including the widest cable-stayed bridge in the world, the largest slurry wall application in the country, and the most extensive use of concrete-immersed tube tunnels in the United States. Other innovations included the first installation of jacked vehicle tunnels in North America (and one of the largest in the world), the second greatest use of soil mix construction on the East Coast, and the largest geotechnical investigation, testing, and monitoring program in North America. However, it was ridden with challenges, burdens, and obstacles throughout its long life. Transformation involves more than just resolving technological challenges, including changing how to do things from conventional approaches to innovative processes and procedures. The transformation required on the Big Dig to meet daily challenges has probably never been faced on any project before. The many lessons learned on managing this transformation will be available for researchers to ponder and examine for decades to come.

4. Set up a Partnering Environment

> If you do not seek out allies and helpers, then you will be isolated and weak.
>
> —*Sun Tzu, "The Art of War"*

Leadership was built into every job description at the project through the concept of partnering. A cooperative, collaborative culture was essential to good leadership. First used by the U.S. Army Corps of Engineers in public construction, partnering is now widely used by numerous government and construction entities around the world. It involves an agreement in principle to share project risks and to establish and promote partnership relationships. On the Big Dig, partnerships were used to improve schedule adherence, quality, safety, and project performance, as well as to reduce costs, claims, disputes, and litigation.

Partnering occurred at two levels on the project, at both the contract team and the executive levels. For the most part, the project focused on extensive amounts of successful problem-solving endeavors. Partnering at the Big Dig was initially implemented in 1992, primarily on construction contracts, but its success in construction later led to its use in design contracts, community groups, and development of internal and interagency partnerships. Almost 100 partnerships existed on the Big Dig based on contract values ranging from $4 million to a half a billion. Megaproject partnering can be contrasted in many ways with outsourcing because you are trying to cut costs, such as labor, regulatory, and training, by bringing in outside experts. Thus, partnering plays an important role in fostering new relationships with external partners unfamiliar with the internal culture. Though partnering is not always contractually required, on the Big Dig it was included in all construction contracts with a duration of at least one year and a value of $1 million or more. The partnering approach was designed to prevent or resolve disputes before they escalated into far more serious problems.

In addition to the partnering approach, when disputes arose among engineers and contractors, they had the option of using the project's dispute review board (DRB) process. The DRB is a unique, nonadversarial process used to proactively resolve disputes while construction continues. Attempts were made to resolve disputes at the field level first, manager to manager, before elevating them to higher levels (CA/T 2003). As noted in the literature, the most prevalent use of the DRB process in the United States, as of 2009, was on the Big Dig project (Harmon 2009). An extensive study of the Big Dig's dispute resolution process revealed "that the DRB process can be effective if disputing parties are compelled to learn the facts and evaluate not only their own positions but that of the opposition; when they do so contemporaneously their chance[s] for settlement are far greater than if they waited a year or more" (Harmon 2009).

5. Provide Your Teams with Unlimited Moral Support

> I am not interested in power for power's sake, but I'm interested in power that is moral, that is right and that is good.
>
> —*Martin Luther King, Jr.*

Leaders should always view themselves as investors, developers, and strategists. Leaders have the responsibility to provide project managers with the resources to effectively perform their jobs, including gathering sufficient project information so that reliable estimates of cost and schedule can be developed and sufficient resources to manage quality, risk, and uncertainty can be arranged. Simply stated, leaders must (1) develop goals that create an environment for success, (2) ensure that appropriate oversight processes are established and functioning, and (3) position the right people for the right tasks. Though these responsibilities are sometimes thought of as managerial, it is the leader who must create the environment and the support necessary for project managers to be effective.

This also means moral support when things go wrong and mistakes are made because of the pressures of meeting schedule-driven project deadlines. Moral support is a concept rarely discussed in the project management literature, or in practice; nonetheless, it looms large over a megaproject environment. On the Big Dig, moral support was critical due to the vast amount of public scrutiny and stakeholder demands that were relentless throughout the life of the project. Some examples of moral support demonstrated on the project were team leaders who took the blame when things went wrong and did not penalize for errors that were fully disclosed and acknowledged. Sharing responsibility and taking the lead when things go wrong is an essential characteristic of leadership on megaprojects.

6. Encourage Out-of-the-Box Thinking

Despite the long history of project management, the focus on cost and schedule as the leading drivers of project decision making on a worldwide basis continues. However, experience has taught us that the integration of scientific evaluation of projects and the growth of a culture of quality management is essential to success in complex projects. Leading the change from the focus on cost and schedule to quality and design not only adds value to projects but creates innovative solutions to project challenges and conflicts.

Scientific evaluation and innovative thinking were used frequently on the Big Dig to solve problems, even though this resulted in serious cost escalations and schedule delays. Some examples of innovative thinking include (1) the important role of value engineering in developing creative solutions to complex problems such as the Fort Point Channel and the Charles River Crossing; (2) the project's innovative wrap-up insurance program that maintained excellence in safety and health; (3) delivering the first "dynamic" finance plan in the nation, which employed unique tools for measuring performance; and (4) development of a "design-to cost" program, in which project designers contractually commit to a construction cost budget.

7. Empower the People

> We need to move from the leader as hero, to the leader as host.
>
> —*Margaret Wheatley*

Margaret J. Wheatley, the inspirational author on leadership and the future, reminds us that leadership means creating an environment where others can succeed. Significant ways of doing this in the project setting are to encourage participation through team decision making, partnering with internal and external stakeholders, and conducting multiple stakeholder sponsored forums and processes. Permit the community to be the voice of the project by raising concerns and dissatisfaction, as well as recognizing accomplishments, as appropriate. Most important, create the governance structure so that stakeholders can perform and participate in a manner that adds value to the endeavor as well as giving responsibility and accountability to the local community.

The many efforts that were undertaken by the project visionaries to incorporate the expectations and desires of the local residents, businesses, community advocates, environmentalists, and all the citizens of the Commonwealth of Massachusetts demonstrate a strong commitment to local community values and community leadership. Once project implementation begins, vesting power in those who have an interest in the project is an important attribute of transformative leadership and is central to creating a perception of trustworthiness and transparency.

8. View Political Problems as Challenges and Opportunities

Project managers frequently claim they can get nothing done because of politics. What does this mean, and how do strong leaders handle what, to some, seem insurmountable obstacles? As one of the greatest wartime leaders of the century famously said:

> Politics is not a game. It is an earnest business.
>
> —*Sir Winston Churchill*

Managing politics is an emerging area of project management that the Project Management Institute (PMI) and other institutions have begun to focus on. Unique aspects of managing the politics of projects from a megaproject perspective include the importance of making values transparent and energizing project teams.

If we follow Churchill's sound advice and pursue responses to political problems in the same manner as we do all other business problems, solutions can be found without losing favor with those we must count on for future support. Political problems can arise in multiple ways, including battles over public financing, changes in the law that make a project more difficult or expensive, or a change of administration that may impact the future viability of the project. Political problems occur not only in publicly controlled projects but also in privately controlled organizations where projects compete for scarce resources or CEOs are fighting battles with the board of directors. Whatever the political problem, projects can move forward by demonstrating their value and focusing on their mission. Rarely are projects cancelled or terminated because of political battles; more often, projects end because of failure of leadership or failure to perform as promised (Pinto and Mantel 2002).

9. Build Teams That Are Lasting and Effective

> Getting together is a beginning, keeping together is progress, working together is success.
>
> —*Henry Ford*

The importance of team leadership is no more heightened than on large-scale projects where team members must work across multiple projects, with diverse team members, to solve impossible problems yet find ways to develop innovative solutions. All of this, and these leaders also operate in often culturally diverse environments, with virtual teams, with different communication styles and unknown risks.

Team building has been defined as "the process of taking a collection of individuals with different needs, backgrounds, and expertise and transforming them into an integrated, effective work unit" (Cleland and Ireland 2002). The most important part of delegating authority or empowering team members is ensuring that they understand the vision of both the project leader and the project's constituents (Thoms and Kerwin 2004). If the vision is understood, the team member must gain experience by managing small aspects of the project and moving up to larger and larger amounts of responsibility. For example, a team member might start by designing a procurement process that will attract small businesses. If the outcome is successful, the team member will move on to activities with even greater responsibility.

On the Big Dig, teamwork was critical to project success. The sheer size and complexity of the project required that teamwork be elevated to the highest priority of the project manager's agenda. Agile project management, project maturity, improvisation, and a shift from hierarchical management to interdynamic structures are critical to the implementation of innovative processes and procedures and reaching goals. Teams on complex projects cannot operate in isolation but have interdependencies with other teams, networks, and organizations. They operate within both internal program and project networks and external networks of regulatory authorities, community organizations, and technical experts, building alliances and multiple relationships across disciplines.

Building teams on the Big Dig required consistent training, shared goals, lessons learned and information sharing, incentivizing management and teams through frequent recognition, and developing a culture of interactivity, accountability, and support.

Team building was perhaps best demonstrated through the project's highly successful Safety and Health Awards for Recognized Excellence (SHARE) Program. The SHARE Program was an integral part of ensuring a safe workplace that not only prevented and reduced accidents but improved productivity, schedule, morale, and individual job satisfaction, and ultimately provided substantial cost savings to the owner and all project participants. This program required a vision and leadership at the top levels of the project and was a continuous model for a shared commitment to safety and health throughout the life of the project. It is critical that shared credit be measurable and verifiable so that the real benefits are transparent to all stakeholders. Respect from both the internal and the external environment is critical to team building, problem solving, and support.

10. Create an Environment Where Transformation and Change Can Occur with Minimal Contest or Obstruction

> No institution can possibly survive if it needs geniuses or
> supermen to manage it. It must be organized in such a way
> as to be able to get along under a leadership composed of
> average human beings.
>
> —*Peter Drucker*

In describing an essential trait of leadership, Peter Drucker reminds us that no leader alone has the capacity to put out all of the fires all of the time. Nor should that be the job of the leader. All leaders must have an organizational and governance structure that provides the framework for successful outcomes and results. More important, successful leaders also must have the intuition to know when it is time to change the organization and strategically restructure so that the project can progress naturally and be led from the lowest possible levels of the project hierarchy. However, leaders must first assess the organization's capacity for change and provide the preparedness and readiness for change.

As we have learned from Enron and Worldcom and the major corporate collapses of the past decade, when undertaking a very large project without an adequate governance regime, most organizations are exposed to a high probability of failure and the resulting significant negative impacts. Because megaprojects are more complex and riskier, they require governance frameworks that are different from those of more routine and less risky endeavors. Governance frameworks, including policies, procedures, regulations and standards, have been described in the research as vitally important to project success. Since the signs of trouble are not always easily recognizable, leaders must have an instinctive ability to identify undercurrents that will result in tidal waves if not immediately corrected. Being willing to admit you are on the wrong path, and changing that path despite the political, economic, and financial repercussions, are traits of true leadership. Megaproject owners and other sponsors require assurance that their projects are positioned for success.

The Future of Project Management and the Leaders of Tomorrow

> The future of space exploration project management will rely on the innovations and ideas of the people involved in the space program. They will dream what can be possible, and then go about the task of making it happen.
>
> —*Dorothy Tiffany, former chief,*
> *Project Management Excellence and Innovation Office*
> *at NASA Goddard Space Flight Center*

Project management is evolving in theory and practice. Understanding the future of project management, and how project management processes and tools will be applied, is critical for every project management professional and student. In their scholarly treatise on the future of project management, *Project Management Circa 2025*, the authors provide important examples of how projects will be utilized to resolve such diverse issues and problems as nanotechnology and energy resources, sustainable manufacturing, conquering new frontiers in space exploration, and monitoring the planet, extreme weather response, and climate control (Cleland and Bidanda 2009).

The Projects of Tomorrow   To understand the types of leaders that will be needed in the world of tomorrow, it is helpful to take a look at the projects of tomorrow and how the changing needs of the world will require a change in leadership skills and focus. Some examples of innovative initiatives in the field of project management are highlighted as follows.

The transportation sector accounts for more than 10 percent of the U.S. gross domestic product, behind only housing, food, and health care. Across the country, taxpayers are pumping billions of dollars into innovative transportation initiatives including the Next Generation Air Transportation System (NextGen) to track aircraft with greater accuracy, integrity, and reliability. Also, the fourth year of the Department of Transportation's implementation of the American Recovery and Reinvestment (ARRA) Act of 2009 was reached in 2012. The \$48.1 billion appropriated to DOT has been used to support more than 15,000 infrastructure projects (USDOT 2010). These investments have improved the safety and efficiency of the nation's system of highways, transit, ports, and airports. Just as important, these projects generated tens of thousands of jobs in transportation and related sectors in a difficult economic environment. Funds have also been designated for transportation infrastructure, including transit capital assistance, high-speed rail, pavement improvements, and bridge repair, as well as the preservation and creation of jobs, to promote economic recovery.

Other U.S.-based initiatives include a surge in wind energy production and manufacturing, the development of biofuel technologies, projects advancing innovative clean coal technology, and the growth of natural shale gas projects across the country, which have popularized the word *fracking* in the United States.

Despite the global economic crisis, megaprojects also continue to be of importance to the developing world. According to the World Bank, in the coming decades the number of international projects will increase exponentially. As an example, Qatar is expected to launch megaprojects worth more than \$185 billion over the next decade. Countries like China, Egypt, Indonesia, Malaysia, Bangladesh, India, Peru, the Ukraine, and the Philippines are also expected to have rapid growth rates over the next decade (World Bank 2011).

Megaprojects of the future include the exploration of cyberspace, advancing human understanding of the laws of nature, and the exploration of physics and nuclear fusion research, as demonstrated by the following international projects:

1. The Large Hadron Collider (LHC) constructed across Switzerland and France is the world's largest and highest-energy particle accelerator, built by the European Organization for Nuclear Research (CERN) from 1998 to 2008, with the aim of allowing physicists to test the predictions of different theories of particle physics and high-energy physics. It contains six detectors, each designed for a specific kind of exploration. The LHC is expected to address some of the most fundamental questions of physics and advance human understanding of the deepest laws of nature.
2. The International Thermonuclear Experimental Reactor (ITER) is presently building the world's largest and most advanced experimental

tokamak nuclear fusion reactor in the south of France. The project's goal is to make the long-awaited transition from experimental studies of plasma physics to full-scale electricity-producing fusion power plants. This is a true international endeavor run by seven member entities: the European Union (EU), India, Japan, China, Russia, South Korea, and the United States. Though the project faces numerous technological challenges, recent advances devoted to controlling the configuration of the plasma have led to the achievement of substantially improved energy and pressure confinement.

3. The International Space Station (ISS) has been described as the greatest human endeavor in the history of the world in terms of complexity and meeting the challenges presented. The ISS serves as a microgravity and space environment research laboratory in which crew members conduct experiments in biology, human biology, physics, astronomy, meteorology, and other fields. The station is suited for the testing of spacecraft systems and equipment required for missions to the Moon and Mars. The station has been continuously occupied for more than 11 years, having exceeded the previous record of almost 10 years (or 3644 days) held by *Mir*, in 2010. It has been visited by astronauts and cosmonauts from 15 different nations. On May 25, 2012, Space Exploration Technologies Corporation (or SpaceX) became the world's first privately held company to send a cargo load, the Dragon spacecraft, to the International Space Station.

BEST PRACTICES

1. Leadership arises from vision and the fostering of innovation, creativity, and a laboratory for learning. Shared knowledge is a powerful asset for any organization, but particularly for projects with short lives, limited budgets, and innovative technology and processes.
2. Value your project teams and stakeholders, and recognize, encourage, and reward new ideas and technological advancement.
3. Leadership comes from successful teams and not from individual accomplishments. Building a coalition of supporters and collaborators is essential for team success.
4. Recruit talent and instill an environment that develops and leverages competent team members, managers, and stakeholders.
5. Build teams that are lasting and effective by empowering the team members.
6. Replace traditional notions of leadership with collective or distributive leadership ideas.
7. Recognize the characteristics of successful leadership and how these characteristics may evolve through the phases and life of the project.
8. Understand how to negotiate across project cultures and break down the barriers.

9. Create a project environment that instills a culture of openness and transparency that permeates the entire organization.
10. Inspire others to develop ideas that will advance the goals of the project and, ultimately, the organization.

SUMMARY

In order to provide value in the coming decades, project managers must grow to be leaders, rather than managers, because the organizations they serve will no longer be siloed functional entities crying out for coordination. Instead they will be project-based organizations that require leadership.
—*Belle Collins Brown (Cleland and Bidanda 2009)*

Based on the future needs of projects and the types of projects that will be built in a global society and a virtual world, it is important to end this book by describing the types of leaders that will be needed to tackle these difficult missions. Remarkably, very little focus has been given to this topic. Perhaps because we are so immersed in process and procedure, we have not had the time to step back and think about the future. The time is surely now, as our global society continues to expand and competition demands higher standards and better-quality products, projects, and services and at a much faster speed. Transformative leaders, who have prepared their organizations well for change through a clearly articulated vision, will be the ones who survive in this environment, and they will also prepare the future leaders of our world.

ETHICAL CONSIDERATIONS

To maintain credibility with stakeholders, it is important to always convey the truth about project cost and identify the precision of estimate values. Transparency in estimate communication is sometimes difficult because external stakeholders often want "one number" before an accurate estimate can be made by even the best estimators and engineers; however, transparency of costs will be best over the duration of a project. Management of project cost through proper communication has implications for the other global strategies of scope/schedule, risk, delivery, estimate quality, and, particularly, the integrity strategy.

As a project leader, how would you instill a culture to ensure that transparency and disclosure were values that were understood and enforced by all project managers?

DISCUSSION QUESTIONS

1. If you were to prioritize characteristics that are essential for a director of project management for a large infrastructure project, what would be your top three, in order of importance. Explain for each characteristic why you feel it is important for effective leadership.
2. What are the skills required to manage change in a complex project?
3. Assess the following problems and describe the most important skill a project manager would need to resolve each of these problems:
   a. A conflict between a project sponsor and the project's management consultant
   b. A change in project goals and mission from a schedule-driven project to a quality-driven project
   c. A shortfall in funding due to increased project cost and scope
   d. Team members who are not motivated and are government employees with protections from being terminated that are not available to private-sector employees
   e. An ethical problem involving a bribe paid by one contractor to a government official to secure the contract
4. Do you believe Hall is correct in his assumptions about culture, as described in your reading? If so, what examples can you give that demonstrate high- and low-context cultures? How would context help explain instances of miscommunication between North Americans and Japanese? How could you become a better international communicator?
5. Explain the difference between a project manager and a leader by analyzing each of the following scenarios from the perspective of the manager and the leader. For example, if a project is running late, the manager might try to find ways to accelerate the schedule or determine the cost of the delay. A leader would look at the systemic problem causing the delay and make sure the problem was corrected to prevent future delays.
   Scenarios
   a. The project has been over budget for six months.
   b. A serious accident occurred on the project, causing permanent injuries to three workers.
   c. The project revenues and financing are insufficient to meet $1 billion in new costs.
   d. The project procurement process requires that the lowest bidder win the contract. Each month, the same contractor wins the bid, creating a perception of favoritism.
   e. The local residents file a complaint because the construction noise keeps them awake at night.
6. Will new leadership be required for the projects of tomorrow described in this chapter? If so, what skills do you see as essential for the innovative projects of our future? How will we manage projects in cyberspace, if we have difficulty managing projects within our present physical

space? Will current organizational and project structures satisfy the needs of tomorrow? In their book, Cleland and Bidanda lay out some of these needs; however, the real challenge is to anticipate and educate project management leaders for the innovation that is about to take place.

REFERENCES

Ancona, D., T. W. Malone, W. J. Orlikowski, and P. J. Senge. 2007. "In Praise of the Incomplete Leader." *Harvard Business Review* (February):92–100.

CA/T (Central Artery Tunnel Project). 2003. *Steps in Claims Dispute Resolution*. Boston: Massachusetts Turnpike Authority.

Cleland, D. I., and B. Bidanda. 2009. *Project Management Circa 2025*. Newtown Square, PA: Project Management Institute.

Cleland, D. I., and L. R. Ireland. 2002. *Project Management: Strategic Design and Implementation*. 4th ed. New York: McGraw-Hill, 517–524.

Covey, S. R. 1990. *The Seven Habits of Highly Effective People*. New York: John Wiley & Sons.

Crawford, L. W. 2007. "Developing the Project Management Competence of Individuals." In *Gower Handbook of Project Management*, edited by J. R. Turner. 4th ed., 678–694. Aldershot, UK: Gover Publishing.

Dulewicz, V., and M. Higgs. 2005. "Assessing Leadership Dimensions, Styles and Organizational Context." *Journal of Managerial Psychology* 20(2): 105–123.

Flyvbjerg, B., N. Bruzelius, and W. Rothengatter. 2003. *Megaprojects and Risk: An Anatomy of Ambition*. Cambridge, UK: Cambridge University Press.

Geoghegan, L., and V. Dulewicz. 2008. "Do Project Managers' Leadership Competencies Contribute to Project Success?" *Project Management Journal* 39(4):58–67.

Hall, E. T. 1976. *Beyond Culture*. New York: Doubleday.

Harmon, K. M. J. 2009. "Case Study as to the Effectiveness of Dispute Review Boards on the Central Artery/Tunnel Project." *Journal of Legal Affairs and Dispute Resolution in Engineering and Construction*. Reston, VA: American Society of Civil Engineers.

Hofstede, G. 2001. *Culture's Consequences*. 2nd ed. Beverly Hills, CA: Sage.

Keegan, A., and D. N. Den Hartog. 2004. "Transformational Leadership in a Project Based Environment: A Comparative Study of the Leadership Styles of Project Managers and Line Managers." *International Journal of Project Management* 22(8):609–617.

Kotter, J. P. 2001. "What Leaders Really Do." *Harvard Business Review*. Cambridge, MA: Harvard Business School Publishing. (First published in 1990.)

Kouzes, J. M., and B. Posner. 2012. *The Leadership Challenge: How to Make Extraordinary Things Happen in Organizations*. 5th ed. San Francisco: Jossey-Bass.

Miller, R., and B. Hobbs. 2005. "Governance Regimes for Large Complex Projects." *Project Management Journal* 36(3):42–50.

Müller, R., and R. Turner. 2010. "Leadership Competency Profiles of Successful Project Managers." *International Journal of Project Management* 28 (2010):437–448.

Mumford, M. D. 2000. "Managing Creative People: Strategies and Tactics for Innovation." *Human Resource Management Review* 10(3):313–351.

Nahavandi, A. 2012. *The Art and Science of Leadership*. 6th ed. Upper Saddle River, NJ: Prentice Hall.

Naveh, E. 2007. "Formality and Discretion in Successful R & D Projects." *Journal of Operations Management* 25(1):110–125.

Pearce, C.L. and J.A. Conger. 2003. *Shared Leadership: Reframing the hows and why of leadership*. Thousand Oaks, CA: Sage Publications.

Pelegrinelli, S., D. Partington, and J. G. Geraldi. 2011. "Program Management: An Emerging Opportunity for Research and Scholarship." In *The Oxford Handbook of Project Management*, edited by P. W. G. Morris, J. D. Pinto, and J. Soderlund, Chapter 10, p. 264. Oxford, UK/New York: Oxford University Press.

Pinto, J. K., and S. K. Mantel. 2002. "The Causes of Project Failure." *IEEE Transactions in Engineering Management* 37(4):269–276. (First published in 1990).

PMI (Project Management Institute). 2013. *A Guide to the Project Management Body of Knowledge (PMBOK® Guide)*—Fifth Edition. Newtown, Square, PA: Project Management Institute, 240.

Salacuse, J. 2003. *The Global Negotiator: Making, Managing, and Mending Deals Around the World in the Twenty-First Century*. New York: Palgrave Macmillan.

Salvucci, F. 2012. Interview with former Massachusetts secretary of transportation. May 25.

Schein, E.H. 1984. *Coming to a New Awareness of Organizational Culture*. Sloan Management Review, 25:2, 3. Cambridge, MA: Massachusetts Institute of Technology, Sloan School of Management.

Thomke, S., and A. Nimgade. 2001. "Siemens AG: Global Development Strategy (A)." *Harvard Business Review*. Cambridge, MA: Harvard Business School Publishing.

Thoms, P., and J. Kerwin. 2004. "Leadership of Project Teams." In *The Wiley Guide to Managing Projects*, edited by P. W. G. Morris and J. K. Pinto, Chapter 40, 1027. New York: John Wiley & Sons.

USDOT (U.S. Department of Transportation). 2010. *Agency Financial Report*. Washington, DC.

World Bank. 2011. *World Bank Annual Report 2011*. Washington, DC, World Bank.

Appendix

Engineering and Construction Excellence Awards for the Central Artery/Tunnel Project

The list that follows incorporates selected awards granted the Central Artery/Tunnel Project and its designers and contractors for technological advancement during the long life of the Big Dig. These advancements demonstrate excellence in leadership, governance and team innovation.

2004

The American Society of Civil Engineers (ASCE) awarded the Zakim Bunker Hill Bridge its Outstanding Civil Engineering Achievement Award, credited to Swiss bridge designer Christian Menn, who designed the widest cable-stayed bridge in the world, a design that ties cables from the roadbed directly to the support towers.

Bechtel/Parsons Brinckerhoff (B/PB) joint-venture management team and AIG Consultants, Inc., received the Arthur Quern Quality Award from the Risk and Insurance Management Society for the venture's development on the Big Dig of an electronic personnel-tracking system for use in emergency tunnel evacuations.

The successful execution and completion of the Boston Jacked Tunnels set a new precedent in the world, becoming the largest and most complex set of tunnels ever installed using this method. These tunnels were actually 10 times the size of any jacked tunnels previously attempted within the United States. Through its team of engineers from Mott MacDonald, the project was awarded the prestigious NOVA Award from the Construction Innovation Forum.

2003

The tunnel jacking team, through its team of engineers, received the Quality in Construction Awards and the International Achievement prize in the 2003 Building Awards.

2002

The Central Artery/Tunnel and Route 128 were named Massachusetts's Top Transportation Infrastructure Projects of the 20th Century.

The tunnel jacking team received the 2002 British Construction Industry International Award and the American Society of Civil Engineers' top recognition award for innovation, the Charles Pankow Award.

The project received the British Construction Industry International Award for tunnel jacking.

2001

The Storrow Drive Connector Bridge received the National Steel Bridge Alliance Prize Award for Medium Long Span Bridge, presented to HNTB Corporation and the Massachusetts Turnpike Authority (MTA).

The New England Chapter of the American Concrete Institute (ACI) and the New England Ready Mixed Concrete Associations presented the Heavy Construction Award for Creative Use of Concrete in New England to Bechtel/Parsons Brinckerhoff (B/PB).

The Precast/Prestressed Concrete Institute (PCI) presented the Robert J. Lyman Award to Vijay Chandra, Anthony Ricci, Keith Donington, Paul Towell, Jennifer Hill, Peter Mainville, Rushu Hsu, Ted Wisniewski, and Ellie Homsi as authors and coauthors of articles on the Big Dig that were published in the May-June 2000 and March-April 2001 issues of *PCI Journal* that contributed to the advancement of design, production, and erection of precast and prestressed concrete.

The American Council of Engineering Companies of Massachusetts presented the Grand Conceptor Award—Engineering Excellence Awards to the joint venture of Fay, Spofford and Thorndike (FST) Inc. and HNTB Corporation for CA/T Project Contract C17A2: I-93 State Street to North Street. The purpose of the contract was to build the I-93 Tunnel without disrupting traffic.

2000

The Central Artery/Tunnel Project and the Massachusetts Turnpike Authority received the Association for Computer Transportation (ACT)/Patriot Chapter Transportation Demand Management Award for Creative TDM Strategies (Transportation Management Associations) and for Outstanding Public Service.

The Engineers' Society of Western Pennsylvania (ESWP), in association with *Roads & Bridges* magazine, presented the George S. Richardson Medal to HNTB Corporation for the Massachusetts Turnpike Authority in recognition of the Storrow Drive Connector Bridge.

U.S. Secretary of Transportation Rodney E. Slater presented the Design for Transportation National Awards—Honor Award for the Memorial Tunnel Fire Ventilation Test Program to the Massachusetts Highway Department, the Federal Highway Administration, and Bechtel/Parsons Brinckerhoff.

The Boston Society of Landscape Architects presented its Honor Award for the completion of Spectacle Island's new landscape to Brown, Richardson & Rowe, Landscape Architects & Planners.

1999

The City of Boston and the Boston Society of Architects/American Institute of Architects (AIA) presented the Harleston Parker Award for the Design Excellence of Ventilation Building No. 7 to Bechtel/Parsons Brinckerhoff and designers TAMS, Wallace/Floyd, and Stull & Lee.

1998

The American Association of State Highway and Transportation Offices (AASHTO) National Value Engineering Award for Most Cost Effective Proposal in Construction was given to the Massachusetts Turnpike Authority and the Central Artery/Tunnel Project VECP Program Coordinator for Ramp L in the I-90/I-93 South Bay Interchange: Tunnel Design and Construction Method.

The Memorial Tunnel Fire Ventilation Test Program was named the Parsons Brinckerhoff Project of the Year, presented to the Massachusetts Turnpike Authority and the Federal Highway Administration (FHWA).

1997

The Boston Society of Architects Chapter of the American Institute of Architects (AIA) Honor Award for Design Excellence went to Wallace/Floyd Design Group, TAMS, Stull & Lee, and Bechtel/Parsons Brinckerhoff for Ventilation Building #7.

The Consulting Engineers Council of Pennsylvania (CECPA) presented the Diamond Award for Engineering Excellence to Bechtel/Parsons Brinckerhoff for the Memorial Fire Ventilation Test Program Standard.

The International Downtown Association Downtown Achievement Award of Merit for Surface Transportation Action Forum (STAF) and Streetscape Design was presented to the Central Artery/Tunnel Project, C.R. Johnson Assoc., Inc., Wallace/Floyd, the Massachusetts Highway Department, the City of Boston, Bechtel/Parsons Brinckerhoff.

1996

The American Society of Civil Engineers (ASCE) Outstanding Civil Engineering Achievement Award was presented to the Central Artery/Tunnel Project and the Massachusetts Highway Department for the Ted Williams Tunnel.

The American Consulting Engineers Council (ACEC) of New England, presented the 1996 Outstanding Civil Engineering Achievement Award to the Central Artery/Tunnel Project and the Massachusetts Highway Department for the Ted Williams Tunnel.

The Federal Highway Administration (FHWA) and the U.S. Department of Transportation (USDOT) presented the Award of Merit—Biennial Awards: Excellence in Highway Design—Urban Highways to the Massachusetts Highway Department and the Massachusetts Turnpike Authority for the Ted Williams Tunnel.

1993

The American Institute of Architects (AIA) presented the Urban Design Award of Excellence to Wallace/Floyd Design Group, Bechtel/Parsons Brinckerhoff, and the Massachusetts Highway Department for the Charles River Crossing/Interchange.

Ford foundation and the John F. Kennedy School of Government at Harvard University named the Central Artery/Tunnel Project a semi-finalist for Innovations in State and Local Government for its Artery Arts Program, CA/T Project, Commonwealth of Massachusetts.

Parsons Brinckerhoff was the Minority Enterprise Development (MED) Week Award Winner, New York Region: U. S. Department of Commerce, Regional Corporation of the Year for outstanding support in fostering Minority Business Development.

SOURCES

1. Central Artery/Tunnel Project Public Information Office.
2. *The Big Dig: Engineering and Construction Excellence Recreates a City*. Special Edition. McGraw-Hill Construction Regional Publications.

Glossary

This glossary of terms is intended as a reference aid and should not be considered an exhaustive or complete list of all the terms set forth in this book or in the project management literature on the topics discussed herein.

A

Abutter: A person (or entity) whose property is adjacent to the property of another. On the Big Dig, abutters included local businesses, residents, and utility sites.

Accountability: Broadly defined, accountability is the acknowledgment and assumption of responsibility for actions, projects, decisions, and policies including the administration, governance, and implementation within the scope of the role in a project or employment position and encompassing the obligation to report, explain, and be answerable for consequences. In a project, governments are accountable to their citizens, and management consultants and contractors are accountable to the project owner.

Activity: Any work performed on a project. *Activity* may be synonymous with *task*, but in some cases it refers to a specific level in the work breakdown structure (WBS) whereby a phase is broken down into a set of activities, and activities into a set of tasks. An activity must have duration and result in one or more deliverables. An activity generally has cost and resource requirements. See also **Task**.

Agile Project Management: Agile methods promote a process that encourages development iterations, teamwork, stakeholder involvement, objective metrics, and effective controls.

A Guide to the Project Management Body of Knowledge (PMBOK® Guide)—**Fifth Edition:** The Project Management Institute's *Body of Knowledge* comprises the sum of knowledge within the profession of project management that is generally recognized as good practice.

Alternative Dispute Resolution: Provides procedures for settling disputes by means other than litigation and includes such mechanisms as negotiation, mediation, arbitration, and mini trials.

Analogous Estimating: Estimating using similar projects or activities as a basis for determining the effort, cost, and/or duration of a current one. Usually used in top-down estimating.

Architecture Governance: The principles, standards, guidelines, contractual obligations, and regulatory framework within which goals are met at an enterprise-wide level.

As-Builts: The latest changes in blueprints that have been shown on new drawings to indicate the way something was built as opposed to the way it was designed.

Association of Project Management (APM): The APM is a U.K.-based organization committed to developing and promoting project and program management.

Assumption: Something taken as true without proof. In planning, assumptions regarding staffing, complexity, learning curves, and many other factors are made to create plan scenarios. These provide the basis for estimating. Assumptions are not facts. Alternative assumptions should be made to get a sense of what might happen in a given project.

Audit: An independent examination of the financial statements or project studies or projections.

Australian Institute of Project Management (AIPM): The AIPM is the primary body for project management in Australia. Formed in 1976 as the Project Managers' Forum, the AIPM has been instrumental in progressing the profession of project management in Australia in the decades since.

Authority: The ability to get other people to act based on your decisions. Authority is generally based on the perception that a person has been officially empowered to issue binding orders.

B

Baldrige Performance Excellence Program: This program provides some key elements for analyzing an organization's governance system. These elements include organizational governance, legal and ethical behavior, and societal responsibilities and community support.

Baseline: A point of reference. The plan used as the comparison point for project control reporting. There are three baselines in a project: schedule baseline, cost baseline, and product (scope) baseline. The combination of these is referred to as the *performance measurement baseline*.

Bechtel/Parsons Brinckerhoff (B/PB): The joint venture comprising Bechtel Corporation and Parsons Brinckerhoff Quade and Douglas hired in 1985 to manage, design, and construct the Central Artery/Tunnel Project. Also referred to as the "management consultant."

(The) Big Dig: Popular name for the Central/Artery Tunnel Project. Also called the "CA/T Project." See also **Central Artery/Tunnel Project**.

Bottom-up Estimating: Approximating the size (duration and cost) and risk of a project (or phase) by breaking it down into activities, tasks, and subtasks; estimating the effort, duration, and cost of each; and rolling them up to determine the full estimate. Determining duration through a bottom-up approach requires sequencing and resource leveling to be done as part of the scheduling process.

Brainstorming: A general data gathering and creativity technique used to identify risks, solutions or ideas by using team members or subject-matter experts.

Budget: The amount allotted for the project that represents the estimate of planned expenditures and income. The budget may be expressed in terms of money or resource units (effort).

Builders Risk Insurance: Covers physical damage to construction work in progress.

Building Information Model (BIM): A digital representation of physical and functional characteristics of a facility. It serves as a shared knowledge resource for information about a facility, constituting a reliable basis for decisions during its life cycle, from inception onward.

Build-Operate-Transfer (BOT): A popular form of project delivery whereby the project is transferred back to the owner or party granting the concession after it has been built and operated for a period of time stated in the concession.

Build-Own-Operate (BOO): A private contractor constructs and operates a facility while retaining ownership. The private sector is under no obligation to the government to purchase the facility or take title.

Business Case: The information that describes the justification for a project. The project is justified if the expected benefits outweigh estimated costs and risks. The business case is often complex and may require financial analysis, technical analysis, organization impact analysis, and a feasibility study.

Business Continuity Institute (BCI): Along with the Disaster Recovery Institute International (DRII), BCI formulates the common body of knowledge that provides a structured and systematic approach to business continuity.

Business Continuity Management: Business continuity management seeks to identify potential risks or threats to an organization and allows it to plan and develop ways to react and recover from major risk events. Today's business continuity management is tied closely to crisis management that systematically deals with a disaster or a risk event as it arises.

C

Catastrophic Loss: One or more related losses whose consequences are extremely harsh in their severity, such as total loss of assets or loss of life.

Central Artery/Tunnel Project: The Central Artery/Tunnel Project in Boston, often referred to as the "CA/T Project" or the "Big Dig," was the country's largest publicly funded construction project, costing $14.8 billion. It was known for its technological advancement of slurry wall construction, ground freezing, and the world's widest cable-stayed bridge. The CA/T Project is also the largest inner-city construction project ever built in the world.

Change: Difference in an expected value or event. The most significant changes in project management are related to scope definition, availability of resources, schedule, and budget.

Change Management: The process of identifying, documenting, approving, and implementing changes within a project. It is a structured and systemic approach to achieve a sustainable change in human behavior within an organization.

Change Request: A documented request for a change in scope or other aspects of the plan.

Charter: A high-level document usually issued by the project initiator or sponsor that describes the purpose of a project, the manner in which it will be structured, and how it will be implemented, and that provides the authorization for the project.

Client: The person or organization that is the principle beneficiary of the project, sometimes called the "project owner." Generally, the client has significant authority regarding scope definition and whether the project should be initiated and/or continued.

Closing: The process of gaining formal acceptance for the results of a project or phase and bringing it to an orderly end, including the archiving of project information and postproject review.

Communications Management: The process of identifying, creating, reviewing, and distributing communications to stakeholders within a project, as well as receiving feedback and information.

Communications Planning: The process of identifying the information needs of project stakeholders and scheduling communications activities to meet those needs within the project.

Conceptual Phase: A period of time in which the description of how a new product will work and meet its performance requirements is formulated.

Concession Agreement: The agreement with a government body that entitles a private entity to undertake an otherwise public service.

Configuration Management: Adopted by the U.S. Air Force (USAF) in the 1950s as a technical management discipline, it is a process for establishing and maintaining consistency of a project's performance, both functional and physical attributes of its design and operational requirements throughout the project's life cycle.

Consensus: Unanimous agreement among the decision makers that everyone can at least live with the decision (or solution). To live with the decision, one has to be convinced that the decision will adequately achieve objectives. As long as someone believes that the decision will not achieve the objectives, there is no consensus.

Consortium: A consortium is an association of two or more individuals, companies, organizations or governments (or any combination of these entities) with the objective of participating in a common activity or pooling their resources for achieving a common goal.

Constraints: The factors that must be considered during the life of the project that cannot be changed. These may include deadlines, regulatory requirements, and dependencies on other projects to deliver.

Construction Contract: The contract between the project company, owner, or sponsor and the construction contractor for the design, construction, and commissioning of the project works.

Construction Contractor: The project participant responsible for the construction and commission of the project works. The contractor can also be the designer, depending on the project agreement.

Construction Management Responsibilities: On the Big Dig, this involved providing construction planning services, including performing constructability reviews on all conceptual, preliminary, and final design packages to provide recommendations for construction staging and sequencing, maintenance of traffic, cost mitigation, and claims and conflict avoidance. It also involves providing construction management services including area office services, resident field office, construction support services, partnering program, and changes and claims administration.

Construction Manager at Risk: The construction manager (CM) begins work on the project during the design phase to provide constructability, pricing, and sequencing analysis of the design. The CM becomes the design-build contractor when a guaranteed maximum price is agreed upon by the project sponsor and the CM.

Constructor: On a project, the party responsible for performing and overseeing construction by its own and/or hired forces.

Contingency: An additional amount/percentage set aside against cash flow for liabilities and exposures that may arise during the course of the project. On the Big Dig, there were three contingency accounts: one for construction, one for costs that arose in the project's nonconstruction cost centers, and a third for management reserves.

Contingency Reserve: A designated amount of time and/or budget to account for parts of the project that cannot be fully predicted. For example, it is relatively certain that there will be some rework, but the amount of rework and where it will occur in the project (or phase) are not known. These are sometimes called "known unknowns." The purpose of the contingency reserve is to provide a more accurate sense of the expected completion date and cost of the project (or phase). Some project managers separate contingency reserves from management reserves, while others combine the two into a single reserve. The better practice is to separate the contingency and management reserves, as they serve two different purposes. Reserves for changes and issues may be part of the contingency reserve or separate reserves. See also **Management Reserve**.

Contractor Backcharge: The right of the project owner to bill a contractor for work that was not performed in accordance with the contract requirements.

Control: The process of monitoring, measuring, and reporting on progress and taking corrective action to ensure project objectives are met.

Corporate Governance: The system by which an organization is overseen and controlled by its shareholders.

Corporate Social Responsibility (CSR): CSR is defined by the World Bank as the commitment of business to contribute to sustainable economic development, working with the employees, their families, the local community, and society at large to improve quality of life in ways that are both good for business and good for development.

Corrective Action: The process of bringing expected future performance of the work in line with the project management plan.

Cost-Benefit Analysis: Used to show that the expected benefits of a project are sufficient to warrant the cost of carrying it out. Monetary units are usually used for the comparison.

Cost Centers: These are the major cost elements based on the project's budget and requirements. On the Big Dig, there were seven major cost centers: design, construction, program management, force accounts, insurance, right-of-way, and contingency.

Cost Management: The process of monitoring and controlling the costs incurred within a project.

Cost Recovery: The process by which public and private owners file claims against design and construction management professionals for the costs claimed to be attributable to errors, omissions, or other "deficient" or unsatisfactory performance.

Critical Chain Project Management (CCPM): A method of planning and managing projects that puts more emphasis on the resources needed to carry out project tasks. It is the theory of constraints (TOC) applied to projects.

Critical Infrastructure: As defined by the U.S. National Infrastructure Protection Plan (NIPP), critical infrastructure includes systems and assets, whether physical or virtual, so vital that the incapacity or destruction of such may have a debilitating impact on the security, economy, public health or safety, environment, or any combination of these matters, across any federal, state, regional, territorial, or local jurisdiction.

Critical Path: The critical path is the sequence of activities that must be completed on time for the entire project to be completed on schedule. It is the longest-duration path through the work plan. If an activity on the critical path is delayed by one day, the entire project will be delayed by one day unless another activity on the critical path can be finished a day earlier than planned. There may be more than one critical path, and the critical path(s) may change during the project.

Critical Risk Exposures: These are major risks that can impact a project's cost and schedule if they occur—for example, design development, hazardous material removal, complexity of interfaces between contracts, unanticipated site conditions such as underground utilities, unexpected ground conditions, and archeological sites. Critical risk exposures can cause the conversion of a noncritical path to a critical path and can also impact project milestones if the exposure occurs on the critical path.

Critical Success Factor: A factor identified as essential to achieving a successful project.

Crossrail Project: The $25 billion Crossrail Project, in London, is presently the largest rail network expansion project in Europe.

Culture: Socially learned behaviors and assumptions of social interaction and problem solving.

D

Debt Service: Required payments on borrowings including state bonds and notes.

Decision Tree: Type of tree diagram used in determining the optimum course of action, in situations having several possible alternatives with uncertain outcomes. The resulting chart or diagram (which looks like a cluster of tree branches) displays the structure of a particular decision, and the interrelationships and interplay between different alternatives, decisions, and possible outcomes.

Decomposition: Dividing the overall project into successively smaller components at defined levels through a tool known as the *work breakdown structure* (WBS).

Deficiency Report: The deficiency report process used on the Big Dig was critical in accounting for the contractor's compliance with specifications and also as a warning that failure to comply with contractual requirements could result in temporary suspension from the project or, for high-risk situations, termination from the project permanently.

Deliverable: Any item produced as the outcome of a project or any part of a project. The project deliverable is differentiated from interim deliverables that result from activities within the project. A deliverable must be tangible and verifiable. Every element of the WBS (activity or task) must have one or more deliverables.

Delphi Technique: A method used to estimate the likelihood and outcome of future events. A group of experts exchange views, and each individually gives estimates and assumptions to a facilitator who reviews the data and issues a report. This process continues until consensus is reached.

Dependency: A relationship between two or more tasks. A dependency may be logical (see **Logical Relationship**) or resource based (see **Resource Dependency**).

Design (Conceptual): The period during which public hearings are held, financing is authorized, environmental approvals are obtained, and right-of-way plans are developed to describe how a new project will be structured and how it will meet its performance requirements.

Design (Final): Requires multiple separate design contracts ranging from less than $1 million to over $50 million. Activities can include right-of-way (ROW) acquisitions, traffic control plans, utility drawings, permits and licensing, final cost estimates, and contractor bid solicitation.

Design (Preliminary): A transitional phase in which the design moves from the schematic phase to the contract document phase. In this phase, drawings and other presentation documents are completed to crystallize the design concept and describe it in terms of architectural, electrical, mechanical, and structural systems. Also, the probable project cost statement is developed.

Design-Bid-Build: The traditional project delivery method used on the Big Dig whereby design and construction are sequential steps in the project development process.

Design-Build: It is a method to deliver a project in which the design and construction services are contracted by a single entity known as the design-builder or design-build contractor. In contrast to design–bid–build, design-build relies on a single point of responsibility contract and is used to minimize risks for the project owner and reduce the delivery schedule by overlapping the design phase and construction phase of a project.

Design to Budget: This process requires designers to provide construction cost estimates. The design to budget methodology assists in developing the baseline and also defines and estimates the basic construction components necessary to meet the project's requirements plus any nonproject costs.

Design Development: Design development is the evolution of design during the life of the project. There are many potential reasons for design changes, including environmental, risk, quality, cost, and schedule issues. Design professionals must balance process and structural considerations with regulatory, maintainability, and human factors.

Design Error: Change in work attributed to a mistake in judgment or work incorrectly done during design.

Design Omission: Oversight in the design that result in additional work that should have been included in the original contract document.

Design Professional: The term *design professional* refers to the project architect and/or engineer. For purposes of the Massachusetts Highway Department's Central Artery/Tunnel Cost Recovery Procedure, the term refers to Bechtel/Parsons Brinckerhoff and any other entity performing professional services in connection with the design of the CA/T Project (including construction phase services) and should include section design consultants, area geotechnical consultants, and any other professional consultants or subconsultants supporting the CA/T Project design effort.

Developing Country: Defined by the World Bank in terms of gross national income per capita.

Differing Site Conditions: These are conditions that can occur on a project that were not anticipated in the project's design and drawings. Differing site conditions can also shift the risk on a project from the contractor to the owner if they are materially different than represented in the contract drawings.

Disadvantaged Business Enterprise (DBE): A DBE is a business entity so certified in the United States by the government of the state in which it is located. The Safe, Accountable, Flexible and Efficient Transportation Equity Act (SAFETEA) provides that the secretary of transportation will provide uniform criteria for certification, and that at least 10 percent of the amounts made available for any federal-aid highway, mass transit, and transportation research and technology program be expended with certified DBEs. The purpose of the DBE program is to stimulate small disadvantaged businesses to improve the economic climate overall.

Disaster Recovery Institute International (DRII): Along with the Business Continuity Institute (BCI), the DRII formulates the common body of knowledge that provides a structured and systematic approach to business continuity.

Dispute Review Board (DRB): A panel of experienced, respected, and impartial reviewers that takes in all the facts of a dispute and makes recommendations on the basis of those facts and the board's own expertise.

Duration: The length of time required or planned for the execution of a project activity. Measured in calendar time units—days, weeks, months.

E

Early Start: The earliest time a task can begin. The time at which all the task's predecessors have been completed and its resources are planned to be available.

Earned Value: An approach whereby you monitor the project plan, actual work, and work-completed value to see if a project is on track. Earned value shows how much of the budget and time should have been spent for work done, and what are the variances from the budget, the estimate to complete, and the budget at completion.

Electronic Identification: The program that provided for notification to contract management upon entry or exit on the work site.

Emergency Preparedness: The project's plan for responding to emergencies, including force majeure events, disasters, catastrophes, shutdowns, and fatalities and serious injuries.

Empirical Research: Empirical research is a way of gaining knowledge by means of direct and indirect observation or experience. Empirical evidence (the record of one's direct observations or experiences) can be analyzed quantitatively or qualitatively. Through quantifying the evidence or making sense of it in qualitative form, a researcher can answer empirical questions, which should be clearly defined and answerable with the evidence collected (usually called *data*). Research design varies by field and by the question being investigated.

Enterprise Governance: The entire accountability framework of the organization.

Errors and Omissions (E&O) Insurance: Professional liability or malpractice insurance, which covers the professional negligence of design professionals.

Estimate: An assessment of the required duration, effort, and/or cost to complete a task or project. Since estimates are not actuals, they should always be expressed with some indication of the degree of accuracy.

Estimate to Completion: The expected effort, cost, and/or duration to complete a project or any part of a project. It may be made at any point in the project's life.

Ethics: The basic concepts and fundamental principles of human conduct. It includes study of universal values such as the essential equality of all men and women, human or natural rights, obedience to the law of the land, concern for health and safety, and, increasingly, concern for the natural environment.

European Bank for Reconstruction and Development (EBRD): Located in London, the EBRD serves as the primary lender to the developing world, particularly Eastern Europe and Russia, on behalf of its membership.

Eurotunnel: The company that was formed on August 13, 1986, to finance, build, and operate a tunnel between Britain and France. Groupe Eurotunnel S.A. presently manages and operates the car shuttle services and earns revenue on other trains passing through the tunnel. It is listed on both the London Stock Exchange and Euronext Paris.

Events and Causal Factors Analysis (ECFA): An integral and important part of the management oversight and risk tree (MORT-based) accident investigation process. It is often used in conjunction with other key MORT tools, such as MORT tree analysis, change analysis, and energy trace and barrier analysis, to achieve optimum results in accident investigation.

Executing: The process of coordinating the people and other resources in the performance of a project.

Exposures: The affected loss elements, such as third-party injury, worker injury, damage to property and equipment or to the work itself, natural environment, agencies, or governments representing the public.

Expropriation: The taking over by a state of a company or investment project, with compensation usually being paid. Creeping expropriation occurs when a government gradually takes over an asset by taxation, regulation, access, or change in the law.

F

Fast-Track Construction: Involves the commencement of construction before all of the design is completed.

Feasibility Study: A document that confirms the likelihood that a range of alternative solutions will meet the requirements of the customer.

Federal False Claims Act (31 U.S.C.A. sec. 3729): Rewards a whistle-blower who brings a lawsuit against a company that makes a false claim or commits fraud against the government.

Federal Highway Administration (FHWA): The entity within the U.S. Department of Transportation that oversees state-level projects that receive federal-aid highways funds, including the Big Dig.

Finance Plan: A project's semiannual report to the public on the project's design and construction status, cost center status, audits, insurance and safety and health program, and the project financing and budget.

Financial Planning: The process of identifying, quantifying, and scheduling the financial resources required to undertake a project.

Financial Structure: The manner in which the project is funded, whether through public or private financing, equity, debt, or revenue streams.

Float: The time a task can be delayed without impacting the project end date. Tasks on the critical path have no float.

Force Accounts: Management of third-party accounts, such as utility accounts or government agency accounts, based on work requested by these third parties during the course of the project.

Force Majeure: An event that is not foreseeable and is beyond the control of the parties, such as a hurricane, earthquake, act of war, or change in the law that will excuse the parties from fulfilling their contractual obligations. Projects generally obtain insurance to protect against these events.

Four T's Approach to Risk Management: Adopted by the U.K. Office of Government Commerce, it provides the following four primary mechanisms for managing risk: (1) Transfer, (2) Tolerate, (3) Treat, and (4) Terminate.

Freedom of Information Act (FOIA): A federal freedom of information law that allows for the full or partial disclosure of previously unreleased information and documents controlled by the United States government.

Functional Manager: A manager responsible for the activities of an organizational unit (department, work group, etc.), which provides some specialized products, services, or staff to projects. For example, the manager of an engineering group, testing department, or procedures development department. Also called a *line manager*.

Funder: The person or group, often called *sponsor*, that provides the financial resources, in cash or in kind, for a project. The Big Dig was 100 percent funded by the federal and state government, requiring active participation in the reviewing of the project scope, timeline, costs, risk, quality, finance plans, and the project budget.

G

Gantt Chart: A bar chart that depicts a schedule of activities and milestones. Generally, activities (which may be projects, operational activities, project activities, tasks, etc.) are listed along the left side of the chart, and the timeline along the top or bottom. The activities are shown as horizontal bars of a length equivalent to the duration of the activity. Gantt charts may be annotated with dependency relationships and other schedule-related information. When first developed in 1917, the Gantt chart did not show the relationships between tasks. In current use, both time and interdependencies between tasks are tracked.

General Liability and Excess Liability Insurance Coverage: Third-party coverage for injury and property damage.

General Obligation Bonds: Debt instruments issued by state and local governments to fund highway and infrastructure projects. Massachusetts Department of Transportation (MADOT), the Commonwealth's transportation agency, spends approximately $155 million, or about 21 percent, of its operating budget annually in debt service payments.

Goal: A desired end result, often synonymous with *objective*. May be a high-level objective that has less-than-complete definition. See also **Objective**.

Governance: A set of relationships between a company's management, its board, its shareholders, and other stakeholders. Corporate governance also provides the structure through which the objectives of the company are set, and the means of attaining those objectives and monitoring performance are determined. The process of developing, communicating, implementing, monitoring, and ensuring the policies, procedures, organizational structures, and practices associated with a given program. Simply stated, governance is oversight and control.

Governance Structure: An oversight and control function that can change to adapt to the emerging context of the project. Megaprojects are unique in that traditional hierarchical structures are replaced by a unique blending of vertical and horizontal engagements that require coordination.

Government Accountability Office (GAO): The U.S. Government Accountability Office (GAO) is an independent, nonpartisan agency that works for Congress. Often called the "congressional watchdog," the GAO investigates how the federal government spends taxpayer dollars. The head of the GAO, the comptroller general of the United States, is appointed to a 15-year term by the president from a slate of candidates Congress proposes.

Grant Anticipation Notes (GANs): The GANs program was an innovative financing program of the U.S. Department of Transportation that leveraged future federal highway funds to provide current cash for Central Artery/Tunnel Project costs without a general obligation pledge from the Commonwealth of Massachusetts. Its purpose was to reduce the funding variance between immediate construction cost needs and future federal highway reimbursements without creating any adverse cost or schedule impacts and without impacting the state's credit ratings.

Greenfield Sites: An area of agricultural or forest land, or some other undeveloped site, earmarked for commercial development or industrial projects—unlike the Big Dig, which was built in the middle of a major city.

Groundwater: Water found beneath the earth's surface.

H

Hazards: The real or potential conditions (natural, accidental, or human) that cause injury to people or loss or damage to property, or which interfere with the operations of a project or the government owner.

I

Implementation: *Implementation* may refer to a phase in a project's life cycle in which a product is put into use. The term may also be used as a synonym for *development*.

Improvisation: Improvisation has been defined as the practice of reacting and of making and creating. Improvisation is linked with aspects of time, and, particularly, pressure to achieve to a demanding or compressed timetable, which is a typical attribute of most megaprojects. Improvisation is a developing theory of project management and is not recognized universally by all the professional bodies.

Incentive/Disincentive (I/D) for Early Completion: A contract provision that compensates the contractor a certain amount of money for each day identified on which critical work is completed ahead of schedule and assesses a deduction for each day the contractor overruns the I/D time.

Incremental Delivery: A project life cycle strategy used to reduce the risk of project failure by dividing projects into more manageable pieces. The resulting subprojects may deliver parts of the full product or product versions. These will be enhanced to increase functionality or improve product quality in subsequent subprojects.

Inflation: In economics, inflation is a rise in the general level of prices of goods and services in an economy over a period of time. Inflation also reflects an erosion in the purchasing power of money. In construction projects, a chief measure of price inflation is the inflation rate, the annualized percentage change in the price index—normally, the *Engineering News-Record*'s Building Cost Index (BCI)—and the Construction Cost index (CCI)) over time. In megaprojects, schedule delays can have a huge impact on the rate of inflation if a project is delivered substantially later than expected.

Initiating (Project): The process of describing and deciding to begin a project (or phase) and authorizing the project manager to expend resources, effort, and money for those that are initiated.

Innovative Contracting: Contract practices meant to improve the efficiency and quality of roadway construction, maintenance, or operation. Examples of innovative contracting include: A+B contracting, lane rental, the use of warranties, design-build, design-build-operate, and design-build-finance-operate-maintain.

Innovative Finance: Innovative methods of financing construction, maintenance, or operation of transportation facilities. The term *innovative finance* covers a broad variety of nontraditional financing, including the use of private funds or the use of public funds in a new way, for example, grant anticipation notes or special tax districts.

Insolvency: The inability to pay debts as they become due.

Institutional Learning: Institutional learning is proposed as a process through which adaptations can be made to accommodate shortcomings in the prevailing institutional environment.

Integrated Change Control: A centralized organization within a project to manage all claims and changes that arise during the course of the project. This centralized system provides many benefits, including more informed decision making, consistency in decision making, important data for the prevention and mitigation of risk, and finance and budget controls.

Integrated Project Delivery (IPD): Integrated Project Delivery (IPD), as defined by the American Institute of Architects (AIA), is a project delivery approach that integrates people, systems, business structures, and practices into a process that collaboratively harnesses the talents and insights of all participants to optimize project results, increase value to the owner, reduce waste, and maximize efficiency through all phases of design, fabrication, and construction (AIA). Integrated projects are distinguished by highly effective collaboration among the owner, the prime designer, and the prime contractor or management consultant, commencing at the early design phase and continuing through to project turnover.

Integrated Project Management: Defined by the Project Management Institute (PMI) to include the processes and activities needed to identify, define, combine, unify, and coordinate the various processes and project management activities within the Project Management Process Groups. Commonly defined as the combining of all of the major dimensions of project management under one umbrella and involves applying a set of knowledge, skills, tools, and techniques to a collection of projects.

Integrated Project Organization (IPO): An organization where both the owner's employees and the management consultant's employees work under one organization structure.

Integration: The coming together of primary participants (which could include owner, designer, constructor, design consultants, and trade contractors, or key systems suppliers) at the beginning of a project, for the purpose of designing and constructing the project together as a team. Also includes the integration of processes and programs such as integrated change control, quality control, and risk management.

Interest: Cash amounts paid by borrowers to lenders for the use of their money.

Interface: The objective of the interface management process is to facilitate agreements with other stakeholders regarding roles and responsibilities, timing for providing interface information, and identification of critical interfaces early in the project through a structured process. The overall goal is the early identification of issues with potential for impact to cost or schedule and to minimize or remove their impact and promote clear, accurate, timely, and consistent communication with other organizations for exchanging interface information.

International Chamber of Commerce (ICC): An organization based in Paris that represents the interests of the global business community. For example, it provides a variety of international dispute resolution services through its International Court of Arbitration.

International Finance Corporation (IFC): Established in 1956 as the private sector arm of the World Bank Group to advance economic development by investing in strictly for-profit and commercial projects which reduce poverty and promote development.

International Project Finance Association (IPFA): An international, independent, not-for-profit association established in 1998. The IPFA aims to raise awareness and understanding about project finance and public-private partnerships (PPPs), and their crucial role in infrastructure and economic development.

International Project Management Association (IPMA): The IPMA is a nonprofit, Swiss-registered organization for the promotion of project management internationally. The IPMA is a federation of more than 50 national and internationally oriented project management associations with over 120,000 members worldwide as of 2012.

Ishikawa Fishbone Control Charts: Ishikawa diagrams (also called *fishbone diagrams, herringbone diagrams, cause-and-effect diagrams*, or *Fishikawa*) are causal diagrams created by Kaoru Ishikawa (1968) that show the causes of a specific event. Common uses of the Ishikawa diagram are product design and quality defect prevention, to identify potential factors causing an overall effect. Each cause or reason for imperfection is a source of variation. Causes are usually grouped into major categories to identify these sources of variation.

Issue: An event that currently affects a project's ability to produce the required deliverables.

Issue Management: The process of identifying, quantifying, and resolving project-related issues.

K

Kaizen: Japanese for "improvement" or "change for the better." Refers to a philosophy or practices that focus upon continuous improvement of processes in manufacturing, engineering, and business management, and is commonly used on megaprojects, including the Big Dig.

Kickoff Meeting: A meeting at the beginning of the project or at the beginning of a major phase of the project to align people's understanding of project objectives, procedures, and plans, and to begin the team-building and bonding process.

L

Late Start: The latest time a task can start before it causes a delay in the project end date.

Leaders: Those who create a vision, develop strategies to achieve the vision, and implement the vision. Leaders must impact human emotion, change minds, and motivate and inspire individuals to do things they have never done before, or do things in a different way.

Lenders: The entities providing debt contributions to the project company.

Life Cycle Costs: The costs of a project over its entire life—from project inception to the end of a transportation facility's design life.

Link: A relationship between two or more tasks. See also **Logical Relationship**.

Liquidated Damages: The daily amount set forth in the contract to be deducted from the contract price to cover additional costs incurred by a state highway agency (SHA) because of the contractor's failure to complete all the contract work within the number of calendar days or workdays specified or by the completion date specified.

Logical Relationship: A dependency relationship between two or more tasks or between tasks and milestones, such that one cannot start or finish before another has started or finished.

Loss Control: An organized and usually continuous effort to help decrease the possibility of unforeseen losses and the impact of those that do occur. Loss control can be applied to all kinds of losses on a construction project such as those caused by contractor negligence, design error, fires, electrical surges, hurricanes, or just about anything that results in unexpected harm, injuries, or damage.

Loss Scenario: Scenario analysis is one of the most common techniques used for analyzing risk. The disciplines of management science and scenario building form the backbone of risk management. These scenarios are used to prevent, mitigate, allocate, monitor, and control risk throughout the life of the project.

M

Management Consultant: The party responsible for overseeing the project construction. On the Big Dig, the management consultant was a joint venture (JV) between the project's constructor (Bechtel) and the project's designer (Parsons Brinckerhoff). The name given to the JV was Bechtel/Parsons Brinckerhoff (B/PB).

Management Reserve: A designated amount of time and/or budget to account for parts of the project that cannot be predicted. These are sometimes called "unknown unknowns." Use of the management reserve generally requires a change to the total budget. See also **Contingency Reserve**.

Market Risk: Changes to the amounts sold or the price paid for a product or services, which generally can impact project procurement.

Massachusetts Department of Transportation (MassDOT): In June 2009, "An Act Modernizing the Transportation Systems of the Commonwealth of Massachusetts, (as amended by Chapter 26 of the "Act.") was established requiring that the Commonwealth integrate transportation agencies and authorities into a new, streamlined Massachusetts Department of Transportation (MassDOT) responsible for overseeing four new divisions: Highway, Mass Transit, Aeronautics and the Registry of Motor Vehicles (RMV), in addition to an Office of Planning and Programming.

Massachusetts Highway Department (MHD): Formerly known as the Massachusetts Department of Public Works, the MHD is the official designated recipient for federal-aid highway funds to Massachusetts for the Big Dig and other projects.

Massachusetts Port Authority (Massport): Commonly known as Logan Airport, Massport is the most active airport in New England and provides both international and domestic commercial service. Located in Boston, Logan serves the 8th largest domestic origin-destination air travel market in the U.S. The Central Artery/Tunnel Project was responsible for completion of $300 million of Airport construction.

Massachusetts Turnpike Authority (MTA): The independent state entity responsible for owning, operating, and maintaining the Metropolitan Highway System (MHS), including project-related facilities as each segment is completed. Under a 1997 agreement with the Massachusetts Highway Department (MHD), the MTA oversaw the Bechtel/Parsons Brinckerhoff (B/PB) consulting contract for management, design, and construction of the Big Dig project.

Massachusetts Water Resources Authority (MWRA): The quasi-independent state authority created by the Massachusetts state legislature to manage the court-ordered cleanup of Boston Harbor—another multi-billion-dollar publicly funded megaproject—among other responsibilities.

Materials: Consumable and nonconsumable items used to produce deliverables, such as equipment, tools, machinery, and supplies.

Matrix Organization: A business structure in which people are assigned both to a functional group (departments, disciplines, etc.) and to projects or processes that cut across the organization and require resources from multiple functional groups. Matrix organizations can be strong (project manager reports directly to CEO), balanced (project manager reports to CEO but may not have dedicated staff), or weak (project manager does not report to CEO and staff report to both project and functional managers).

Megaproject: The Federal Highway Administration (FHWA) characterizes megaprojects as any projects costing $1 billion or more, and they are commonly distinguished by size, duration, uncertainty, and significant political and external influences.

Methodology: A system of practices, techniques, procedures, and rules used by those who work in a discipline.

Metrics: Metrics are quantitative measures, such as the number of on-time projects. They are used in improvement programs to determine whether improvement has taken place or whether goals and objectives have been met.

Metropolitan Highway System: The Metropolitan Highway System (MHS) includes the Boston Extension from Route 128/I-95 to the terminus of I-90 in East Boston, The Sumner, Callahan, and Ted Williams Tunnels and all other roadways built as part of the CA/T Project.

Milestone: A point in time when a deliverable or a set of deliverables is available. Generally used to denote a significant event such as the completion of a phase of the project or of a set of critical activities. A milestone is an event; it has no duration or effort. It must be preceded by one or more tasks.

MOD Contract Modifications (MODs): Written notices to a contractor that identify proposed contract changes. An approved MOD contains the scope, cost, and estimated time impact of the change. See also **Pending Change Notices (PCNs)**.

Monte Carlo Simulation: A technique used to estimate the likely range of outcomes from a complex process by simulating the process under randomly selected conditions a large number of times.

MORT Risk Factor Analysis: MORT (management oversight and risk tree) was developed for the Department of Energy in the 1970s by Bill Johnson. The chart consists of 1500 items arranged into a large/complex fault tree, which is used primarily for accident investigation.

Mozal Project: A successful construction project in the war-torn country of Mozambique that was built ahead of schedule and under budget and delivered many benefits to the people of Mozambique.

Murphy's Laws: The law that says "If anything can go wrong, it will go wrong," named after Captain Edward A. Murphy, an engineer working on U.S. Air Force Project MX981 in 1949. Variations of Murphy's Law: Nothing is as easy as it looks. Everything takes longer than you think. If there is a possibility of several things going wrong, the one that will cause the most damage will be the one to go wrong. Corollaries: If there is a worse time for something to go wrong, it will happen then. If anything simply cannot go wrong, it will anyway.

N

National Transportation Safety Board (NTSB): An independent U.S. federal government agency charged with determining the probable cause of transportation accidents and promoting transportation safety, as well as assisting victims of transportation accidents and their families.

Net Present Value (NPV): Net present value (NPV) is an estimate that helps organizations determine the financial benefits of long-term projects. NPV compares the value of a pound today to the value of that same pound in the future, taking inflation and returns into account.

Network Diagram: A graphic tool for depicting the sequence of and relationships between tasks in a project. The Program Evaluation and Review Technique (PERT) diagram, critical path diagram, arrow diagram, and precedence diagram are all forms of network diagrams.

O

Objective: Something to be achieved. In project management, the objectives are the desired outcomes of the project or any part of the project, in terms of both concrete deliverables and behavioral outcomes (e.g., improved service, more money).

Occupational Safety and Health Administration (OSHA): OSHA is a federal government agency that continuously monitors and studies the reasons for project failures. Each year, OSHA identifies the most frequently cited violations of its own standards.

Operation and Maintenance Agreement: The agreement allocating to the operator the obligation to operate and maintain the project in accordance with its requirements.

Operator: The project participant who undertakes the operation and maintenance obligations. On the Big Dig, the Massachusetts Turnpike Authority (MTA) became the ultimate operator.

Organizational Project Management Maturity Model (OPM3): The Project Management Institute's global best practice standard for enterprise improvement.

Organizational Structure: An enterprise environmental factor that can affect the availability of resources and how projects are conducted. Organizational structures can range from functional to projectized, with a variety of matrix structures between them.

Organization for Economic Co-operation and Development (OECD): A multilateral organization based in Paris and focused on the harmonization of the international trade laws and the advancement of international trade and development.

(Executive) Oversight Coordination Commission (OCC): Established by the Massachusetts state legislature to coordinate the oversight of the Big Dig among the Commonwealth's major oversight agencies, including the Office of the Inspector General, the State Auditor's Office, and the Office of the Attorney General.

Owner: Usually the owner of a project's assets in a public project that is usually the government agency responsible for funding the project.

Owner-Controlled Insurance Program (OCIP): A comprehensive, project-specific insurance program obtained by the owner and intended to cover all key project participants commonly used on megaprojects. An OCIP is managed by the project owner and has the benefits of economies of scale and centralized control. An OCIP can include coverage for builder's risk, workers' compensation, comprehensive general liability, and professional liability. The specific details of coverage and the allocation of premium cost are unique to a specific project. In some instances, similar coverage can be obtained by the contractor on behalf of the project as a contractor-controlled insurance program (CCIP). OCIP and CCIP are sometimes generically referred to as "wrap-up insurance."

P

P3M3: Also known as the Portfolio, Programme, and Project Management Maturity Model, P3M3 is a reference guide for structured best practice. It breaks down the broad disciplines of portfolio, programme and project management into a hierarchy of Key Process Areas (KPAs). P3M3 is owned by the United Kingdom's Office of Government Commerce (OGC).

Parametric Estimating: Estimating using an algorithm in which parameters that represent different attributes of the project are used to calculate project effort, cost, and/or duration. Parametric estimating is usually used in top-down estimating.

Pareto Principle: Named after Italian economist Vilfredo Pareto, the Pareto Principle is the idea that by doing 20 percent of the work, you can produce 80 percent of the benefit of doing the whole job. For quality improvement, the Pareto Principle means that most problems are produced by a few key causes.

Partnering: Establishing a long-term win-win relationship based on mutual trust and teamwork and sharing of both risks and rewards. Partnering arrangements can be between labor and management, government owners and management consultants, subordinates and executives, suppliers and customers, designers and contractors, and contractors and contractors. The objective is to focus on what each party does best, by sharing financial and other resources, and establishing specific roles for each participant.

Partnership: An arrangement in which two or more persons place their money, efforts, labor, and skill in lawful commerce or business with the understanding that there will be a proportional sharing of profits and losses between them.

Penalty Clause: See **Liquidated Damages**.

Pending Change Notices (PCNs): Written notices to a contractor that identify proposed contract changes. An approved change order contained the scope, cost, and estimated time impact of the change.

Performance Bond: A bond payable if a project is not completed as specified. Some performance bonds require satisfactory completion of the contract, while other performance bonds provide for payment of a sum of money for failure of the contractor to perform under the contract.

PERT Chart: A tool used to schedule, organize, and coordinate tasks within a project. PERT stands for Program Evaluation Review Technique, a method developed by the U.S. Navy in the 1950s to manage the Polaris submarine missile program. Also known as a *precedence diagram, a network chart,* or a *logic diagram.*

PEST Analysis: A strategic planning tool used to evaluate the impact that political, economic, social, and technological factors might have on a project. It involves an organization considering the external environment before starting a project.

Phase: A set of project activities and tasks that usually result in the completion of one or more project deliverables.

Phase Review: A checkpoint at the end of each project phase to ensure that a project has achieved its stated objectives and deliverables as planned. Sometimes called *stage gates* or *gateway approvals*.

Planning: The process of establishing and maintaining the definition of the scope of a project, the way the project will be performed (procedures and tasks), roles and responsibilities, and the time and cost estimates.

Policy: A definite course or method of action selected from among alternatives and in light of given conditions to guide and determine present and future decisions.

Political Risk: Risks associated with cross-border investing usually comprising currency inconvertibility, expropriation, war and terrorism, nongovernment activists, and legal approvals. In the United States, it is often referred to as *regulatory* or *financial risk*.

Portfolio: A combination of projects and programs both related and unrelated and other matters managed under the organization's strategic plan.

Power: The ability to influence the actions of others. Power may come from formal delegation of authority, reference power, subject matter expertise, the ability to influence, rewards and penalties, as well as other sources.

Practice: A specific type of professional or management activity that may employ one or more techniques or tools.

Present Value: The value today of a future payment, calculated by discounting at a specified discounted rate.

PRINCE2: An approach to project management, released in 1996 as a generic project management method. It provides a method for managing projects within a clearly defined framework. PRINCE2 describes procedures to coordinate people and activities in a project, how to design and supervise the project, and what to do if the project has to be adjusted if it doesn't develop as planned.

Process: Establishes the total scope of the effort, defines and refines the objectives, and develops the course of action required to attain those objectives.

Procurement Management: A component of a project or program management plan that describes how a project team will acquire goods and services from outside the performing organization. On the Big Dig, all construction contracts were procured through an open procurement and low-bid process.

Product: A project's material outcome. It may be a service, event, or any material object (a machine, highway, bridge, building, etc.). The product includes all necessary aspects of the deliverable (training, documentation, etc.).

Program: A group of related projects managed as a whole to obtain benefits not available from managing them individually. The Big Dig was managed as a program, though it was called a project.

Program Governance: The structure by which related projects and other work are integrated, coordinated, and managed among all stakeholders in alignment with the strategic goals of the parent organization.

Program Management: The centralized coordinated management of a program to achieve the program's strategic objectives and benefits.

Program Management Office (PMO): An organization or department that oversees and mentors groups of projects. Often, the PMO is responsible for setting up policies and standards for the projects in the organization, reviewing and consolidating project reports for external stakeholders, and checking project performance against the organization's standards.

Program Management Plan: The full set of documents required to manage the program. The program management plan is distinct and separate from the project management plans required to manage the individual projects within the program.

Project: In the project management literature, *project* is generally defined as being temporary in nature; undertaken to create a unique project, service, or result; and completed when the goals are achieved or when the project is no longer viable.

Project Director: Person who leads, manages, or supervises a project or program. On the Big Dig, the project director was the top position in the project organizational structure.

Project Finance: The financing of long-term infrastructure, industrial projects, and public services based upon a nonrecourse or limited-recourse financial structure whereby project debt and equity used to finance the project are paid back from the cash flow generated by the project (International Project Finance Association).

Project Governance: The system by which projects are managed to ensure benefits are received and requirements are met in alignment with the organization's and/or the program's goals.

Projectized Organization: Any organizational structure in which the project manager has full authority to assign priorities, apply resources, and direct the work of persons assigned to the project.

Project Life Cycle: The full set of activities from the beginning to the end of a project. Generally associated with a set of phases, which are determined based on the major parts of project performance (e.g., requirements definition, design, construction, operation) and the need for control by the client or owner's organization.

Project Management: The discipline of planning, organizing, and managing resources to bring about the successful completion of specific project goals and objectives.

Project Management Institute (PMI): PMI is the world's leading not-for-profit membership association for the project management profession, with more than 600,000 members and credential holders in more than 185 countries. PMI issues standards and guideline publications developed through a voluntary consensus standards development process.

Project Management Knowledge Area: Defined by Project Management Institute (PMI) as an identified area of project management defined by its knowledge requirements and described in terms of its component processes, practices, inputs, outputs, tools, and techniques.

Project Management Monthly (PMM): A monthly status update report, which was used during the Big Dig megaproject. The PMM served to keep all departments updated regarding the tasks and milestones of the project.

Project Management Process Group: As defined by the Project Management Institute (PMI), a process group is a logical grouping of project management inputs, tools and techniques, and outputs. It includes initiating, planning, executing, monitoring and controlling, and closing processes.

Project Management Professional (PMP): A globally recognized certification in project management. It is managed by the Project Management Institute and is based on the PMP Examination Specification.

Project Management Team: The members of the project team who are directly involved in project management activities. On megaprojects, there are generally hundreds of teams that represent the various contracts on the project.

Project Manager (PM): The person assigned by the performing organization who has the overall responsibility for the successful planning, execution, and closure of a project. Project managers work in the construction industry, architecture, information technology, and many different occupations that produce a product or service.

Publicist: On the Big Dig, the government was the ultimate promoter of the project with the community, legislators, stakeholders, and the various government agencies and auditors involved in the project. The state government agencies involved often served as their own lobbyists in influencing Congress and the executive branch about the continuous need for additional funds.

Public-Private Partnership (PPP): The public and the private sector work together to design, construct, finance, operate, and maintain infrastructure projects. PPPs are usually, but not always, funded in part by the private sector and part by the public sector. While the public sector usually retains ownership in the facility or system, the private party will be given additional decision rights in determining how the project or task will be completed.

Q

Qualitative Risk Assessment: The reactive assessment of risk that does not assign hard financial values to assets, expected losses, and cost of controls. Instead, one calculates relative values. Risk analysis is usually conducted through a combination of data analysis, questionnaires, brainstorming sessions, and collaborative workshops involving people from a variety of groups within, as well as external to, the organization. As described in the *PMBOK®️ Guide*, the process of qualitative risk analysis is to assess the likelihood that a specific risk will occur and the impact on cost, quality, or performance, including both negative effects for threats and positive effects for opportunities if it does occur.

Quality: The extent to which the final deliverable conforms to the customer requirements.

Quality Assurance: A structured review of the project, usually by an external resource, to determine the overall project performance (e.g., against schedule and budget) and conformance (i.e., to the management processes specified for the project).

Quality Control: The internal monitoring and control of project deliverables, to ensure that they meet the quality targets set for the project.

Quality Management: The process by which the quality of the deliverables and management processes is ensured and controlled on a project.

Quality Planning: The process of identifying and scheduling quality assurance and quality control activities to improve the level of quality within a project.

Quality Review: A structured independent review of the project, to determine the overall project performance (e.g., against schedule and budget) and the project conformance (i.e., to the management processes specified for the project).

Quantitative Risk Assessment: The mathematical assessment of the likelihood and gravity of a given risk, usually by probability analysis.

R

Rating: An evaluation of creditworthiness provided by a rating agency such as Standard & Poor's Corporation, Fitch Group, or Moody' Investor Service.

Request for Information: A tender document issued to potential suppliers to enable them to describe how they will meet the procurement requirements of a project.

Request for Proposal (RFP): A document that describes a need for products and/or services and the conditions under which they are to be provided. The purpose of the RFP is to solicit bids or proposals from prospective suppliers. Also called a *request for quote* (RFQ).

Requirements: The statement of detailed product objectives that describes the features, functions, and performance constraints to be delivered in the product. The requirements provide the basis for accepting the product.

Resident Engineer: The individual assigned as the authorized representative for the owner's construction contracts on a project and interagency agreements.

Residual Risks: The risks that have been accepted and for which contingency plans and fallback plans can be related. Residual risks should be documented and reviewed throughout the project to determine whether their priority has changed.

Resource: Any tangible support, such as a person, tool, supply item, or facility, used in the execution of a project.

Resource Dependency: A dependency between tasks in which the tasks share the same resources and therefore cannot be worked on simultaneously. Resource-dependent tasks can be scheduled at the same time but are limited by the availability of the shared resources.

Resource Leveling: The part of the scheduling process in which the start and end dates of tasks are driven by resource limitations (e.g., limited availability of resources or difficult-to-manage resource levels). Among the scheduling objectives is ensuring that resources are not overburdened and there are not significant peaks and valleys in the resource schedule.

Retrospective Rating Plan: A plan in insurance programs that reflects actual loss experience used to maximize potential savings from an owner-controlled insurance program. The insurance premium for a retrospective rating plan is based on incurred loss at the expiration of a rating period.

Rework: Work that an owner requires the designer or the contractor to do over again because the original work contained design errors, omissions, or deficient construction work. The cost of rework is generally allocated to the party at fault and not to the owner.

Right-of-Way (ROW): ROW includes development, route layout, design criteria, utility locations, surveys, geometric alignments, and property easements and takings.

Risk: Any event that is likely to adversely affect a project's ability to achieve the defined objectives or an event that creates an opportunity.

Risk Allocation: The process of allocating responsibility for a risk to the party best able to manage the risk. Sometimes the best allocation is to share a risk.

Risk Assessment: The part of risk management in which planners identify potential risks and describe them, usually in terms of their symptoms, causes, probability of occurrence, and potential impact.

Risk Avoidance: A risk response planning technique for a threat that creates changes that are designed to eliminate the risk or to protect the project from its impact.

Risk Breakdown Structure (RBS): A hierarchical representation of risks according to their risk categories.

Risk Identification: Determining what risks or hazards exist or are anticipated, their characteristics, remoteness in time, duration period, and possible outcomes.

Risk Management: The process of identifying, quantifying, mitigating, responding to, and controlling risks throughout a project.

Risk Mitigation: The actions taken to avoid, transfer, or mitigate risks within a project.

Risk Monitoring and Control: Defined in PMI's the *PMBOK® Guide* as the process of identifying, analyzing, and planning for newly arising risks, keeping track of the identified risks and those on the watch list, reanalyzing existing risks, monitoring trigger conditions for contingency plans, monitoring residual risks, and reviewing the execution of risk responses while evaluating their effectiveness.

Risk Planning: The identification and scheduling of actions needed to reduce the level of risk within a project.

Risk Response: Action that can be taken to address the occurrence of a risk event. Contingency plans are collections of risk responses. Typical risk response methodologies include avoidance, loss prevention, loss reduction, separation, duplication, and risk transfer.

Risk Sharing: A risk management method in which the cost of the consequences of a risk is distributed among several participants in an enterprise, such as in syndication.

Root-Cause Analysis: Identification and analytical evaluation of the reason for nonconformance, a variance or defect, a risk, an undesirable condition, or a problem. The Department of Energy defines root-cause analysis as any analysis that identifies underlying deficiencies in a safety management system that, if corrected, would prevent the same and similar accidents from occurring, and to identify the lessons to be learned to promote the achievement of better consequences.

S

Safety and Health Awards for Recognized Excellence (SHARE): An awards program used on the Big Dig to incentivize workers to exercise safe behaviors resulting in reduced lost time incidents and reduced Occupational Safety and Health Administration (OSHA) recordables.

Scenario Analysis: A process of analyzing possible future events by considering alternative possible events, thus giving a scope of possible future outcomes.

Schedule: The project timeline, identifying the dates (absolute or relative to a start date) that project tasks will be started and completed, that resources will be required, and upon which milestones will be reached.

Schedule Recovery: The initiatives implemented to overcome serious obstacles to the critical or near-critical paths.

Scope: The overall definition of what the project should achieve and a specific description of what the result should be. A major ingredient of scope is the quality of the final product.

Scope Change: Any change in the definition of the project scope. Scope change can result from changes in client needs, discovery of defects or omissions, or regulatory changes.

Scope Change Control: Also called *scope change management*. The process of making sure that all changes to the project scope are consciously evaluated and their implications to the project plan are considered in making a decision to make the change, postpone it, or reject it.

Scope Creep: The uncontrolled growth of the project scope resulting from constant changes to requirements without consideration of the impact on resources or schedule.

Scope Definition: Breaking down the project's major deliverables into smaller, more manageable components to make verification, development, and project control easier. This may be part of requirements definition and/or design.

Scope Planning: Development of a statement of the principal deliverables of a project along with the project's justification (business case) and objectives. Part of requirements definition.

Scope Verification: The Project Management Institutes's *PMBOK® Guide* defines this as the process to ensure that all project deliverables have been completed satisfactorily. It is associated with acceptance of the product by clients and sponsors.

Secondment: The process or state of being seconded; the temporary transfer of a person from his or her normal duty to another assignment, such as a project.

Section Design Consultant (SDC): The professional consultant(s) on a project responsible for performing and overseeing design in specific areas of the work (i.e., structural, mechanical, landscape, electrical, civil).

Sequencing Tasks: A part of the scheduling process in which the tasks are positioned serially or parallel to one another based on dependencies between them. Sequencing results in a task network.

Shared Values: Those principles or beliefs that the project participants agree are the most important and will be given priority over all other principles that may arise as the project evolves.

Shareholder: An equity holder in the project company.

Single-Purpose Entity (SPE): An independent legal entity created to accomplish a specific project. Often a limited-liability company or a limited-liability partnership, the single-purpose entity is generally dissolved once the project is completed and its financial goals achieved.

Six Sigma: A management philosophy developed by Motorola that emphasizes setting extremely high objectives, collecting data, and analyzing results to a fine degree as a way to reduce defects in products and services.

Slack: See **Float**.

Specifications: Detailed statements of project deliverables that result from requirements definition and design. Specifications generally describe the deliverables in terms of appearance, operational constraints, and quality attributes. Specifications are the basis for acceptance criteria used in scope verification and quality control. In some organizations and industries, specifications may be qualified as requirements specifications and design specifications. See also **Requirements**.

Sponsor: The person who typically has authority over the project and provides funding, approves scope changes, provides high-level direction, and champions the project within an organization.

Stage Gate Review: The evaluation process by which a project is authorized to progress from one life cycle phase to the next. It is a collaborative practice in which all participants play an important role in assessing the project's overall health and quality of execution to empower the governance organization or delegated authority to make an informed decision as to whether the project is ready to enter the next phase of its life cycle and receive further resource commitments.

Stakeholder: Anyone, internal or external to an organization, who has an interest in a project or will be affected by its deliverables. The International Finance Corporation (IFC) of the World Bank Group defines partners and stakeholders to include "a wide range of groups that have a stake in their projects, are affected by their work, or help strengthen impact on sustainable private sector development."

Stakeholder Engagement: The involvement of stakeholders in the program and the measurement of stakeholder impact based on issue and prioritization tracking.

Stakeholder Expectation Management: The process of managing stakeholder communications to satisfy the requirements of, and resolve issues with, program stakeholders.

Stakeholder Governance: The process by which stakeholders or external groups or committees are involved in the project's decision making or oversight.

Stakeholder Identification: The systematic identification and analysis of program stakeholders.

Stakeholder Management Planning: The process of planning how stakeholders will be identified, analyzed, engaged, and managed throughout the life of the program.

Stakeholder Mapping: A list of all stakeholders, with their interests. Indicates for whom the project causes problems and for whom the project offers something attractive.

Stakeholder Matrix: A stakeholder matrix informs the project of the interests and influence of those involved in a project. Good stakeholder analysis matrices should display each person (or group's) interest in the project as well as their influence and should include an axis for influence and an axis for interest in the project.

Standard of Care: A designer's normal standard of care is "exercis[ing] that standard of reasonable care required of members of [his or her] profession" (*Anthony's Pier Four, Inc. v. Crandall Dry Dock Engineers*, 396 Mass. 818, 823, quoting *Klein v. Catalano*, 386 Mass. 701, 719 [1982]).

Statement of Work (SOW): The top-level document for the work the project must produce. The SOW is a key governance tool: Whether it is being used to direct work for a vendor or contractor or to direct the work internally, the SOW must contain a description of all the work that is expected. On the Big Dig, the SOW was called the Technical Scope Statement.

Strategy: A direction in a project that contributes to the success and survival of the project in its environment and aligns with the goals of the project's parent organization. Strategy is all about gaining (or being prepared to gain) a position of advantage over adversaries or best exploiting emerging possibilities. As there is always an element of uncertainty about the future, strategy is more about a set of options (*strategic choices*) than a fixed plan.

Subcontractor: A group or individual providing products or services to the project. Commonly, subcontractors are considered to be suppliers. However, there is a growing understanding that any internal group that provides products or services is a subcontractor to the project manager.

Subject Matter Expert (SME): An expert in some aspect of the project's content who is expected to provide input to the project team regarding business, scientific, engineering, or other subjects. Input may be in the form of requirements, planning, resolutions to issues, and/or review of project results.

Substance Abuse Prevention Program: A drug testing program established for all project construction workers to ensure a drug-free construction environment.

Sustainable Development: The meeting of present needs without compromising the ability of future generations to meet their own needs.

Sustainable Programs: A strategy for maintaining programs over the long haul during the product's life.

SWOT Analysis: A strategic planning tool used to evaluate the strengths, weaknesses, Opportunities, and threats (SWOT) of a project. It involves specifying the objective of the project and identifying the internal and external factors that are favorable and unfavorable to achieving that objective.

T

T5 Project: The Terminal 5 (T5) Project increased the annual capacity of London's Heathrow Airport from 67 million to 95 million passengers. The project was unusual in that it achieved its goals of delivering a high-quality project within schedule and a budget of $8.5 billion, and the project maintained an exemplary safety record.

Task: A piece of work requiring effort and resources and having a concrete outcome (a deliverable). A task may be of any size. Sometimes the term is used to denote a piece of work at a particular level in a work breakdown structure (WBS) hierarchy—for example, a phase that is broken into a set of activities, and an activity that is broken into a set of tasks. Except for this hierarchical usage, *activity* is synonymous with *task*.

Technical Scope Statement (TSS): A document that defines and guides any major project. Usually includes a section on risk analysis and management. The TSS on the Big Dig included the applicable design and construction contracts.

Technology Transfer Program: In an effort to expand the knowledge gained from the Big Dig, the U.S. Department of Transportation's, Federal Highway Administration (FHWA) developed a technology transfer program to share project management lessons with audiences throughout the United States and the international transportation community.

Termination: The right of one of the parties to bring a contract to an end in accordance with applicable law or the terms of the contract.

Theory: Derives primarily from concepts and causal relationships that relate these concepts, and contributes to understanding as well as providing a prediction of future behavior.

Tolling: The process of collecting revenue whereby road users are charged a fee. Tolls may be collected on a flat-fee basis, a time basis, or a distance basis and may vary by type of vehicle.

Top-down Estimating: Approximating the size (duration and cost) and risk of a project (or phase) by looking at the project as a whole and comparing it to previously performed similar projects. The comparison may be made directly using "*analogous estimating*, through an algorithm as in *parametric estimating*, or from the memory of estimating experts.

Total Quality Management (TQM): The TQM concept was developed by a number of American management consultants, including W. Edwards Deming, Joseph M. Juran, and Armand V. Feigenbaum. TQM functions on the premise that the quality of products and processes is the responsibility of everyone who is involved with the creation or consumption of the products or services offered by an organization. TQM capitalizes on the involvement of management, workforce, suppliers, and customers, in order to meet or exceed customer expectations.

Transportation Infrastructure Fund: The Central Artery/Tunnel Project and Statewide Road and Bridge Transportation Infrastructure Fund (TIF) was created within the Commonwealth of Massachusetts and relied on a variety of revenue sources to fund project costs, including bonds, grants, notes, and revenue streams from tolls, motor vehicle fees, and other sources.

Triple Constraint: The concept of triple constraint is based on the premise that if any one of the project elements changes (cost, scope, or time), this may have an impact on the other two. Careful analysis of these three factors must be done on every contract to identify the solution that has the least undesirable impact. Quality, which is defined in the *PMBOK®️ Guide* as "conformance to requirements" is often impacted by the triple constraint. Quality is sometimes referred to as the fourth constraint, since it is an important factor in project success and can be compromised with an increase in scope or a decrease in budget or time.

Turnkey Construction: The design and construction of a project to completion, so that it is ready to produce cash flow.

V

Value Engineering (VE): VE is a systematic method for improving the value of goods or products and services. It was developed at General Electric Corporation during World War II and is widely used in industry and government, particularly in areas such as defense, transportation, construction, and health care. VE is an effective technique for reducing costs, increasing productivity, and improving quality.

Value Engineering Change Proposal (VECP): A construction contract provision that encourages the contractor to propose changes in the contract requirements to accomplish the project's functional requirements at less cost or to improve value or service at no increase or a minor increase in cost. On federal government projects, the contractor and the government often split the savings.

Variance: The difference between estimated cost, duration, or effort and the actual result of performance. In addition, variance can be the difference between the initial or baseline product scope and the actual product delivered.

W

Warranty: Used in public-private partnerships for the construction of roads and other infrastructure. Warranty clauses guarantee that the roadway will meet a certain level of quality or else repairs will be made at the private contractor's expense. There are currently two types of warranties used in highway construction: (1) materials and workmanship warranties and (2) performance warranties. Under the first type, the contractor is responsible only for defects caused by poor materials and workmanship. Under the latter, the contractor is responsible for the product meeting certain agreed-upon performance thresholds, regardless of whether materials and workmanship met state standards.

Whistle-blower: A whistle-blower is a person who tells the public or someone in authority about alleged dishonest or illegal activities or misconduct occurring in a government department, a public or private organization, or a company. In the United States, the Occupational Safety and Health Administration Agency (OSHA) Whistleblower Protection Program enforces the whistle-blower provisions of 21 whistle-blower statutes, protecting employees who report violations of various workplace safety, airline, commercial motor carrier, consumer product, environmental, financial reform, food safety, health care reform, nuclear, pipeline, public transportation agency, railroad, maritime, and securities laws. Rights afforded by these whistle-blower acts include, but are not limited to, worker participation in safety and health activities; reporting a work-related injury, illness, or fatality; and reporting a violation of the statutes.

Work Breakdown Structure (WBS): An exhaustive, hierarchical tree structure of deliverables and activities that need to be performed to complete a project. A WBS is a common project management tool and the basis for much project planning.

Workers' Compensation: Covers injury to contractors and management consultant employees while working on a project.

Work Package: A task at a low level of the work breakdown structure at which project accounting is performed.

Work Program: One of a series of 15 contracts between the project owner (Massachusetts Highway Department/Massachusetts Turnpike Authority) and the management consultant (Bechtel/Parsons Brinckerhoff) to manage the Big Dig project.

World Bank (WB): A multilateral agency based in Washington, D.C., whose primary mission is to lend to developing countries to assist in reducing the poverty level. The bank consists of the following groups: (1) the International Bank for Reconstruction and Development (IBRD), (2) the International Development Association (IDA), the International Finance Corporation (IFC), the Multilateral Guarantee Association (MIGA), and the International Center for the Settlement of Investment Disputes (ICSID).

Wrap-up Insurance Program: See **Owner-Controlled Insurance Program (OCIP)**.

Abbreviations and Acronyms

ABC: Artery Business Committee
AG: Attorney General
AIPM: Australian Institute of Project Management
ANSI: American National Standards Institute
APM: The U.K. Association for Project Management
ASQ: American Society for Quality
BOT: Build-Own-Transfer
B/PB: Bechtel/Parsons Brinckerhoff
CA/T: Central Artery/Tunnel Project
CMR: Construction Manager at Risk
CPS: Construction Phase Services
CSR: Corporate Social Responsibility
C/SU: Cost/Schedule Update
DB: Design-Build
DBB: Design-Bid-Build
DBE: Disadvantaged Business Enterprise
DQM: Director of Quality Management
DR: Deficiency Report
EBRD: European Bank for Reconstruction and Development
ECA: Export Credit Agency
EIB: European Investment Bank
EIS: Environmental Impact Statement
EPA: Environmental Protection Agency
EV: Earned Value
FE: Field Engineer
FEIS: Final Environmental Impact Statement
FDI: Foreign Direct Investment
FHWA: Federal Highway Administration

FOIA: Freedom of Information Act

FP: Finance Plan

FY: Fiscal Year

GANs: Grant Anticipation Notes

GAO: [U.S.] Government Accountability Office

GOBs: General Obligation Bonds

IFC: International Finance Corporation (of the World Bank Group)

IHS: Interstate Highway System

IPFA: International Project Finance Association

IPMA: International Project Management Association

ISO: International Standards Organization

ISTEA: Intermodal Surface Transportation Efficiency Act of 1991

JV: Joint Venture

MassDOT: The Massachusetts Department of Transportation

MHD: Massachusetts Highway Department

MHS Bonds: Metropolitan Highway System Bonds

MTA: Massachusetts Turnpike Authority

NASA: National Aeronautics and Space Administration

NIST: National Institute of Standards and Technology

NTSB: National Transportation Safety Board

OCC: Oversight Coordination Commission

OCIP: Owner-Controlled Insurance Program

OECD: Organization for Economic Co-operation and Development

OIG: Office of the Inspector General

OSA: Office of the State Auditor

OSHA: Occupational Safety and Health Administration

PCA: Potential Change Allowance

PF: Potential Forecast

PMBOK®: *A Guide to the Project Management Body of Knowledge (PMBOK® Guide)*—Fifth Edition

PMI: Project Management Institute

PMM: Project Management Monthly

PMO: Program Management Office

PPP: Public-Private Partnership

QA: Quality Assurance

QAM: Quality Assurance Manager

QC: Quality Control

QCM: Quality Control Manager
QCP: Quality Control Plan
RE: Resident Engineer
RFP: Request for Proposal
RM: Risk Manager
ROI: Return on Investment
SAFETEA: Safe, Accountable, Flexible and Efficient Transportation Equity Act
SDC: Section Design Consultant
SHARE: Safety and Health Awards for Recognized Excellence
TEA-21: Transportation Efficiency Act for the 21st Century
TIF: Transportation Infrastructure Fund
TQM: Total Quality Management
TRB: Transportation Research Board
USAID: United States Agency for International Development
USDOT: United States Department of Transportation
VE: Value Engineering
VECP: Value Engineering Change Proposal
WBS: Work Breakdown Structure

Index